# Multilateral Asian Security Architecture

This book provides a comparative assessment of the material and ideational contributions of five countries to the regional architecture of post-Cold War Asia.

In contrast to the usual emphasis placed on the role and centrality of the Association of Southeast Asian Nations (ASEAN) in Asia's multilateral architecture and its component institutions, this book argues that the four non-ASEAN countries of interest here – Australia, Japan, China and the United States – and Indonesia have played and continue to play an influential part in determining the shape and substance of Asian multilateralism from its pre-inception to the present. The work does not contend that existing scholarship overstates ASEAN's significance to the successes and failures of Asia's multilateral enterprise. Rather, it claims that the impact of non-ASEAN stakeholders in innovating multilateral architecture in Asia has been understated. Whether ASEAN has fared well or poorly as a custodian of Asia's regional architecture, the fact remains that the countries considered here, notwithstanding their present discontent over the state of that architecture, are key to understanding the evolution of Asian multilateralism.

This book will be of much interest to students of Asian politics, international organisations, security studies and IR more generally.

**See Seng Tan** is associate professor, Deputy Director and Head of Research of the Institute of Defence and Strategic Studies at the S. Rajaratnam School of International Studies (RSIS), Nanyang Technological University, Singapore. He is the author of *The Making of the Asia Pacific: Knowledge Brokers and the Politics of Representation* (2013).

## Asian Security Studies

Series Editors:
Sumit Ganguly, *Indiana University, Bloomington*,
Andrew Scobell, *Research and Development (RAND) Corporation, Santa Monica*
and Joseph Chinyong Liow, *Nanyang Technological University, Singapore*.

Few regions of the world are fraught with as many security questions as Asia. Within this region it is possible to study great power rivalries, irredentist conflicts, nuclear and ballistic missile proliferation, secessionist movements, ethno-religious conflicts and inter-state wars. This book series publishes the best possible scholarship on the security issues affecting the region, and includes detailed empirical studies, theoretically oriented case studies and policy-relevant analyses as well as more general works.

**China and International Institutions**
Alternate paths to global power
*Marc Lanteigne*

**China's Rising Sea Power**
The PLA Navy's Submarine Challenge
*Peter Howarth*

**If China Attacks Taiwan**
Military strategy, politics and economics
*Edited by Steve Tsang*

**Chinese Civil-Military Relations**
The transformation of the People's Liberation Army
*Edited by Nan Li*

**The Chinese Army Today**
Tradition and transformation for the 21st Century
*Dennis J. Blasko*

**Taiwan's Security**
History and prospects
*Bernard D. Cole*

**Religion and Conflict in South and Southeast Asia**
Disrupting violence
*Edited by Linell E. Cady and Sheldon W. Simon*

**Political Islam and Violence in Indonesia**
*Zachary Abuza*

**US-Indian Strategic Cooperation into the 21st Century**
More than words
*Edited by Sumit Ganguly, Brian Shoup and Andrew Scobell*

**India, Pakistan and the Secret Jihad**
The covert war in Kashmir, 1947–2004
*Praveen Swami*

**China's Strategic Culture and Foreign Policy Decision-Making**
Confucianism, leadership and war
*Huiyun Feng*

**Chinese Military Strategy in the Third Indochina War**
The last Maoist war
*Edward C. O'Dowd*

**Asia Pacific Security**
US, Australia and Japan and the New Security Triangle
*Edited by William T. Tow, Mark J. Thomson, Yoshinobu Yamamoto and Satu P. Limaye*

**China, the United States, and Southeast Asia**
Contending perspectives on politics, security, and economics
*Edited by Evelyn Goh and Sheldon W. Simon*

**Conflict and Cooperation in Multi-Ethnic States**
Institutional incentives, myths, and counter-balancing
*Brian Shoup*

**China's War on Terrorism**
Counter- insurgency, politics and internal security
*Martin I. Wayne*

**US Taiwan Policy**
Constructing the triangle
*Øystein Tunsjø*

**Conflict Management, Security and Intervention in East Asia**
Third-party mediation in regional conflict
*Edited by Jacob Bercovitch, Kwei-Bo Huang, and Chung-Chian Teng*

**South Asia's Cold War**
Nuclear weapons and conflict in comparative perspective
*Rajesh M. Basrur*

**The Rise of China and International Security**
America and Asia Respond
*Edited by Kevin J. Cooney and Yoichiro Sato*

**Nuclear Proliferation in South Asia**
Crisis behaviour and the bomb
*Edited by Sumit Ganguly and S. Paul Kapur*

**Nuclear Weapons and Conflict Transformation**
The case of India-Pakistan
*Saira Khan*

**Managing the China Challenge**
Global Perspectives
*Edited by Quansheng Zhao and Guoli Liu*

**India and Counterinsurgency**
Lessons learned
*Edited by Sumit Ganguly and David P. Fidler*

**Cooperative Security in the Asia-Pacific**
The ASEAN Regional Forum
*Edited by Jürgen Haacke and Noel M. Morada*

**US–China–EU Relations**
Managing the new world order
*Edited by Robert S. Ross, Øystein Tunsjø and Zhang Tuosheng*

**China, Europe and International Security**
Interests, roles and prospects
*Edited by Frans-Paul van der Putten and Chu Shulong*

**Crime-Terror Nexus in South Asia**
States, security and non-state actors
*Ryan Clarke*

**US-Japan-North Korean Security Relations**
Irrepressible Interests
*Anthony DiFilippo*

**Pakistan's War on Terrorism**
Strategies for Combating Jihadist Armed Groups since 9/11
*Samir Puri*

**Indian Foreign and Security Policy in South Asia**
Regional power strategies
*Sandra Destradi*

**Sri Lanka and the Responsibility to Protect**
Politics, ethnicity and genocide
*Damien Kingsbury*

**The Chinese Army Today, Second Edition**
Tradition and transformation for the 21st century
Second edition
*Dennis J. Blasko*

**Understanding Security Practices in South Asia**
Securitization Theory and the role of non-state actors
*Monika Barthwal-Datta*

**Autonomy and Ethnic Conflict in South and South-East Asia**
*Edited by Rajat Ganguly*

**Chinese Industrial Espionage**
Technology acquisition and military modernisation
*William C. Hannas, James Mulvenon and Anna B. Puglisi*

**Power Transition and International Order in Asia**
Issues and challenges
*Edited by Peter Shearman*

**Afghanistan, Pakistan and Strategic Change**
Adjusting Western regional policy
*Edited by Joachim Krause and Charles King Mallory, IV*

**The Arms Race in Asia**
Trends, causes and implications
*Andrew T.H. Tan*

**Globalization and Security Relations across the Taiwan Strait**
In the shadow of China
*Edited by Ming-chin Monique Chu and Scott L. Kastner*

**Multilateral Asian Security Architecture**
Non-ASEAN stakeholders
*See Seng Tan*

# Multilateral Asian Security Architecture
Non-ASEAN stakeholders

**See Seng Tan**

LONDON AND NEW YORK

First published 2016
by Routledge
2 Park Square, Milton Park, Abingdon, Oxon OX14 4RN

and by Routledge
711 Third Avenue, New York, NY 10017

*Routledge is an imprint of the Taylor & Francis Group, an informa business*

© 2016 See Seng Tan

The right of See Seng Tan to be identified as author of this work has been asserted by him in accordance with sections 77 and 78 of the Copyright, Designs and Patents Act 1988.

All rights reserved. No part of this book may be reprinted or reproduced or utilised in any form or by any electronic, mechanical, or other means, now known or hereafter invented, including photocopying and recording, or in any information storage or retrieval system, without permission in writing from the publishers.

*Trademark notice*: Product or corporate names may be trademarks or registered trademarks, and are used only for identification and explanation without intent to infringe.

*British Library Cataloguing-in-Publication Data*
A catalogue record for this book is available from the British Library

*Library of Congress Cataloging-in-Publication Data*
Tan, See Seng, 1965-
Multilateral Asian security architecture : non-Asean stakeholders / See Seng Tan.
pages cm. -- (Asian Security Studies)
Includes bibliographical references and index.
1. Security, International--Asia. 2. National security--Asia. 3. Asia--Foreign relations. I. Title.
JZ6009.A3T34 2016
355'.03305--dc23
2015003898

ISBN: 978-1-138-90240-4 (hbk)
ISBN: 978-1-315-69678-2 (ebk)

Typeset in Times
by Saxon Graphics Ltd, Derby

# Contents

|   | *Acknowledgements* | xi |
|---|---|---|
|   | *Glossary* | xii |
| 1 | Introduction | 1 |
| 2 | Multilateralism in Asia | 4 |
| 3 | ASEAN | 18 |
| 4 | Australia | 41 |
| 5 | Japan | 63 |
| 6 | China | 87 |
| 7 | United States | 110 |
| 8 | Indonesia | 130 |
| 9 | Conclusion | 155 |
|   | *Bibliography* | 168 |
|   | *Index* | 204 |

# Acknowledgements

This book would not have been written were it not for the serendipitous coalescing of factors, forces and friends that made it possible. Writing it gave me the opportunity to develop and piece together disparate ideas and things I have long studied and written about and debated with colleagues and students over endless brews of coffee (and considerably more potent beverages). My thanks to the following individuals: Joseph Liow, dean of the S. Rajaratnam School of International Studies (RSIS), Nanyang Technological University, for his counsel, friendship and unstinting support; James Tang, dean of social sciences at the Singapore Management University, who kindly facilitated my short sabbatical in 2014 where I began work on this book; Andrew Humphrys, Senior Editor at Routledge, and his editorial team for backing this project; and two reviewers for their helpful comments. My utmost gratitude is reserved for Trina and Elisabeth, lovely wife and daughter respectively, for their forbearance, indulgence and diligence in keeping husband and dad on the straight and narrow.

# Glossary

| | |
|---|---|
| A2/AD | anti-access/anti-denial |
| ADB | Asian Development Bank |
| ADF | Australian Defence Forces |
| ADIZ | air defence identification zone |
| ADMM | ASEAN Defence Ministers' Meeting |
| ADMM-Plus | ASEAN Defence Ministers' Meeting Plus |
| AEC | ASEAN Economic Community |
| AFTA | ASEAN Free Trade Area |
| AICHR | ASEAN Intergovernmental Commission on Human Rights |
| AIIB | Asian Infrastructure Investment Bank |
| AIPO | ASEAN Inter-Parliamentary Organization |
| AMF | Asian Monetary Fund |
| ANZUS | Australia, New Zealand, United States Security Treaty |
| APC | Asia-Pacific Community (Kevin Rudd's proposal) |
| APEC | Asia-Pacific Economic Cooperation |
| APSC | ASEAN Political-Security Community |
| APT | ASEAN Plus Three |
| ARF | ASEAN Regional Forum |
| ASEAN | Association of Southeast Asian Nations |
| ASEAN-PMC | ASEAN Post-Ministerial Conference |
| ASEM | Asia–Europe Meeting |
| C2 | Coordination 2 |
| CEPEA | Comprehensive Economic Partnership for East Asia |
| CICA | Conference on Interaction and Confidence-Building Measures |
| CLMV | Cambodia, Laos, Myanmar and Vietnam |
| CMI | Chiang Mai Initiative |
| CMIM | Chiang Mai Initiative Multilateralization |
| COC | Code of Conduct for the South China Sea |
| CSCAP | Council for Security Cooperation in the Asia-Pacific |
| CSCE/OSCE | Conference (now Organization) for Security Cooperation in Europe |
| CSI | Container Security Initiative |
| DFAT | Department of Foreign Affairs and Trade (of Australia) |

| | |
|---|---|
| DOC | Declaration on the Conduct of Parties in the South China Sea |
| DPJ | Democratic Party of Japan |
| EAC | East Asian Community or East African Community |
| EAEC | East Asian Economic Caucus |
| EAFTA | East Asia Free Trade Area |
| EAS | East Asia Summit |
| ECOWAS | Economic Community of West African States |
| EDSM | Enhanced Dispute Settlement Mechanism (of ASEAN) |
| EEC | European Economic Community |
| EMEAP | Executives' Meeting of East Asia and Pacific Central Banks |
| EU | European Union |
| FTA | Free Trade Agreement |
| FTAAP | Free Trade Area of the Asia-Pacific |
| G20 | Group of Twenty |
| GATT | General Agreement on Tariffs and Trade |
| GWOT | global war on terrorism |
| HADR | humanitarian assistance and disaster relief |
| ICJ | International Court of Justice |
| IMET | International Military Education and Training (of the United States) |
| IMF | International Monetary Fund |
| IOR-ARC | Indian Ocean Rim Association for Regional Cooperation |
| ITLOS | International Tribunal for the Law of the Sea |
| JDA | Japan Defense Agency |
| JIIA | Japan Institute of International Affairs |
| *Kemlu* | Indonesia's Ministry of Foreign Affairs |
| LDP | Liberal Democratic Party (of Japan) |
| MAFLAFS | Multilateral Agreement for Full Liberalization of Air Freight Services |
| Mercosur | Common Market of the South |
| MITI | Ministry of International Trade and Industry (of Japan) |
| MOFA | Ministry of Foreign Affairs (of Japan) |
| MPAC | Master Plan in ASEAN Connectivity (of ASEAN) |
| NAFTA | North American Free Trade Area |
| NAM | Non-Aligned Movement |
| NATO | North Atlantic Treaty Organization |
| NTS | Non-traditional security |
| P5 | UN Security Council's Permanent Five Members |
| PAFTAD | Pacific Trade and Development forum |
| PBEC | Pacific Basin Economic Council |
| PD | Preventive diplomacy |
| PECC | Pacific Economic Cooperation Council |
| PKI | Indonesian Communist Party |
| PLA | People's Liberation Army (of China) |
| PSI | Proliferation Security Initiative |

| | |
|---|---|
| RCEP | Regional Comprehensive Economic Partnership |
| ROO | rules of origin |
| S&ED | (Sino-US) Strategic and Economic Dialogue |
| SCO | Shanghai Cooperation Organization |
| SEANWFZ | Southeast Asia Nuclear Weapons Free Zone |
| SEATO | Southeast Asia Treaty Organization |
| SLD | Shangri-La Dialogue |
| SPT | Six Party Talks |
| TAC | Treaty of Amity and Cooperation |
| TPP | Trans-Pacific Partnership |
| UN | United Nations |
| UNCLOS | United Nations Convention on the Law of the Sea |
| WTO | World Trade Organization |
| ZOPFAN | Zone of Peace, Freedom and Neutrality |

# 1 Introduction

The development of East Asian regionalism presents students of international relations with an intriguing puzzle. In each of the major regional groupings outside of East Asia, the regionalism project has been promoted and shaped by the region's major powers... However, in East Asia, despite the presence of two major powers in the region, Japan and China, as well as the continuing influence of the United States, it has been the members of ASEAN that have led the way in building East Asian regional cooperation.[1]

The prevailing scholarly orthodoxy regarding recent diplomatic initiatives in the Asia-Pacific assumes that East Asia is evolving into a distinctive regional community. The orthodoxy attributes this development to the growing influence of the diplomatic practices espoused by the Association of Southeast Asian Nations (ASEAN) and its related institutions. However, a paradox remains, namely: despite the failure of ASEAN's distinctive practice to fulfil its rhetorical promise in Southeast Asia both immediately prior to and in the aftermath of the Asian financial crisis in 1997, it is nevertheless considered sufficient to validate the projection of ASEAN defined norms onto a wider Pacific canvas.[2]

It has become commonplace to attribute the origins and state of Asia's multilateral enterprise and the region's still evolving institutional architecture principally to the effort of the Association of Southeast Asian Nations' (ASEAN) in regional cooperation and integration, institution-building, and norm creation and diffusion. Gratuitous claims about 'ASEAN centrality' and ASEAN's occupancy of the 'driving seat' of Asian regionalism have added to the notion – academically contested, to be sure – that the impressive complex of institutional arrangements that form a not insignificant part of Asia's broader architecture – such as the ASEAN Regional Forum (ARF), ASEAN Plus Three (APT), East Asia Summit (EAS), and indeed even the Asia-Pacific Economic Cooperation (APEC) – and the way they operate and the outcomes they have engendered, have a whole lot to do with ASEAN.

Indeed, ASEAN has been roundly praised for the perceived successes and, in more recent years, pilloried for the failures of Asia's multilateral architecture. The design and conventions of Asian multilateralism – its apparent incoherence, the emphasis on process over results, the making of decisions by consensus, and the sanctity of so-called 'legal' norms (sovereignty, non-intervention and/or non-interference) – have increasingly been viewed as constraints against deeper regional integration. They are also seen as an excuse to do nothing by states that lack the will to commit to institutional change and bear its associated risks, since multilateralism in Asia is viewed by its stakeholder countries as adjunct or supplementary to their preferred strategies and structures. And, more often than not, proposals for architectural reform allude, indirectly or otherwise, to ASEAN's purported ineffectiveness as the driver of regionalism even as they (or most of them at least) continue to pay lip service to the purported relevance of ASEAN's centrality.

While not incorrect, the above received wisdom is however incomplete, not least because it ignores the significant contributions to the establishment and maintenance of the regional architecture by its non-ASEAN stakeholders. For example, Australia's and Japan's contributions to the establishment of the APEC are well documented. And while the ad hoc manner in which the ARF, the APT, and the EAS have emerged has often been attributed to the pragmatic approach by the ASEAN states to different regional challenges, it could just as readily be ascribed to the proactive pragmatism of the non-ASEAN states, whose ostensible roles in those arrangements have at times been reduced inadvertently and unfairly in some analyses to passive actors who 'bought in' to an architecture they had little to no part in constructing. By contrast, the central thesis of this book is: *far from mere norm-takers, non-ASEAN stakeholders have arguably had just as much influence as ASEAN, if not more, in defining the shape and substance of Asia's multilateral architecture.* It contends that non-ASEAN stakeholders – as much as, if not more than, their ASEAN counterparts – have from early on sought proactively to shape Asian multilateralism for a variety of purposes, whether to engage, cooperate with, hedge against or to balance one another. Crucially, the argument here is not that the impact of ASEAN has been overstated without justification but rather that the impact of non-ASEAN stakeholders in innovating multilateral architecture in Asia has been understated. Whether ASEAN has fared well or poorly as a custodian of Asia's regional architecture, the fact remains that non-ASEAN powers and stakeholders also played key roles in making and maintaining (and, where conceivable, remaking) Asian multilateralism, and as such share responsibility for its successes and failures.

In fairness, the extant academic literature, including that which argues the primacy of ASEAN in Asian multilateralism, includes acknowledgment of the impact of non-ASEAN powers on regional order and architecture in Asia. That said, apart from specific works focused on a particular nation's engagement with multilateralism, there has to date been no book-length, cross-national comparative analysis of the material and ideational contributions of non-ASEAN powers to Asia's multilateral architecture. Here is where this present work seeks to provide added value. While much has been made of America's preference for '*a la carte* multilateralism'[3] – that is, the adoption of a selective and instrumental approach to multilateral diplomacy and institution-building – it is fair to say that this condition also affects most if not all stakeholders of Asia's multilateral architecture to varying extents. Five national case studies comprising four non-ASEAN stakeholders (Australia, Japan, China and the United States) and one ASEAN stakeholder (Indonesia) form the basis for a comparative assessment of their respective contributions to making Asia's regional architecture the way it is today.

The book's architecture (pardon the pun) consists in the following. Chapter 2 surveys the evolution of the multilateral enterprise in Asia and its attributes and processes. In particular, it focuses on the intramural dynamics and the tensions that define Asia's 'multi-multilateral' character and the diplomatic-security model, the so-called 'ASEAN Way', which ostensibly guides the region's institutional practices. Chapter 3 examines the role and place of ASEAN in Asian multilateralism, paying close attention to the ways in which its putative 'centrality' in the regional architecture has been understood. Chapters 4 and 5 look at the contributions of two highly proactive stakeholders, Australia and Japan, whose multilateral contributions have been equally prodigious in their respective ways. Chapters 6 and 7 compare the contributions of two great powers, China and the United States, whose respective progressions from countries highly apprehensive about the proposition of multilateralism in Asia – for different reasons, to be sure, but both equally concerned over how multilateralism might constrain their freedom of manoeuvre – to committed (and at times frustrated) multilateral actors. Chapter 8 looks at the multilateral contributions of an ASEAN 'insider', Indonesia, whose own trajectory from the *de facto* leader of ASEAN to, in recent times, an emerging power in its own right, seeking to transcend its regional and organizational moorings, raises intriguing (and, where ASEAN's future is concerned, alarming) ramifications for Asian multilateralism. In their own ways, each of those five countries find their participation in regional arrangements useful to their respective interests even if their contributions may not have been entirely helpful at times to enhancing the multilateral enterprise's overall effectiveness. Finally, the concluding chapter categorizes the various multilateral ideas and innovations of the five countries and their counterparts according to three ideal types of multilateralism (namely, 'command', 'functional' and 'laissez faire'), and reflects briefly and preliminarily on what the foreseeable future of multilateral Asia might look like.

## Notes

1 Richard Stubbs, 'ASEAN's Leadership in East Asian Region-Building: Strength in Weakness', *The Pacific Review*, Vol. 27, No. 4 (2014), pp. 523–41, on p. 524.
2 David Martin Jones and Michael L. R. Smith, 'Constructing Communities: The Curious Case of East Asian Regionalism', *Review of International Studies*, Vol. 33, No. 1 (2007), pp. 165–86, on p. 165.
3 Stewart Patrick, 'Prix Fixe *and* à la Carte: Avoiding False Multilateral Choices', *The Washington Quarterly*, Vol. 32, No. 4 (2009), pp. 77–95.

# 2 Multilateralism in Asia

This chapter addresses two interrelated issues. First, it discusses Asia's evolving regional architecture, particularly the intramural dynamics and the tensions that define its so-called 'multi-multilateral' character. Second, it elaborates on the institutional design of the architecture, paying close attention to the facets that comprise what analysts have referred to as the 'ASEAN Way' or even more broadly, the 'Asian Way' or 'Asia-Pacific Way'.[1] Regionalism in contemporary Asia is in many ways a paradox. Against received wisdom at the end of the Cold War concerning the absence therein of any dense web of institutions for mitigating the potentially disastrous impact of persistent security dilemmas, power balances and economic vulnerabilities in the region,[2] today's Asian landscape teems with institutional arrangements – intergovernmental or 'top down' for the most part rather than 'bottom up', it should be said – whose origins date back both to the Cold War and to the rise of the 'new regionalism' after the Cold War. (Notably, the original 'new regionalism' literature is predominantly concerned with *regionalization* – transnational 'bottom up', non-state processes that interconnect a constellation of societies along economic, socio-cultural and other functionally defined lines.[3] Although there has been some been some notable work on 'bottom up' regionalization in Asia, the 'new regionalism' in the Asian context mostly refers, however, to 'top down' processes – intergovernmental institutions – with some consideration of 'bottom up' processes.[4])

Be that as it may, the density, deepening and intrusiveness of these Asian institutions continue to lag behind the European Union (EU), which remains for many the 'gold standard' of regional integration.[5] Indeed, it has been argued that Asian countries have for the most part neither been willing to invest resources commensurate to their express collective visions and proposals for regionalism, nor are they given to seeking institutional innovation in view of their apparent preference for keeping the regional status quo.[6] And to the extent a stable regional environment is what they most desire, there is less incentive for them to seek reform of their regional institutions even if there are obvious benefits to be had from such change.[7] Even then, despite its relatively underdeveloped character, it has been described by past political leaders from Asia variously as 'complicated enough' (Han Sung-Joo, former foreign minister of South Korea) and as 'an idea that would not go away' (Lee Kuan Yew, founding prime minister and most recently 'minister mentor' of Singapore).[8]

## Asia's 'multi-multilateral' architecture

One thing supporters and critics of Asian regionalism alike do not quibble over is the shared perception that the region's security architecture is messy and disjointed. Since the Asia-Pacific Economic Cooperation trade forum was established in 1989, East Asia – or, more specifically, the Association of Southeast Asian Nations (ASEAN) – has gone on a spawning spree, giving birth to one institution after another. (Not all regional arrangements in the Asian region have their origins in ASEAN, to be sure.) Today, the institutional landscape fosters the impression of a crowded and cluttered region. Institutional arrangements overlap each other in membership and potentially also in remit and interest. It has been described variously as a 'complex', an 'ecosystem', a 'multiplex', and/or a 'patchwork' of institutional arrangements.[9] With no semblance of grand architectural or of strategic coherence,[10] the regional 'house' that the stakeholders have built, most of which is centred upon ASEAN, is far from the finished article. That said, the bits and pieces of its still evolving architecture – one analyst has identified at least five distinct institutional complexes within the Asian region, each with its own ensemble of arrangements[11] – have been added in an ad hoc and pragmatic fashion in response to specific historical challenges and crises, and as such have their own contingent rationale.

But while the experience of the EU and European integration might have led its advocates to advance institutional singularity as destiny, the global landscape paints a different picture altogether. More like Asia than Europe, multilateralism worldwide has developed into a plethora of formal standing multilateral institutions as well as interest-based coalitions referred to by scholars as 'mini-laterals'.[12] Making the case for 'multi-multilateralism', Francis Fukuyama, observing that the world is 'far too diverse and complex to be overseen properly by a single global body', has argued: 'A truly liberal principle would argue not for a single, overarching, enforceable liberal order but rather for a diversity of institutions and institutional forms to provide governance across a range of security, economic, environmental, and other issues'.[13] With its overlapping concentric circles and 'variable geometries' – at its most basic, the idea that countries mutually engaged in regional integration may integrate respectively at different speeds and to different extents relative to one another[14] – multi-multilateralism might appear to its critics as the embodiment of inefficiency and ineffectiveness owing to the high possibility for rivalry, replication, and redundancy between and among institutions.[15]

### *Equity versus efficiency*

The debate over whether regional institutions are effective and legitimate because they are comprehensively represented by all countries within the region or because they are efficient performers in fulfilling institutional goals is a long-standing one. In this respect, institutional design – how members are selected, the procedures by which decisions are made and power exercised and so on – matters (as discussed in the following section). On the one hand, to the extent that they ensure that all states within the region enjoy equal stakes within the institution and their interests are adequately represented therein, what could be termed 'input-oriented' legitimacy is guaranteed (i.e. equity).[16] Formal standing institutions such as the United Nations (UN) and the World Trade Organization (WTO), with their global memberships, are typical illustrations of input-oriented or representative legitimacy. On the other hand, institutions are regarded as effective on the basis of the relevance and quality of their performance (i.e. efficiency).[17] The formation of the Group of Twenty (G20) in 1999 was welcomed precisely by those who favour efficiency over equity given, in their view, the aptness in gathering the twenty economic powerhouses which together account for nearly 80 per cent of the world's wealth and resources.[18]

Advocates of equity decry the purported exclusiveness of output-oriented global institutions, no matter how efficient they might be. More often than not, they highlight the ostensible lack of correspondence between exclusivity and efficiency by pointing to the apparent inability or unwillingness of elitist institutions to manage much less resolve serious international diplomatic and/or economic crises as a result of political differences among them – as evidenced, say, by the strategic divergences among the UN Security Council's Permanent Five (P5) members over the crisis in Syria and the relative weakness of the G20 in its response to the global financial crisis. On their part, advocates of efficiency see large institutions such as the UN as problematic because their input-oriented or democratic legitimacy does not guarantee their output-oriented or performance legitimacy. Likewise, the death of the Doha Round of world trade talks has been attributed by the former US trade representative, Susan Schwab, to the 'lumping together of all emerging and developing economies in the Doha negotiating structure', which in her view allowed emerging economies disinclined to open their markets to undermine any prospect for progress.[19]

The controversy surrounding then Prime Minister Kevin Rudd of Australia's 2008 proposal for an 'Asia-Pacific Community' (APC), discussed at length in chapter 4, merits a brief mention here given its direct bearing on the equity–efficiency debate. Frustrated by the lack of progress in regional institutions, particularly the ASEAN Regional Forum, Rudd and his Australian colleagues called for an overhaul of Asia's security architecture.[20] However, some regional countries took umbrage with subsequent iterations of Rudd's APC idea which advocated the formation of what amounted to a concert of powers – whose membership would include the extant great power and middle power stakeholders of Asia's architecture – that would presumably co-manage the APC.[21] If realized, a concert arrangement could lead to improved regional governance in Asia as hoped by those who prioritize efficiency of regional architecture over equity, but it could also effectively marginalize countries within the APC that are not part of the concert from having a say in the decision-making process – a concern very much at the heart of regional opposition against Rudd's proposal.[22]

### *Inter-stakeholder dynamics*

The proliferation of institutions in Asia has not only been driven by the political imperative for collective action among regional states – defined largely in terms of regional integration and trade liberalization for economic-oriented institutions[23] and multilateral dialogue, cooperative security, the building of mutual confidence and transparency, preventive diplomacy, and normative socialization for security-oriented institutions[24] – in response to challenges common to all. The perceived need to balance as well as hedge against one another within their respective institutional cum intramural contexts has equally been a key driver.[25] While the formation and maintenance of Asia's 'multi-multilateral' architecture has been driven in part by the perceived need to mobilize collective action among regional states and to ensure regional coordination and collaboration, those institutional settings have also become arenas where states engage with as well as balance against each other. On the one hand, they pursue diplomatic engagement and economic cooperation with one another. On the other hand, they balance each other using diplomatic and institutional means to counter against and constrain the power and influence of those they deem threatening.[26] Such 'soft' balancing is somewhat similar to the notion of 'associative' balancing, where states collectively exercise self-restraint and mutual regulation of each other's power and intentions as was the case, so argued, with the Concert of Europe in the nineteenth century.[27] In times of relative strategic stability and/or uncertainty, states may opt to hedge using a combination of engagement and balancing.[28]

A concern for Asian multilateralism as such is what happens when conditions which favour engagement, soft balancing and hedging no longer exist. Arguably, this is a potential outcome for Asia in the light of China's inexorable rise, America's 'pivot' or 'rebalancing' to Asia, and the push-and-pull effect that has had on regional states as they struggle to strengthen their existing alignments or establish new ones. If the resulting tensions are not mitigated, the net outcome could well be the wholesale adoption of hard military balancing by one and all. Critics of soft balancing also contend that the conceptual line between soft and hard balancing is a slippery slope.[29] The risk of escalation from soft to hard is also compounded by the conclusion of some that balancing does not necessarily produce moderation and restraint among states as conventional balance of power theory has presupposed. Instead, an effective balance of power system depends on the pre-existence of moderation and restraint.[30] Given the pervasiveness of balancing and hedging within Asian multilateralism, the effectiveness of the region's institutions depends on the shared willingness of its participants to exercise restraint even if they stand to incur costs to themselves in the short term. While the region's institutional woes are many, the lack of restraint by states, many whose security outlooks are increasingly coloured by nationalistic sentiments, has become a key cause of interstate tensions.[31]

What is true for effective multilateralism is true also for interstate stability more generally: a sustained mutual exercise in restraint and the formation of healthy and ambitious bilateral relationships among key actors and great powers. Received wisdom has it that the success of European integration would not have been possible without restraint and rapprochement between Europe's two key powers, France and Germany.[32] The very existence of ASEAN would not have been possible without Indonesia's moderation following its undeclared war against

Malaysia and Singapore (1963–6) known as Confrontation.[33] 'Any solution must improve bilateral relationships and base institutional cooperation on a pre-existing commonality of interest', as Thomas Wright has argued about effective multilateralism. 'States should work to convert their strongest bilateral relationships into multilateral arrangements. Beyond mere shared commitment to an aspirational goal, true common interests are rooted in considerable overlap of how countries see and reach solutions to problems'.[34]

The dynamics of balancing, engagement, and hedging are not restricted to state-to-state interactions within institutions, however. The multiplicity of institutions in Asia – the 'oversupply of region', according to one formulation[35] – also enables states to balance one another *across* institutions. In this respect, the complex character of Asia's multi-multilateralism in effect allows states to mitigate the impact of the predominance of any single state in one institutional context by shifting the locus of regional activity and attention to other institutional contexts.[36] By the same token, it has also been argued that interstate relations that face gridlock in one institution could be taken up in other institutional settings where breakthroughs could be sought.[37] This also presupposes a level of instrumental and normative commitment on the part of countries to Asia's suite of institutions. While states will always be tempted to pursue *à la carte* multilateralism for pragmatic and strategic reasons, they will do well to avoid making false choices between and among institutions, say, by unequivocally and uncritically favouring and choosing institutions built for efficiency over those built for equity. After all, recent history – for example, the United States' foreign policy unilateralism during the first term of George W. Bush's presidency – suggests that a state's marginalizing of institutions can carry tangible costs, such as squandering its legitimacy to have a say (much less lead) and lost opportunities for it to encourage burden sharing with its counterparts in cooperative enterprises, which could lead ultimately to the erosion of international order.[38]

## Institutional design

There is no shortage of regional arrangements in Asia, whose institutional landscape appears multi-layered and overlapping. There are formal or standing multilateral institutions such as the Asia-Pacific Economic Cooperation (APEC), the ASEAN Regional Forum (ARF), the ASEAN Plus Three (APT), the East Asia Summit (EAS) and the ASEAN Defence Ministers' Meeting Plus (ADMM-Plus). There are also functionally oriented or interest-based arrangements where like-minded countries band together to collaborate on particular concerns – as noted earlier, so-called 'mini-lateral' or 'pluri-lateral' arrangements[39] – which include regional trade pacts like the Trans-Pacific Partnership (TPP) and the Regional Comprehensive Economic Partnership (RCEP), or so-called 'natural economic regions' such as the Greater Mekong Sub-region and the Greater Tumen Initiative, or security arrangements like the Six Party Talks (SPT) and the US-led Proliferation Security Initiative (PSI) and Container Security Initiative (CSI). Crucially, multilateralism in Asia was not planned but an ad hoc phenomenon, where institutions were formed spontaneously to address immediate challenges and specific problem areas. It also means there is no overarching structure or process – a kind of 'top level management' endowed with steering capacity – to link and coordinate disparate institutions and initiatives together. In other words, Asia lacks robust institutions: far from institution-*light* (not lacking in institutions), the region is instead institution-*lite* (with relatively weak institutions).[40] Amitav Acharya has argued that from the Asian Relations Conference of 1947 on and through the Afro-Asian Conference (more commonly known as the Bandung Conference) of 1955, ideas such as non-interference, national sovereignty, and the rejection of collective defence have served as a sort of region-wide 'cognitive prior' which, by the logic of path dependence, have normatively influenced the design of most if not all institutions in the Asian region.[41] Whether that has indeed been the case is debatable, but what is incontrovertible is the broad similarity in institutional characteristics – with some notable nuances, to be sure – throughout the region.

Generally speaking, the following attributes can be noted of Asia's institutions. First, they are predominantly intergovernmental or 'top down' in character. Most if not all are convened at the level of either annual summits of Heads of Government/ State or ministerial meetings. Important nuances exist, however. ASEAN is a good example of a highly centralized arrangement. Part of the reason why ASEAN has not invested heavily in a strengthened secretariat is because it wants to retain all decision-making prerogatives in the hands of the national leaders and policymakers. This is equally true of the 'ASEAN complex' of institutions – that is, ASEAN plus its suite of pan-Asia spin-offs – at the cross-regional level.[42]

Second, they make decisions based on consensus and/or unanimity, not majority-voting. All Asian institutions, bar none, are consensus-based. Here too there are nuances, as most if not all exercise flexible consensus. The 'ASEAN minus x' and 'two plus x' principles are a good example, where latitude is given to member states of ASEAN willingly to decide on the terms of their involvement in cooperative ventures. Accordingly, countries that are ready to undertake cooperation can proceed without having to get the unanimous approval of all their fellows.[43] Based on the same principle, the ASEAN Charter allows subgroups of ASEAN countries to push ahead with more ambitious agreements so long as consensus among them exists.[44] Two related concepts used in studies of European integration are useful here, namely, variable geometries and concentric circles.[45]

Variable geometry refers to the idea that countries participate in regional integration efforts at different speeds, to different extents, and in different issue areas. The subgroup of ready countries may wish to push forward with cooperation, while the subgroup of not yet ready countries can join later. The *ARF Annual Security Outlook*, an annual series of white paper-styled statements by ARF members on their national and regional security perspectives, is an example of variable geometry since submission is done on a purely voluntary basis. The enterprise still does not enjoy regular participation by all ARF members. Concentric circles – 'ASEAN inside APT inside EAS', according to one analyst[46] – refer to the prospect of a hard core or inner circle of countries proceeding with integration first, with the outer circle following later when they are ready or as and when the core group 'invites' or 'permits' them to do so.[47] Arguably, ASEAN's aim to establish a regional community in Southeast Asia by 2015 – the ASEAN Community with distinct economic, political-security and socio-cultural communities as its pillars – with the likelihood of a larger community at the East Asian (or, for that matter, Asia Pacific) level to follow, can be considered an illustration of a concentric circles approach to regional integration. Another example, though a considerably more implicit and negative one, is the possibility of China, as the pre-eminent force in the APT, potentially feeling squeezed by the inner ASEAN circle and the outer EAS circle.[48] An entirely different example is the oft-cited complaint by non-ASEAN members of the ARF that they feel treated by their ASEAN counterparts as 'second-class citizens' within the ARF.[49] In other words, the logic of concentric circles could serve as a form of exclusion.

Further, despite their design as flexible consensus organizations,[50] decision-making in Asian institutions can prove inflexible as well, however. The failure of the ARF to agree on and implement preventive diplomacy underscores the difficulty in cutting flexible consensus deals so long as there is no 'buy in' from powerful or influential members in the ARF.[51] The free rider problem – the notion that if others are cooperating for mutual benefit and one benefits from their cooperation, then one has an obligation to do one's share[52] – could also be a likely disincentive against interested members who otherwise might have jointly pursued preventive diplomacy as a subgroup within the ARF if the conditions were ripe. Probably, decisions based on flexible consensus are easier to achieve in economic rather than security cooperation because of the greater preoccupation over sovereignty and non-interference concerns in Asian security affairs. Also, consensus decision-making becomes more complicated in sizeable groupings, where the tendency in decision-making to seek the lowest common denominator and keep the comfort level of all concerned is likely to produce unimpressive and grossly diluted outcomes.[53]

Third, their institutional mandates and modalities are largely advisory rather than regulatory. As intergovernmental consensus-driven organizations, Asian institutions lack the regulative and punitive mechanisms for impelling wayward member states to comply with agreed-upon norms, rules and regulations. As such, the only way such institutions have been able to make decisions historically is through social persuasion.[54] True, ASEAN is gradually moving towards a regulatory model, particularly as the sub-region integrates economically. But it is still early days. It is not the removal of tariff barriers but rather of non-tariff and other regulatory impediments ('behind the border' barriers) that is at issue.[55] Indeed, even the former secretary-general of ASEAN, Surin Pitsuwan, has publicly conceded that ASEAN is unlikely to meet its express goal of realizing the formation of the ASEAN Economic Community (much less that of the ASEAN Political-Security Community and/or the ASEAN Socio-Cultural Community) by 2015.[56] Given the premium placed on sovereignty and the general treatment of legalization and institutionalization by Asian states as matters of strategic choice (that is, pursued solely according to whether it meets one's national interests and priorities, including enhancing one's relative power position over others, especially perceived rivals) rather than normative necessity (that is, a good thing worth pursuing on its own terms),[57] the reliance on dialogue as the modus operandi of regionalism has meant that the mandates and approach of the region's institutions remains advisory and process-oriented, rather than regulatory and outcomes-oriented.[58] This is not to imply the region's institutions will stay this way. In Southeast Asia, efforts are underway gradually to transform the region's extant 'soft' form of regionalism to a 'hard' or rules-based one. That said, while ASEAN has signalled its intent to develop a rules-based, regulatory regionalism (particularly in support of economic integration), the lack of provision within its dispute settlement mechanism to ensure rule compliance and enforcement — in this respect, Article 27 of the ASEAN Charter on compliance is non-comprehensive and deficient — and the retention of the 'ASEAN Way' in the charter — both its 'legal' norms (national sovereignty and non-intervention/non-interference principles) and 'social' norms (consultation and consensus)[59] — has raised questions about whether ASEAN, arguably the most established and progressive of the Asian institutions, is truly ready for regulatory regionalism.

Fourth, the agreements Asian multilateral institutions make have primarily been voluntary and non-binding. Perhaps more than any other reason, it is this fourth factor that best explains the relatively slow pace of security cooperation in East Asia. All regional institutions are voluntary non-binding arrangements that rely on the force of suasion to move cooperation forward.[60] What is striking about the ASEAN Charter that was established in 2007 and ratified fully by all ten member countries in 2008 — 'a legally binding agreement among the ten ASEAN Member States', as the language of the Charter has it — is the absence of robust compliance provisions, despite the inclusion of an article on compliance within the Charter. This basically means no country can legally be held accountable for 'failures', real or perceived, to satisfy the terms of regional agreements. Indeed, most such agreements come with escape clauses. Morally and politically, of course, states that have behaved in ways contrary to what the majority of its fellow institutional members might have preferred — Myanmar during its crackdown on the so-called Saffron Revolution in August 2007 and Cambodia's perceptibly pro-China stance at the ASEAN ministerial meeting in July 2012 are two recent examples[61] — face the ire of the others for their perceived dissension. In lieu of an obligatory system and culture taking root any time soon, regional institutions have had to adopt imaginative ways to circumvent the problem of non-compliance to consensus decisions. For example, in the economic area, APEC officials initiated a peer review process of the annual submission of members' individual action plans (IAPs) of measures in thirteen areas to achieve the so-called 'Bogor Goals', the two sets of goals set by APEC for its developed and developing member economies.[62] Interestingly, the peer review process has, as hoped, created a system of peer pressure to nudge member countries towards taking the progressive steps necessary for accelerating growth. In the ARF, there is an ongoing attempt to get ARF states to consider enhancing the *Annual Security Outlook* to which they contribute on a voluntary basis.

Fifth, Asia's institutions have few dispute and feedback mechanisms available. Until the ASEAN Charter, Asian institutions did not have explicit mechanisms for dispute settlement. Nor, for that matter, the ability to enforce compliance following settlement – a concern that still dogs the grouping's charter to this day. ASEAN has three putative mechanisms for dispute settlement, namely, the High Council of the Treaty of Amity and Cooperation (TAC), the Protocol for Enhanced Dispute Settlement Mechanism (EDSM) for disputes relating to ASEAN economic agreements, and of course the ASEAN Charter. To date, neither the High Council nor the EDSM have been used by member states.[63] This exercise may be seen as a way to develop a feedback mechanism that appears to be more systematic than the ad hoc review processes employed by ASEAN and its suite of regional arrangements.

Sixth and lastly, institutions in Asia have weak secretariats and are, with few exceptions, generally weak in their delegation of power to non-governmental agencies. The preceding points – institutions as intergovernmental, advisory, non-binding, weak in dispute settlement, and the like – militate against any impetus for strong secretariats. In the case of ASEAN, the gap between its institutional ambition as expressed in its documents and developmental blueprints, on the one hand, and the capacity of its secretariat to implement them on the other is tellingly wide. As one analyst has observed:

> The need for an ASEAN-dedicated civil service is compelling – a regional bureaucracy capable of planning, introducing and managing reforms, rules and regulations to be adopted in compliance with the Charter and the ASEAN Community Blueprints. Capacity-building programs on technical and regional matters are needed not only for personnel working in ASEAN institutions, but also (and mainly) for staff in national agencies involved in ASEAN affairs. Increasing awareness of how regional cooperation can strengthen the national interest would be an important aspect of such training.[64]

ASEAN's reliance on a system of equal contributions – where wealthy Singapore contributes the same amount as the poorest ASEAN member, Laos – rather than relative to country Gross Domestic Product (GDP) effectively diminishes any prospect for an enhanced secretariat (unless external funding is available).[65] Granted, some ASEAN member countries provide developmental assistance to one another. Singapore, for example, gives mostly but not exclusively to the CLMV countries (Cambodia, Laos, Myanmar and Vietnam) through a variety of modalities such as the Singapore Cooperation Programme and the Initiative for ASEAN Integration.[66]

## Conclusion

This chapter has provided a sense of what Asia's multi-multilateral architecture looks like, the conditions under which that architecture has emerged and the various political-strategic purposes its stakeholders hope that architecture would serve, and the institutional design and outcomes that have arisen as a consequence of the predominantly ad hoc manner in which those stakeholders have approached the multilateral enterprise in Asia. The following chapters address the question of who has been responsible for shaping that architecture and the way its component parts have turned out. That ASEAN has played a key part in that process is not in question here. But so have non-ASEAN stakeholders as well.

## Notes

1 Amitav Acharya, 'Ideas, Identity and Institution-Building: From the "ASEAN Way" to the "Asia-Pacific Way"?', *The Pacific Review*, Vol. 10, No. 3 (1997), pp. 319–46; Simon Chesterman and Kishore Mahbubani, 'The Asian Way of Handling the World', *The Guardian*, 4 March 2010, www.theguardian.com/commentisfree/2010/mar/04/global-problem-solving-asian-way; Michael Haas, *The Asian Way to Peace: A Story of Regional Cooperation* (Portsmouth, NH: Greenwood Publishing Group, 1989).
2 Richard K. Betts, 'East Asia and the United States after the Cold War', *International Security*, Vol. 18, No. 3 (1993/94), pp. 34–77; Barry Buzan and Gerald Segal, 'Rethinking East Asian Security', *Survival*, Vol. 36, No. 2 (1994), pp. 3–21; Aaron L. Friedberg, 'Ripe for Rivalry: Prospects for Peace in a Multipolar Asia', *International Security*, Vol. 18, No. 3 (1993/94), pp. 5–33.
3 Shaun Breslin, Christopher Hughes, Nicola Phillips and Ben Rosamond, eds., *New Regionalisms in the Global Political Economy: Theories and Cases* (London: Routledge, 2002); Björn Hettne and András Inotai, eds., *The New Regionalism: Implications for Global Development and International Security* (Helsinki: United Nations University/World Institute for Development Economics Research, 1994).
4 Ellen L. Frost, *Asia's New Regionalism* (Boulder, CO: Lynne Rienner, 2008); See Seng Tan, ed., *Regionalism in Asia Vol. 3: Regional Order and Architecture* (Abingdon: Routledge, 2009).
5 Tanja A. Börzel and Thomas Risse, *Diffusing (Inter-)Regionalism: The EU as a Model of Regional Integration*, KFG Working Paper, No. 7 (Berlin: Free University, September 2009); Amitav Acharya and Alastair Iain Johnston, 'Comparing Regional Institutions: An Introduction', in Amitav Acharya and Alastair Iain Johnston, eds., *Crafting Cooperation: Regional International Institutions in Comparative Perspective* (Cambridge: Cambridge University Press, 2007), pp. 1–31.
6 Paul Evans, 'Between Regionalism and Regionalization: Policy Networks and the Nascent East Asian Institutional Identity', in T. J. Pempel, ed., *Remapping East Asia: The Construction of a Region* (Ithaca, NY: Cornell University Press, 2005), pp. 195–215, at p. 196; Michael Leifer, *ASEAN's Search for Regional Order* (Singapore: Faculty of Arts and Social Sciences, National University of Singapore, 1987), p. 21.
7 As Brent Scowcroft once observed, 'It's easy in the name of stability to be comfortable with the status quo'. Cited in Jeffrey Goldberg, 'Breaking Ranks: What Turned Brent Scowcroft against the Bush Administration?', *The New Yorker*, 31 October 2005, www.newyorker.com/archive/2005/10/31/051031fa_fact2?currentPage=all.
8 Evans, 'Between Regionalism and Regionalization', p. 195; Samuel S. Kim, 'Regionalization and Regionalism in East Asia', *Journal of East Asian Studies*, Vol. 4, No. 1 (2004), pp. 39–68, see pp. 18–19.
9 Amitav Acharya, *The End of American World Order* (Oxford: Polity Press, 2014); Victor D. Cha, 'Complex Patchworks: U.S. Alliances as Part of Asia's Regional Architecture', *Asia Policy*, No. 11 (2011), pp. 27–50; Stephen D. Haggard, 'The Organizational Architecture of the Asia-Pacific: Insights from the New Institutionalism', in Miles Kahler and Andrew MacIntyre, eds., *Integrating Regions: Asia in Comparative Context*, (Stanford, CA: Stanford University Press, 2013), pp. 195–221, on p. 195; T. J. Pempel, 'Soft Balancing, Hedging, and Institutional Darwinism: The Economic-Security Nexus and East Asian Regionalism', *Journal of East Asian Studies*, Vol. 10, No. 2 (May–August 2010), pp. 209–38.

10. William T. Tow and Brendan Taylor, 'What is Asian Security Architecture?', *Review of International Studies*, Vol. 36, No. 1 (2010), pp. 95–116.
11. Haggard, 'The Organizational Architecture of the Asia-Pacific', p. 195.
12. Moisés Naím, 'Minilateralism: The Magic Number to Get Real International Action', *Foreign Policy*, 22 June 2009, www.foreignpolicy.com/articles/2009/06/18/minilateralism; Stewart Patrick, 'Prix Fixe *and* à la Carte: Avoiding False Multilateral Choices', *The Washington Quarterly*, Vol. 32, No. 4 (2009), pp. 77–95; Thomas Wright, 'Toward Effective Multilateralism: Why Bigger May Not Be Better', *The Washington Quarterly*, Vol. 32, No. 3 (2009), pp. 163–80.
13. Francis Fukuyama, *America at the Crossroads: Democracy, Power, and the Neoconservative Legacy* (New Haven, CT: Yale University Press, 2007), p. 163.
14. F. Merand and S. Hofmann, 'Regional Institutions à la Carte: Mechanisms of Variable Geometry in Europe', paper presented at the annual meeting of the International Studies Association Annual Conference, Montreal, 16 March 2011; John A. Usher, 'Variable Geometry or Concentric Circles: Patterns for the European Union', *International and Comparative Law Quarterly*, Vol. 46, No. 2 (1997), pp. 243–73.
15. Joseph Camilleri, 'East Asia's Emerging Regionalism: Tensions and Potential in Design and Architecture', *Global Change, Peace and Security*, Vol. 17, No. 3 (2005), pp. 253–61; Allan Gyngell, 'Design Faults: The Asia Pacific's Regional Architecture', *Lowy Institute Policy Brief*, 18 July (Sydney, NSW: Lowy Institute for International Policy, 2007).
16. Andrew Potter, 'Two Concepts of Legitimacy', *MacLean's*, 3 December 2008, www.macleans.ca/general/two-concepts-of-legitimacy/.
17. Dingxin Zhao, 'The Mandate of Heaven and Performance Legitimation in Historical and Contemporary China', *American Behavioral Scientist*, Vol. 53, No. 3 (2009), pp. 416–33.
18. Naím, 'Minilateralism'.
19. Susan C. Schwab, 'After Doha: Why the Negotiations Are Doomed and What We Should Do About It', *Foreign Affairs*, Vol. 90, No. 3 (2011), pp. 104–77, at p. 104.
20. Tim Colebatch, 'Rudd's Grand Vision for Asia-Pacific', *The Age*, 5 June 2008.
21. Graeme Dobell, 'An Asia Pacific Concert by Another name', *Lowy Interpreter*, 11 October 2011, www.lowyinterpreter.org/post/2011/10/11/The-Asia-Pacific-concert-by-another-name.aspx?COLLCC=4060986791&.
22. Amitav Acharya, 'Asia-Pacific Security: Community, Concert or What?', *PacNet*, No. 11, 12 March 2010.
23. Peter Drysdale and Shiro Armstrong, 'Does APEC Matter?', *East Asia Forum*, 8 November 2009, www.eastasiaforum.org/2009/11/08/does-apec-matter/; K. Kesavapany and Hank Lim, eds., *APEC at 20: Recall, Reflect, Remake* (Singapore: Institute of Southeast Asian Studies, 2009); Charles E. Morrison and Eduardo Pedrosa, eds., *An APEC Trade Agenda? The Political Economy of a Free Trade Area of the Asia-Pacific* (Singapore: Institute of Southeast Asian Studies, 2007); John Ravenhill, *APEC and the Construction of Pacific Rim Regionalism* (Cambridge: Cambridge University Press, 2002).
24. Kevin P. Clements, 'Common Security in the Asia-Pacific Region: Problems and Prospects', *Alternatives: Global, Local, Political*, Vol. 14, No. 1 (1983), pp. 49–76; Ralph A. Cossa, *Multilateral Dialogue in Asia: Building on a Strong Bilateral Base* (Honolulu, HI: Pacific Forum CSIS, 1994); David B. Dewitt, 'Common, Comprehensive, and Cooperative Security', *The Pacific Review*, Vol. 7, No. 1 (1994), pp. 1–15; Ralf Emmers, *Cooperative Security and the Balance of Power in ASEAN and the ARF* (London: Routledge, 2003); Harry Harding, 'Cooperative Security in the Asia-Pacific', in Janne E. Nolan, ed., *Global Engagement: Cooperation and Security in the 21st Century* (Washington, D.C.: The Brookings Institution Press, 1994), pp. 419–46; Hiro Katsumata, *ASEAN's Cooperative Security Enterprise: Norms and Interests in the ASEAN Regional Forum* (London: Palgrave Macmillan, 2010); Takeshi Yuzawa, 'The

Evolution of Preventive Diplomacy in the ASEAN Regional Forum: Problems and Prospects', *Asian Survey*, Vol. 46, No. 5 (September/October 2006), pp. 785–804.
25 Yuen Foong Khong, 'Coping with Strategic Uncertainty: The Role of Institutions and Soft Balancing in Southeast Asia's Post-Cold War Strategy', in J. J. Suh, Peter J. Katzenstein, and Alan Carlson, eds., *Rethinking Security in East Asia: Identity, Power, and Efficiency* (Stanford, CA: Stanford University Press, 2004), pp. 172–298; Evan S. Medeiros, 'Strategic Hedging and the Future of Asia-Pacific Stability', *The Washington Quarterly*, Vol. 29, No. 1 (2005/6), pp. 145–67; Pempel, 'Soft Balancing, Hedging, and Institutional Darwinism'.
26 Robert A. Pape, 'Soft Balancing against the United States', *International Security*, Vol. 30, No. 1 (Summer 2005), pp. 7–45; T. V. Paul, 'Soft Balancing in the Age of US Primacy', *International Security*, Vol. 30, No. 1 (Summer 2005), pp. 46–71.
27 Richard Little, 'Deconstructing the Balance of Power: Two Traditions of Thought', *Review of International Studies*, Vol. 15, No. 2 (1989), pp. 87–100.
28 Medeiros, 'Strategic Hedging and the Future of Asia-Pacific Stability'.
29 Stephen G. Brooks and William C. Wohlforth, 'Hard Times for Soft Balancing', *International Security*, Vol. 30, No. 1 (Summer 2005), pp. 72–108.
30 Inis L. Claude, 'The Balance of Power Revisited', *Review of International Studies*, Vol. 15, No. 2 (1989), pp. 77–85.
31 William A. Callahan, *China: The Pessoptimist Nation* (Oxford: Oxford University Press, 2012); Stephen van Evera, 'Hypotheses on Nationalism and War', *International Security*, Vol. 18, No. 4 (Spring 1994), pp. 5–39; John A. Hall and Siniša Malešević, eds., *Nationalism and War* (Cambridge: Cambridge University Press, 2013).
32 Mette Eilstrup-Sangiovanni and Daniel Verdier, 'European Integration as a Solution to War', *European Journal of International Relations*, Vol. 11, No. 1 (2005), pp. 99–135.
33 Michael Leifer, *ASEAN and the Security of South East Asia* (London: Routledge, 1989).
34 Wright, 'Toward Effective Multilateralism', p. 164.
35 Shaun Breslin, 'Comparative Theory, China, and the Future of East Asian Regionalism(s)', *Review of International Studies*, Vol. 36, No. 3 (July 2010), pp. 709–29.
36 Christopher W. Hughes, 'Japan's Response to China's Rise: Regional Engagement, Global Containment, Dangers of Collision', *International Affairs*, Vol. 85, No. 4 (2009), pp. 837–56.
37 Cha, 'Complex Patchworks'.
38 Patrick, 'Prix Fixe *and* à la Carte', p. 84.
39 Miles Kahler, *International Institutions and the Political Economy of Integration* (Washington, D.C.: The Brookings Institution, 1995), p. 5.
40 See Seng Tan, 'Is Asia-Pacific Regionalism Outgrowing ASEAN?', *The RUSI Journal*, Vol. 156, No. 1 (2011), pp. 58–62.
41 Amitav Acharya, *Whose Ideas Matter? Agency and Power in Asian Regionalism* (Ithaca, NY: Cornell University Press, 2009), pp. 69–111. On path dependence, see James Mahoney, 'Path Dependence in Historical Sociology', *Theory and Society*, Vol. 29, No. 4 (2000), pp. 507–48.
42 On the other hand, the SAARC is slightly more decentralized with a system of regional centres, albeit for implementing facets of economic (i.e. non-security-related) cooperation. Muhammad Jamshed Iqbal, 'SAARC: Origin, Growth, Potential and Achievements', *Pakistan Journal of History & Culture*, Vol. 26, No. 2 (2006), pp. 127–40.
43 Amitav Acharya, *Constructing a Security Community in Southeast Asia: ASEAN and the Problem of Regional Order* (London: Routledge, 2000), p. 263; Denis Hew, 'Introduction: Roadmap to an ASEAN Economic Community', in Denis Hew, ed., *Roadmap to an ASEAN Economic Community* (Singapore: Institute of Southeast Asian Studies, 2005), pp. 1–12, on p. 3; Lee Jones, *ASEAN, Sovereignty and Intervention in Southeast Asia* (London: Palgrave Macmillan, 2011), p. 31; Rodolfo C. Severino, *Southeast Asia in Search of an ASEAN Community: Insights from the Former ASEAN*

Secretary-General (Singapore: Institute of Southeast Asian Studies, 2006), p. 353; Barry Desker, 'Is the ASEAN Charter Necessary?', *RSIS Commentaries*, No. 77/2008, 17 July 2008.
44 See Chapter VII, Article 21, Paragraph 2 of the ASEAN Charter.
45 Merand and Hofmann, 'Regional Institutions *à la Carte*'; Usher, 'Variable Geometry or Concentric Circles'.
46 Donald K. Emmerson, *Asian Regionalism and US Policy: The Case for Creative Adaptation*, RSIS Working Paper, No. 193 (Singapore: S. Rajaratnam School of International Studies, Nanyang Technological University, 2010), p. 5.
47 Yasumasa Komori, 'Asia's Institutional Creation and Evolution', *Asian Perspective*, Vol. 33, No. 3 (2009), pp. 151–82.
48 Emmerson, *Asian Regionalism and US Policy*, p. 5.
49 Michael Leifer, *The ASEAN Regional Forum: Extending ASEAN's Model of Regional Security*, Adelphi Paper, No. 302 (Oxford: Oxford University Press for International Institute for Strategic Studies, 1996).
50 Alastair Iain Johnston, 'Socialization in International Institutions: The ASEAN Way and International Relations Theory', in G. John Ikenberry and Michael Mastanduno, eds., *International Relations Theory and the Asia-Pacific* (New York: Columbia University Press, 2003), pp. 107–62.
51 Ralf Emmers and See Seng Tan, 'The ASEAN Regional Forum and Preventive Diplomacy: Built to Fail?', *Asian Security*, Vol. 7, No. 1 (2011), pp. 44–60.
52 H. L. A. Hart, 'Are There any Natural Rights?', *Philosophical Review*, Vol. 64 (1955), pp. 175–91, on pp. 185–6; John Rawls, *A Theory of Justice* (Cambridge, MA: Harvard University Press, 1971), p. 96. However, philosophers like Robert Nozick feel that this proposition is not as straightforward as it sounds because it assumes that others could impose an obligation on us by dint of their acting cooperatively to provide some good from which we also benefit. Robert Nozick, *Anarchy, the State, and Utopia* (New York: Basic Books, 1974), pp. 90–5.
53 Miles Kahler, 'Multilateralism with Small and Large Numbers', *International Organization*, Vol. 46, No. 3 (Summer 1992), pp. 681–708.
54 See Seng Tan, 'Herding Cats: The Role of Persuasion in Political Change and Continuity in the Association of Southeast Asian Nations (ASEAN)', *International Relations of the Asia-Pacific*, Vol. 13, No. 2 (2013), pp. 233–65.
55 Maria Monica Wihardja, 'Second-Generation Reform in Asia', *East Asia Forum*, 18 August 2011, www.eastasiaforum.org/2011/08/18/second-generation-reforms-the-key-to-deeper-regional-cooperation/.
56 Yang Razali Kassim, 'ASEAN Community: Losing Grip over Vision 2015?', *RSIS Commentaries*, No. 87/2011, 2 June 2011.
57 Miles Kahler, 'Legalization as Strategy: The Asia-Pacific Case', *International Organization*, Vol. 54, No. 3 (2000), pp. 549–71.
58 David Martin Jones and Michael L. R. Smith, 'Making Process, Not Progress: ASEAN and the Evolving East Asian Regional Order', *International Security*, Vol. 32, No. 1 (2007), pp. 148–84.
59 Matthias Baier, ed., *Social and Legal Norms: Towards a Socio-legal Understanding of Normativity* (Farnham: Ashgate, 2013); Shaun Narine, 'The English School and ASEAN', in Amitav Acharya and Richard Stubbs, ed., *Theorizing Southeast Asian Relations: Emerging Debates* (Abingdon: Routledge, 2013), pp. 71–89, see pp. 74–5.
60 Alice D. Ba, 'Who's Socializing Whom? Complex Engagement in China–ASEAN Relations', *The Pacific Review*, Vol. 19, No. 2 (2006), pp. 157–79; Alastair Iain Johnston, *Social States: China in International Institutions, 1980–2000* (Princeton, NJ: Princeton University Press, 2007).
61 Don Emmerson, 'ASEAN Stumbles in Phnom Penh', *PacNet*, No. 45, 19 July 2012; Christopher Roberts, *ASEAN's Myanmar Crisis: Challenges to the Pursuit of a Security Community* (Singapore: Institute of Southeast Asian Studies, 2010), p. 173.

62 Ippei Yamazawa, *How to Meet the Mid-term Bogor Goal?*, ISEAS Paper, May 2009, www.iseas.edu.sg/apec/D1S1S3_Paper_Yamazawa.pdf.
63 Acharya, *Whose Ideas Matter?*, p. 141; Paul J. Davidson, *The Legal Framework for International Economic Relations: ASEAN and Canada* (Singapore: Institute of Southeast Asian Studies, 1997), p. 156; Denis Hew, *Brick by Brick: The Building of an ASEAN Economic Community* (Singapore: Institute of Southeast Asian Studies, 2007), p. 212. In the case of SAARC, the South Asian Free Trade Agreement (SAFTA) provides a settlement mechanism, which remains unused since SAFTA itself has not taken off. Indeed, SAARC patently avoids discussing certain contentious bilateral issues (read Indo-Pakistani affairs). Feedback mechanisms in the region have tended to be ad hoc in nature. The use of Eminent Persons Groups (EPGs) as an ad hoc review process is a relatively common practice. For instance, the decision by the ARF officially to produce a preventive diplomacy work plan in 2011 was preceded by an exhaustive review conducted by the ARF EPG – with the aid of the work of research institutes – of best practices by international institutions around the world on preventive diplomacy. The Pacific Islands institutions have come up with an innovative way to obtain feedback: the Council of Regional Organizations in the Pacific (CROP) has adopted a review exercise on the effectiveness of these institutions under the so-called Regional Institutional Framework (RIF). Kaliopate Tavola et al., *Reforming the Pacific Regional Institutional Framework*, SOPAC Paper, August 2006, www.sopac.org/sopac/docs/RIF/07_RIF%20study,%20final_Tavola%20et%20al.pdf.
64 Giovanni Capannelli, 'Time to Create an ASEAN Academy', *East Asia Forum*, 22 November 2013, www.eastasiaforum.org/2013/11/22/time-to-create-an-asean-academy/.
65 Michael Ewing-Chow and Tan Hsien-Li, *The Role of the Rule of Law in ASEAN Integration*, EUI Working Paper RSCAS 2013/16 (Badia Fiesolana: European University Institute, 2013), p. 17.
66 Ong Keng Yong, 'Asian Economies Now Providing More Aid and Development Assistance: The Case of Singapore', Keynote Address at the International Volunteer Cooperation Organization (IVCO), 4 October 2010, p. 2, www.spp.nus.edu.sg/ips/docs/enewsletter/Dec2010/OKY_Asian%20Economies%20Now%20Providing%20More%20Aid_011210.pdf. In Central Asia, the lack of financial, administrative and technical capacities has meant reliance on the Asian Development Bank (ADB) to act as secretariat for that sub-region's institutions. Regarding the delegation of powers, the region is generally weak, but here too important nuances exist where governance in non-security areas is concerned. For example, the SAARC secretariat exercises oversight of regional centres created to advance economic cooperation. Zahid Shahab Ahmed, *Regionalism and Regional Security in South Asia: The Role of SAARC* (Farnham: Ashgate, 2013), ch. 3. These centres enjoy a limited measure of autonomy not shared by the various 'offshoots' of ASEAN that manage similar areas of technical cooperation. In the area of resource pooling as a building block of regional economic integration, SAARC's regional centres and the Pacific Islands' South Pacific Commission (SPC) play important implementing roles.

# 3  ASEAN

The idea that ASEAN is principally responsible for the regional institutional architecture in Asia is today commonplace. This is understandable given the oft-heard refrains about 'ASEAN centrality'[1] and ASEAN being in the 'driver's seat'[2] of regionalism in East Asia (and/or the Asia-Pacific). This situation has long been seen as incongruous by realist-minded analysts, who view the professed aim of a group of relatively weak most if not all of the world's great powers – China, Japan, India, Russia, and the United States – as a 'structural flaw'.[3] 'For many IR scholars, ASEAN is an anomaly', as Amitav Acharya has observed:

> It is a group of weak states that has managed to gain the attention of all the major powers. If you look at the list of ASEAN's dialogue partners, which includes all the great powers of the day: China, United States, Japan, the European Union, Russia, India and middle powers like Australia and Canada. This is really unprecedented, for a regional institution to engage all powers in this way. For realism it really is a structural anomaly; weak powers are supposed to be objects rather than subjects of great power attention.[4]

The notion that ASEAN has effectively possessed a measure of local agency if not relative autonomy going back as far as the Cold War years has become a cottage industry. Much of that has focused on the apparent success ASEAN has had in engendering interstate peace and stability in Southeast Asia. Writing in 1982, Donald Zagoria, taking issue with the doomsday predictions of the domino theorists following the fall of South Vietnam, noted that the five non-communist countries of Southeast Asia and founding members of ASEAN – Indonesia, Philippines, Malaysia, Singapore and Thailand – had become one of the fastest growing, relatively stable, and dynamic groups of countries in the Third World: 'They have, moreover, come together in a successful regional organization, ASEAN, which has diminished the likelihood of resort to violent methods to resolve interstate conflicts and has greatly enhanced their overall influence and position in the international community'.[5] Despite questioning the direct impact of ASEAN on economic development in Southeast Asia, Hans Blomqvist concluded in his 1993 article that ASEAN had nonetheless been instrumental in the preservation of peace and stability in the region, wherein the 'patient, gradual deepening of relations between the member countries ... seems to have prepared the ground for more substantial future cooperation and integration'.[6] For Blomqvist, the lesson to be gleaned from the ASEAN experience was that the organization's accomplishments by the early 1990s were extensive because 'its ambitions were realistic and not overly far-reaching in the first place'.[7] And as noted in a recent study,[8] ASEAN, fairly or otherwise, has been lauded at various times as 'the most successful regional organization of its kind in the third world',[9] 'a body without parallel in the developing world',[10] and an institution worthy of attention because it has 'proved durable' and 'fit for purpose'.[11]

This chapter addresses the place and role of ASEAN in Asian regionalism and the regional multilateral architecture in Asia, as portrayed in the relevant academic and policy debates. What is 'ASEAN centrality', and how is it expressed within the context of Asian multilateralism? How central is ASEAN to Asia's regional architecture? The historical importance of ASEAN to regionalism is not in doubt; what is unclear, however, is its current place and role particularly in the light of the growing disenchantment non-ASEAN stakeholders (and, for that matter, some non-official actors in ASEAN countries) feel over what they, fairly or otherwise, see as ASEAN's increasing inability and ineffectiveness to drive regionalism. Needless to say, the issue of the centrality of ASEAN is (no pun intended) central here. In that regard, at least five ways to understand ASEAN centrality are discussed below.

## The house that ASEAN built

A recent commentary by Evelyn Goh on what has arguably been ASEAN's greatest success in Asian multilateralism and, paradoxically, increasingly its most fundamental challenge nicely sums up the general scholarly consensus over the dilemma confronting the regional organization and its member states today. As Goh has noted, on the one hand, 'ASEAN's vital contribution to regional order was in persuading the great powers to commit to a supplementary supporting structure of multilateral confidence-building at a critical juncture of strategic transition after the Cold War ended'.[12] On the other hand, ASEAN's brand of multilateral diplomacy and institutionalism has grown less effective as regional strategic challenges have evolved over the last two decades. 'Increasingly', as Goh has also noted,

> ASEAN's approach to enmeshing the great powers in regional multilateral institutions may be out-dated, as it cannot help to bring about the negotiation of modus vivendi among the great powers themselves so necessary to managing regional stability over the medium- to long-term.[13]

This section will focus on the first aspect, ASEAN's role in securing great power commitment to engaging the region through multilateralism – an approach of which not every great power, not least China and the United States, were particularly supportive for different reasons.

As the orthodoxy on Asian multilateralism has it, a key part of ASEAN's perceived success has to do with its involvement in the formation – an ad hoc and incremental, even (in the view of some) haphazard process, it might be said – of the regional multilateral architecture in post-Cold War Asia. As noted in the previous chapter, the ad hoc approach to institution-building in Asia – 'the tortured course of multilateralism in Asia', according to one view[14] – has produced a multi-multilateral collage of overlapping institutions that implies a serious lack in architectural much less strategic coherence. But incoherence did not mean the absence of strategic motivations which impelled the stakeholders of Asia's architecture to build as they have hitherto done (and, if the occasion warrants it, would probably continue to do). Despite lacking in material or structural power as a group of relatively weak states – in fairness, the ten member countries of ASEAN together comprise a market of 600 million people with a combined annual gross domestic product of US$2.1 trillion, a track record of reasonably solid growth, low manufacturing costs and a rising middle class[15] – ASEAN is arguably an example of an institution that combines what Oran Young has termed 'entrepreneurial' and 'intellectual' types of leadership, where the former involves bringing willing parties together to work for the benefit of all and the latter the use of ideas to shape the way participants understand the issues at hand and the options available to them.[16] Entrepreneurial leadership has much to do with what has been referred to the power to convene. 'Call the right people, and encourage them to come up with a solution', as a US politician once noted. 'Generally, when leaders invite people to the table to work on an issue, they are willing to come'.[17] The notion of intellectual leadership builds on a body of literature on the complex ties between ideas, on the one hand, and on foreign policy and the foreign policy institutions that host them on the other.[18] Crucially, ideas neither float freely nor do they persuade purely on the basis of their merits. As Jeff Checkel has noted, the advocates of new concepts and ideologies do not operate in a vacuum. Rather, they act within institutional and political settings that at different times either constrain or augment their ability to influence policy.[19]

Using the aforementioned understandings of entrepreneurial and intellectual leadership, Richard Stubbs has argued that ASEAN served during the Cold War years as a framework for a number of things, namely: negotiations over regional conflicts; coordination of bargaining positions among the member countries at international forums such as the General Agreement on Tariffs and Trade (GATT); negotiations with the European Economic Community (EEC) and countries such as Australia and Japan over trade and aid concerns; and, collective dissuasion of the major powers from using non-communist Southeast Asian states as proxies in the Cold War.[20] And while the effort at the end of the Cold War to establish the APEC trade forum was largely driven by countries such as Australia and Japan (see chapters 4 and 5) – alternatively, it has also been argued that the ASEAN Post-Ministerial Conference (ASEAN-PMC) process, which brought together foreign ministers from ASEAN countries and five developed Asia-Pacific countries, served as a building block as well for the APEC.[21] The effort rendered by the architects of APEC to assuage the anxieties of ASEAN states that their organization could be diluted or overshadowed by the APEC led to a key concession: the APEC meeting would be held in an ASEAN country every second year – beginning with Singapore in 1990 – and the APEC secretariat would be based in an ASEAN country, Singapore.[22] Furthermore, ASEAN threw its support behind the APEC with the Kuching Consensus of 1990, which urged for increased sensitivity in the APEC process to the wide variances in economic development and socio-political systems among the member economies in the region, as well as the need for consultation on economic issues rather than the adoption of mandatory directives that all members must implement.[23] With the agenda of APEC driven each year by the host country, the arrangement has not only given the ASEAN countries considerable experience in the conduct of large-scale multilateral intergovernmental meetings but also in influencing the direction and substance of regional trade discussions.[24]

Unlike the formation of the APEC, the founding of the ARF involved the direct commitment of participation of ASEAN, whose experience with the former could have presumably impressed on the ASEAN states the benefits of establishing and managing a new regionalism rather than having somebody else do it. While countries such as Australia, Japan and Canada provided the intellectual ballast behind the formation of the ARF – indeed, it is questionable whether intellectual leadership of the sort Stubbs had in mind could at all be attributed to ASEAN where the ARF is concerned – it has been established that the ARF is essentially the outgrowth of the ASEAN–PMC process, ASEAN's annual consultation with its dialogue partners. Unlike the ASEAN–PMC, however, which some have argued was in effect a dialogue among the likeminded, the ARF, at least for its architects, would be more 'inclusive' in bringing together regional actors which have different and perhaps conflicting perspectives on regional security issues.[25] In this respect, the decision by the ASEAN Summit in 1992 to include political and security issues in the ASEAN–PMC agenda, which had hitherto emphasized economic issues, proved to be a critical step towards the eventual formation of the ARF.[26] ASEAN would also play a key role in defining the institutional design and diplomatic convention adopted by the ARF.

Yet as the subsequent country chapters show, ASEAN's insistence on 'retaining the central diplomatic role in the ARF' has engendered both criticism and support from within the ranks of the non-ASEAN members of the ARF.[27] Barely a couple of years in existence, the ARF under ASEAN's leadership was already being dismissed as unable and/or unwilling to contribute to regional security 'because ASEAN insists on its primacy in [the ARF]',[28] and that 'ASEAN is an inappropriate model for the ARF [because] the political, economic, and strategic considerations that have made ASEAN a success within Southeast Asia do not necessarily apply to the more powerful states of the Asia-Pacific region'.[29] A case in point is the attitudinal divide between the so-called 'activist' members – such as Australia, Canada, Japan, the United States and the European Union – that want the ARF to implement preventive diplomacy measures as anticipated in the forum's three-staged roadmap for security cooperation laid out in its 1995 concept paper, on the one hand, and the 'reluctant' member countries – China and most Southeast Asian states, among others – that worry over the ramifications such a direction could mean for their national sovereignty.[30] Despite that, 'it is unlikely that any of the present ARF participants, including those who are increasingly and frustratingly dissatisfied with the "ineffectiveness", utility, and progress of the grouping, would soon desert and quit the ARF', according to Rizal Sukma. 'In other words, it seems that ASEAN will continue to manage the ARF, and non-ASEAN states will keep on participating in the process'.[31]

While the formation of the APT can be considered as East Asia's institutional response to the Asian financial crisis of 1997–8, its development can also be traced back to the Asia–Europe Meeting (ASEM) – established in 1996 as a joint initiative of France and Singapore – where the need to develop a common East Asian position led to regularized consultations between the ASEAN countries and their Northeast Asian counterparts, China, Japan, and South Korea.[32] Early editions of the APT gatherings would further engender the collective sense of the need to develop institutional links between Southeast Asia and Northeast Asia, as well as for a working group to study the merits of an East Asian free trade and investment area. Even then, there was interest among some that the APT could over time become a summit-level gathering and the vehicle through which a future East Asian community could be forged. Others however counselled against moving too quickly in that direction, presumably out of concern over what a new regional summit could mean for ASEAN's pride of place in the evolving regional architecture. As Goh Chok Tong, the then prime minister of Singapore, noted at the APT gathering in Singapore in November 2000, 'I see no problem in ASEAN Plus Three evolving, if that's the desire of leaders, into some kind of East Asia Summit. But there are implications. I myself would not recommend a hasty evolution'.[33]

As things would have it, the EAS – with the inclusion of Australia, India, and New Zealand to the thirteen APT member states – was formed in late 2005, and expanded subsequently in 2011 with Russia and the United States coming on board. Finally, it should be noted that the formation of the ADMM-Plus in 2010, whose membership corresponds with that of the EAS – and prior to that, the ADMM in 2006 – is arguably in response to the Shangri-La Dialogue (SLD), an annual non-official forum for defence ministers and military leaders convened by the London-based International Institute for Strategic Studies (IISS) and held in Singapore since 2002.[34] Modelled after the Munich Conference on Security Policy, the SLD was promoted by some as a plausible official defence gathering, an idea which ASEAN leaders strongly resisted. Be that as it may, it provided the needed impetus for ASEAN to develop its forum for defence ministers.[35]

## What is ASEAN centrality?

Perhaps no concept underscores better the significance of ASEAN to Asian regionalism and Asia's regional architecture than its ostensible *centrality*. Arguably, the incorporation of Russia and the United States into the EAS in 2011 has not only confirmed ASEAN's claim to centrality in East Asian regionalism but also underscored the futility of building formal regional institutions in East

Asia that are neither based on nor originate from ASEAN.[36] For that matter, whether it is the APEC or the ARF or the EAS or the ADMM-Plus, the experiences with all these respective formations of regional frameworks and institutions leave one with the conclusion that any promotion of ideas for new regionalism in Asia, if it is to succeed, has to have the endorsement and support of ASEAN.[37] Given the ad hoc way in which the process of institution-building has taken place, it is unlikely that ASEAN's privileged position in Asia's security architecture was a planned outcome much less a foregone conclusion. Rather, the increasingly central role played by ASEAN in Asian regionalism has emerged more as 'an outcome of its pragmatic approach to problem-solving and its own evolution' in response to the changing international political and economic environment.[38] But as noted earlier, the fundamental challenge confronting ASEAN's ostensible stewardship of Asia's architecture today is the purported disillusionment of non-ASEAN stakeholders over not only their place in that architecture but ASEAN's apparent inability to drive regional cooperation and broker intraregional disputes. The ostensible centrality of ASEAN in Asian regionalism and its continued viability is a fundamental part of the issue.

If the Cold War aim of NATO, as its first Secretary-General Lord Ismay famously said, was to 'to keep the Russians out, the Americans in, and the Germans down',[39] then it could presumably be said that the broad aim of Asian regionalism, as envisaged and executed by ASEAN, has been to keep the Americans on board, the Chinese in check, and ASEAN in charge. The ASEAN Charter, established in 2007 and ratified by all ten ASEAN countries a year later, stresses the need to 'maintain the centrality and proactive role of ASEAN as the primary driving force in its relations and cooperation with its external partners in a regional architecture that is open, transparent and inclusive'.[40] In the organization's report of its Forty-third ASEAN Ministerial Meeting in Hanoi in July 2010, much was made about ASEAN's dialogue partner countries reaffirming 'their unequivocal support for ASEAN Centrality', as well as their declared hope that 'ASEAN would continue to play a central role in the emerging regional architecture'.[41] The centrality of ASEAN is therefore best understood as the perceived default mechanism – a perception ASEAN, above all, has laboured long and hard to maintain, it has been argued[42] – for regional order and stability in the absence of a single power or group of powers which could be accepted by one and all to lead the formation of an Asia-wide agenda, promote regional cooperation and integration, and drive the provision of public goods for the entire region.[43] It is also viewed as a benchmark for the shaping of external relations with other powers and international bodies.[44] As Ernest Bower has put it, ASEAN 'is the glue that binds key actors together, either through direct membership or via regional structures' – such as the various ASEAN plus one arrangements, APT, ARF, ADMM-Plus, EAS, and indeed even APEC.[45]

Beyond the aforementioned broadly defined points, there remains little clarity even among those who support the idea of ASEAN centrality regarding its exact meaning. There are at least five interrelated understandings in the extant scholarly debate and policy discourse regarding the regional organization's role in Asian multilateralism and regionalism. Centrality has been defined in terms of ASEAN as leader or driver, as convenor or facilitator, as hub or key node, and as an agent of (proposed) progress (and not just process). On the other hand, a fifth and much less sympathetic rendition of ASEAN centrality sees it as little more than an expedient device to preserve ASEAN's primacy in Asian regionalism and to ward off any form of architectural renovation which could lead to its marginalization.

## *ASEAN as regional leader*

The most common conception of centrality is in terms of ASEAN as regional *leader*. This conception is most commonly associated with the notion of ASEAN as the *driver* of regionalism.[46] Holders of this perspective are clear that ASEAN's perceived leadership does not derive from the combined material or structural power of its member states, which, while not insignificant, lack the collective policy consensus if not shared sovereignty in order to be effectively deployed. Further, ASEAN's *primus inter pares* (first among equals) position in the ARF – where a regional grouping of developing nations lead an institution whose members include the world's most powerful nations – flies in the face of conventional wisdom on regional order and power.

Received wisdom has it that the construction of regions and the shaping of regional order are roles for global and great powers rather than small, weak and/or marginal actors.[47] Asia (or more accurately, East Asia) has also been defined as a 'regional security complex' that nonetheless differs from other regional security complexes in that it comprises a number of great powers, thereby making it a 'great power complex'.[48] Thus understood, regions are essentially defined by powers of various kinds, be it 'the sole superpower and its imperium, great powers including "core states" that serve the power and purpose of the imperium and, to a lesser extent, regional powers'.[49] In contrast, it has been argued that 'local responses to power may matter even more in the construction of regional orders'.[50] Accordingly, Asia has been constructed 'more from within than from without' through the leadership of ASEAN.[51] In the same way, it has been argued that though none of the ASEAN countries can be considered a major economic or military power, yet 'through ASEAN they have been at the heart of the key advances in East Asian regionalism'.[52] Making a similar point about ASEAN as a default leader ostensibly acceptable to the broader community of stakeholders, the former foreign minister of Indonesia, Marty Natalegawa, has argued that the organization earned its centrality through 'its intellectual leadership and capacity to engage and serve as equilibrium-maker'.[53] The apparent primacy of ASEAN goes against the grain of who the prime movers and shakers behind the economic regionalisms in different regions tend to be, namely, great and/or regional powers – Germany and France in the case of the EEC and European Union; Brazil and Argentina in the case of Mercosur; the United States in the case of the North American Free Trade Area (NAFTA). Thus understood, the 'puzzle' in the case of East Asian regionalism is why, despite the presence of two major powers, China and Japan, in the region, ASEAN has emerged as the leader.[54]

## *ASEAN as regional convenor*

A second way to understand ASEAN centrality is in terms of ASEAN's contribution as a *convenor* and/or *facilitator*. It has been argued that ASEAN's most important contribution to Asia's stability and security has been to serve as the region's convenor or facilitator through providing an assortment of multilateral mechanisms – 'meeting places', as two leading analysts once put it[55] – which bring together great powers, regional powers, and small and/or weak states in Asia for regular consultation and confidence-building. Arguably, ASEAN's menu of modalities has also helped to facilitate the institutionalization of relations between China and the United States, the most crucial bilateral relationship in international security today in the view of many.[56] Thus understood, ASEAN's effort to mobilize and bring regional stakeholders together, to keep them participating and persevering when negotiations prove complex and difficult, to avoid taking sides and to try to find solutions that all sides can embrace can also be viewed as a form of leadership.[57]

On the other hand, it has been argued that 'ASEAN's central role as East Asia and the Asia-Pacific's regional convenor has not been matched by ASEAN regional leadership'.[58] Though critical of the extent and depth of ASEAN's regional leadership, this perspective acknowledges nonetheless the importance of ASEAN's role as the region's convenor or facilitator. There are, to be sure, risks to such a conception of centrality where the relevance of ASEAN to Asia lies squarely with its ability to ensure that the consultative frameworks and mechanisms for economic and security cooperation which it has created are seen by their stakeholders as effective. The alternative has been to keep seizing the initiative to spawn more frameworks and mechanisms without necessarily having given careful thought to how they are supposed to complement one another. Commenting on the potential cleavages and competition that could arise between and among the various component parts of Asia's evolving architecture – in this instance, the TPP and the RCEP regional trade pacts – Beginda Pakpahan has observed:

> Such division will profoundly influence the centrality of ASEAN. ASEAN aims to preserve its centrality to economic cooperation within Southeast and East Asia through initiatives such as the EAS and [APT]. If ASEAN does not respond effectively to any potential competition between the TPP and RCEP, ASEAN's role as a driving force in the various regional arrangements is more likely to decline. The rivalry between the US and China could also undermine the crucial role that ASEAN plays. So, in order to maintain its centrality, ASEAN must focus on the creation of RCEP while furthering its regional consolidation through the ASEAN Community. If it does not do this, ASEAN may find that its role as a proactive, central player in fostering political and economic arrangements in East and Southeast Asia declines.[59]

Not taking sides and working to find common solutions agreeable to all is also something ASEAN has sought to maintain. Forged in the crucible of Cold War

Southeast Asia where residual anxieties about neo-colonialist designs and external power intervention ran deep, ASEAN emerged as an (undeclared) institutional expression of collective political, not military, defence against communism where its proposed neutrality – documented in the Zone of Peace, Freedom and Neutrality (ZOPFAN) of 1971 and the Southeast Asia Nuclear Weapons Free Zone (SEANWFZ) of 1995 (entered into force in 1997) – was viewed as a necessity, rendered more acute in the wake of the failure of the Southeast Asia Treaty Organization (SEATO), to counter Vietnam's accusation that ASEAN was a Western-supported military bloc. After the Cold War, ASEAN neutrality would come to be seen as critical to ASEAN's role as a convenor of Asian regionalism through its provision of 'meeting places'. According to the Singaporean diplomat Tommy Koh, the neutrality of ASEAN is a key reason why the regional institution is 'acceptable to all':

> For the past two decades, ASEAN has taken the initiative to bring these key powers, as well as other regional countries, together in various ASEAN-centred institutions and forums. The objective has been to develop mutual confidence, to reduce mutual suspicions, to deepen economic linkages and to nurture a culture of cooperation. *ASEAN is acceptable to all the stakeholders as the region's convenor and facilitator because it is neutral, pragmatic and welcoming.*[60]

Likewise, ASEAN has resolutely insisted on its neutrality insofar as its institutional position on the South China Sea disputes, in which four of its member countries (Brunei, Malaysia, the Philippines, and Vietnam) are involved directly as territorial claimants, is concerned.[61] Arguably, China has actively supported ASEAN neutrality since 1979, which the Chinese putatively viewed as a device to limit Soviet and (less probably) American influence on the Southeast Asian region.[62] For example, when ASEAN Secretary-General Le Luong Minh commented in May 2014 that China had purportedly 'encroached' upon Vietnam's territorial integrity and thereby 'violated' the Declaration on the Conduct of Parties in the South China Sea (DOC) – Le, a former Vietnamese deputy foreign minister, reportedly said that ASEAN had to 'get China out of the territorial waters' of Vietnam before formal talks could proceed in the South China Sea dispute[63] – a Chinese foreign ministry spokesperson retorted that ASEAN neutrality over the dispute should be observed.[64] The incident brings to mind the debacle at the ASEAN ministerial meeting in July 2012, where the organization failed for the first time in its history to issue a joint communique as a consequence of Cambodia's insistence in its role as chair of ASEAN – and, in the impolitic view of some, as the lackey of China[65] – to not include views on the South China Sea disputes out of concern that the communique could offend China. Crucially, Cambodia justified its position on the basis that ASEAN ought to remain neutral.[66] As Amitav Acharya has argued:

> The major powers of Asia do not trust each other enough to develop a Concert of Powers, instead these powers, including US and China, have accepted ASEAN's centrality in the regional security architecture. But ASEAN will be

doomed if it loses its unity and takes sides with one great power against another. So ASEAN will need to provide the role of honest, neutral broker particularly when the great powers do not trust each other.[67]

Be that as it may, not unlike the apparent readiness of ASEAN states to 'interfere' in one another's domestic affairs in contravention of ASEAN's principle of non-interference when it is in their interest to do so,[68] it has been argued that ASEAN's nominal neutrality should not become an excuse not to do anything especially if ASEAN's inaction could severely undermine its interests down the road.[69] In this regard, an editorial for the Singapore's *The Sunday Times* argued in May 2014 that ASEAN neutrality 'should not and does not mean caving in to Chinese maritime assertiveness'.[70] Others have gone as far as to claim that ASEAN, at least where the South China Sea disputes are concerned, has transcended – if only temporarily – its neutrality norm and putatively underscored its centrality. For instance, commenting on the joint agreement in July 2011 between ASEAN and China to nonbinding guidelines for settling competing territorial claims in the South China Sea, a noted pundit from the region, Simon Tay, argued that ASEAN was 'moving from neutrality to a new centrality'.[71]

### *ASEAN as regional hub and/or node*

Viewing ASEAN as the hub and/or prime node of Asia's regional architecture is a third way to understand centrality. Arguing that ASEAN's engagement with the wider regional groupings it has helped spawned has been less about wanting to lead and drive them than avoiding being marginalized by their more powerful non-ASEAN stakeholders, one scholar has suggested that it is far more accurate to speak of ASEAN as the 'hub' than as the leader of those groupings.[72] This contention is particularly popular with economists who see deeper intra-ASEAN integration as a necessary precondition for a broader East Asian integration. For example, it has been claimed that 'ASEAN functions as a "hub" with linkages or spokes to countries (the dialogue partners); at the same time, the hub serves as a platform for networks of production involving all countries connected through the hub (or ASEAN)'.[73] It has also been argued that ASEAN makes good sense as a 'regional hub' for free trade agreements (FTAs) given its FTAs with various East Asian countries; however, others have pointed to the fact that ASEAN's relatively small economic size and export market, the disparate character of the ASEAN Free Trade Area (and, in time, the ASEAN Economic Community) – ten economies as opposed to a single economy – and other constraints limit ASEAN's potential to become an important regional hub relative, say, to China.[74]

The idea that ASEAN is not necessarily the most important hub in Asian regionalism might anger its advocates, but nowhere is the disjuncture between how other regional stakeholders and ASEAN supporters see ASEAN's place and role more apparent than in the way various pundits repeatedly quote (or, perhaps more accurately, misquote) former US Secretary of State Hillary Clinton's by now clichéd – and intriguingly, often misrepresented – reference to the matter in an address given in October 2010. It has often been assumed that Clinton referred to ASEAN as '*the* fulcrum' of Asia's regional architecture – a perspective which grants ASEAN primacy in Asian regionalism.[75] The notion has also been picked up by policy practitioners as well. For example, Surin Pitsuwan, the former secretary-general of ASEAN, reportedly warned that 'ASEAN cannot afford to be complacent if it wants to continue to be *the* fulcrum of the regional architecture in East Asia and a locomotive for the rise of Asia'.[76] However, as Clinton said in her October 2010 speech:

> And let me simply state the principle that will guide America's role in Asian institutions. If consequential security, political, and economic issues are being discussed, and if they involve our interests, then we will seek a seat at the table. That's why we view ASEAN as *a* fulcrum for the region's emerging regional architecture. And we see it as indispensable on a host of political, economic, and strategic matters.[77]

To be sure, ASEAN supporters could be forgiven for assuming that if ASEAN is regarded by Clinton as 'indispensable' on a host of regional issues, then it should logically be considered *the* (rather than a) fulcrum of Asia's architecture. Yet the distinction, no matter how trivial, provides a sense of the nuances in the perceptions held by ASEAN and non-ASEAN stakeholders regarding ASEAN's place in Asian regionalism.

Analysts who use a social network approach have pointed to the importance of nodes in networks and their relations with other nodes.[78] Three analytical elements are especially noteworthy, namely, 'between-ness' (the extent to which a node lies between other notes in a network), 'closeness' (the degree to which a node is near other nodes in the network) and 'degree' (the count of the number of ties to other nodes in the network).[79] This is best conceptualized by way of the image of overlapping concentric circles of memberships of various regional institutions in Asia, where ASEAN is more often than not pictured as the common point where all those circles overlap and converge. So too, it could be said, the position of ASEAN within each wider regional grouping, which purportedly allows ASEAN to dictate the shape and substance of each grouping. With the EAS as a case study, Caballero-Anthony has argued that ASEAN has succeeded in maintaining its centrality in the EAS through its ability to decide the summit's membership and to set its agenda. 'Despite its lack of material power', she concluded,

> ASEAN has been able to claim centrality because of its position as a node in a cluster of networks, and this condition of 'high between-ness' allows ASEAN to exercise influence in regional processes with the tacit acceptance of the major powers.[80]

### ASEAN as agent of regional progress

A fourth way to understand ASEAN's centrality emphasizes the need for ASEAN member states to take seriously the implementation of the stated aims and plans in the organization's concords and roadmaps. Critics and supporters of ASEAN alike do not disagree over the fact that Asian regionalism, with ASEAN as leader, convenor or hub, has long emphasized process over results. For instance, a recent assessment of the proposed RCEP trade pact by a China-based analyst contends that 'ASEAN does not intend to deviate from its approach of "putting process over progress"' where its implementation of the RCEP is concerned, which, so far as that analyst is concerned, essentially means the RCEP's anticipated achievements would at best be minimal.[81] As David Martin Jones and Michael L. R. Smith have concluded, 'the norms and practices that ASEAN promotes, rather than creating an integrated community, can only sustain a pattern of limited intergovernmental and bureaucratically rigid interaction'.[82] Contending that ASEAN-led Asian regionalism is a severely flawed enterprise, Jones and Smith had on another occasion dismissed the regional enterprise as full of talk but empty of substance, where ASEAN and the regional community it aspires to establish are little more than 'a rhetorical and institutional shell'.[83] Advocates of the ASEAN Way understandably dispute that interpretation, with one assessment insisting that to date, the African Union, the Gulf Cooperation Council, the Organization of American States, and the Shanghai Cooperation Organization still lag behind ASEAN in terms of institutional comprehensiveness, inclusiveness or maturity, whilst groupings like Mercosur and the South Asian Association for Regional Cooperation continue to look to ASEAN for encouragement and inspiration.[84]

Be that as it may, officials past and present of the ASEAN Secretariat understand ASEAN centrality in terms of the need for the institution to fulfil its pledges and successfully implement its stated purposes and action plans, the most immediately critical of which is the ASEAN Economic Community (AEC).[85] As Sundram Pushpanathan, the former deputy secretary-general of ASEAN for the AEC, argued in 2010:

> While 'process-based regionalism' – the series of meetings, dialogues, consultations and engagements that ASEAN has put in place for internal economic integration and relations with its major trading partners – has produced spectacular results for ASEAN as convenor of regional meetings and pace-setter for ASEAN+1, [APT], and East Asia Summit these institutional processes alone may not be adequate to maintain ASEAN's centrality and to achieve the AEC by 2015. To meet its goals, ASEAN must ensure the substantive implementation of its economic agreements, declarations, plans and programs. I call this form of regionalism supported by concrete results and outcomes based on a structured and rules-based regime 'results-based regionalism' ... To maintain ASEAN's centrality in the region and to achieve the goal of AEC by 2015 it is imperative that ASEAN shifts aggressively towards 'result-based regionalism'. We must act now.[86]

Thus understood, ASEAN centrality is inextricably tied to the notion of an ASEAN that 'walks its talk', as it were. Likewise, Mely Caballero-Anthony, who once directed external relations for ASEAN at the Secretariat, has observed, while [ASEAN] centrality has been achieved, maintaining centrality in a rapidly changing regional environment compels ASEAN to address challenges to its centrality. This would necessarily include its ability to maintain consensus, carry out collective action and achieve its stated goals.[87]

Or, as Surin Pitsuwan, the former secretary-general of ASEAN, has put it, ASEAN must provide a 'centrality of substance' in Southeast Asia, not just a 'centrality of good will'.[88] For those who share the aforementioned views, it is less about moving beyond the ASEAN Way of consultation and consensus – no different really from how the world of sovereign states conducts its affairs, according to another former secretary-general of ASEAN, Rodolfo Severino[89] – than the ongoing evolution of the ASEAN Way from a process-driven regionalism to, in time to come, a rules-based and results-based regionalism as foreshadowed by the establishment of the ASEAN Charter. Such appeals, from officials of ASEAN no less, should not be taken to imply the absence of change in ASEAN, however. Rather, they highlight the abiding concern that change is not taking place deep and fast enough. As Acharya has intimated:

> You have seen the ability of ASEAN to shift and adapt over the past few years. ASEAN in recent years has departed somewhat from its non-interference doctrine. It has adopted a Charter and it has developed mechanisms for dealing with transnational challenges and regional conflict. It has come out on the side of political reform in Burma, when traditionally it was very hands off, and has begun a limited regional mechanism for human rights. It has also developed mechanisms for engaging all the great powers of the world as we discussed above. So ASEAN is adopting and adapting but the questions is [is] whether it can adapt enough to keep up with the fast moving economic and political transnational environment – is ASEAN going to be too slow? At this stage it really remains to be seen whether it will be overtaken by events or whether it will be able to adapt.[90]

Fundamentally, the constraints against change are structural as much as attitudinal. To move from process-based regionalism to a results-based one – if the results are the substantive sort stakeholders hanker after – could involve significant reform well beyond what the existing intergovernmental structures and conventions which ASEAN has long justified can deliver. The same holds true for ASEAN's professed aim to establish a 'people-centred' regional community. For example, recent research has suggested that the creation of putatively transnational bodies such as the ASEAN Inter-Parliamentary Organization (AIPO) and the ASEAN Intergovernmental Commission on Human Rights (AICHR) has not significantly undermined ASEAN's intergovernmental character but arguably reinforced it, not least because these were formed in part to retain ASEAN's 'cognitive prior' – that is, an existing set of ideas, belief systems, and norms which determine and condition an individual or collective subject's receptivity to new ideas and norms[91] – which rests upon deeply entrenched corporatist norms and ideas.[92] Treading well beyond the simplistic rote responses regarding ASEAN's resistance to democratization pressures using the norms of sovereignty and non-interference, Jürgen Rüland's research suggests that ASEAN has skilfully countered external democracy promotion and domestic pressures for democratizing regional governance through variable strategies including 'rejection', 'isomorphic adaptation' and 'localization', which, for Rüland, significantly dim the prospects for a wholesale liberal-pluralist transformation of ASEAN's system of interest representation.[93] All this implies that much as ASEAN leaders desire change and work collectively to effect it, the pace, depth and extent of institutional adaptation might not be sufficient for ASEAN to pass future stress tests levelled against it – so long as extant structures remain.

Related to the perceived need for ASEAN to prove its legitimacy by way of institutional performance is the equally worrying question of the cohesion of its member countries. Oddly, the preservation of ASEAN unity has not been a key priority in the foreign policies of ASEAN states, not all of the time and especially not when their national interests have been directly at odds with those of the organization. Such parochialism at the expense of intramural accord has hitherto not posed serious difficulties for Southeast Asia; in any case, ASEAN members rarely see ASEAN as an institution of first resort for meeting their vital interests.[94] Of late, however, leaders and officials of member countries have acknowledged with greater urgency the need for a strong and united ASEAN if their respective economies and societies are to avoid being left behind in an increasingly competitive and complex global milieu and/or, for that matter, in dealing with a perceptibly assertive China over the South China Sea. For example, according to a leaked US Statement Department cable detailing an exchange between US and Singapore diplomats, the Singaporean interlocutor acknowledged that the responsibility for ASEAN's failure to remain united in its future dealings with China lies solely with ASEAN.[95] Similarly, as Kishore Mahbubani, commenting on rising tensions between China and the United States and the strategic ramifications that could have on ASEAN, has observed, 'Quite naturally, ASEAN countries are being pulled in different directions. ASEAN has to work twice as hard to ensure that this new geopolitical contest doesn't split the grouping'.[96] Likewise, Acharya has noted that despite the rise of powers in Asia like China and India, 'ASEAN will survive if it manages to maintain a certain degree of cohesiveness'.[97]

Moreover, episodes such as the debacle at the Phnom Penh ministerial meeting mentioned earlier, or the Cambodian–Thai border conflict in 2011, reflect ASEAN members' tendency continually to undermine their organization. At any rate, such incidents undermine ASEAN's efforts (which, by its own secretary-general's admission, are difficult and likely to be delayed) to transform itself into an economic, political-security and socio-cultural community.[98] Ultimately, a divided and weak ASEAN is inimical to ASEAN centrality.[99] No claim to centrality makes sense if the putative centrepiece and cornerstone of Asia's architecture itself, ASEAN, cannot hold itself together. And without its central position in the regional architecture, Southeast Asians stand to lose their prerogative to influence the shape and substance of Asian regionalism. But is ASEAN centrality essential to Southeast Asia? Member countries themselves appear divided on the matter, not least where their practical attitudes and actions are concerned. When asked privately, leading ASEAN watchers and practitioners often point, among other things, to the divide between the founding member countries (Indonesia, Malaysia, the Philippines, Singapore and Thailand, and Brunei, on the one hand) and the newer members (Cambodia, Laos, Myanmar and Vietnam) that joined the organization in the 1990s. The more established 'ASEAN-6' are clearly not without their differences, but have learnt over the years to shelve them and circle their wagons in support of a member nation in need, as happened for Thailand following Vietnam's occupation of Cambodia in the 1980s, or Myanmar since it joined ASEAN in 1997. In that regard, Cambodia's recent actions – blocking an ASEAN joint declaration in 2012, 'interfering' in Thailand's domestic affairs by hosting the fugitive former Thai leader Thaksin Shinawatra and even appointing him in an advisory capacity in 2009 – are, as Acharya has observed, ironic given that Cambodia probably owes its very sovereignty to ASEAN's role in seeking a negotiated solution to the third Indochina war.[100]

## Centrality as a device of expedience

A fifth way to understand ASEAN centrality has been to see it as a contrivance to ensure ASEAN remains in charge. If Michael Leifer were right to insist that ASEAN regionalism – and, by extension, its complex of Asia-wide institutions – is principally about conservation rather than innovation,[101] then critics who contend that ASEAN-led regional initiatives are all about maintaining ASEAN's pride of place and little else – 'clinging to the driver's seat', according to one formulation[102] – clearly have a point. If ASEAN states seek to avoid marginalization in regional and global affairs, that provides ample motivation for them to preserve ASEAN's position in the regional architecture, particularly in the face of a recent slew of proposals for alternative regionalisms by the then leaders of the non-ASEAN stakeholder countries – from Kevin Rudd's 'Asia-Pacific Community' to Lee Myung-bak's 'New Asia Initiative' to Yukio Hatoyama's 'East Asian Community'[103] – all of which not only signal a disenchantment with ASEAN's leadership of Asian regionalism but which go the extra mile in their readiness to relax the extant axiom about ASEAN's centrality. Besides such proposals from regional leaders, ASEAN also had to contend with efforts by various 'second track' communities and networks urging for a major overhaul of the existing regional architecture. For example, a report drafted by a task force commissioned by the Pacific Economic Cooperation Council (PECC), the Track 2 complement to the APEC, on regional institutional architecture called for the establishment of an 'Asia-Pacific Summit' comprising the nineteen APEC participant states and India (not an APEC economy) for high-level discussions on key issues. The report also urged the creation of an informal 'G10', a caucus consisting of the Asia-Pacific members of the G20, which could ostensibly voice the collective concerns of all Asia-Pacific countries.[104] Noting that both the ARF and APT have suffered from their 'southeast Asia-centric leadership' – ASEAN, in other words – the report conceded that ASEAN's position in the 'driving seat' of Asian regionalism is by default alone and not based on merit, given that it is the only option politically acceptable to all regional stakeholders.[105]

Increasingly, even analysts from China, a stakeholder that has traditionally and quite robustly supported the centrality of ASEAN, have begun questioning that wisdom. Commenting on the RCEP trade pact, arguably a proposal to assuage Chinese anxieties over the US-backed TPP as an American-led form of economic containment against China,[106] a Chinese scholar has contended that 'ASEAN has sometimes hidden its true motivations. It is evident that ASEAN's efforts to advance the RCEP are geared towards boosting the often-addressed "centrality" of its organization rather than deepening regional economic cooperation'. Noting that the RCEP idea 'is [already] winning support from all sides', Yuzhu Wang lamented that the RCEP 'has begun to play its role in safeguarding ASEAN "centrality"'.[107] Views like this and those discussed above underscore the rising expectations (and growing frustrations) being heaped on ASEAN, whose performance must now keep up with its claims.

## Conclusion

There is no question over the historical significance of ASEAN to the formation and instantiation of Asia's regionalism and its supporting architecture. That being said, the foregoing analysis has shown that the centrality of ASEAN, despite receiving the support of all the stakeholder countries in the regional arrangements discussed above – with the APEC as the sole exception – remains a contested principle, in terms of both its meaning and the apparent willingness of some non-ASEAN stakeholders to challenge it. 'ASEAN's centrality, or place in the driving seat, is not a given', according to Marty Natalegawa.[108] Ultimately, the centrality of ASEAN does not reveal much of what those other stakeholders, despite their acknowledgement – increasingly reluctant, perhaps – of ASEAN's centrality, have in fact contributed respectively to multilateralism and regionalism in Asia.

## Notes

1 Amitav Acharya, 'The End of ASEAN Centrality?', *Asia Times Online*, 8 August 2012, www.atimes.com/atimes/Southeast_Asia/NH08Ae03.html; 'ASEAN Centrality Maintained, Says Yudhoyono', *AntaraNews.com*, 19 November 2011, www.antaranews.com/en/news/77754/aseans-centrality-maintained--says-yudhoyono; Mely Caballero-Anthony, 'Understanding ASEAN's Centrality: Bases and Prospects in an Evolving Regional Architecture', *The Pacific Review*, Vol. 27, No. 4 (2014), pp. 563–84; Yose Rizal Damuri, 'East Asia Economic Integration and ASEAN Centrality', *The Jakarta Post*, 16 November 2012; Benjamin Ho, *ASEAN's Centrality in a Rising Asia*, RSIS Working Paper No. 249 (Singapore: S. Rajaratnam School of International Studies, Nanyang Technological University, 2012); and Peter A. Petri and Michael G. Plummer, *ASEAN Centrality and the ASEAN-US Economic Relationship*, Advance Copy of Policy Studies No. 69 (Honolulu, HI: East-West Center, 2013).

2 Yevgeny Kanaev, 'The Driver's Seat Phenomenon', *International Affairs*, Special Issue (2010), pp. 29–36; Lee Jones, 'Still in the "Drivers' Seat", But for How Long?

ASEAN's Capacity for Leadership in East-Asian International Relations', *Journal of Current Southeast Asian Affairs*, Vol. 29, No. 3 (2010), pp. 95–113; Paul Lim, 'ASEAN's Role in the ASEAN Regional Forum: Will ASEAN Remain in the Driver's Seat? A European Perspective', *Cooperation & Dialogue*, No. 2 (2003), pp. 5–11.
3 Michael Leifer, *The ASEAN Regional Forum: Extending ASEAN's Model of Regional Security*. Adelphi Paper, No. 302 (Oxford: Oxford University Press for International Institute for Strategic Studies, 1996). Also see, Amitav Acharya, *Asian Regional Institutions and the Possibilities for Socializing the Behaviour of States*, ADB Working Paper Series on Regional Economic Integration, No. 82 (Manila: Asian Development Bank, 2011), p. 8; See Seng Tan, 'Spectres of Leifer: Insights on Regional Order and Security for Southeast Asia Today', *Contemporary Southeast Asia*, Vol. 34, No. 3 (2012), pp. 309–37, on p. 316.
4 S. Clifford, 'Theory Talk #42: Amitav Acharya on the Relevance of Regions, ASEAN, and Western IR's False Universalisms', *Theory Talks*, 8 October 2011, pp. 1–11, on p. 5, www.theorytalks.org/2011/08/theory-talk-42.htmlm.
5 Donald S. Zagoria, 'Regional Organization and Order in South-East Asia: Understanding ASEAN', *Foreign Affairs*, Vol. 67, No. 1 (1982), www.foreignaffairs.com/articles/36778/donald-s-zagoria/regional-organization-and-order-in-south-east-asia-understanding.
6 Hans C. Blomqvist, 'ASEAN as a Model for Third World Regional Economic Cooperation?', *ASEAN Economic Bulletin*, Vol. 10, No. 1 (1993), pp. 52–67, on p. 52.
7 Blomqvist, 'ASEAN as a Model for Third World Regional Economic Cooperation?', p. 52.
8 David Martin Jones, Michael Lawrence Rowan Smith and Nicholas Khoo, *Asian Security and the Rise of China: International Relations in an Age of Volatility* (Cheltenham: Edward Elgar, 2013), pp. 69–70.
9 Frank Frost, 'Introduction: ASEAN since 1967', in Alison Broinowski, ed., *ASEAN in the 1990s* (London: Macmillan, 1990), pp. 1–31.
10 Anthony L. Smith, 'ASEAN's Ninth Summit: Solidifying Regional Cohesion, Advancing External Linkages', *Contemporary Southeast Asia*, Vol. 26, No. 3 (2004), pp. 416–33, on p. 417.
11 Mark Beeson, 'ASEAN's Ways: Still Fit for Purpose?', *Cambridge Review of International Affairs*, Vol. 22, No. 3 (2009), pp. 333–43, on p. 333.
12 Evelyn Goh, 'ASEAN-led Multilateralism and Regional Order: The Great Power Bargain Deficit', *The Asan Forum* (Special Forum), 23 May 2014, www.theasanforum.org/asean-led-multilateralism-and-regional-order-the-great-power-bargain-deficit/.
13 Goh, 'ASEAN-led Multilateralism and Regional Order'.
14 Kent E. Caulder and Francis Fukuyama, 'Introduction', in Kent E. Caulder and Francis Fukuyama, eds., *East Asian Multilateralism: Prospects for Regional Stability* (Baltimore, MD: The Johns Hopkins University Press, 2008), pp. 1–12, on p. 3.
15 Noel Quinn, '600 million reasons to invest in Asean', *South China Morning Post*, 7 October 2013.
16 Oran Young, 'Political Leadership and Regime Formation: On the Development of Institutions in International Society', *International Organization*, Vol. 45, No. 3 (1991), pp. 281–308, on p. 288.
17 Cited in Christine Carlson and Greg Wolf, 'The Power to Convene', *State News*, November/December 2005 (Lexington, KY: The Council of State Governments, 2005), p. 12. An example of the 'convening power' of particular individuals is Klaus Schwab who founded the World Economic Forum held annually in Davos. Erika Karp, 'The Power to Convene', *Forbes*, 10 December 2012, www.forbes.com/sites/85broads/2012/12/10/the-power-to-convene/.
18 Judith Goldstein and Robert O. Keohane, eds., *Ideas and Foreign Policy: Beliefs, Institutions, and Political Change* (Ithaca, NY: Cornell University Press, 1993); Peter

A. Hall, *The Political Power of Economic Ideas* (Princeton, NJ: Princeton University Press, 1989); Richard Higgott, 'Introduction: Ideas, Interests and Identity in the Asia-Pacific', *The Pacific Review*, Vol. 7, No. 4 (1994), pp. 367–79; John S. Odell, *U.S. International Monetary Policy: Markets, Power, and Ideas as Sources of Change* (Princeton, NJ: Princeton University Press, 1982); Kathryn Sikkink, *Ideas and Institutions: Developmentalism in Brazil and Argentina* (Ithaca, NY: Cornell University Press, 1991); Albert. S. Yee, 'The Causal Effects of Ideas on Policy', *International Organization*, Vol. 50, No. 1 (1996), pp. 69–108.
19 Jeff Checkel, 'Ideas, Institutions, and the Gorbachev Foreign Policy Revolution', *World Politics*, Vol. 45, No. 2 (1993), pp. 271–300, on p. 273.
20 Richard Stubbs, 'ASEAN's Leadership in East Asian Region-Building: Strength in Weakness', *The Pacific Review*, Vol. 27, No. 4 (2014), pp. 523–41, on p. 530.
21 John McKay, 'APEC: Successes, Weaknesses, and Future Prospects', in Daljit Singh and Anthony L. Smith, eds., *Southeast Asian Affairs 2002* (Singapore: Institute of Southeast Asian Affairs, 2002), pp. 42–53, on p. 44.
22 Naoko Munakata, *Transforming East Asia: The Evolution of Regional Economic Integration* (Washington, D.C.: The Brookings Institution, 2006), p. 70.
23 Man-jung Mignonne Chan, 'APEC's Eye on the Prize: Participants, Modality, and Confidence-Building', in K. Kesavapany and Hank Lim, eds., *APEC at 20: Recall, Reflect, Remake* (Singapore: Institute of Southeast Asian Studies, 2009), pp. 41–54, on p. 45.
24 Robert Gilpin, 'APEC in a New International Order', in Donald C. Hellmann and Kenneth B. Pyle, eds., *From APEC to Xanadu: Creating a Viable Community in the Post-War Pacific* (Armonk, NY: M. E. Sharpe, 1997), pp. 34–35; Jeff Loder, Jean Michel Montsion and Richard Stubbs, 'East Asian Regionalism and the European Experience', in Alex Warleigh-Lack, Nick Robinson and Ben Rosamond, eds., *New Regionalism and the European Union: Dialogues, Comparisons and New Research Directions* (Abingdon: Routledge, 2011), pp. 80–96, on p. 82.
25 Peter Ho Hak Ean, 'The ASEAN Regional Forum: The Way Forward', paper presented to the Third Workshop on ASEAN-UN Cooperation in Peace and Preventive Diplomacy, Bangkok, 17–18 February 1994.
26 Rodolfo C. Severino, *The ASEAN Regional Forum* (Singapore: Institute of Southeast Asian Studies, 2009), p. 4.
27 Leifer, *The ASEAN Regional Forum*, p. 59.
28 Robyn Lim, 'The ASEAN Regional Forum: Building on Sand', *Contemporary Southeast Asia*, Vol. 20, No. 2 (1998), pp. 115–36, on p. 115.
29 Shaun Narine, 'ASEAN and the ARF: The Limits of the "ASEAN Way"', *Asian Survey*, Vol. 37, No. 10 (1997), pp. 961–78, on p. 962.
30 Ralf Emmers and See Seng Tan, 'The ASEAN Regional Forum and Preventive Diplomacy: Built to Fail?', *Asian Security*, Vol. 7, No. 1 (2011), pp. 44–60; Takeshi Yuzawa, 'The Evolution of Preventive Diplomacy in the ASEAN Regional Forum: Problems and Prospects', *Asian Survey*, Vol. 46, No. 5 (2006), pp. 785–804.
31 Rizal Sukma, 'The Accidental Driver: ASEAN in the ASEAN Regional Forum', in Jürgen Haacke and Noel M. Morada, eds., *Cooperative Security in the Asia-Pacific: The ASEAN Regional Forum* (Abingdon: Routledge, 2010), pp. 111–23, on p. 111.
32 David Camroux and Christian Lechervy, 'Close Encounter of a Third Kind? The Inaugural Asia-Europe Meeting of March 1996', *The Pacific Review*, Vol. 9, No. 3 (1996), pp. 442–53; Richard Stubbs, 'ASEAN Plus Three: Emerging East Asian Regionalism?', *Asian Survey*, Vol. 42, No. 3 (2002), pp. 440–55.
33 Cited in Hadi Soesastro, 'Whither ASEAN Plus Three?', paper for the Pacific Economic Cooperation Council (PECC) Trade Policy Forum on Regional Trading Arrangements: Stocktake and Next Steps', Bangkok, 12-13 June 2001, p. 2.
34 David Capie and Brendan Taylor, 'The Shangri-La Dialogue and the Institutionalization of Defence Diplomacy in Asia', *The Pacific Review*, Vol. 23, No. 3 (2010), pp. 359–76, at pp. 371–2.

35 See Seng Tan, '"Talking Their Walk"? The Evolution of Defence Regionalism in Southeast Asia', *Asian Security*, Vol. 8, No. 3 (2012), pp. 232–50.
36 Malcolm Cook, *ASEAN's Triumph*, Policy Brief, No. 4, June 2011 (Adelaide, SA: Indo-Pacific Governance Research Centre, The University of Adelaide, 2011).
37 Stubbs, 'ASEAN's Leadership in East Asian Region-Building', p. 530.
38 *ASEAN 2030: Toward a Borderless Economic Community* (Tokyo: Asian Development Bank Institute, 2014), p. 191.
39 Cited in Geoffrey Wheatcroft, 'Who Needs NATO?', *The New York Times*, 15 June 2011.
40 See, paragraph 15 of Article 1 of the ASEAN Charter, www.aseansec.org/21069.pdf.
41 'ASEAN Centrality and EAS Tops AMM Agenda Ha Noi, July 20, 2010', *Association of Southeast Asian Nations*, 20 July 2010, www.asean.org/news/item/asean-centrality-and-eas-tops-amm-agenda-ha-noi-20-july-2010#.
42 Alice D. Ba, *(Re)Negotiating East and Southeast Asia: Region, Regionalism, and the Association of Southeast Asian Nations* (Stanford, CA: Stanford University Press, 2009); Hiro Katsumata, 'What Explains ASEAN's Leadership in East Asian Community Building?', *Pacific Affairs*, Vol. 87, No. 2 (2014), pp. 247–64.
43 *ASEAN 2030*, pp. 191–92; Katsumata, 'What Explains ASEAN's Leadership in East Asian Community Building?', p. 247. Also see Wendy Dobson, 'Asia's Evolving Economic Institutions: Roles and Future Prospects', *East Asia Forum*, 21 August 2011, www.eastasiaforum.org/2011/08/21/asia-s-evolving-economic-institutions-roles-and-future-prospects/.
44 Peter A. Petri and Michael G. Plummer, *ASEAN Centrality and the ASEAN–US Economic Relationship*, Advance Copy of Policy Studies, No. 69, 22 November (Honolulu, HI: East-West Center, 2013), p. ii.
45 Ernest Z. Bower, 'The Quintessential Test of ASEAN Centrality: Changing the Paradigm in the South China Sea', *Center for Strategic and International Studies (CSIS)*, 21 June 2011, csis.org/publication/quintessential-test-asean-centrality-changing-paradigm-south-china-sea.
46 See, for example, Kanaev, 'The Driver's Seat Phenomenon'; Jones, 'Still in the "Drivers' Seat", But for How Long?'; Lim, 'ASEAN's Role in the ASEAN Regional Forum'; Sukma, 'The Accidental Driver'.
47 Barry Buzan and Ole Wæver, *Regions and Powers: The Structure of International Security* (Cambridge: Cambridge University Press, 2003); Peter J. Katzenstein, *A World of Regions: Asia and Europe in the American Imperium* (Ithaca, NY: Cornell University Press, 2005); David A. Lake and Patrick M. Morgan, eds., *Regional Orders: Building Security in a New World* (University Park, PA: Pennsylvania State University Press, 1997); Etel Solingen, *Regional Orders at Century's Dawn: Global and Domestic Influences on Grand Strategy* (Princeton, NJ: Princeton University Press, 1998).
48 A regional security complex or RSC 'refers to the level where states or other units link together sufficiently closely that their securities cannot be considered separate from each other'. Buzan and Ole Wæver, *Regions and Powers*, p. 43.
49 Amitav Acharya, 'Review Article: The Emerging Regional Architecture of World Politics', *World Politics*, Vol. Vol. 59, No. 4 (July 2007), pp. 629–52, on p. 630.
50 Acharya, 'Review Article', p. 630.
51 Amitav Acharya and See Seng Tan, 'Betwixt Balance and Community: America, ASEAN, and the Security of Southeast Asia', *International Relations of the Asia-Pacific*, Vol. 6, No. 1 (2006), pp. 37–59.
52 Stubbs, 'ASEAN's Leadership in East Asian Region-Building', p. 524.
53 Marty Natalegawa, 'Aggressively Waging Peace: ASEAN and the Asia-Pacific', *Strategic Review: The Indonesian Journal of Leadership, Policy and World Affairs*, Vol. 1, No. 2 (2011), pp. 40–46, on p. 40.

54 Stubbs, 'ASEAN's Leadership in East Asian Region-Building', p. 524.
55 Evelyn Goh and Amitav Acharya, 'The ASEAN Regional Forum and US–China Relations: Comparing Chinese and American Positions', paper prepared for the Fifth China-ASEAN Research Institutes Roundtable on Regionalism and Community-Building in East Asia, University of Hong Kong, Hong Kong, 2002.
56 See Seng Tan, *Facilitating China–U.S. Relations in the Age of Rebalancing: ASEAN's 'Middle Power' Diplomacy*, EAI MPD Working Paper, No. 1 (Seoul: East Asia Institute, October 2013).
57 Christine Carlson, 'Using Political Power to Convene', *National Civic Review*, Vol. 95, No. 3 (2006), pp. 57–60, on p. 57.
58 Cook, *ASEAN's Triumph*, p. 1.
59 Beginda Pakpahan, 'Will RCEP compete with the TPP? *East Asia Forum*, 28 November 2012, www.eastasiaforum.org/2012/11/28/will-rcep-compete-with-the-tpp/.
60 Tommy Koh, 'Rudd's Reckless Regional Rush', *The Australian*, 18 December 2009, emphasis added.
61 Ralf Emmers, 'ASEAN's Search for Neutrality in the South China Sea', *Asian Journal of Peacebuilding*, Vol. 2, No.1 (2014), pp. 61–77.
62 C. Y. Chang, 'ASEAN's Proposed Neutrality: China's Response', *Contemporary Southeast Asia*, Vol. 1, No. 3 (1979), pp. 249–67, on p. 249.
63 Cited in 'Editorial: Asean's Neutrality is its Strength', *The Sunday Times*, 23 May 2014.
64 'China Demands Asean Neutrality over South China Sea', *The Straits Times*, 19 May 2014.
65 According to the eminent Southeast Asia watcher Donald Emmerson, no ASEAN leader is more sensitive to China's views and demands than Cambodia's prime minister Hun Sen. As Emmerson has written about Cambodia's controversial management of the final draft of the joint communique that the ASEAN ministerial meeting at Phnom Penh in July 2012,

> By refusing to read a statement that mentions Scarborough Shoal, [the Cambodian leadership] acted in a manner consistent with China's positions. In Beijing's view, ASEAN has no business trying to resolve the disputes, which can only be settled bilaterally between China and each of the four claimants. China is Cambodia's largest foreign investor. Beijing has lavished money on high-profile aid projects, including paying for the Peace Palace in Phnom Penh where the ASEAN ministers met. There is no question that Hun Sen has tried to use his country's chairmanship of ASEAN in 2012 to keep the SCS off the group's agenda. An observer might conclude that China has effectively hired the Cambodian government to do its bidding.
> Don Emmerson, 'ASEAN Stumbles in Phnom Penh', *PacNet*, No. 45, 19 July 2012, csis.org/files/publication/Pac1245.pdf.

66 Simon Tay, 'ASEAN, Neutral or Neutered?', *Today*, 17 July 2012, pp. 8, 10–11, on p. 8.
67 Clifford, 'Theory Talk #42', pp. 5–6.
68 Lee Jones, 'ASEAN's Unchanged Melody? The Theory and Practice of "Non-Interference" in Southeast Asia', *The Pacific Review*, Vol. 23, No. 4 (2010), pp. 479–502.
69 Aileen S. P. Baviera, 'South China Sea Disputes: Why ASEAN Must Unite', *East Asia Forum*, 26 July 2012, www.eastasiaforum.org/2012/07/26/south-china-sea-disputes-why-asean-must-unite/; Supalak Ganjanakhundee, 'Asean Must Unite on South China Sea: Kerry', *The Nation*, 29 September 2013, www.nationmultimedia.com/national/Asean-must-unite-on-South-China-Sea-Kerry-30215874.html; Luke Hunt, 'Can ASEAN Unite on South China Sea?', *The Diplomat*, 17 November 2012, http://thediplomat.com/2012/11/can-asean-unite-on-south-china-sea/.
70 'Editorial: Asean's Neutrality is its Strength'.

71 Cited in Thomas Clouse, 'ASEAN Moves Closer to Political Cohesion', *Global Finance*, 29 August 2011, http://www.gfmag.com/magazine/julyaugust-2011/asean-moves-closer-to-political-cohesion.
72 Amitav Acharya, *Whose Ideas Matter? Agency and Power in Asian Regionalism* (Ithaca, NY: Cornell University Press, 2009).
73 Dionisius Narjoko, 'Why Indonesia Needs to Lead in Economic Integration', *East Asia Forum*, 3 March 2014, www.eastasiaforum.org/2014/03/03/why-indonesia-needs-to-lead-in-economic-integration/.
74 Yung Chul Park and Inkyo Cheong, 'The Proliferation of FTAs and Prospects for Trade Liberalization in East Asia', in Barry Eichengreen, Yung Chul Park and Charles Wyplosz, eds., *China, Asia, and the New World Economy* (Oxford: Oxford University Press, 2008), ch. 4.
75 Ernest Bower, '"After Hillary" Era concerns Southeast Asia', *East Asia Forum*, 30 March 2011, www.eastasiaforum.org/2011/03/30/after-hillary-era-concerns-southeast-asia/; Matthew Harrison, 'What Role Does ASEAN Play in the US Pivot to Asia?', *Asia House*, 20 August 2013, www.futureforeignpolicy.com/what-role-does-asean-play-in-the-us-pivot-to-asia-2/; Roger Mitton, 'The "Pacific Secretary" Needs to Ensure her Regional Legacy', *The Phnom Penh Post*, 21 March 2011.
76 Cited in Sundram Pushpanathan, 'Opinion: No Place for Passive Regionalism in ASEAN', *The Jakarta Post*, 7 April 2010, www.thejakartapost.com/news/2010/04/07/no-place-passive-regionalism-asean.html, emphasis added.
77 Hillary Clinton, 'Clinton's Speech on America's Engagement in the Asia-Pacific, October 2010', *Council on Foreign Relations*, 28 October 2010, www.cfr.org/asia-and-pacific/clintons-speech-americas-engagement-asia-pacific-october-2010/p23280, emphasis added.
78 Mely Caballero-Anthony, 'Understanding ASEAN Centrality: Bases and Prospects in an Evolving Regional Architecture', *The Pacific Review*, Vol. 27, No. 4 (2014), pp. 563–84.
79 Lindon C. Freeman, 'Centrality in Social Networks: Conceptual Clarification', *Social Networks*, Vol. 1 (1979), pp. 215–39, discussed in Caballero-Anthony, 'Understanding ASEAN Centrality', p. 567. In the same way, Miles Kahler has argued that power in networks 'depends on structural positions [of a node] in a field of connections to other agents, as well as actor capabilities or attributes'. Miles Kahler, *Networked Politics: Agency, Power, and Governance* (Ithaca, NY: Cornell University Press, 2009), p. 3.
80 Caballero-Anthony, 'Understanding ASEAN Centrality', p. 563.
81 Yuzhu Wang, 'The RCEP Initiative and ASEAN "Centrality"', *China Institute of International Studies (CIIS)*, 6 December 2013, www.ciis.org.cn/english/2013-12/06/content_6518129.htm
82 David Martin Jones and Michael L. R. Smith, 'Making Process, Not Progress: ASEAN and the Evolving East Asian Regional Order', *International Security*, Vol. 32, No. 1 (Summer 2007), pp. 148–84, on p. 148.
83 David Martin Jones and Michael L. R. Smith, 'The Changing Security Agenda in Southeast Asia: Globalization, New Terror, and the Delusions of Regionalism', *Studies in Conflict and Terrorism*, Vol. 24, No. 4 (2001), pp. 271–88, on p. 285.
84 Bunn Nagara, 'Misunderstanding the "Asean Way"', *The Jakarta Post*, 2 December 2013, www.thejakartapost.com/news/2013/12/02/misunderstanding-asean-way.html.
85 Author's personal communication with Termsak Chalermpalanupap, who formerly directed the ASEAN Political-Security Community (APSC) project at the ASEAN Secretariat, in Singapore on 29 August 2014.
86 Pushpanathan, 'Opinion'.
87 Caballero-Anthony, 'Understanding ASEAN Centrality', p. 563.
88 'Concepts for the East Asia Summit: Connectivity, Security & ASEAN Centrality', *Center for Strategic and International Studies (CSIS)*, 20 May 2011, csis.org/event/concepts-east-asia-summit.

89 Against the notion that sovereignty, non-interference and the like are specific to the ASEAN Way, Rodolfo Severino writes, 'It must be noted at the outset that the so-called "ASEAN Way" is actually the way of the world, the world being, like ASEAN, made up of sovereign states that are not subject to any extra-national authority'. Rodolfo C. Severino, 'Regional Institutions in Southeast Asia: The First Movers and their Challenges', Background Paper, No. 24, Asian Development Bank Study Finalization Workshop on Institutions for Regionalism in Asia and the Pacific, Shanghai, 2–3 December 2009, p. 6.
90 Clifford, 'Theory Talk #42', p. 6.
91 Amitav Acharya, *Whose Ideas Matter?*, pp. 21–23.
92 Alan Collins, *Building a People-Oriented Security Community the ASEAN Way* (Abingdon: Routledge, 2013), pp. 79–106; Jones, 'ASEAN's Unchanged Melody?'; Jürgen Rüland and Karsten Bechle, 'Defending State-Centric Regionalism through Mimicry and Localization: Regional Parliamentary Bodies in the Association of Southeast Asian Nations (ASEAN) and Mercosur', *Journal of International Relations and Development*, Vol. 17, No. 1 (2014), pp. 61–88.
93 Jürgen Rüland, The Limits of Democratizing Interest Representation: ASEAN's Regional Corporatism and Normative Challenges', *European Journal of International Relations*, Vol. 20, No. 1 (2014), pp. 237–61.
94 See the results of surveys of Asia's elites in Bates Gill, Michael Green, Kiyoto Tsuji and William Watts, *Strategic Views on Asian Regionalism: Survey Results and Analysis* (Washington, D.C.: Center for Strategic and International Studies, 2009).
95 'Confidential Section 01 of 02 Singapore 000852 SIPDIS Department for EAP/MTS – M. Coppola E.O. 12958: Decl: 09/04/2019 Tags: Prel, SN Subject: Singapore MFA's Tommy Koh Talks China, SE Asia with STAFFDEL (Keith) Luse Singapore 00000852 001.2 of 002 Classified By: E/P Counselor Joel Ehrendreich for reason 1.4(d)', in 'Singapore, Malaysia and the WikiLeaks', *Asia Sentinel*, 20 January 2011, www.asiasentinel.com/politics/singapore-malaysia-and-the-wikileaks/.
96 Cited in Jeremy Grant, Ben Bland and Gwen Robinson, 'South China Sea Issue Divides Asean', *Financial Times*, 16 July 2012.
97 Clifford, 'Theory Talk #42', p. 5.
98 Dr Surin Pitsuwan's remarks on whether ASEAN can succeed in fulfilling its goal of becoming an economic community by its 2015 deadline, rendered in Singapore on 1 June 2011. Cited in Yang Razali Kassim, 'ASEAN Community: Losing Grip over Vision 2015?', *The Nation*, 6 June 2011.
99 See Seng Tan, 'ASEAN Centrality', in Desmond Ball, Anthony Milner, Rizal Sukma and Yusuf Wanandi, eds., *CSCAP Regional Security Outlook 2013* (Singapore: Booksmith Productions for Council for Security Cooperation in the Asia-Pacific, 2012), pp. 26–29.
100 Acharya, 'The End of ASEAN Centrality?'.
101 Michael Leifer, *ASEAN's Search for Regional Order* (Singapore: Faculty of Arts and Social Sciences, National University of Singapore, 1987), p. 21.
102 Donald K. Emmerson, *Crisis and Consensus: American and ASEAN in a New Global Context*, Working Paper (Bangkok: American Studies Program, Chulalongkorn University, 2009), p. 11.
103 In March 2009, President Lee Myung-bak of South Korea presented his New Asia Initiative, which also envisaged key responsibilities for regional powers in Asian regionalism and a presumably global role for his own country. Cheong Wa Dae, 'President Announces "New Asia Initiative"', *Korea.net*, 8 March 2009, www.korea.net/news/News/NewsView.asp?serial_no=20090308001&part=101&SearchDay=. Not to be outdone, former Japanese premier Yukio Hatoyama, during a visit to Beijing in September 2009, called for a European Union-like community for East Asia, one centred on a Sino-Japanese core that presupposed a potential reconciliation and condominium between the two Asian powers, not unlike European regionalism's reliance on the

Franco-German base. 'Japan's New Premier Pitches East Asia Union', *China Daily*, 29 September 2009, www.chinadaily.com.cn/world/2009-09/23/content_8724372.htm.
104 Hadi Soesastro, Allan Gyngell, Charles E. Morrison, and Mr Jusuf Wanandi, 'Report of Regional Task Force on Regional Institutional Architecture', report prepared for the Pacific Economic Cooperation Council (PECC) Standing Committee, June 2009.
105 Soesastro, Gyngell, Morrison, and Wanandi, 'Report of Regional Task Force on Regional Institutional Architecture', p. 16.
106 Sanchita Basu Das, 'The Trans-Pacific Partnership as a Tool to Contain China: Myth or Reality?', *East Asia Forum*, 8 June 2013, www.eastasiaforum.org/2013/06/08/the-trans-pacific-partnership-as-a-tool-to-contain-china-myth-or-reality/.
107 Wang, 'The RCEP Initiative and ASEAN "Centrality"'.
108 Natalegawa, 'Aggressively Waging Peace'.

# 4 Australia

Australia's contributions to the building of Asia's multilateral architecture are not in question. As Surin Pitsuwan, the former secretary-general of ASEAN, remarked in 2008, 'Australia has always been a catalyst and strong pillar of [Asia's] regional architectures of cooperation and prosperity in the past'.[1] Australian policymakers have consciously sought to construct a regional architecture favourable to Australia's efforts to engage deeply with the established and emerging powers of the world, and where peaceful and cooperative relations between China and the United States could be nurtured and advanced in the interest of regional peace and stability. Australia's participation in the emerging multilateralism of post-Cold War Asia has been defined implicitly by a focused and sustained attentiveness to the evolving strategic and economic milieu of Asia, and in that regard, the growing power and influence of China. Five decades ago, Sir Shane Paltridge, the former defence minister of Australia, argued that Australian strategic thinking has been defined by two key concerns – one, Canberra's acute awareness of the region's relative weakness and imbalance in economic and security resources, and two, its uneasiness over China's strategic ambitions over Southeast Asia – both of which hold implications for Australia's security.[2]

In many respects, that logic has remained relatively unchanged over the years, notwithstanding the fact that China has been the top trading partner of Australia since 2007.[3] On the other hand, Australia continues to maintain its longstanding robust military alliance with the United States, fighting alongside the latter in the recent wars in Afghanistan and Iraq (including the current campaign against the Islamic State rebels in northern Iraq).[4] The divide of economic reliance on a China which could pose a strategic threat to Australia, on the one hand, and military reliance on the United States on the other has become a matter of grave concern among some in Australia's strategic circles. But as one analyst has put it, '[Australia's] strategic interactions with the two major powers are not mechanistic "zero sum games" in which cooperation with one country automatically comes at the expense of the other'.[5] This has rendered the imperative of big power diplomacy, which has historically animated and defined Australia's contributions to regionalism in Asia, even more crucial in the foreseeable future. For the same reason, Australia will in all likelihood seek to revise what it sees as an increasingly ineffective regional architecture in the hands of ASEAN.

Australia is surely not alone in putting its ties with great powers at the heart of its contributions to regionalism in Asia; the ASEAN countries share the same aim.[6] That said, Australia's support for ASEAN's centrality in Asia's regional architecture arguably waxes and wanes depending on its perception of whether ASEAN's 'ecosystem' of regional institutions,[7] which Australia played a key part in fostering, remains relevant to its engagement of China and the United States. Despite its multi-multilateral character, ASEAN's suite of regional arrangements has furnished ample regular opportunities for Australia to engage the great powers in high-level security dialogue and defence cooperation beyond what it can do on its own. 'In no multilateral fora would our Prime Minister sit with the leaders of the United States, Japan, China, Indonesia or any of the states of South East Asia. The leadership of those countries occupied a world beyond us', as Paul Keating once conceded in the context of Australian participation in Asia's regional architecture.[8] If anything, involvement in the ARF, EAS and ADMM-Plus, no matter how flawed those bodies are in the view of many Australians, has allowed Australia to 'walk amongst giants'.[9] This is not to imply Australia harbours big power aspirations, even if former Australian foreign minister Alexander Downer, when rubbishing references to Australia as a 'middle power' and the purported existence among his peers of a 'middle child complex when it comes to [Australia's] place in the world', reportedly insisted that Australia is 'not "middling" or "average" or "insignificant"' but 'a considerable power and a significant country'.[10]

Middle power or otherwise, Australia – arguably since Gough Whitlam's visit, as opposition leader, to China in 1971, and his normalization of ties, as prime minister, with China in 1972 – has sought a role for itself as an honest though interested broker to the great powers. 'We cannot hope to have sensible relations with China unless we recognise that this proud and purposeful people will never again submit to international humiliation', as Whitlam has himself intimated. 'We understand that one great fact. Australia can play a significant part in helping China fulfil its destiny as a leader in international cooperation'.[11] Furthermore, to the extent ASEAN – the regional organization, not the region – is increasingly viewed these days by many as an ineffective driver of regionalism and unreliable trustee of the regional architecture, Australia's 'irrepressibly activist' diplomacy – which, according to a respected Australian academic/practitioner, has shaped their alliance strategies, military engagements and multilateral diplomacy[12] – has led Canberra in the recent past to seek more credible regional alternatives. In this regard, Australia's partnership with ASEAN and other stakeholder countries becomes even more crucial as they work to render those multilateral institutions into 'effective mechanisms to manage regional and transnational security issues and risks arising from rivalries and the possibilities of miscalculation'.[13] For these reasons, Australia's 2013 defence white paper has indicated Australia's strong continued support for the ARF and the EAS and its intention to 'take a leading role' in the ADMM-Plus.[14]

## Australia's 'Asia pivot'

It has been said, with good reason, that Australia's international history has left it fearful of abandonment by its allies ('great and powerful friends', as Canberra's official argot has it) – the United Kingdom for a fair part of the twentieth century, followed by the United States for the latter half of that century to the present – rather than entrapment in their conflicts and wars which Australia might otherwise prefer to avoid.[15] Even as the Labor government under Prime Minister Julia Gillard released a white paper in 2012 entitled *Australia in the Asian Century* which acknowledged the fundamental economic and political significance of the Asian region – and, in particular, of China – to Australia, the appropriate assurances and evidence of commitment were rendered to its key ally, the United States. By most accounts, official or otherwise, Australians accept that growing engagement with Asia has become a categorical imperative. 'The Asian century is an Australian opportunity', as the executive summary of *Australia in the Asian Century* has put it.

> As the global centre of gravity shifts to our region, the tyranny of distance is being replaced by the prospects of proximity. Australia is located in the right place at the right time – in the Asian region in the Asian century.[16]

Yet Australia's 'pivot' to Asia, if only in aspirational terms, is by no means novel. As Gareth Evans, foreign minister in the Hawke and Keating governments, argued back in 1992:

> The great turn-around in Australia's contemporary history has been our response to developments in Asia. This dynamic, changing region, from which we sought to protect ourselves in the past, is now the region that offers Australia the most. Economically, there is now a widespread recognition in Australia that Asia is the region where we can best guarantee our prosperity. The same historic shift is clear in terms of security. The need to live in Asia strategically has led us to realize that we must seek security *with* Asia rather than *from* it.[17]

Ramesh Thakur has made the following contention:

> In the end, Australia needs and will continue to need Asia more than Asia will need Australia. The burden of adjustment falls unevenly in the Australia–Asia relationship. As an actor of modest means and influence, Australia can but try to mould the contours of great-power economic and security interactions – hence the twin emphases in Australian foreign policy on coalition-building and concentration of efforts on areas and issues where Australia can make a difference. Australia is so isolated geographically that it cannot be isolationist in foreign policy. Regional engagement is the solution to this dilemma – the path to salvation from economic marginalization, political loneliness and, ultimately, strategic irrelevance.[18]

Be that as it may, there is good reason to suppose that by 'Asia', most Australian strategic thinkers are in fact referring to China. Australia's efforts to seek security with rather than from China, its key economic partner but whose strategic intentions it doubts, has led it to pursue, in April 2013, a 'strategic partnership' and 'new bilateral architecture' with China that comprise high-level political and economic dialogues between their two nations.[19] At the same time, however, Australians have sought to reassure their American friends – as Gillard did before the American Congress in March 2011 – that Australia 'is an ally [of the United States] for all the years to come'.[20] Given the resource constraints that have limited Australia's ability to provide for its own security – an issue that scuttled national plans for naval force modernization delineated in its 2019 defence white paper and which now lies at the core of the anticipated defence white paper which the Coalition Government led by Prime Minister Tony Abbott will publish in 2015 – reliance on the extended military deterrence furnished by the United States is understandable. In short, defence and security bilateralism would remain critical for Australia for the foreseeable future.

That being said, Australia's continued reliance on the United States for its security has raised warning flags for advocates of a hedging strategy. Mourning the supposed passing of Australia's 'era of effective foreign policy activism', Paul Keating argued as recently as 2012 that Australian diplomacy, in his view, has turned back the clock in gravitating to the United States.

> Our sense of independence has flagged and as it flagged, we have rolled back into an easy accommodation with the foreign policy objectives of the United States. More latterly, our respect for the foreign policy objectives of the United States has superimposed itself on what should otherwise be the foreign policy objectives of Australia.[21]

Indeed, Nick Bisley has gone further in arguing that Australia has, for all intents and purposes, dispensed with all pretence of strategic hedging by hewing even more closely to the United States politically and militarily: 'Australia has made up its mind about its strategic policy: it has bound itself to the United States and will do all it can to support America's conception of regional and global order'.[22] Anthony Milner has urged against allowing Australian interests to be submerged in the United States' global agenda.[23] For Keating, however, it is not just the Howard government's willingness to play 'deputy sheriff' to America,[24] but also the Rudd government's shared preoccupation with Washington over the military threat China purportedly poses to the region and the Gillard government's 'facilitation' of America's 'rebalancing' strategy towards Asia which President Barack Obama spoke about when he addressed the Australian Parliament in November 2011.[25] For his part, as noted earlier, Hugh White has called for a rethink of the existing bifurcation – ultimately detrimental to Australia's interests, in his view – of economic reliance on China, on the one hand, and military reliance on the United States on the other.[26] For that matter, Malcolm Fraser, the former prime minister who arguably did the most to expand Australia's alliance with the United States, argued in 2014 for an end to strategic dependence and the establishment of 'a truly independent Australia'. Urging his successors to adopt a much greater degree of independence in foreign policy, he believes Australia should no longer merely follow other nations – even if they happen to be 'great and powerful friends', into wars of no direct bearing on Australia or Australia's security.[27] 'Australia is too important to define itself in terms of one great power, rising, falling, or in between', as another observer has put it. 'No need, no possibility, no benefit in having a single star illumine our way'.[28]

Australia's engagement with regionalism in Asia – with engagement of China and the United States at its core – has taken place within a historical context of domestic ambivalence towards Asia.[29] The vigorous national debate sparked by the release of *Australia in the Asian Century* reflects not only the policy differences among Australians concerning their country's relationship with the Asian region, but also an enduring deep-seated angst about Australia's identity that has hitherto remained unresolved despite serious if at times uneven efforts by Canberra to engage the Asian region – efforts that existed well before Labor leader Paul Keating's spirited 'turn' towards Asia.[30] At different times, Australians have questioned the value, appropriateness and consequences of engagement with Asia.[31] Although Australian attitudes toward Asia have undoubtedly evolved from early fears and ignorance about the region and worries over Asian immigration to Australia, to growing, perhaps even grudging, acceptance of multiculturalism as a foundation of Australian society, there have however been enough hints to suggest that the purported perception shift 'from White Australia to part of Asia'[32] has neither been comprehensive nor holistic, but defined by and pursued largely and pragmatically on economic grounds.[33] Granted, there are social, cultural and other aspects to that historical engagement – there are significant exceptions, to be sure, as the failed Chinalco–Rio Tinto deal in 2005, or the Singaporean telecommunications giant SingTel's failed bid for Australia's Optus in 2001, owing to Australian allegations of spying by the Singapore government, have shown[34] – but they generally lack the unequivocal and unambiguous rationale undergirding economic cooperation.[35] (Be that as it may, SingTel was in the news in late 2013 for reportedly facilitating the efforts by Western powers – the so-called 'Five Eyes' including Australia – to conduct electronic surveillance on certain Southeast Asian leaders, including the alleged monitoring by Australia of Indonesian President Susilo Bambang Yudhoyono's cell phone.[36]) Even so, it has been argued that Australians have not made enough economic investment in Asia to warrant the claim of being 'in the Asian Century', so to speak. As Jenny McGregor has queried:

> The real measure of a genuine desire to understand the Asian region, and comprehend the opportunities, is people on the ground and financial commitment. Australia still invests more in Europe, the United States and New Zealand than we do in Asia, by a significant margin, despite the enormous growth opportunities and proximity and time zone advantages we enjoy in our own neighbourhood. There is a disconnect here. We know that Asia saved us from the [Global Financial Crisis] and we assert that our economic future lies with this region but are we willing to put more in?[37]

46  *Australia*

Others have taken umbrage with such pragmatism, however. 'We are chasing our own tail regarding engagement with Asia', as Australian academic Ying Zhu has commented in response to concerns raised in *Australia in the Asian Century*.

> We know the issues that are holding Australia back still relate to a lack of awareness and deep understanding of Asian cultures and societies. We treat our Asian partners as business clients, not cooperative partners. Our engagement seems superficial and lacks real trust.[38]

## Present at the creation

In more respects than one, the ending of the Cold War proved a crucial time for Australian economic and foreign policy through opening new 'fronts' which Cold War ideological and security concerns either discouraged or simply ignored.[39] Despite the existence of a persistent domestic debate over Australia's place and role in Asia, there is little question that the country has had and continues to have a strong if at times controversial involvement in Asian experimentations in regional cooperation and integration.[40] Australia's contributions to Asian regionalism are indisputable. Whether in terms of regional visions and intellectual ideas, as well as the hard and oft-times behind-the-scenes work of establishing institutional arrangements in support of regional security and/or economic collaboration, Australian innovation has been characterized by vibrancy and vigour, as in the case of former prime minister Bob Hawke's initiation in 1989 – the inaugural ministerial meeting in Canberra that November was chaired by Gareth Evans, then foreign minister of Australia, while Andrew Elek also played a key role as inaugural chairperson of the APEC Senior Officials[41] – of a process that would eventuate in the formation of the APEC trade forum and the works of Australian National University economists Peter Drysdale and Ross Garnaut on 'open regionalism'.[42] As much a slogan for rallying support against the worrying trend of the early post-Cold War period towards regional trade blocs, such as the North American Free Trade Agreement (NAFTA) and the ASEAN Free Trade Agreement (AFTA) – as Arthur Dunkel, director-general of the General Agreement on Tariffs and Trade (GATT), the predecessor to the WTO, once declared concerning the ostensible threat posed to the Uruguay Round of world trade talks by the rise of economic regionalism, 'multilateralism and regionalism will either live together or die together!'[43] – open regionalism became the overarching concept for APEC trade liberalization. More broadly, Australian scholarship on APEC has also theorized on the trade forum's importance to regional architecture building in Asia.[44] To be sure, Australia did not work alone in initiating the APEC but enjoyed significant collaboration with Japan, particularly the Japanese Ministry of International Trade and Industry (MITI).[45] Less welcomed by Asia but no less important for Asian regionalism has been former prime minister Kevin Rudd's introduction in 2008 of his vision for an overarching regional architecture in Asia[46] and the subsequent efforts by Australian policy intellectuals and practitioners to develop and embellish further Rudd's ideas.[47] The idea has proved particularly controversial for ASEAN member countries because of its implications for ASEAN's future place and role in regional architecture. Controversy aside, the Rudd government can probably take some credit for proposing in late 2009 the inclusion of Russia and the United States in the EAS.[48]

As noted, a key contribution of Australia to Asian multilateralism has been to ensure the presence and participation of the relevant major post-Cold War powers, namely China and the United States, in regional order and architecture. One motivation for this could have been the apparent lack of participation by Australia in multilateral diplomacy of the sort that allowed Australian leaders to commingle intimately with the leaders of established great powers and emerging Asian powers.[49] Prior to the start of the post-Cold War era, Australian leaders, apart from participating at the United Nations, tended only to attend international gatherings such as the British Commonwealth Heads of Government Meeting and the South Pacific Forum. That would change with Australia's role – together with that of Japan, as discussed in the subsequent chapter – in initiating the APEC. Already, there was a clear sense, in the strategic uncertainty of the immediate post-Cold War period even as the Gorbachev-led Soviet Union started to unravel, that America, the soon-to-be sole global power, and rising China had to be engaged. As Bob Hawke, former Australian prime minister, once reminisced about the political haggling over the proposed membership of the inaugural APEC meeting in 1989:

> Some people didn't want China, and some people didn't want the United States. To my mind, this was absurdity. You couldn't with any sense of intelligent purpose talk about the Asia-Pacific region without either of them not being part of it. And we had to do quite a bit of, not arm-twisting, you know, but a lot of discussion and negotiation to bring about a point where the organization that did emerge encompassed both.[50]

In July 1990, Australian Foreign Minister Gareth Evans advocated the convening of a security conference for the Asia-Pacific modelled on the Conference for Security Cooperation in Europe (CSCE), an idea the Canadian Foreign Minister Joe Clark subsequently proposed as well.[51] Evans's proposal did not receive the support of Japan, whose security planners felt that the European common security model would not adequately address Asia's distinct security concerns, nor that of the United States, whose Secretary of State James Baker argued that 'bilateral security arrangements were sufficient to meet regional security needs'.[52] Washington's other related worry, as it turned out, also had to do with residual Cold War considerations, particularly the prospect of Russia's appropriation of such a regional security forum to prevent freedom of navigation in the Pacific. '[W]e don't want to allow the Soviets to get either the framework or the agenda for the security of Asia', Baker reportedly wrote Evans in late 1990 to explain Washington's resistance to Evans' proposal. 'Advocacy of a "common security approach" provides the wedge they need to achieve their long-held goal of naval arms control in the Pacific. Constraints on our navy would not, in my view, enhance regional security at all'.[53]

The formation of the ARF in 1993 – the forum's formal inauguration would take place a year later – and the development of elements of its three-staged 'roadmap' of security cooperation have also involved, at the policy and intellectual dimensions, critical contributions by Australians. While key Department of Foreign Affairs and Trade (DFAT) and Department of Defence officials such as Evans and Richard ('Ric') Smith[54] worked alongside their intergovernmental counterparts from other countries, leading Australian academics and analysts such as Desmond Ball, Sam Bateman, Sandy Duncan, Alan Dupont, Richard Higgott, Andrew Mack, Anthony Milner, Geoffrey Wiseman and many others, researching independently as well as in collaboration with fellow Australian and/or non-Australian scholars – including in 'second track' settings such as the Council for Security Cooperation in the Asia-Pacific (CSCAP), just as their economist colleagues did in the Pacific Economic Cooperation Council (PECC) on behalf of the APEC[55] – contributed to the conceptual development of security ideas such as confidence building, preventive diplomacy, cooperative security, common security, maritime security, and so forth. Not unlike the APEC trade forum, the ARF amounted to a security version of open regionalism, whereby political-security dialogue among the major and regional powers and ASEAN states is institutionalized on a multilateral basis using the diplomatic-security convention of ASEAN as a guide.[56] Indeed, where engaging China is concerned, the ARF has been viewed by some as having facilitated China's gradual evolution from revolutionary regime to a 'normal' state.[57] That said, it is also the failure of the ARF, already two decades old, to fulfil its stated objective of implementing preventive diplomacy (PD) that led to growing disenchantment with the ARF among its 'activist' members – Australia among them – seeking to advance security cooperation but unable to overcome stonewalling by their 'reluctant' counterparts fearing the erosion of sovereignty given the potentially intrusive and interventionist nature of PD.[58] And while Australia has no official role in the APT, the political-strategic issues behind the formation of that framework have served as a relevant if convenient backdrop to Australian intellectual contributions to the broader concern surrounding Asian anxieties, in the immediate aftermath of Asia's financial crisis in 1997–8, over structural 'conditionalities' imposed on them by Western countries (primarily the United States) and Western-led international financial institutions, and related questions over the continued feasibility of the 'Washington Consensus' and the neoliberal economic system.[59]

## Of concerts and communities

The controversial releases of thousands of diplomatic cables in 2010 by WikiLeaks included details of a conversation between then Prime Minister Kevin Rudd and US Secretary of State Hillary Clinton in March 2009 regarding Australia's view and policy on China. Describing himself as a 'brutal realist on China', Rudd reportedly informed his interlocutor that Australia's strategy consisted in 'integrating China effectively into the international community and allowing it to demonstrate greater responsibility, all while also preparing to deploy force if everything goes wrong'.[60] Critically, Rudd saw his Asia-Pacific Community (APC) initiative, which sought to promote a new vision of regional architecture, as an important element in what would conceivably be a collective effort to balance against China. As Rudd informed Clinton, the APC was (in the language of the leaked US diplomatic cable)

> an effort to ensure Chinese dominance of the East Asia Summit (EAS) did not result in a 'Chinese Munroe Doctrine' and an Asia without the United States. Expressing appreciation for US reengagement in the region, Rudd said China could succeed only if the United States ceded the field.[61]

Rudd the 'brutal realist' also sought, as he had promised Clinton, to enhance Australia's naval capabilities as a response to China's growing ability to project force 'beyond the scope of what would be required for a conflict over Taiwan', in the words of Australian 2009 defence white paper.[62] Thanks reportedly to efforts by Australian diplomats to stave off expected Chinese disquiet through deft consultations with the Chinese before the white paper went public, official Chinese reaction to it was relatively subdued with a Chinese Ministry of Foreign Affairs statement noting that 'China is a peaceful force that forms no threat to any other countries [sic]', and that Beijing's hope was that 'neighbour countries will view China's military build-up objectively, without bias'.[63] The most recent defence white paper released by Australia in 2013 implies that Australian worries over China have not dissipated – indeed, it clarified that its threat assessment, accounting for nuances, has fundamentally remained unchanged from that furnished by its 2009 predecessor and it was committed to delivering the core military capabilities promised in 2009[64] – and highlights a key challenge for Australia's so-called 'outgoing maritime strategy', for which China's recent assertiveness in regional waters and its formidable anti-access cum anti-denial capabilities have understandably proved worrisome. 'Australia is thoroughly enmeshed in a global sea-based trading system, not least as a major supplier of commodities to China', as maritime expert Geoffrey Till has argued. 'A threat to the system's operation represents an indirect threat to Australia's interests'.[65]

However, even if Australia's aim to provide a military counterpoint to China seemed sufficiently unambiguous in its defence white paper of 2009, the counterbalancing narrative was largely absent in Rudd's launch of his APC initiative in 2008. 'The Rudd initiative, at least in the form it was introduced rather than its subsequent iterations, arguably fits what this book's Conclusion (see p. 159) describes as *command multilateralism*, that is, a hierarchical conception of architecture in the form of either a single comprehensive institution or an overarching or lead institution which is authorized to steer all other institutions and constitutive elements of the regional architecture'. It is motivated by the belief that the existing multi-multilateral architecture helmed by ASEAN – or at least aspects of that architecture – no longer works. It was, as the veteran Australian envoy Richard Woolcott has noted, disenchantment with the ARF which partly led Rudd to promote the APC. The ARF, Woolcott argued, 'is too large and has made insufficient progress since its inception'.[66] At a meeting in Singapore in August 2008, Rudd made the following observation:

> All of our existing regional mechanisms have a critical role to play now and into the future – including ASEAN, APEC and the EAS. But, at the same time, we need to begin our conversation on where our wider region goes from here. And this is where the wider region needs to learn from ASEAN's success – how to build the institutions, habits and practices of cooperation across the policy spectrum and across historically uncomfortable national divides ...[67]

Rudd's remark, glaring for its omission of the ARF, more or less echoed his foreign minister Stephen Smith's perspective which the latter shared a month before his prime minister's speech in Singapore. In July 2008, Smith argued that the 'conversation' initiated by his prime minister on revising regional architecture 'doesn't diminish any of the existing regional bodies. On the contrary, they will continue to play their essential roles'. Nonetheless, he proceeded to add, 'There could be a new piece of architecture, as ASEAN and APEC once were. Or it could evolve and emerge from and through the existing architecture, as the ASEAN Regional Forum and the East Asia Summit have'.[68] The notion that there is need for a 'new piece of architecture' has also captured the imaginations of Australian academics and policy intellectuals who appeal for the streamlining or overhauling of the existing architecture.[69] For that matter, it has led to deeper rumination on the language of regionalism and the proclivity of contributors to that debate to occasional or even common misappropriations of terms such as 'architecture'.[70] Arguably, while Rudd viewed his proposal as an invitation to an evolving regional conversation – 'Australia remains open to the suggestions of our regional partners as this discussion unfolds', as he noted in 2008[71] – the lieutenants to whom he entrusted the task of moderating that conversation evidently saw things differently, or so some representatives of ASEAN countries believed. At a regional meeting convened by Richard Woolcott on behalf of his prime minister in Sydney in December 2009, the sense, correct or otherwise, some invited participants to that gathering had of the proceedings was one of being herded against their inclinations towards an involuntary consensus. As Tommy Koh, the veteran diplomat from Singapore, recollected of the Sydney meeting,

> One of the findings of Woolcott's extensive consultations with regional leaders was that the region had no appetite for a new institution. Notwithstanding this, the organisers tried to push the contrary view that we agreed *existing institutions were inadequate and ineffective*.[72]

Koh's insinuation that regional leaders harbour 'no appetite for a new institution' implies – in contrast to the Australian desire for command multilateralism – that the region's putative preference is for either the *functional* or *laissez faire* variants of multilateralism (see the concluding chapter of this book)'.

The sense of a disconnect between Rudd's publicly declared support for ASEAN and the apparent disregard for ASEAN by the convenors of the Sydney meeting centred on the advocacy by Michael Wesley, who co-chaired the meeting, of a concert of powers arrangement comprising the region's great powers and a number of smaller powers (including Australia), and an annual 'leaders-level coordinating body' that would presumably replace ASEAN centrality.[73] And when the EAS admitted Russia and the United States as members in 2011, suggestions were offered – by Rudd himself no less at the EAS gathering in July 2011 – that the expanded EAS, as a summit-level arrangement, was what Rudd had in mind as a leaders-level coordinating body.[74] Reportedly, Wesley claimed at the Sydney meeting that both those ideas (power concert and coordinating body) enjoyed growing support within the region, a claim which some participants from the ASEAN countries, particularly Singapore, have vehemently disputed. As Amitav Acharya has noted:

> According to Singaporean diplomat Tommy Koh, 'The idea to replace ASEAN with a G8 of the Asia Pacific is both impractical and a violation of the Pacific ethos of equality and consensus'. Koh argued that there was nothing wrong with the region's current multi-layered or 'multiplex' system, which also existed in Europe ... His Singaporean colleague, Simon Tay, who used the term 'directorate' to describe the concert, joined in: 'there is, in my view, a strong case *against* – not for – a non-inclusive fora [sic] among the major powers to seek to direct events in all fields'.[75]

Further, Rudd's APC vision, on the one hand, appears to conflict with the community-challenged, elitist model of a power concert advocated by Wesley on the other.[76] There is delicious irony here given Wesley's seeming disregard for conceptual clarity over the meaning of *community* in the face of criticism over a similar disregard by regional participants in their relatively loose use of the word *architecture*.[77] Hence the suggestion by Baogang He that Australia, despite its significant contributions to Asian regionalism, nonetheless comes across an 'awkward partner' to the region. As He has observed about Rudd's vision, 'The main critical analysis of the proposal has focused on institutional building or architecture, or its relationship with existing regional institutions, but overlooks a host of often fraught questions about culture, norms, identities, and international power relations'.[78] And despite Australia's attempts to punch above its weight in regional forums and to be a regional leader', He argues that Australia 'is still not regarded as a full member or as quite fitting into the region. It is an "awkward partner" in the Asian context, and has experienced the "liminality" of being neither here nor there'.[79] As John Blaxland has likewise argued:

> To engage with Asia we need to know who we are and where we have come from. Too often Australians venture into Asia with a brash, informal and culturally unaware approach that does much to undermine prospective

relations. Australians try to fit in, but it often falls flat. Our informality and directness (which we consider one of our strengths) blinds us to the significance in Asia of form, appearances, and 'face'.[80]

Blaxland, He, and those who share their view have a point. Is Australia primarily concerned about results and not process, the latter of which seems to preoccupy the ASEAN states?[81] For example, concerning his celebrated jibe at the APEC as 'four adjectives in search of a noun', Gareth Evans has admitted his attempt at mirth-making was intended to be dismissive of the APEC, but 'was an acknowledgement that this is a work in progress and the need to shrug off many of the inhibitions that have [delayed] progress'.[82]

Other Australians, most notably the practitioner turned academician Hugh White, have also argued that Asia's security is best provided for by way of a concert of powers, although White, unlike Wesley, is more circumspect about which other nation – other than China and the United States whom White urges ought to share power with one another – deserves a trusteeship in the co-management of regional order.[83] But as has also been argued, a Sino-US condominium for co-managing Asia, whether conceived as a 'G2' or a 'Coordination 2' (C2) partnership, is unlikely to be sufficient because of the multipolar structure of contemporary Asia.[84] Indeed, both Beijing and Washington have dispelled the notion of a 'G2', where the two great powers would supposedly forge 'a two nation clearinghouse for international disputes'.[85] However, prior to the Sino-US Strategic and Economic Dialogue (S&ED) of 2012, State Councillor Dai Bingguo of China noted that 'China is not seeking after G2, but is willing to build C2, or the two in coordination with the US' – a prospect offered by the S&ED and ancillary bilateral processes between the two countries, but yet to be realized.[86] Unlike those who argue for concerts and/or condominiums of power, Baogang He however demurs, believing ASEAN deserves neither to be marginalized nor excluded in Australian strategic calculations, but whose involvement should be incorporated with the relevant concert arrangement to form a composite or 'hybrid' regionalism.[87] Intriguingly, whether and how Rudd's claim that 'ASEAN, given its positive history and its contribution for the future, should be very much at the core of any future Asia-Pacific community'[88] figures in the sort of hybrid regionalism He is referring to remains to be seen. This raises the question, hitherto unanswered, whether the expanded EAS, presumably Rudd's 'gift to the world'[89] – indeed, Rudd himself suggested as much in April 2012 during an interview with Australian media[90] – represents in Australians' minds the hybrid regionalism He has advocated, or an elitist arrangement within which ASEAN is merely a junior partner.[91] Beyond conceptual speculation on architecture, there is concern among some Asians over the practical but fundamental challenge of ensuring regular annual participation by the American president, be it Barack Obama or his successors, to the EAS. (Ironically, Obama would miss both the EAS and APEC meetings in 2013 as a result of the federal government shutdown which resulted from the US Congress's inability to resolve the budgetary crisis.) This is especially a worry for ASEAN states who remember all too well the absences of former US Secretary of State Condoleeza Rice at the 2005 and 2007 ARF meetings.

Neither China nor the United States supported Rudd's proposal.[92] In a way, this undermines suggestions that the enlarged EAS is in effect Rudd's APC realized. Perhaps equally telling is the inclusion in the 2013 defence white paper of the ARF as a regional arrangement which Australia – or at least its defence ministry – ostensibly regards as significant. Yet, the emphasis on a putative concert of power arguably serves as an implicit clue as to what Rudd and his colleagues had in mind regarding how they perceived China's rising power and influence – both Australia's 'meal ticket' as well as its prospective threat simultaneously, as one pundit has put it[93] – and what was therefore needed to deal with that. For them, Asia's evolving architecture provided both an institutional space for multilateral collaboration as well as an institutional constraint against China, whose proposal to render the EAS a 'two-tiered, exclusionary and discriminatory' structure – effectively creating a China-dominated sphere of influence – was viewed by Canberra, fairly or otherwise, as proof positive of China's aspiration for regional hegemony.[94] Indeed, Australia's very inclusion into the EAS in 2005 was made with those same objectives in mind.[95] It presumably also implies – given the disappointment felt by many in Australia's strategic circles regarding the ARF – that Rudd and his colleagues did not believe the ARF had sufficiently succeeded in constraining China's growing diplomatic assertiveness, leading them to seek an alternative multilateral mechanism that could fulfil that objective. Rudd's efforts were reportedly acknowledged by Singapore's foreign minister at the EAS meeting in July 2011.[96] Whether this was a result of the WikiLeaks revelation regarding Rudd's aspiration for the APC as a forum to soft-balance against China or his 'success' at bringing the United States into East Asian regionalism remains unclear. For its part, Singapore had proposed an alternative to enlarging the EAS, namely, a separate 'ASEAN plus eight' arrangement that would comprise the eighteen member countries that today make up the expanded EAS, except it would function as an informal arrangement that would meet on a triennial or biennial basis as and when the need arises – an effort, more than anything else, to accommodate US engagement in the region. Ultimately, the Singaporean proposal was rendered moot when Indonesia, Laos, Malaysia, and Vietnam expressed their preference for an expansion of the EAS over Singapore's proposal and when President Obama committed the United States to joining the EAS.[97]

Be that as it may, whichever form of regional architecture and whether ASEAN plays a key part in it, the strategic aim for Australia's investment has been and remains the same – effectively to engage the major powers of the day. Few would disagree that it is the proverbial 'elephants' in the room – China, Indonesia, increasingly India, and of course the United States, as former foreign minister Gareth Evans has pointed out[98] – that truly matter to Australia, and for whom successive Australian governments, Labor and Liberal/Coalition alike, have conscientiously laboured to build and improve the regional architecture as they have understood it.

## Do Southeast Asia and ASEAN (still) matter?

The foregoing analysis suggests an Australia increasingly less inclined, over time, to rely on ASEAN to helm Asian regional architecture, owing to the latter's perceived inability. While the episode of the Rudd initiative appears to have been settled if only because of the shared anxieties both Australia and many ASEAN states harbour regarding China's strategic ambitions, the debate over the remit and role of the EAS, now enlarged and increasingly urged by non-ASEAN stakeholders to assume a managerial and/or coordinating function for the entire regional architecture, puts at risk the principle of ASEAN centrality that ASEAN and its member states have fought hard to preserve.

To be sure, ASEAN still has its supporters within Australian policy and academic circles who do not doubt the organization's continued relevance to regional security despite their worries over its member states' apparent inability to cohere.[99] Some have taken umbrage with Canberra's evident lack of focus on ASEAN and Southeast Asia more broadly even in the 2012 white paper, *Australia in the Asian Century*. As Michele Ford shared of her impressions of that white paper, 'I have a sinking feeling that this shopping list of initiatives lacks the kind of comprehensiveness and coherence needed if we are to truly engage with the complex and diverse place that is Southeast Asia'.[100] At times, the antipathy has been mutual. It would not surprise us if some Southeast Asians and ASEAN in particular continue to question Australia's commitment to Asia. ASEAN countries have not always been ready to welcome, much less reciprocate, Australian overtures.[101] Indeed, some ASEAN leaders have at times shown outright antagonism towards Australia and its leaders, such as former Singapore premier Lee Kuan Yew's infamous putdown of Australia in the 1980s as the 'poor white trash of Asia' and ex-Malaysian leader Mahathir Mohamad's many verbal jousts with Australian leaders – with Hawke over Malaysia's 'barbaric' hanging of two Australian men for drug-related offences, Keating over Mahathir's absence at the inaugural APEC meeting in Seattle in 1993, and Howard over Australia's 'deputy sheriff' tag and the Howard government's talk about a 'pre-emption' strategy in its response to terrorism.

As the very first dialogue partner of ASEAN – a relationship dating back to 1974 – Australia clearly remains interested in its dealings with Southeast Asian countries and with the ASEAN region as a whole. Together with ASEAN and New Zealand, Australia established a tripartite free trade agreement that entered into force between January 2010 and January 2012 (with Indonesia as the last country to come on board). Australia is also a participating economy in the Regional Comprehensive Economic Partnership (RCEP) and a member of the ADMM-Plus,[102] both important ASEAN-based frameworks for facilitating economic and security cooperation respectively between ASEAN dialogue partners and the ASEAN region. Individual ASEAN member nations remain significant for Australia for economic, political and security reasons. Of these, there is none more crucial than Indonesia, once viewed by Australian strategic thinkers as the place 'from or through which a military threat to Australia could most easily be posed',[103] but more and more so today as a country whose 'strengths as a potential partner for Australia … are increasing'.[104]

From a security perspective, Southeast Asia has arguably grown in salience and significance for Australia as reflected in Australian defence white papers of the past three decades. While the 1987 paper stressed self-reliance in the direct defence of Australia, the 2000 paper, mindful of the prospect for rising instability in Australia's near abroad – East Timor in 1999, among others, comes to mind – rationalized and urged the expansion of Australia's military-to-military diplomacy in the Asia-Pacific region in addition to its existing peacekeeping commitments. Crucially, the 'concentric circles' approach of the 2000 white paper placed Indonesia – together with Timor Leste, Papua New Guinea, New Zealand and the South Pacific islands – within the second priority circle, but for all intents and purposes 'relegated' Southeast Asia to the third or next outer circle. Although the concentric circles approach has more or less been retained within the white papers of 2009 and 2013, the place of Southeast Asia however appears to have been 'upgraded' in Canberra's strategic thinking. If anything, Southeast Asia looms large in the 2013 white paper and has in fact become central to Australia's defence diplomacy efforts.[105] While the *Australia in the Asian Century* white paper has been criticized for its relative silence on Southeast Asia and ASEAN, the same cannot be said of its 2013 defence counterpart.

With Southeast Asia standing between it and its largest trading partner, Australia cannot afford to ignore Southeast Asia. Deepening ties with ASEAN states – and not just with Indonesia[106] – has been critical not only to maintaining the region as a buffer against inappropriate Chinese ambitions should they manifest, but provides Australia with an economic alternative or hedge. As a pundit has put it, Australia's 'newly found love of regional engagement is all about winning over the half billion souls that live between [it] and China over to [its] way of thinking'.[107] Furthermore, it could be argued that Southeast Asia and ASEAN are critical to Australia because the region and the organization have grown in significance for the United States, Australia's key ally. As US support for Japan's military normalization (discussed at length in chapter 5) has underscored, enhanced burden-sharing among America's Asian allies has become an expectation from which no one, not least Australia, is exempt.[108] According to a study on Australian defence diplomacy, what stood out among a host of policy recommendations on how the Australian Defence Forces (ADF) could enhance their military-to-military engagement with Southeast Asian countries were proposals to enhance ADF contributions in areas where US forces might draw down in the future, such as counterinsurgency assistance to the Philippines.[109] While such readiness to plug gaps left by the Americans could encourage allegations that Canberra is again playing Washington's 'deputy sheriff' in the region,[110] it is clearly in Australia's interest to assist the region and deepen its ties with it.

## Conclusion

From very early on, Australia has played and continues to play a key role in the shaping of Asia's multilateral architecture, whose arrangements have provided Canberra with opportunities to engage deeply with great and regional powers in ways it might otherwise not been able to do on its own. However, with rising tensions between China and some of its fellow stakeholders – and, crucially, the growing sense that ASEAN is not only unable to provide the requisite regional leadership but unwillingly to forego its privilege of centrality – Australia, particularly under Rudd, has sought to revise the regional status quo. Despite the regional backlash against the Rudd initiative, it has become clear, as subsequent chapters show, that other non-ASEAN stakeholder countries are equally concerned about the perceived paucity of regional leadership and, in varying degrees, view the enlarged EAS as a prospective 'game changer' in Asian regionalism – a message which ASEAN may find hard to stomach (for the reasons explained in chapter 3).

## Notes

1. 'ASEAN Secretary General's Welcoming Speech on the Occasion of the Visit of the Hon. Kevin Michael Rudd, Prime Minister of Australia, to the ASEAN Secretariat, Jakarta, June 13, 2008', cited in Frank Frost, 'Australia's Proposal for an "Asia Pacific Community": Issues and Prospects', Parliamentary Library Research Paper, 1 December 2009 (Canberra, ACT: Department of Parliamentary Services, Parliament of Australia, 2009), p. 12.
2. Shane Paltridge, 'Australia and the Defence of Southeast Asia', *Foreign Affairs*, Vol. 49 (1965), pp. 49–61.
3. David Uren, 'China Emerges as Our Biggest Trade Partner', *The Australian*, 6 May 2007, www.theaustralian.com.au/news/nation/china-emerges-as-our-biggest-trade-partner/story-e6frg6nf-1111113474544?nk=9cb1cc6b01a3ac696353ec4443b7bb5e (accessed 27 August 2014).
4. Nick Bisley, 'No Hedging in Canberra: The Australia–US Alliance in the "Asian Century"', *Asia-Pacific Bulletin*, No. 157, 3 April 2012 (Honolulu, HI: East-West Center, 2012), pp. 1–2; Paul McGeough, 'Australia still at America's Beck and Call', *The Sydney Morning Herald*, 31 August 2014, www.smh.com.au/federal-politics/political-opinion/australia-still-at-americas-beck-and-call-20140831-10albb.html.
5. Benjamin Schreer, 'Walking among Giants: Australia and Indonesia between the US and China', *The Strategist*, 24 May 2013, www.aspistrategist.org.au/walking-among-giants-australia-and-indonesia-between-the-us-and-china/.
6. See Seng Tan, *Facilitating China–US Relations in the Age of Rebalancing. ASEAN's 'Middle Power' Diplomacy*, EAI MPDI Working Paper No. 1 (Seoul: East Asia Institute, October 2013).
7. T. J. Pempel, 'Soft Balancing, Hedging, and Institutional Darwinism: The Economic–Security Nexus and East Asian Regionalism', *Journal of East Asian Studies*, Vol. 10, No. 2 (2010), pp. 209–38.
8. Paul Keating, 'Asia in the New Order: Australia's Diminishing Sphere of Influence', The Keith Murdoch Oration, State Library of Victoria, 14 November 2012, p. 5.
9. Ross Babbage, 'Learning to Walk amongst Giants: The New Defence White Paper', *Security Challenges*, Vol. 4, No. 1 (2008), pp. 13–20.
10. Alexander Downer (former Australian foreign minister), 'Should Australia Think Big or Small in Foreign Policy?', Address to the Centre for Independent Studies: The Policymakers Forum, 10 July 2006, Sydney, www.foreignminister.gov.au/speeches/2006/060710_bigorsmall.html.
11. Gough Whitlam, cited in 'Transcript of Remarks by Senator the Hon Bob Carr, Minister for Foreign Affairs, Launch of the 40th Anniversary of Australia China Diplomatic Relations, Capital M, Beijing, May 15, 2012', www.china.embassy.gov.au/bjng/20120605Carrremarks-eng.html.

12 Allen Gyngell, 'What Happened to Diplomacy?', Address to the Australian Institute of International Affairs, ACT Branch, 7 May 2012, p. 9, www.ona.gov.au/media/39310/aiia-address_7-may-2012.pdf.
13 Paragraph 6.5 in *2013 Defence White Paper* (Canberra, ACT: Department of Defence, Commonwealth of Australia, 2013), p. 55.
14 Paragraph 6.37 in *2013 Defence White Paper*, p. 60.
15 Derek McDougall, *Australian Foreign Relations: Entering the 21st Century* (FrenchsForest: Pearson, 2009), pp. 3–11. Also see, Gareth Evans and Bruce Grant, *Australia's Foreign Relations: In the World of the 1990s*, 2nd edn (Melbourne, VIC: Melbourne University Press, 1995). On abandonment and entrapment in alliance dynamics, see Glenn H. Snyder, *Alliance Politics* (Ithaca, NY: Cornell University Press, 2007).
16 'Executive Summary', *Australia in the Asian Century*, Australian Government White Paper, October 2012, p. 1.
17 'Australia's Economic Engagement with Asia', Address by Senator Gareth Evans, Minister for Foreign Affairs and Trade, to the Australian Institute of Company Directors, 27 March 1992, Sydney, www.gevans.org/speeches/old/1992/270392_fm_auseconomicengage.pdf.
18 Ramesh Thakur, 'Is Australia Serious About Asia?', *Global Brief*, 5 March 2013, pp. 1–6, on p. 6, http://globalbrief.ca/blog/2013/03/05/is-australia-serious-about-asia/print/.
19 Sid Maher, 'China Deal the Cornerstone of Julia Gillard's Asian Century', *The Australian*, 10 April 2013.
20 Cited in Nick Bisley, 'No Hedging in Canberra: The Australia–US Alliance in the "Asian Century"', *Asia-Pacific Bulletin*, No. 157, 3 April (Honolulu, HI: East-West Center, 2012).
21 Keating, 'Asia in the New Order', p. 8.
22 Bisley, 'No Hedging in Canberra', p. 1.
23 'Such an image will not do', Milner cautions, 'especially in the "Asian Century"'. Anthony Milner, 'Think Again About ASEAN', *The Asialink Essays 2012*, Vol. 4, No. 2 (2012), pp. 1–4, on p. 1.
24 See, Mark Baker, 'Mahathir Advises Australia to Stop Giving Advice', *The Age*, 28 November 2002, www.theage.com.au/articles/2002/11/27/1038386202475.html; and David Wright-Neville, 'Fear and Loathing: Australia and Counter-Terrorism', ARI No. 156/2005, 21 December (Madrid: Real Instituto Elcano, 2005).
25 Keating, 'Asia in the New Order', p. 8.
26 White, *The China Choice*; White, 'Power Shift'.
27 Malcolm Fraser with Cain Roberts, *Dangerous Allies* (Melbourne, VIC: Melbourne University Press, 2014).
28 Ross Terrill, CAPS? 'We Shouldn't Be Marching to the Beat of our New "Great and Powerful Friend"', *The Sydney Morning Herald*, 30 March 2013.
29 See, for example, Victor J. Callen, 'Anglo-Australian Attitudes toward Immigrants: A Review of Survey Evidence', *International Migration Review*, Vol. 17, No. 1 (1983), pp. 120–37; Joseph V. D'Cruz and William Steele, *Australia's Ambivalence towards Asia: Politics, Neo/Post-Colonialism, and Fact/Fiction* (Melbourne, VIC: Monash Asia Institute, Monash University, 2003); Carol Johnson, Paul Ahluwalia and Greg McCarthy, 'Australia's Ambivalent Re-imagining of Asia', *Australian Journal of Political Science*, Vol. 45, No. 1 (2010), pp. 59–74; and, James Jupp, 'From "White Australia" to "Part of Asia": Recent Shifts in Australian Immigration Policy towards the Region', *International Migration Review*, Vol. 29, No. 1 (1995), pp. 207–28.
30 Amanda Vanstone, 'Does Labor Really Think It Started Our Engagement with Asia?', *The Sydney Morning Herald*, 12 November 2012, www.theage.com.au/federal-politics/political-opinion/does-labor-really-think-it-started-our-engagement-with-asia-20121111-29689.html.

31 Pumendra Chandra Jain, 'Australia's Attitude toward Asian Values and Regional Community Building', *Politics & Policy*, Vol. 35, No. 1 (2007), pp. 26–41.
32 Jupp, 'From "White Australia" to "Part of Asia"'.
33 In this regard, the Australian predicament is not unlike the general attitudes of Canadians toward Asia, not least according to a recent poll published by the Asia Pacific Foundation of Canada, which showed that while Canadians (or at least British Columbians) value Asia for economic reasons, they do not seem to 'like it much'. Dan Cayo, 'Opinion: B.C. values Asia – We Just Don't Like It Much', *Vancouver Sun*, 30 May 2013.
34 Juliet Pietsch and Hadyn Aarons, 'Australian Engagement with Asia: Towards Closer Political, Economic and Cultural Ties', in Juliet Pietsch and Hadyn Aarons, eds., *Australia: Identity, Fear and Governance in the 21st Century* (Canberra, ACT: ANU E-Press, 2012), pp. 33–46.
35 Becky Gaylord, 'In Optus Deal, Australians Ponder How to Trust Singapore', *The New York Times*, 13 August 2001; Shujie Yao, 'China will Learn Its Lessons from the Chinalco Fiasco', *The Age*, 18 June 2009.
36 'Malaysia summons Singapore envoy over Spying Reports', *Reuters*, November 25, 2013, www.reuters.com/article/2013/11/26/us-malaysia-singapore-spying-idUSBRE9AP03P20131126.
37 Jenny McGregor, 'An "Asia Capable" Australia for the Coming Century', *The Melbourne Review*, March 2013, www.melbournereview.com.au/features/article/an-asia-capable-australia-for-the-coming-century-2012.
38 Ying Zhu, 'Australia's Engagement in Asia', Paper for the CPA International Forum for Academics, Melbourne, 28 June 2012, p. 2.
39 As Dennis Rumley has argued, Australia's regional relations in the late-Cold War and post-Cold War periods expanded outwards towards four fronts: a 'cooperative security front' to its north; an 'aid front' to its east; an 'environmental security front' to its south; and, a 'trade front' to its west. Dennis Rumley, *The Geopolitics of Australia's Regional Relations* (New York: Springer, 1999), p. 1.
40 This and the next sections draw partly from See Seng Tan, 'Hobnobbing with Giants: Australia's Approach to Asian Regionalism', in Sally Percival Wood and Baogang He, eds., *The Australia–ASEAN Dialogue: Tracing 40 Years of Partnership* (New York: Palgrave Macmillan, 2014); pp. 33–48.
41 Andrew Elek, 'APEC paves the way for greater regional connectivity', *East Asia Forum*, 21 October 2013, www.eastasiaforum.org/2013/10/21/apec-paves-the-way-for-greater-regional-connectivity/.
42 See Peter Drysdale, *Open Regionalism: A Key to East Asia's Economic Future*, Pacific Economic Papers, No. 197 (Canberra, ACT: Australia–Japan Research Centre, Australian National University, 1991); and, Ross Garnaut, *Open Regionalism and Trade Liberalization: An Asia-Pacific Contribution to the World Trade System* (Singapore: Institute of Southeast Asian Studies, 1996).
43 Arthur Dunkel, 'Don't Make "the Best Become Enemy of the Good"', Address delivered at the Pacific Economic Cooperation Council (PECC) IX, 25 September 1992, www.sunsonline.org/trade/process/during/uruguay/dunkel/09250092.htm.
44 Mark Beeson, *Institutions of the Asia-Pacific: ASEAN, APEC and Beyond* (Abingdon: Routledge, 2009); John Ravenhill, *APEC and the Construction of Pacific Rim Regionalism* (Cambridge: Cambridge University Press, 2002).
45 Takashi Terada, *The Genesis of APEC: Australia–Japan Political Initiatives*, Pacific Economic Papers, No. 298 (Canberra, ACT: Australia–Japan Research Centre, Australian National University, 1999).
46 Tim Colebatch, 'Rudd's Grand Vision for Asia-Pacific', *The Age*, 5 June 2008, www.theage.com.au/national/rudds-grand-vision-for-asiapacific-20080604-2lw1.html.
47 I refer specifically to a 'Track 1.5' regional meeting held in Sydney in December 2009. Convened by respected Australian envoy, Richard Woolcott, the meeting was

in a sense a promotional exercise that advanced Rudd's 'Asia Pacific Community' vision to a regional audience.
48 This was acknowledged by Singapore's veteran diplomat Tommy Koh in his article, 'Rudd's Reckless Regional Rush', *The Australian*, 18 December 2009, www.theaustralian.com.au/opinion/rudds-reckless-regional-rush/story-e6frg6zo-1225811530050.
49 Keating, 'Asia in the New Order'.
50 Bob Hawke, former Australian prime minister, in Chuck Thompson, 'Interview: Bob Hawke and Gareth Evans, APEC architects', *CNN Global NewsView*, 12 November 2009, travel.cnn.com/singapore/none/interview-bob-hawke-and-gareth-evans-apec-architects-295654.
51 David Capie and Paul Evans, *The Asia-Pacific Security Lexicon*, 2nd edn (Singapore: Institute of Southeast Asian Studies, 2007), p. 61. Also see Amitav Acharya, *Whose Ideas Matter? Agency and Power in Asian Regionalism* (Ithaca, NY: Cornell University Press, 2009), p. 114.
52 Cited in Takeshi Yuzawa, *Japan's Security Policy and the ASEAN Regional Forum: The Search for Multilateral Security in the Asia-Pacific* (Abingdon: Routledge, 2007), p. 20.
53 Cited in James L. Lacy, *Stonework or Sandcastle? Asia's Regional Security Forum*, IDA Paper No. P-3110, July 1995 (Alexandria, VA: Institute of Defense Analyses, 1995), p. 9.
54 On Smith, see chapter 6, 'The Reluctant Chief: Ric Smith, Department of Defence', in Paul Malone (ed.), *Australian Department Heads under Howard: Career Paths and Practice* (Canberra, ACT: Australian National University E-Press, 2006), http://press.anu.edu.au/anzsog/dept_heads/mobile_devices/ch06.html.
55 For a recent book-length treatment of the CSCAP and PECC, see See Seng Tan, *The Making of the Asia Pacific: Knowledge Brokers and the Politics of Representation* (Amsterdam: Amsterdam University Press, 2013).
56 Michael Leifer, *The ASEAN Regional Forum: Extending ASEAN's Model of Regional Security*, Adelphi Papers No. 302 (Oxford: Oxford University Press for the International Institute for Strategic Studies, 1996). Also see Amitav Acharya, 'Ideas, Identity, and Institution-Building: From the "ASEAN Way" to the "Asia-Pacific Way"?', *The Pacific Review*, Vol. 10, No. 3 (1997), pp. 319–46.
57 Alice D. Ba, 'Who's Socializing Whom? Complex Engagement in China–ASEAN Relations', *The Pacific Review*, Vol. 19, No. 2 (2006), pp. 157–79; Alastair Iain Johnston, 'The Myth of the ASEAN Way? Explaining the Evolution of the ASEAN Regional Forum', in Helga Haftendorn, Robert O. Keohane, and Celeste A. Wallander, eds., *Imperfect Unions: Security Institutions over Time and Space* (New York: Oxford University Press, 1999), pp. 287–324; Ron Huisken, 'Civilizing the Anarchical Society: Multilateral Security Processes in the Asia-Pacific', *Contemporary Southeast Asia*, Vol. 24, No. 2 (2002), pp. 187–202.
58 Ralf Emmers and See Seng Tan, 'The ASEAN Regional Forum and Preventive Diplomacy: Built to Fail?', *Asian Security*, Vol. 17, No. 1 (2011), pp. 44–60.
59 For example, see Mark Beeson, *Competing Capitalisms: Australia, Japan and Economic Competition in the Asia Pacific* (London: Macmillan, 1999); Mark Beeson and Iyanatul Islam, 'Neoliberalism and East Asia: Resisting the Washington Consensus', *The Journal of Development Studies*, Vol. 41, No. 2 (2005), pp. 197–219; and, Garry Rodan and Kevin Hewison, eds., *Neoliberalism and Conflict in Asia after 9/11* (London and New York: Routledge, 2006).
60 Geoffrey Garrett, 'Rudd's Chinese Whispers Will Have Been Heard Loud and Clear', *The Sydney Morning Herald*, 7 December 2010, www.smh.com.au/federal-politics/political-opinion/rudds-chinese-whispers-will-have-been-heard-loud-and-clear-20101206-18mpa.html.
61 Cited in Joel Atkinson, *Australia and Taiwan: Bilateral Relations, China, the United States, and the South Pacific* (Leiden: Brill, 2010), p. 122.
62 Paragraph 4.27 in *Defending Australia in the Asia Pacific Century: Force 2030*, Defence White Paper 2009 (Canberra, ACT: Commonwealth of Australia, 2009), p. 34.

60  *Australia*

63 Michael Sainsbury and Cameron Stewart, 'China a "Peaceful Force" in Beijing's Response to Defence Paper', *The Australian*, 6 May 2009, www.theaustralian.com.au/news/nation/china-a-peaceful-force/story-e6frg6nf-1225710310338?nk=24297064718cd878e720eac78a4d6b65.
64 Paragraph 1.22 in *2013 Defence White Paper*, p. 3.
65 Geoffrey Till, 'Outgoing Australia?', *Centre of Gravity* Series Paper, No. 14, February 2014 (Canberra, ACT: Strategic Defence Studies Centre, Australian National University, 2014) p. 4.
66 Richard Woolcott, 'Towards an Asia Pacific Community', *Asialink Essays*, No. 9 (2009), p. 3.
67 Kevin Rudd, 'The Singapore Lecture: Building on ASEAN's Success – Towards an Asia Pacific Century', 12 August 2008, Singapore, www.pm.gov.au/media/Speech/2008/speech_0419.cfm.
68 Stephen Smith, 'Australia, ASEAN and the Asia Pacific', 18 July 2008, Lowy Institute, Sydney, www.foreignminister.gov.au/speeches/2008/080718_lowy.html.
69 For example, see Joseph Camilleri, 'East Asia's Emerging Regionalism: Tensions and Potential in Design and Architecture', *Global Change, Peace and Security*, Vol. 17, No. 3 (2005), pp. 253–61; and, Allan Gyngell, 'Design Faults: The Asia Pacific's Regional Architecture', *Lowy Institute Policy Brief*, 18 July (Sydney, NSW: Lowy Institute for International Policy, 2007). Gyngell has also contributed to an unpublished report by Hadi Soesastro, Allan Gyngell, Charles E. Morrison, and Jusuf Wanandi, 'Report of Regional Task Force on Regional Institutional Architecture', report for the Pacific Economic Cooperation Council (PECC) Standing Committee. The online outlet, *East Asia Forum*, has also been a significant platform for debate and discussion by Australians (and non-Australians as well) on the state of and prospective directions for regionalism and regional architecture in Asia. See, for example, Alison Broinowski, 'Why Do We Want an Asia Pacific Community?', *East Asia Forum*, 2 May 2009, www.eastasiaforum.org/2009/05/02/why-do-we-want-an-asia-pacific-community/; Peter Drysdale, 'Rudd in Singapore on the Asia Pacific Community Idea', *East Asia Forum*, 31 May 2009, www.eastasiaforum.org/2009/05/31/rudd-in-singapore-on-the-asia-pacific-community-idea/; Joel Rathus, 'Squaring the Japanese and Australia Proposals for an East Asian and Asia Pacific Community: Is America In or Out?', *East Asia Forum*, 4 November 2009, www.eastasiaforum.org/2009/11/04/scuaring-the-japanese-and-australia-proposals-for-an-east-asian-and-asia-pacific-community-is-america-in-or-out/; Carlyle Thayer, 'Kevin Rudd's Multi-layered Asia Pacific Community Initiative', *East Asia Forum*, 22 June 2009, www.eastasiaforum.org/2009/06/22/kevin-rudds-multi-layered-asia-pacific-community-initiative/.
70 William T. Tow and Brendan Taylor, 'What is Asian Security Architecture?', *Review of International Studies*, Vol. 36, No. 1 (2010), pp. 95–116.
71 Rudd, 'The Singapore Lecture'.
72 Koh, 'Rudd's Reckless Regional Rush', emphasis added.
73 For a slightly different take on the same episode, see David Hundt, 'Middle Powers and the Building of Regional Order: Australia and South Korea Compared', in Jehoon Park, T. J. Pempel, Geng Xiao, eds., *Asian Responses to the Global Financial Crisis: The Impact of Regionalism and the Role of the G20* (Cheltenham: Edward Elgar, 2012), pp. 193–211, on pp. 203–6.
74 Daniel Flitton, 'My Dream of Asia is Here Now, Says Rudd', *The Sydney Morning Herald*, 24 July 2011; Thom Woodroofe, 'Is the East Asia Summit Rudd's Gift to the World?', *Australian Policy Outline*, 12 January 2012, http://apo.org.au/commentary/east-asia-summit-rudd%E2%80%99s-gift-world.
75 Amitav Acharya, 'Asia's Competing Communities and Why Asian Regionalism Matters', amitavacharya.com, pp. 3–4, www.amitavacharya.com/sites/default/files/Competing%20Communities.pdf.

76 Acharya, 'Asia's Competing Communities and Why Asian Regionalism Matters'.
77 Tow and Taylor, 'What is Asian Security Architecture?'.
78 Baogang He, 'The Awkwardness of Australian Engagement with Asia: The Dilemmas of Australian Idea of Regionalism', *Japanese Journal of Political Science*, Vol. 12, No. 2 (2011), pp. 267–85, on p. 267.
79 He, 'The Awkwardness of Australian Engagement with Asia', p. 267.
80 John Blaxland, 'The Australian Mindset in Asia', *Lowy Interpreter*, 30 October 2012, www.lowyinterpreter.org/?d=D - Reactions to 'Australia in the Asian Century' White Paper.
81 David Martin Jones and Michael L. R. Smith, 'Making Process, Not Progress: ASEAN and the Evolving East Asian Regional Order', *International Security*, Vol. 32, No. 1 (2007), pp. 148–84.
82 Gareth Evans, in Thompson, 'Interview: Bob Hawke and Gareth Evans, APEC Architects', p. 2.
83 Hugh White, *The China Choice: Why America Should Share Power* (Melbourne, VIC: Black Inc., 2012); Hugh White, 'Power Shift: Rethinking Australia's Place in the Asian Century', *Australian Journal of International Affairs*, Vol. 65, No. 1 (2011), pp. 81–93.
84 See Seng Tan, 'Spectres of Leifer: Insights on Regional Order and Security for Southeast Asia Today', *Contemporary Southeast Asia*, Vol. 34, No. 3 (2012), pp. 309–337, on p. 316.
85 Geoff Dyer and Daniel Dombey, 'Shadow Cast over Hopes for US–China 'G2'', *Financial Times*, 14 January 2010.
86 Wang Qi, 'China and US not G2, but C2', *Sina English*, 4 May 2012, http://english.sina.com/china/2012/0503/464519.html.
87 He Baogang, 'A Concert of Powers and Hybrid Regionalism in Asia', *Australian Journal of Political Science*, Vol. 47, No. 4 (2012), pp. 677–90.
88 Cited in Koh, 'Rudd's Reckless Regional Rush'.
89 Woodroofe, 'Is the East Asia Summit Rudd's Gift to the World?'.
90 Liam Cochrane, 'Kevin Rudd Claims Asia-Pacific Community Success', *Radio Australia*, 17 April 2012, www.radioaustralia.net.au/international/radio/program/asia-pacific/kevin-rudd-claims-asiapacific-community-success/914668.
91 The issue is examined in Tan, 'Spectres of Leifer', pp. 316–17.
92 See, Peter Hartcher, 'Rudd Asia Plan Stirs Tensions with US, China', *Sydney Morning Herald*, 28 June 2008, www.smh.com.au/news/national/rudd-asia-plan-stirs-tensions-with-us-china/2008/06/27/1214472770870.html; Peter Symonds, 'WikiLeaks Cables Expose US Hostility to Rudd's Asia Pacific Community Plan', *World Socialist Web Site*, 31 December 2010, www.wsws.org/en/articles/2010/12/rudd-d31.html.
93 Garrett, 'Rudd's Chinese Whispers Will Have Been Heard Loud and Clear'.
94 Mohan Malik, *China and the East Asia Summit: More Discord than Accord*, APCSS Working Paper (Honolulu, HI: Asia-Pacific Center for Security Studies, 2006), p. 4.
95 Ralf Emmers, Joseph Chinyong Liow and See Seng Tan, *The East Asia Summit and the Regional Security Architecture*, Maryland Series in Contemporary Asian Studies No. 3-2010 (202) (College Park, MD: University of Maryland, 2011), pp. 27–29.
96 Flitton, 'My Dream of Asia is Here Now, Says Rudd'.
97 Emmers, Liow and Tan, *The East Asia Summit and the Regional Security Architecture*, pp. 30–1.
98 Gareth Evans, 'No Power? No Influence? Australia's Middle Power Diplomacy in the Asian Century', 2012 Charteris Lecture by Professor the Hon Gareth Evans AO QC, to the Australian Institute of International Affairs (AIIA), New South Wales Branch, Sydney, 6 June 2012, www.gevans.org/speeches/speech472.html.
99 For example, see, Milner, 'Think Again about ASEAN'.

100 Michele Ford, 'White Paper: Searching for Southeast Asia', *Lowy Interpreter*, 1 November 2012, www.lowyinterpreter.org/?d=D – Reactions to 'Australia in the Asian Century' White Paper.
101 Alison Broinowski, *About Face: Asian Accounts of Australia* (Melbourne, VIC: Scribe, 2003)
102 See Seng Tan, '"Talking Their Walk"? The Evolution of Defence Regionalism in Southeast Asia', *Asian Security*, Vol. 8, No. 3 (2012), pp. 232–50
103 Paul Dibb, *Review of Australia's Defence Capabilities: Report to the Minister for Defence by Mr. Paul Dibb* (Canberra, ACT: Australian Government Publishing Service, 1986), p. 4.
104 Allan Gyngell, 'Australia-Indonesia', in Brendan Taylor, ed., *Australia as an Asia Pacific Regional Power: Friendship in Flux* (Abingdon: Routledge, 2007), pp. 97–115, on p. 114.
105 Rod Lyon, 'The Southeast Asian Emphasis in DWP2013', *The Strategist*, 21 June 2013, www.aspistrategist.org.au/the-southeast-asian-emphasis-in-dwp2013/.
106 Tim Huxley, 'Australian Defence Engagement with Southeast Asia', *Centre of Gravity* Series Paper, No. 2, November 2012 (Canberra, ACT: Strategic Defence Studies Centre, Australian National University, 2012)
107 Mark Thomson, 'The Defence White Paper: Between the Lines', *The Strategist*, 14 May 2013, www.aspistrategist.org.au/the-defence-white-paper-between-the-lines/.
108 Atlantic Council, 'Obama Warns NATO Allies to Share Defence Burden: "We Can't Do It Alone"', *Atlantic Council*, 3 June 2014, www.atlanticcouncil.org/blogs/natosource/obama-warns-nato-allies-to-share-defense-burden-we-can-t-do-it-alone; Yuka Hayashi, 'Abe's Military Push May Please U.S. but Rattle Neighbours', *The Wall Street Journal*, 22 April 2014.
109 Sam Bateman, Anthony Bergin and Hayley Channer, *Terms of Engagement: Australia's Regional Defence Policy*, Strategy, July 2013 (Barton, ACT: Australian Strategic Policy Institute, 2013), p. 5.
110 Albeit reluctantly, at least according to *The Economist*; see, 'The Reluctant Deputy Sheriff' (Special Report: Australia), *The Economist*, 5 May 2005. Also see, Alan Dupont, 'Inflection Point: The Australian Defence Force after Afghanistan', *Policy Brief*, March (Sydney, NSW: Lowy Institute for International Policy, 2012).

# 5 Japan

The history of Japan's post-war participation in Asia-Pacific security can be described as a mix of entrenched bilateralism (the Japan–US security alliance) and incipient multilateralism (Japan's active membership in and contributions to Asia's regional institutions).[1] Given the closeness of the Japan–US relationship, much of Japan's involvement in Asian multilateralism has also been defined partly by the terms of its partnership with the United States. In that regard, Japan's efforts to construct multilateral structures and conventions useful for its own interests have in a key sense also been shaped by the United States' disposition towards multilateralism in general and Asian multilateralism in particular. Whatever Japan's contributions, past or potential, to multilateral institution-building in post-Cold War Asia have or could have been, America's approval or sanction has often been viewed as essential. This is best seen in Washington's active participation in Asia-Pacific multilateral institutions which Tokyo had a hand in fostering such as the APEC and the ARF. At the same time, Japanese regional initiatives that failed to take off underscore the constraining effect of Japan's partnership with the United States on the former's foreign policy. While this subaltern status might have suited the 'pragmatists' of the mould of Shigeru Yoshida – some would have chafed at it but accepted it as the price for living under the extended military deterrence furnished by the Americans – 'revisionists' since former premier Junichiro Koizumi,[2] including so-called 'normal nationalists' who believe alliance with the United States is good for Japan and ought to be continued and even strengthened,[3] have not only urged a revision of the terms of the alliance to make Japan an equal rather than junior partner to the United States, but even sought at times to limit US influence and involvement in Asian multilateralism.

It is fair to say that the since the *fin de siècle*, Japan, in an incremental though not always smooth fashion, has – with the support of the Americans – undertaken steps towards becoming a normal military power. While it is commonplace these days to attribute Japan's perceived assertiveness to the nationalist thrust of Prime Minister Shinzo Abe – recently re-elected in December 2014 to a new term – the imperative for normalization has in fact been driven by a long and deep concern in Tokyo since the 1990s over the rise of China and its strategic ramifications for Japan, although it is fair to say that Koizumi and his protégés gave military normalization a more determined push than others before them might have done

– a direction expected to continue under Japan's new defence minister, Gen Nakatani.[4] By the same token, this trend also raises important questions regarding Japan's view of and approach to Asian multilateralism. That said, what does not seem likely is any fundamental change in Japan's long-standing identity as a committed advocate and activist for multilateralism. But what could change is a greater propensity of the Japanese to use Asia's multilateral institutions as platforms with which to balance against China rather than merely to engage it. As Abe's remarks at the Shangri-La Dialogue (SLD) 2014 – the international defence forum held annually in Singapore – imply, the issue is less likely to be Japan's prioritizing of its alliance with the United States over Asian multilateralism but rather the likelihood that it will selectively choose among the multilateral structures at hand as to which would prove the most useful to its immediate political and strategic aims, while downplaying other structures. Given Tokyo's security ties – and, by the look of things, growing integration – with Washington, it is highly probable, as evidenced by Prime Minister Abe's focus on the EAS, that a convergence in outlook and effort regarding Asian multilateralism would emerge and has emerged between the two allies not only as to which regional arrangements are most appropriate to realizing their goals, specifically their common cause to engage with but more precisely to balance against China, but also how those arrangements ought to be refashioned in order to achieve that. Such a convergence is likely to lead Japan, in tandem with the United States, to focus its attention, energy and resources on a preferred arrangement at the expense of other arrangements. While Japan's putative turn to '*à la carte* multilateralism'[5] is entirely comprehensible – indeed, most if not all countries engage selectively with multilateralism no matter their avowed support for it – there are potential risks involved, not least those associated with an uncritical adherence to a particular multilateral path favoured and defined by the Americans.[6]

Be that as it may, adopting a selective approach to Asian multilateralism could come at the possible expense of Japan's relations with regional countries which it has carefully nurtured over the years as well as its vision of alternative security that it has long advanced and for which it has come to be admired.[7] At stake here is Japan's very regional leadership, which it will do well to preserve and enhance through maintaining its hitherto broad and normative commitment to multilateralism. To be sure, given the prevalence of strategic hedging in the region, engagement and balancing actions by regional countries clearly coexist within the region's multilateral institutions. And much like any other state actor, Japan has long engaged in all those practices in multilateral settings. While Tokyo's growing transition from quiet diplomacy to a more assertive diplomacy does not fit snugly with engagement, balancing and even containment respectively – that is, from engagers who prefer quiet diplomacy to balancers and/or containers who adopt more assertive approaches – there is reason to assume, with nationalist-minded leaders at the helm at a time of rising tensions with China, that Japan's foreign policy style inevitably changes particularly when its key decision-makers perceive, rightly or otherwise, that Japan's options for engagement with China have been exhausted. It certainly does not mean Japan will from henceforth abandon quiet diplomacy, not least when dealing with other East Asian countries, but it will use both quiet and assertive approaches as Tokyo sees fit. In such conditions, what implications might a 'normal' Japan hold for its future commitment to and involvement in Asian multilateralism?[8]

## Japan and multilateralism in Asia

At a public address given in Washington in February 2013, Prime Minister Abe spoke assuredly of Japan's revival as a putative great power and of his personal commitment to achieving that goal.[9] Signs of economic recovery have since been matched by a diplomatic assertiveness towards China over their East China Sea dispute, a plan to increase defence spending, and the revocation of a ban that since 1945 has disallowed Japanese armed forces from engaging in combat abroad. Fair or otherwise, these developments have led some to inquire whether Abe is a 'dangerous militarist' given to unwarranted adventurism or a 'modernizing reformer' committed to transforming Japan's economic fortunes.[10] Such a question also matters where Japan's approach to Asian multilateralism is concerned.

Far from being a passive regional actor as imagined by some, post-war Japan has in fact been a proactive player whose motives and actions have helped shaped Asia's regional architecture in ways deeper and more intimate than much of the existing scholarship on Asian multilateralism has hitherto acknowledged. Arguably, Japan's contributions to multilateralism in Asia have differed according to the leaders who – or, if you will, the leader-types that – direct Japanese foreign policy. The aims and approaches of Japan's key decision-makers for and to Asian multilateralism have differed from leader to national leader.[11] For example, Japanese leaders wanting to engage their regional neighbours have sought to construct regional multilateral institutions through which they can build confidence and cooperate with their counterparts and, should security dilemmas exist between their countries, to minimize and/or mitigate the negative consequences of their mutual strategic competition. On the other hand, those seeking to balance China have treated Asia's multilateral institutions as arenas for building coalitions to counter – or, in extreme instances, contain – the rising power and influence of China. Second, the way in which leaders (or leader-types) engage in foreign policy also appears to be different. Backed by the Yoshida Doctrine, Japan has been able to focus principally on its economic development and on the economic integration of the East Asian region, while leaving its military security in the hands of its ally, the United States.

During this period of what might be referred to as the 'Japan as peace state' phase, Japan relied largely on a foreign policy strategy of quiet diplomacy, soft power and implicit regional leadership.[12] No less proactive than direct and explicit styles of diplomatic engagement, this form of diplomacy has also been referred to by various scholars as 'directional leadership', leadership by 'stealth' and 'leadership from behind'.[13] Non-military in orientation, directional leadership is an implicit political strategy saddled with security implications, which Japan has been able to pursue relatively unopposed because of its traditional self-image as a 'peace state'.[14] And though post-war Japanese society has been depicted as anti-militaristic – Article 9 of Japan's post-war constitution is regularly invoked by observers as the embodiment of that national sentiment – Japan has presumably been able to maintain such a stance because of its alliance with the United States.[15] However, with the growing influence of nationalistic leaders who see nothing inherently wrong with Japan aspiring to be a normal military power and pursuing a more assertive diplomacy[16] – the roots of this thinking arguably go back to the 'revisionism' inspired by Koizumi[17] – the era of strict adherence to an implicit approach to regional leadership has probably come to an end.

Crucially for Abe, or so it seems, the end to implicit leadership is not equated with a rejection of multilateralism, not least that led by and centred upon ASEAN. As Abe avowed at the SLD 2014: 'Taking our alliance with the United States as the foundation and respecting our partnership with ASEAN, Japan will spare no effort to make regional stability, peace, and prosperity into something rock solid'.[18] To those who would question Abe's sincerity or the wisdom of his strategy, a noted Japanese analyst has offered this assurance: 'Although Japan's identity is complex, the diplomatic strategy of a "normal" middle power is essentially internationalist; its mission is to contribute to the creation of a liberal international order'.[19] Presumably, Japan's continued strong support for Asian multilateralism would be a manifestation of 'its mission'. To that end, Abe's affirmation of the EAS – whose enhancement and 'multi-layered' coordination with the ARF and the ADMM-Plus he has also urged – could go some way to allay concerns which member states of ASEAN might have regarding his disposition toward Asian multilateralism. Significantly, Abe's viewpoint is shared by the United States, not least by an Obama administration known for its advocacy of multilateralism.[20] However, much as Japan's rise as an economic power and its at times ambivalent relationship with its key ally have allowed it to forge its own multilateral path,[21] its recent policy convergence with the United States regarding their shared expectations for Asian multilateralism as tools to manage assertively and counterbalance China could potentially be counterproductive to Japan's liberal internationalist mission, particularly if it ends up destabilizing Asia. But while an enhanced Japan–US partnership is presumably healthy in order for Asian multilateralism to be effective, it could only be so if China goes along with what Japan and the United States expect of it or is given a stake in defining the rules of the road.

### Building Asian multilateralism 'from behind'

Japan's track record in multilateralism in Asia is a strong indictment of any crass caricature of Japan as a passive regional actor and serial 'buck-passer'.[22] It has rendered significant contributions to Asian multilateralism through the sort of implicit leadership style described earlier. There is no question about the importance of the Fukuda Doctrine – wherein Prime Minister Takeo Fukuda famously pledged that Japan will never become a military power – to Japan's policy toward the Southeast Asian region since that doctrine's enunciation in

1977. While it is debatable whether the doctrine played any role in guiding Japan's approach to Asian multilateralism – as Yukio Satoh recently recounted, the Fukuda Doctrine is rarely mentioned these days over three decades since its pronouncement[23] – it is perhaps noteworthy that member states of ASEAN positively remember the doctrine as a watershed that transformed Japan–ASEAN relations.[24] On the other hand, the successful reception by Southeast Asian audiences of the Fukuda Doctrine might not have been possible without the existence of the Yoshida Doctrine (never formally declared[25]), which prioritized economic development while leaving Japan's military defence to the United States. According to the argument of this chapter, if both the Yoshida and Fukuda doctrines facilitated Japan's directional leadership, they have been able to do so because of the military guarantee provided to Japan concerning its national security by the United States, and the strategic assurance provided more broadly to East Asia concerning its regional security by the United States, not least due to the curbing effect its alliance with Japan has (or is supposed to have) on unwelcome expansionist designs the latter may harbour.

Aimed at engaging China in the immediate post-Cold War environment, Japan's most important early contributions to Asian multilateralism have resulted arguably because of Tokyo's directional leadership and Washington's willing albeit selective involvement in multilateralism.[26] As we have seen in chapter 4, the formation of APEC in the late 1980s is a well-traced story, particularly from the Australian angle given the enormously important roles played by Prime Minister Bob Hawke and the Department of Foreign Affairs and Trade (DFAT) of Australia. Indeed, Japanese–Australian collaboration has been critical to the formation of not only APEC but also its three non-official regional predecessors, the Pacific Basin Economic Council (PBEC), the Pacific Trade and Development forum (PAFTAD) and the Pacific Economic Cooperation Council (PECC).[27] However, as Takashi Terada has pointed out, the lesser-known contributions by Japan's Ministry of International Trade and Industry (MITI) – and, for that matter, the regional vision of former Japanese foreign minister and prime minister, Takeo Miki[28] – were no less significant. According to Terada:

> [APEC] was the common goal of Australian Prime Minister Bob Hawke, his Office, the Department of Foreign Affairs and Trade (DFAT) and the Japanese Ministry of International Trade and Industry (MITI) in the late 1980s. Bob Hawke publicly announced the idea in Seoul in January 1989, but his initiative was backed by a solid foundation of cooperation with Japan. In mid-1988, MITI has floated a proposal for regional meetings of economic ministers and DFAT's strong interest in the idea urged coordination between the two countries. In March 1989 a MITI delegation visited the region to sound out reactions to its proposal and the Hawke initiative, and this laid the groundwork for the Hawke proposal's relatively easy acceptance on the Australian delegation's later visit in April and May. Both countries continued to coordinate their approaches toward the organization of the first Asia-Pacific Economic Cooperation (APEC) meeting in Canberra in November 1989.[29]

If both countries played equally significant parts in APEC's formation, why is it that most accounts seem to credit Australia more so than Japan, if at all? Terada explains: 'MITI's proposal was eventually subsumed into the Hawke initiative, but MITI believed the successful establishment of APEC amounted to the success of its own proposal'.[30] The willingness to fold its ideas within another country's initiative, and to do so with as little fanfare and self-promotion as possible, seems to be at the core of Japan's implicit leadership style. The focus here is on ensuring the success of the mission rather than getting the credit for it.

Fair or otherwise, one of the criticisms for APEC's inability to deepen trade liberalization and economic integration has been the apparent distraction of security-related concerns that have been added to the trade forum's institutional agenda. US President George W. Bush's use of the Shanghai summit in 2001, which took place weeks following the 9/11 attacks, to draw attention to the scourge of international terrorism was not the first time security matters had been raised in APEC. In this regard, APEC has also proved to be an equally useful multilateral platform for Japan through which to deliberate security issues.[31] Indeed, given its experience with APEC as a useful forum for discussing issues such as the turmoil in East Timor at the end of the 1990s and North Korea's missile programme – the latter issue, as Christopher W. Hughes has noted, was added to the APEC Statement at the Auckland summit in 1999[32] – APEC has served as a framework through which US commitment to the region could be sustained and strengthened. By the same token, APEC and other regional institutions have also proved useful to Japan as platforms to engage China; for instance, although Japan rejected Malaysia's idea for an East Asian Economic Caucus (EAEC) because realization of the Malaysian proposal would have kept the United States out of East Asia, it subsequently helped form the APT, however.[33] Certainly, the idea of APEC as an instrument of post-Cold War multilateral diplomacy to ensure the regular presence and responsible participation of the relevant big powers – particularly China and the United States – in regional security resonated with Australia, Japan's co-sponsor of APEC. It would also have resonated well with ASEAN leaders, for whom the regional institutional architecture of Asia that they would help to define downstream would be about the furnishing of 'meeting places'[34] wherein the great powers and regional countries can interact according to ASEAN's terms.[35] Indeed, by the time the Asian financial crisis struck in 1997–8, the APEC had by then, fairly or otherwise, come to be seen by regional countries stung by the painful economic restructuring imposed on them by international financial institutions and frustrated by US opposition to alternative proposals from the region (specifically Japan's) as 'a tool for US regional domination'.[36] A contemporary parallel to APEC as a multilateral instrument appropriated – 'hijacked', some might say – by the United States for its own purposes might be the TPP (Trans-Pacific Partnership), a trade pact originally started by Brunei, Chile, New Zealand and Singapore as the Trans-Pacific Strategic Economic Partnership in 2005, but now very much viewed with suspicion, fairly or otherwise, by countries such as China as part of the US pivot/rebalancing strategy to contain China.

If APEC's formation hints at a Japanese contribution to Asian multilateralism that would attract America's 'buy-in', then nowhere is this logic more apparent than in the run-up to the formation of the ARF in 1994. The ARF, fairly or otherwise, has been credited with helping to integrate and socialize a China initially suspicious of multilateralism as a tool of containment, to becoming a sophisticated user of multilateral diplomacy for its own ends.[37] Yet the ARF might not even have been formed if not for a Japanese intervention. At the July 1991 ASEAN Post-Ministerial Conference (PMC), Japan's Foreign Minister Taro Nakayama proposed that the PMC process should in the future become a political forum for political dialogue aimed at discussing mutual security concerns facing Asia-Pacific countries. As Nakayama put it then:

> If there is any anything to add to the mechanisms and frameworks for cooperation in the three fields of economic cooperation, diplomacy and security, the first would be a forum for political dialogue where friendly countries in this region could engage in frank exchanges of opinion on matters of mutual interest ... I believe it would be meaningful and timely to use the ASEAN Post Ministerial Conference as a process of political discussions designed to improve the sense of security among us. In order for these discussions to be effective, it might be advisable to organize a senior officials' meeting [SOM], which would then report its deliberations to the ASEAN Post Ministerial Conference for future discussion.[38]

While the ASEAN countries reacted coolly to Nakayama's proposal, the United States reacted positively to it and officially accepted the principle of multilateral dialogue, thereby paving the way for the July 1993 agreement to establish the ARF. But as the old saying goes, success has many fathers and others have sought to lay claim to having spawned or at least midwifed the ARF. Since then, Japan has actively participated in the ARF. Ministry of Foreign Affairs (MOFA) and Japan Defense Agency (JDA) officials have regularly participated in senior officials' meetings, defence officials' dialogues, and inter-sessional meetings on things ranging from confidence building and preventive diplomacy to peacekeeping. 'Japan has thought highly of ARF activities, and has proactively participated in them', as Japan's then minister for foreign affairs, Masahiko Koumura, noted in 1999. 'Japan will continue to maintain its proactive stance toward ARF activities in order to ensure that the Asian economic crisis, which began in the middle of 1997, will not slow down the efforts to promote such confidence building'.[39]

The Japanese contribution stands out in contrast to what the Australians sought to achieve with Prime Minister Kevin Rudd's proposal in June 2008 for an 'Asia-Pacific Community'. Ironically, the Rudd vision for an overhaul of the ASEAN-led regional security architecture was rendered out of concern that the ARF had become moribund and irrelevant to the region's needs and hence a new security institution – 'a new piece of architecture', as Rudd's foreign minister, Stephen Smith, put it[40] – was deemed necessary. Rudd's proposal – or at least succeeding iterations of it that argued for a concert of powers for co-managing regional order and architecture, presumably at ASEAN's expense[41] – proved much more controversial, even divisive, than Nakayama's 1991 proposal. While both similarly elicited cool reactions from ASEAN, the crucial distinction seems to have been the nature of the American response. As we have seen, the ASEAN-PMC evolved into the ARF in no small part due to strong US support for Nakayama's proposal, which created a *fait accompli* of sorts for ASEAN. On the other hand, Rudd's idea for a revamped regional architecture failed to materialize not only because the ASEAN states rejected the proposal – strenuously, in Singapore's case[42] – but because both China and the United States also rejected it. In a not dissimilar fashion, the region's hand was, in a sense, forced when US President Barack Obama committed the United States to membership in the EAS, leading advocates of Rudd's vision, fairly or otherwise, to lay claim to the enlarged EAS – crucially, with the Americans on board – as the realization of that vision's argument for a 'leaders-level coordinating body'.[43]

Perhaps there is no better example of the acute influence of the United States in constraining Japan's ability to contribute to Asian multilateralism than the latter's attempt to fashion a regional financial mechanism to alleviate the dire consequences of economic crises like the financial crisis that rocked East Asia in 1997. The Ryutaro Hashimoto government's proposal for an Asian Monetary Fund (AMF) was dropped – despite strong support for the idea from hard-hit East Asian economies – in the face of tremendous pressure by the US Treasury and the International Monetary Fund (IMF), both of whom felt the AMF idea would make a mockery of the IMF and global financial regulation in general.[44] The failed AMF proposal stands in stark contrast to the success of Japan's leading role in the 1996 inaugural meeting of central bank governors of member countries of the Executives' Meeting of East Asia and Pacific Central Banks (EMEAP), which led to the formation of the first repurchase lines to address ASEAN's concerns of contagion.[45] While the EMEAP 'repo' lines eventually had no direct role in addressing the financial crisis itself, they would evolve into more complex lines that would form part of the basis of the Chiang Mai Initiative.

Another key but little acknowledged contribution by Japan to the shape and substance of Asia's regional architecture involves the vision and efforts behind the so-called 'East Asian Community' (EAC), and the regional vehicles formed as the building blocks of the EAC, the APT and the EAS. It bears reminding that China, whose perceived dominance of the APT and East Asia at large has caused considerable alarm for Japan and other regional countries, initially welcomed the proposal by Japan and others to form a summit-level gathering, believing its membership would comprise essentially the originally 'ten plus three' of the APT. But what Prime Minister Koizumi had in mind was a bigger grouping (which he referred to using EAC nomenclature[46]) – he sought the inclusion of Australia and New Zealand in particular – out of concern that China's power and influence needed to be balanced against. 'In my heart I truly hope Australia will participate in the East Asia summit', Hitoshi Tanaka, a former vice minister in MOFA, once commented regarding Japan's pursuit of Australian involvement in the proposed EAS.

We have worked very hard to make it possible. We are doing this not for Australia's sake, but for Japan's sake … I have a very strong feeling about our cooperation with Australia and I have been advocating it for a very long time.[47]

Beyond the EAS, Japan also sought to balance China with its proposal for a Comprehensive Economic Partnership for East Asia (CEPEA) covering sixteen countries – the APT states and Australia, India and New Zealand – that rivalled the East Asia Free Trade Area (EAFTA) championed by China.[48] Unlike Prime Minister Yukio Hatoyama's subsequent and considerably hazier version of the EAC (discussed below), however, Koizumi's EAC idea avoided any pretension of being a comprehensive overarching framework in the European Union mould and focused instead on building intraregional collaboration over a number of functional fronts such as energy, the economy and the environment.[49]

In other words, the 'variable geometric' approach which has come to characterize Asia's regional architecture – usually diagrammed as a dizzying complex or patchwork of overlapping circles and ovals – is as much the contribution of Japan as anyone else. Japan that actively supported the ad hoc formation of multiple regional institutions in East Asia out of worry that the APT might end up as the only framework for Japan to deal with China.[50] Thus understood, the oversupply of institutions for which ASEAN, as the self-professed occupant of the 'driving seat' in Asian multilateralism, is often criticized, is in fact equally attributable to efforts by Japan to create political-cum-strategic space for managing China. According to this view, Japan has actively sought to build regional institutions because they have become, in Tokyo's perspective, the preferred grounds on which Japan's political competition with China should take place.[51] If Yoshida-type pragmatists worried over the potential exclusion of the United States from Asian multilateralism, Koizumi-type revisionists-cum-nationalists who chafed at Japan's junior partner status in its alliance with the United States did not seem overly perturbed at the prospect of America's exclusion from at least one regional institution, the EAS (at least before the United States joined the arrangement in 2011). If anything, the Japanese leadership appeared to work toward that end, according to an eminent analyst of Japanese foreign policy.[52] As Richard Samuels has noted, 'Japan responded to the threat of Chinese regional dominance with characteristic ambiguity and a studied ambivalence about its continued dependence on the United States'.[53]

Yet another example of a policy idea contributed by a Japanese official that was met initially with reservations in ASEAN circles, but subsequently proved revolutionary, is that of a regional forum for defence ministers. In March 2002, Gen Nakatani, then director of the Japan Defense Agency (JDA) – the precursor to the Japan Ministry of Defense – suggested that the ARF, predominantly a forum driven by the region's foreign policy establishments, could perhaps be complemented by a parallel defence forum. Nakatani had in mind the then newly formed SLD as a basis for what could evolve into an 'Asian defence ministerial meeting'.[54] Again, as in the case of the Nakayama proposal in 1991, the proposal for a defence forum met with a cool reaction from the ASEAN states. It would take another eight years before the ADMM-Plus – comprising the ten ASEAN states, which formed the ADMM in 2006, and eight dialogue partners of ASEAN, Australia, China, India, Japan, New Zealand, Russia, South Korea and the United States – would be established in 2010.[55]

Finally, Japan has been a diligent participant in non-official multilateral diplomacy in regional security affairs. At the 'Track 2' level, Japan, through the Japan Institute of International Affairs (JIIA), a think tank once affiliated with Japan's MOFA until recently, has actively been involved in the Council for Security Cooperation in the Asia-Pacific (CSCAP).[56] For that matter, Japan has provided arguably the most substantial funding for CSCAP activities, including financing the involvement of North Korean officials (acting in their private capacity, as the Track 2 mantra goes) at CSCAP meetings. Japan has also had strong representation at other semi/non-official epistemic networks such as the Northeast Asia Cooperation Dialogue and the Trilateral Forum on North Pacific Security.

What the foregoing illustrations highlight is not only a long Japanese tradition in furnishing viable and actionable policy recommendations and, should the political conditions prove felicitous, a concomitant willingness to facilitate their fulfilment with apparently little interest in self-promotion or self-aggrandizement. The illustrations also underscore a key ingredient for multilateralism in Asia, namely, America's buy-in, although as our discussion on Koizumi's efforts to implement his EAC vision has shown, Japan has at times proved ambivalent in its attitude towards its principal ally and has even sought to exclude it from particular regional arrangements – despite, crucially, Tokyo's perceived need to balance against Beijing in a specific multilateral institutional context. Granted, US membership in all of Asia's regional institutions is not absolutely vital; the APT is a good example of that. Even then, the APT could be considered *sui generis* in that it was as much an East Asian reaction to perceived unfairness on the part of the Americans to the region in the wake of the 1997–8 financial crisis as an attempt to formulate a regional mechanism for responding to crisis. Moreover, that the EAS emerged partly out of the region's concern that the APT was at risk of being dominated by China only underscores the importance of US involvement in Asian multilateralism, whether to lend it greater legitimacy or as a counterbalance against China and/or other powers wishing to control the multilateral agenda. In contrast to the APEC and ARF illustrations, Hatoyama's 2009 proposal to establish a European Union-like institution in East Asia faced a similar fate as the Australian proposal because, unlike the MITI and Nakayama proposals, it earned highly ambivalent reactions from the United States, China and ASEAN.[57] Moreover, to the extent that the Hatoyama proposal could at all have been motivated by concern over Asia's underperforming regional architecture – the reasons behind the proposal, along with the proposal itself, remained unclear – then it poses a potential conundrum for Japanese foreign policy since, as we have seen, the Koizumi government's contributions to the formation of the EAS arguably had a hand in shaping the design of the regional architecture. In sum, where Japan's contributions to Asia's post-Cold War multilateralism have proved most effective and relevant, they have been achieved through a mix of strong US interest and support and a readiness by Japan to play second fiddle even if its actual role has been considerable. In other words, while Tokyo's involvement in multilateralism goes only as far as Washington is prepared to allow it,[58] Tokyo, partly by resisting Washington's call to it to assume more responsibilities and play a more explicit role in regional leadership, has however succeeded in its efforts to define the shape and substance of multilateralism in Asia.

## *Shaping Asian multilateralism under 'normalization'*

Among analysts of Japan's defence and foreign policy, there is strong agreement that Japan is seeking to become a normal military power, but has no intention of exiting its long-standing security alliance with the United States. For example, Michael Green has written about Japan as a 'reluctant' realist state that, with the end of the Cold War, has been compelled by circumstances to alter its foreign policy approach. No longer able to rely solely on economic power to insure its regional dominance, Green argues that Japan has begun to assert its power – reluctantly in his view –commensurately with its growing concerns over China's growing military power, its increased anxiety about external security threats, and its apparent readiness to disagree with US policy especially over East Asia.[59] Green concludes, however, that these changes ought to foster rather than hinder closer coordination between Japanese and US policy. In like fashion, Christopher Hughes has argued that Japan is seeking to become a more assertive military power, and that this trend has been accelerated in the post-9/11 period.[60] However, he believes that rather than striking out on its own, Japan will opt to integrate its growing military capabilities into its alliance with the United States, rather than pursue options for greater autonomy or multilateralism. Japan's strengthened role will allow it to be the 'defensive shield' to America's 'offensive sword', thereby bolstering US military hegemony in East Asia and globally.[61] Another analyst, Tang Siew Mun, tracing the transition in Japanese grand strategy from the Yoshida premiership to the Koizumi premiership, detects in the latter a concern with achieving structural power, preserving national tranquillity and maintaining Japan's economic competitiveness. The shift 'from the Yoshida Doctrine to the Koizumi Doctrine', as Tang sees it, has arisen out of 'Japan's aspirations and perception of vulnerabilities in the context of domestic and international developments'.[62] Finally, Bhubhindar Singh, using national identity as a handle, argues that Japan's image of itself has evolved from a 'peace state' to an 'international state'.[63] Whichever way one has it, Japan has been undergoing transformation.

Needless to say, China has emerged as the prime rationale for the Abe government's projected increase in defence spending to record levels and its establishment of a US-style national security council – a decision ostensibly motivated by the perceived need to 'counter China'.[64] Arguably, Abe sees Japan's promised economic revival as an effective means of building 'a more powerful, assertive Japan, complete with a full-fledged military, as well as pride in its World War II-era past'.[65] Rather than forge a strategic path independent of the United

States, however, Japan is more likely than not to integrate its growing military capabilities into its alliance with the United States, with potential ramifications for its hitherto strong support for Asian multilateralism. But while that would undoubtedly be the case, there is evidence to suggest that the diplomatic assertiveness expected of Tokyo – the 'new normal' of a normal Japan, if you will – might not be fully appreciated by Washington, particularly if rising tensions with China over the Senkaku/Diaoyu islands pose an entrapment problem for America.[66] In the same way US unilateralism during the first term of George W. Bush's presidency, heavily criticized for its neoconservative orientation, in fact built on the Clinton presidency's equally unilateral foreign policy,[67] Abe's aspiration for a militarily strong Japan is not an *ex nihilo* development but one that builds on what one analyst has referred to as Japan's enduring 'quest for normalcy',[68] one that began well before Abe's emergence. Crucially, this quest for normality does not necessarily imply an assertion for greater Japanese autonomy from US power and influence, even as it changes the terms of their bilateral relationship. In a key sense, Abe's aim to balance against China is clearly shared by the United States – the pivot/rebalancing to Asia strategy of the Obama administration being the latest manifestation of American intent – and closer Japan–US military cooperation toward that end is a logical consequence. As Hughes has noted:

> The result of Japan's perceived exhaustion of its options for engagement, despite its strenuous and innovative regional and global activity, and thus to assert an active hold on China's rise, could be to force it on the defensive and to shift precipitously to a default policy of containment. Japan has already shown signs of this containment founded inevitably on the further enhancement of its own military power, tighter US–Japan security cooperation, and active, if quiet, balancing against China.[69]

Hughes's premonition is supported by an influential policy study co-authored in 2011 by a prominent coterie of 'young guns' of Japan's security studies community, which contended that in place of its long-standing dual strategy of engagement and hedging long adopted vis-à-vis China, Japan ought instead to do the following: first, further integrate China – as opposed to 'engage' since, it is argued, China is already a part of the international order – regionally and globally; second, balance against China through persuading it to comply with international rules and norms; and finally, militarily deter China from attempting to change the status quo by force.[70] Their third recommendation has been echoed by Abe himself, who averred in the context of Chinese assertiveness that Japan 'will never tolerate the change of status quo by force or coercion'.[71] The ready and quite public references to political balancing and military deterrence against China presumably marks the verbal crossing of a political Rubicon of sorts, where Japan's normalization will no longer be something to be pursued haltingly, quietly, and apologetically, but – notwithstanding incessant resistance at home and indeed within Abe's Liberal Democratic Party (LDP) itself[72] – enthusiastically, energetically, and unabashedly.

While efforts to revive Japan's economy are welcomed, not every Japanese voter has necessarily agreed with Abe's and his fellow revisionists' logic regarding normalization, not least when it leads to problems with China and South Korea.[73] Reminiscent of his mentor Koizumi's controversial visits to the Yasukuni war shrine, Abe's own visits to the same shrine have aroused both Beijing's and Seoul's ire. In response to Abe's shrine visit in December 2013, the US Department of State released a statement on the website of its embassy in Tokyo, noting Washington's disappointment with the Japanese leadership for having 'taken an action that will exacerbate tensions with Japan's neighbours'.[74] Reportedly, the US rejoinder came after Tokyo had evidently ignored Washington's attempt to prevent the visit. Yet it is experiences such as this that highlight the limits of US military support for Japan should tensions escalate in the East China Sea and conflict with China becomes a real possibility. And if Washington's irritation with Tokyo stems from the former's worry over entrapment, then it is certainly not inconceivable that the latter may worry over possible abandonment by Washington should tensions between China and Japan over their islands dispute worsen beyond repair. Despite former US Secretary of State Hillary Clinton's assurance conveyed in October 2010 – and reiterated by President Obama in April 2014 – that the Senkaku/Diaoyu islands are covered by the US–Japanese mutual defence treaty, the fact that a number of US policy experts have voiced concerns that such a commitment goes too far and risks a conflict between China and the United States over a useless 'pile of rocks' has raised Japanese fears of US abandonment.[75] Moreover, the Obama administration has stated on a number of occasions that dialogue and consultations remain the best way to ease tensions between China and Japan.[76]

Nor is it in the interest of America, as the 'hub' of its alliance system, to see the system rocked by strife between the 'spokes'. 'If Seoul and Tokyo are at odds, that's a problem for us', according to a noted Washington-based analyst. 'In Washington, when experts debate problems in the Asia-Pacific region, before the Chinese ADIZ [air defence identification zone], the No. 1 topic is what do we do to prevent the Japanese and Koreans from tearing each other apart'.[77] When Abe visited Indonesia in January 2013, he introduced his 'five principles' of Japanese diplomacy, touted fairly or otherwise by some as Japan's first major diplomatic policy since the Fukuda Doctrine.[78] Among them, the so-called 'Abe Doctrine' identifies principles such as protecting freedom of thought, expression and speech in Southeast Asia, and ensuring that the seas ('the most vital commons to us all') are governed by international law, as sharing common cause to the US rebalancing policy.[79] But as an editorial of the Japanese new daily *Asahi Shimbun* has pointed out, at the Japan–ASEAN Summit that took place in mid-December 2013 in Tokyo, Abe advocated the importance of the rule of law in the seas and skies but evidently failed to mention the promotion of human rights and democratization.[80] Abe's selective emphasis raises the prospect that his doctrine is principally about balancing, if not containing, China. A recent study by the Tokyo Foundation suggests that ASEAN states 'are reluctant to define the US role as an external balancer against China in the light of deep, ASEAN–China economic interdependence'.[81] As a consequence, ASEAN, in Japan's perspective, requires external assistance to build its 'own strength and resilience against China's growing maritime pressure [as] an important vanguard for denying China's creeping expansion to the contested territorial waters [in the South China Sea]'.[82] If so, Abe's policy towards Southeast Asia/ASEAN could be at risk of being overly focused on China – an emphasis the Southeast Asian countries, despite their own strategic worries, might not fully appreciate.

A normal and decidedly more assertive Japan – 'return of the Samurai', as a *Time* article has it[83] – would clearly pose challenges for Japan's future participation in Asian multilateralism. On the one hand, it deepens an already entrenched Japan–US security bilateralism at the possible expense of multilateralism. On the other hand, should Japan persist under its current trajectory under Abe's leadership and further vex Japan's ties with China, South Korea and others, there is an outside chance that it could alienate the United States and the ASEAN states. Given, as shown earlier, the importance of the United States to getting most of Asia's multilateral mechanisms off the ground, and ASEAN's place in the 'driving seat' of Asia's regional architecture, an increasingly isolated Japan might opt out of Asian multilateralism altogether, particularly if the Japanese leadership adopts a more independent orientation. In this regard, the judicious appropriation of diplomatic strategies by the Abe government would be of utmost importance to improving Japan's relations with its neighbours and winning the region's trust.[84] As Terada has argued, what proved crucial in winning friends and supporters throughout the region, but especially among the ASEAN states, to Japan's approach to regional diplomacy in the past was Tokyo's robust emphasis on multilateralism and its consultative approach to regional economic and security cooperation.[85] This implies, on the one hand, that directional leadership, once Japan's hallmark and so crucial to Japan's contributions to multilateralism in Asia but now increasingly replaced by assertive diplomacy, still has a role to play. On the other hand, whatever its many flaws and perceived obstacles it places in the way of Japan's realization of its interests, Asian multilateralism still has something to offer.

## Converging multilateralisms *à la carte*?

The growing security integration between Tokyo and Washington is also expressed in their increasingly similar perspectives over which aspects of Asia's regional security architecture matter, the purposes they should serve and how they ought to be utilized. Abe has made clear his desire to support ASEAN and to see the EAS and other regional arrangements strengthened. Japan harbours the hope that Asian multilateralism will function as venues through which interstate transparency and trust can be fostered, not least with China. In Abe's 2014 SLD remarks, the EAS, the ARF, and the ADMM-Plus were all referenced by the Japanese leader as the appropriate mechanisms whereby member countries could engage in the mutual disclosure of their respective military expenditures:

> There is no stage that outshines the East Asia Summit as a venue for heads of state and government to come together and discuss the order that is desirable. Keeping military expansion in check and making military budgets transparent,

as well as enlarging the number of countries that conclude the Arms Trade Treaty and improving mutual understanding between authorities in charge of national defence – there is no lack of issues those of us [who are] national leaders ought to take up, applying peer pressure on each other. I urge the further enhancement of the East Asia Summit, as the premier forum taking up regional politics and security. I propose that we first create a permanent committee comprised of permanent representatives to ASEAN from the member countries and then prepare a road map to bring renewed vitality to the Summit itself, while also making the Summit along with the ARF and the ADMM-Plus function in a multi-layered fashion.[86]

While Japan might not have played a leading role in the TPP – indeed, there were early signs suggesting that domestic opposition at home could dampen Japanese enthusiasm for the regional trade pact, despite Abe's and the former Democratic Party of Japan (DPJ) government's support for it – it has since, in negotiations with the United States, resolved most of its key reservations about the TPP.[87] While it is in Japan's geopolitical interest to join the TPP given the presence of the United States and other security partners of Japan in the TPP, the trade pact also provides Japan with a weighty platform through which it could engage China and, when the time is right, to encourage its participation in the TPP.[88] While the TPP could conceivably be the economic mechanism through which Japan would facilitate China's further integration with the regional and global economy,[89] there is no question concerning its political and strategic value as a tool to (as Abe has put it in another context) apply peer pressure and balance against China. As a former Australian central banker has observed, getting the rules of the TPP set before inviting China to join the party is a strange way of encouraging China to be a responsible stakeholder.[90]

The United States has made clear its support for an effective multilateralism in Asia. According to the Japan–US. Joint Statement released in April 2014:

> The United States and Japan renew our commitment to deepening diplomatic, economic, and security cooperation with the Association of Southeast Asian Nations (ASEAN), recognizing the importance of ASEAN unity and centrality to regional security and prosperity. We are coordinating closely to support ASEAN and its affiliated fora as its members seek to build a regional economic community and address trans-border challenges, including cybersecurity and cybercrime. In this context, the two countries view the East Asia Summit as the premier political and security forum in the region.[91]

In a key respect, the developments highlighted in the above statement satisfy some of the requisite conditions of effective multilateralism – a strong bilateral partnership and commonality of interest, on the one hand, and strong support for a formal standing arrangement, the EAS, without apparently sacrificing others such as the ARF. Indeed, the emphasis on cyber espionage in the above Joint Statement implies those two countries' view of the EAS as an appropriate forum not only for mutually addressing that concern but also for counterbalancing other powers, particularly China.[92] However, it is also possible that the developments highlight a mutual lack in restraint among the three powers in question here, Japan, China and the United States. To be sure, it could be argued that China's policy of 'tailored coercion' (as a study has called it[93]) in the East and South China Seas, an incremental and selective form of low-end coercive diplomacy, is in fact an exercise in restraint. However, the level of competition and risks arising from their respective employments of sea denial strategies and counterstrategies, on the one hand, and the lack of any dedicated maritime code of conduct, incidences at sea agreement and confidence-building measures on the other far exceed any benefit gleaned from occasional and uneven displays in restraint by any power.[94] How Japan, China, the United States, and the ASEAN countries, among others, find ways to improve their bilateral ties and emphasize their common interests will be fundamental to the success of any multilateral framework in facilitating the region's security and stability.

Furthermore, notwithstanding the joint Japan–US affirmations for ASEAN centrality and the EAS's putative relevance, a nagging concern for ASEAN and its member states would be to what extent such an inordinate focus on the EAS and the role it ought to play could mean for their place in the very multilateral house they had constructed. Both the Joint Statement and Abe's SLD remarks were careful to emphasize the import of ASEAN's centrality. At the same time, however, ASEAN's weakness and disunity are seen by many, fairly or otherwise, as a root cause of the relative ineffectiveness of Asian multilateralism. It has been proposed (as Abe also has done) that the EAS should be empowered with the capacity to 'steer' the various regional modalities available. Mindful of the problems former Australian leader Kevin Rudd's 'Asia-Pacific Community' proposal had with regional anxieties over the prospect of the region being co-managed by a concert of powers at the expense of a more representative and equitable community, a leading Indonesian policy intellectual has argued that the EAS 'should function as a sort of steering committee for the Asia-Pacific region [through] coordinating various regional institutions in the region' such as the APT, ARF, ADMM-Plus, and APEC, whilst 'the EAS members of the G20 [should] form an informal caucus to coordinate their policies and interests at the global level'.[95] It is debatable whether other ASEAN states – with the possible exception of Indonesia, the only Southeast Asian member of the G20 [Group of Twenty] – would accept the idea. The challenge for Japan, the United States, and other powers would be to ensure, in the collective quest to enhance the EAS, that the concerns and interests of the smaller players are not ignored. The proposed conferral of steering capacity on the EAS also leaves unanswered the question of whether the EAS would be able to secure the agreement of the ARF and the APEC, not least when their respective memberships include a large number of non-EAS countries, with that idea.

Those concerns aside, Japan's reputation as a regional leader, already in doubt for some in the wake of Japan's persistent irritants – controversial shrine visits, ambivalence on the comfort women issue, resistance against giving a full formal apology for war transgressions, and the like – could be further jeopardized should its future participation in Asian multilateralism be shaped exclusively by the perceived need to counterbalance China through its partnership with the United States. The issue here has less to do with balancing per se – the existence of soft balancing and hedging dynamics within Asia's regional institutions has long been acknowledged[96] – than the risks posed to those institutions by member countries potentially engaged in hard balancing. Moreover, it has been argued that the choices Tokyo makes concerning the frameworks – bilateral alliance, Asian multilateralism, and/or United Nations-centred multilateralism – through which it would deploy its expanded military capabilities could prove decisive for regional stability and the international order as a whole.[97] Even so, it is not entirely certain, should Japan adopt an à la carte multilateralism that is mutually convergent with the US position and narrowly focused on the China threat, whether the future security environment of the region would be any less worrisome than if Japan had decided to go it alone.

Another equally challenging ramification for Japan's regional leadership as a consequence of its military normalization has to do with its long-standing devotion to and championing of alternative security, especially economic, human, and other non-military approaches to security.[98] According to the 2013 interim report by the Japanese commission tasked to review the country's defence guidelines, Japan's security policy is acutely focused on traditional security concerns rather than non-traditional ones – the latter with which, on the other hand, Japan continues to engage proactively in areas like disaster relief, maritime security and military medicine through the ADMM-Plus and the ARF.[99] If anything, it is the area of humanitarian assistance and disaster relief (HADR) that has afforded the most opportunities to foster military-to-military cooperation between Japan and other members of the ADMM-Plus and the ARF, including China.[100] But it is also in such ostensibly non-military areas of regional cooperation that Japan's contributions could potentially destabilize the region by proxy, such as its decision to donate patrol boats to the Philippines amidst rising tensions in the South China Sea. While Japan's turn to hard balancing against China has not quite led it to abandon its support for alternative security approaches, it is nonetheless at risk of hijacking and undermining its own historical legacy by securitizing its contributions to multilateral cooperation.

## Conclusion

This chapter has argued that Japan's present push to become a normal military power is likely to have a lasting impact on Asian multilateralism, though not quite in the way anticipated by those who foresee Japan's prioritization of its alliance with the United States at the expense of its long-standing and largely positive history with the region's multilateral enterprise. The envisaged outcome is likely to be the same, but arguably arrived at not through Japan's rejection or abandonment of multilateralism as much as through its adoption of an instrumental or selective approach to multilateralism that, at its most problematic, risks antagonizing not only China but other regional countries as well. It arguably risks the region's stability as its focus on the perceived threat posed by China to its interests and the lack of restraint on the part of Japan and other powers equally contribute to an ineffective multilateralism. Furthermore, whatever contributions Japan's *à la carte* multilateralism might deliver to the region would not only be undermined by its turn to hard balancing against China, but its leadership in alternative security approaches could itself be jeopardized.

In his 2015 New Year Reflections, Prime Minister Abe's 'message to the world' focused exclusively on re-energizing Abenomics towards the end goal of fashioning Japan into 'a country that once again shines on the world's center stage'[101] – a consistent aim of his that, combined with his leadership and sense of destiny, has engendered the myriad consequences discussed here. It remains to be seen what and how this next term with Abe still at Japan's helm might mean for Asian multilateralism. The foregoing analysis has also shown that the region's multi-multilateral character, which ASEAN has often been criticized for having fashioned, is in fact equally attributable to efforts by Japan, among others, to create political and strategic space for managing and counterbalancing China. While the way forward to an effective multilateralism and a stable and secure Asia will probably need to involve close bilateral (and possibly even trilateral) coordination and cooperation between and among Japan, China and the United States, how those powers can pull that off, while at the same time addressing residual regional worries over existing multilateral institutions being hijacked by a concert of power arrangement, could prove to be the key challenge.

## Notes

1 Nobuo Okawara and Peter J. Katzenstein, 'Japan and Asia-Pacific Security: Regionalization, Entrenched Bilateralism, and Incipient Multilateralism', *The Pacific Review*. Vol. 14, No. 2 (2001), pp. 165–94. For realists and liberals alike, the Japan–US alliance is part of a network of US-based security bilateralisms (i.e. the San Francisco System) that have long provided the strategic foundation for Asia's multilateralism. G. John Ikenberry and Jitsuo Tsuchiyama, 'Between Balance of Power and Community: The Future of Multilateral Security Co-operation in the Asia-Pacific', *International Relations of the Asia-Pacific*, Vol. 2, No. 1 (2002), pp. 69–94; William T. Tow, *Asia-Pacific Security Relations: Seeking Convergent Security* (Cambridge: Cambridge University Press, 2001).
2 On 'pragmatists' and 'revisionists' among Japan's political elite. see Axel Berkofsky, *A Pacifist Constitution for an Armed Empire: Past and Present of the Japanese Security and Defence Policies* (Milan: FrancoAngeli, 2012), pp. 140–4.
3 Richard J. Samuels, 'Japan's Goldilocks Strategy', *The Washington Quarterly*, Vol. 29, No. 4 (2006), pp. 111–27.
4 'China Urges Japan to Pursue Peace under New Defence Chief Gen Nakatani', *South China Morning Post*, 27 December 2014.
5 Stewart Patrick, 'Prix Fixe and à la Carte: Avoiding False Multilateral Choices', *The Washington Quarterly*, Vol. 32, No. 4 (2009), pp. 77–95.
6 Robert Kagan, 'Multilateralism, American Style', *The Washington Post*, 13 September 2002.
7 Bert Edström, *Japan and Human Security: The Derailing of a Foreign Policy Vision*, Asia Paper, March (Stockholm: Institute for Security and Development Policy, 2011);

Peng Er Lam, 'Japan's Human Security Role in Southeast Asia', *Contemporary Southeast Asia*, Vol. 28, No. 1 (2006), pp. 141–59.
8 This chapter draws on the following papers by See Seng Tan: 'Asian Multilateralism in the Age of Japan's "New Normal": Perils and Prospects', *Japanese Journal of Political Science*, accepted for publication; and, 'Japan and Multilateralism in Asia', prepared for the Study Group on 'ASEAN–Japan Strategic Partnership on East Asian Community-Building', co-organized by the Centre for Strategic and International Studies (CSIS) Indonesia and the Japan Center for International Exchange (JCIE), Bali, 13–14 June 2013.
9 'Keynote Address by Shinzo Abe, Prime Minister of Japan', The Thirteenth IISS (International Institute for Strategic Studies) Asia Security Summit, the Shangri-La Dialogue, 30 May 2014, www.iiss.org/en/events/shangri%20la%20dialogue/archive/2014-c20c/opening-remarks-and-keynote-address-b0b2/keynote-address-shinzo-abe-a787.
10 Simon Tisdall, 'Shinzo Abe: Is Japan's PM a Dangerous Militarist or Modernizing Reformer?', *The Guardian*, 16 December 2013, www.theguardian.com/world/2013/dec/16/shinzo-abe-japan-pm.
11 On various categories of political actors in Japanese foreign policy, see, Richard J. Samuels, 'Japan's Goldilocks Strategy', *The Washington Quarterly*, Vol. 29, No. 4 (2006), pp. 111–27.
12 Glenn D. Hook, 'Japan in the World', in William M. Tsutsui, ed., *A Companion to Japanese History* (Malden, MA: Blackwell, 2009), p. 344.
13 Respectively, in Takashi Terada, 'Directional Leadership in Institution-Building: Japan's Approaches to ASEAN in the Establishment of PECC and APEC', *The Pacific Review*, Vol. 14, No. 2 (2001), pp. 195–220; Reinhard Drifte, *Japan's Foreign Policy for the 21st Century: From Economic Superpower to What Power?* (Houndmills, Basingstoke: Palgrave Macmillan, 1998); and, Alan Rix, 'Japan and the Region: Leading from Behind', in Richard Higgott, Richard Leaver and John Ravenhill, eds., *Pacific Economic Relations in the 1990s: Cooperation or Conflict?* (Boulder, CO: Lynne Rienner, 1993), p. 65.
14 Bhubhindar Singh, *Japan's Security Identity: From a Peace State to an International State* (Abingdon: Routledge, 2013).
15 Jennifer M. Lind, 'Pacifism or Passing the Buck? Testing Theories of Japanese Security Policy', *International Security*, Vol. 29, No. 1 (2004), pp. 92–121.
16 Christopher W. Hughes, *Japan's Re-emergence as a 'Normal' Military Power*, Adelphi Series No. 368–9 (Abingdon: Routledge, 2007).
17 Yew Meng Lai, *Nationalism and Power Politics in Japan's Relations with China: A Neoclassical Realist Interpretation* (Abingdon: Routledge, 2014), ch. 3.
18 'Keynote Address by Shinzo Abe, Prime Minister of Japan', pp. 8–9.
19 Yoshihide Soeya, 'China, and Japan's Foreign Policy Posture', *East Asia Forum*, 8 April 2012, www.eastasiaforum.org/2010/02/16/the-us-japan-alliance-beyond-futenma/.
20 Chris Good, 'The Obama Doctrine: Multilateralism with Teeth', *The Atlantic*, 10 December 2009; Richard Gowan and Bruce Jones, 'Mr. Obama Goes to New York: The President and the Restoration of Multilateral Diplomacy', *Brookings Report*, 17 September (Washington, D.C.: Brookings Institution, 2009).
21 Philippe Regnier and Daniel Warner, eds., *Japan and Multilateral Diplomacy* (Farnham: Ashgate, 2001).
22 Lind, 'Pacifism or Passing the Buck?'.
23 Yukio Satoh, 'Foreword', in Lam Peng Er, ed., *Japan's Relations with Southeast Asia: The Fukuda Doctrine and Beyond* (Abingdon: Routledge, 2012), pp. xv–xvi.
24 Sueo Sudo, *The Fukuda Doctrine and ASEAN: New Dimensions in Japanese Foreign Policy* (Singapore: Institute of Southeast Asian Studies, 1992).
25 As Paul Midford has explained, it is difficult to date the start of the Yoshida Doctrine since Prime Minister Yoshida never formally announced his strategy much less

suggested it was his own. Midford further provides a useful distinction between the Yoshida and Fukuda doctrines: the first (Yoshida Doctrine) is an implicit grand strategy, whereas the second (Fukuda Doctrine) is an explicit diplomatic doctrine. Paul Midford, *Rethinking Japanese Public Opinion and Security: From Pacifism to Realism?* (Stanford, CA: Stanford University Press, 2011), p. 193.
26 Patrick, 'Prix Fixe *and* à la Carte'.
27 On PAFTAD, see Takashi Terada, *The Japanese Origins of PAFTAD: The Beginning of an Asia Pacific Economic Community*, Pacific Economic Papers, No. 292 (Canberra: Australia-Japan Research Centre, Australian National University, June 1999).
28 Takashi Terada, 'The Origins of Japan's APEC Policy: Foreign Minister Takeo Miki's Asia-Pacific Policy and Current Implications', *The Pacific Review*, Vol. 11, No. 3 (1998), pp. 337–63.
29 Takashi Terada, *The Genesis of APEC: Australian-Japanese Political Initiatives*, Pacific Economic Papers, No. 298 (Canberra, ACT: Australia–Japan Research Centre, Australian National University, 1999), p. 1.
30 Terada, *The Genesis of APEC*, p. 1.
31 Michael J. Green, *Japan's Reluctant Realism* (Houndmills, Basingstoke: Palgrave Macmillan, 2001), p. 216.
32 Christopher W. Hughes, *Japan's Security Agenda: Military, Economic, and Environmental Dimensions* (Boulder, CO: Lynne Rienner, 2004), p. 198.
33 Christopher W. Hughes, 'Japan's Response to China's Rise: Regional Engagement, Global Containment, Dangers of Collision', *International Affairs*, Vol. 85, No. 4 (2009), pp. 837–56.
34 The term is used in Evelyn Goh and Amitav Acharya, 'The ASEAN Regional Forum and US–China Relations: Comparing Chinese and American Positions', paper for the Fifth China–ASEAN Research Institutes Roundtable on Regionalism and Community Building in East Asia, University of Hong Kong, 17–19 October 2002.
35 See Seng Tan, *Facilitating China–U.S. Relations in the Age of Rebalancing. ASEAN's 'Middle Power' Diplomacy*, EAI MPDI Working Paper No. 1 (Seoul: East Asia Institute, 2013).
36 Helen Nesadurai, 'APEC: A Tool for US Regional Domination?', *The Pacific Review*, Vol. 9, No. 1 (2006), pp. 31–57.
37 See, Alice D. Ba, 'Who's Socializing Whom? Complex Engagement in China–ASEAN Relations', *The Pacific Review*, Vol. 19, No. 2 (2006). pp. 157–79; Alastair Iain Johnston, 'Is China a Status Quo Power?', *International Security*, Vol. 27, No. 4 (2003), pp. 5–56; and, Alastair Iain Johnston and Paul Evans, 'China's Engagement with Multilateral Security Institutions', in Alastair Iain Johnston and Robert Ross, eds., *Engaging China* (London: Routledge, 1999), pp. 235–72.
38 Quoted in Kuniko Ashizawa, *Japan, the US, and Regional Institution-Building in the New Asia: When Identity Matters* (Houndmills, Basingstoke: Palgrave Macmillan, 2013), p. 125.
39 Masahiko Koumura, 'Japan's Leadership for the Future of Asia', *Ministry of Foreign Affairs of Japan*, 3 June 1999 www.mofa.go.jp/announce/fm/koumura/address9906.html.
40 Stephen Smith, 'Australia, ASEAN and the Asia Pacific', 18 July 2008, Lowy Institute, Sydney, www.foreignminister.gov.au/speeches/2008/080718_lowy.html.
41 See Seng Tan, 'Spectres of Leifer: Insights on Regional Order and Security for Southeast Asia Today', *Contemporary Southeast Asia*, Vol. 34, No. 3 (2012), pp. 309–37, on pp. 316–17.
42 Tommy Koh, 'Rudd's Reckless Regional Rush', *The Australian*, 18 December 2009.
43 Thom Woodroofe, 'Is the East Asia Summit Rudd's Gift to the World?', *Australian Policy Outline*, 12 January 2012 http://apo.org.au/commentary/east-asia-summit-rudd%E2%80%99s-gift-world.

44 Phillip Y. Lipscy, 'Japan's Asian Monetary Fund Proposal', *Stanford Journal of East Asian Affairs*, Vol. 3, No. 1 (2003), pp. 93–104, on p. 93.
45 Douglas W. Arner, Paul Lejot and Wang Wei, 'Governance and Financial Integration in East Asia', in Masahiro Kawai, Jong-Wha Lee and Peter A. Petri, eds., *Asian Regionalism in the World Economy: Engine for Dynamism and Stability* (Cheltenham: Edward Elgar, 2010), pp. 209–48, on p. 225.
46 Notably, Koizumi first proposed the EAC idea in 2002, but Malaysia rejected it for Koizumi's inclusion of Australia because of then brewing political tensions between Kuala Lumpur and Canberra, not least those caused by travel warnings covering certain Southeast Asian countries issued by Canberra following the Bali bombings in October 2002. 'Travel Warnings Cause Tension with Malaysia', *Radio Australia*, 6November2002www.radioaustralia.net.au/international/2002-11-06/travel-warnings-cause-tension-with-malaysia/599076.
47 Quoted in Takashi Terada, 'Security Partnership: Toward a Softer Triangle Alliance with the United States?', in G. John Ikenberry, Takashi Inoguchi, Yoichiro Sato, eds., *The U.S.–Japan Security Alliance: Regional Multilateralism* (Houndmills, Basingstoke: Palgrave Macmillan, 2011), pp. 217-32, at p. 222. The bilateral goodwill was reciprocated as recently as October 2013, when Australian Foreign Minister Julie Bishop noted that her government welcomes 'the direction that the Abe government has taken in terms of having a more normal defence posture and being able to take a constructive role in regional and global security'. Quoted in Kirk Spitzer, 'Why Japan Wants to Break Free of its Pacifist Past', *Time*, 22 October 2013, http://world.time.com/2013/10/22/why-tokyo-wants-to-break-free-of-its-pacifist-past/.
48 Japan-sponsored organizations such as the Asian Development Bank (ADB) produced comparative studies on the anticipated economic benefits of the CEPEA and the EAFTA. One such study by two eminent economists from the Tokyo-based ADB Institute concluded, unsurprisingly, that 'consolidation into a Comprehensive Economic Partnership in East Asia at the ASEAN+6 level would yield the largest gains to East Asia among plausible regional trade agreements'. Masahiro Kawai and Ganeshan Wignaraja, 'EAFTA or CEPEA', *ASEAN Economic Bulletin*, Vol. 25, No. 2 (2008), pp. 113–39, on p. 113.
49 Richard J. Samuels, *Securing Japan: Tokyo's Grand Strategy and the Future of East Asia* (Ithaca, NY: Cornell University Press, 2007), p. 166.
50 Hughes, 'Japan's Response to China's Rise'; Takashi Terada, 'The Birth and Growth of ASEAN+3', in Bertrand Fort and Douglas Webber, eds., *Regional Integration in East Asia and Europe: Convergence or Divergence?* (London: Routledge, 2006), pp. 229–33.
51 Samuels, *Securing Japan*, p. 165.
52 Samuels, *Securing Japan*, pp. 165–6.
53 Samuels, *Securing Japan*, p. 166.
54 Glenn D. Hook, Julie Gilson, Christopher W. Hughes and Hugo Dobson, *Japan's International Relations: Politics, Economics, and Security*, 2nd edn (London and New York: Routledge, 2001), p. 263.
55 On the evolution in regional defence cooperation culminating in the formation of the ADMM and ADMM-Plus, see See Seng Tan, '"Talking Their Walk"? The Evolution of Defence Regionalism in Southeast Asia', *Asian Security*, Vol. 8, No. 3 (2012), pp. 232–50.
56 On CSCAP, see See Seng Tan, *The Making of the Asia Pacific: Knowledge Brokers and the Politics of Representation* (Amsterdam: Amsterdam University Press, 2013), pp. 69–75.
57 Ko Hirano, 'China Wary of Hatoyama's "East Asian Community"', *The Japan Times*, 3 October 2009, www.japantimes.co.jp/news/2009/10/03/national/china-wary-of-hatoyamas-east-asian-community/#.VQ04XdGJjVI; Aurelia George Mulgan, 'Hatoyama's East Asia Community and Regional Leadership Rivalries', *East Asia*

Forum, 13 October 2009, www.eastasiaforum.org/2009/10/13/hatoyamas-east-asia-community/; and, Yoshihide Soeya, 'An East Asian Community and Japan-China relations', *East Asia Forum*, 17 May 2010 www.eastasiaforum.org/tag/eac/.
58 Glenn D. Hook, 'Japan and the ASEAN Regional Forum: Bilateralism, Multilateralism or Supplementalism?', *Japanstudien*, Vol. 10 (1998), pp. 159–88.
59 Green, *Japan's Reluctant Realism*.
60 Christopher W. Hughes, *Japan's Security Policy and the War on Terror: Steady Incrementalism or a Radical Leap?*, CSGR Working Paper No. 104/02 (Coventry: Centre for the Study of Globalization and Regionalization, Warwick University, 2002).
61 Hughes, *Japan's Re-emergence as a 'Normal' Military Power*.
62 Tang Siew Mun, 'Japan's Grand Strategic Shift from Yoshida to Koizumi: Reflections on Japan's Strategic Focus in the 21st Century', *Akademika*, No. 70 (2007), p. 117.
63 Singh, *Japan's Security Identity*.
64 Linda Sieg and Kiyoshi Takenaka, 'Japan to Bolster Military, Boost Asia Ties to Counter China', *Reuters*, 17 December 2013 www.reuters.com/article/2013/12/17/us-japan-security-idUSBRE9BG02S20131217. Abe pledged at the December 2012 elections, which he won, to implement a more assertive foreign policy and to build a stronger military. Yuka Hayashi, 'Abe Tells Obama Japan Will Boost Its Defence', *The Wall Street Journal*, 22 February 2013, www.wsj.com/articles/SB10001424127887324503204578320640390164434.
65 Hiroko Tabuchi, 'With Shrine Visit, Leader Asserts Japan's Track from Pacifism', *The New York Times*, 26 December 2013, www.nytimes.com/2013/12/27/world/asia/japanese-premier-visits-contentious-war-shrine.html?_r=0.
66 As Bosco has noted, 'The entrapment problem [for the United States] is occasioned by American worries that longstanding security arrangements could drag the United States into a Chinese–Japanese, Chinese–Taiwanese or Chinese–Filipino conflict'. Joseph A. Bosco, 'Entrapment and Abandonment in Asia', *The National Interest*, 8 July 2013, http://nationalinterest.org/commentary/entrapment-abandonment-asia-8697. On entrapment and abandonment in alliance politics more broadly, see Glenn H. Snyder, *Alliance Politics* (Ithaca, NY: Cornell University Press, 2007).
67 David M. Malone and Yuen Foong Khong, 'Unilateralism and US Foreign Policy: International Perspectives', in Malone and Khong, eds., *Unilateralism and US Foreign Policy* (Boulder, CO: Lynne Rienner, 2003), pp. 1–19
68 Kevin J. Cooney, *Japan's Foreign Policy Maturation: A Quest for Normalcy* (London: Routledge, 2002)
69 Hughes, 'Japan's Response to China's Rise'.
70 Ken Jimbo, Ryo Sahashi, Sugio Takahashi, Yasuyo Sakata, Masayuki Masuda and Takeshi Yuzawa, *Japan's Security Strategy toward China: Integration, Balancing, and Deterrence in the Era of Power Shift* (Tokyo: The Tokyo Foundation, 2011), p. 6.
71 Gerard Baker and Jacob M. Schlesinger, 'Abe's Strategy: Rearrange Region's Power Balance', *The Wall Street Journal*, 26 May 2014, www.wsj.com/articles/SB10001424052702304811904579585702903470312.
72 Tom Clifford, 'Abe and the Re-Militarization of Japan', *Counterpunch*, 1 April 2014 www.counterpunch.org/2014/04/01/abe-and-the-re-militarization-of-japan/; Shunsuke Hirose, 'Shinzo Abe's Biggest Enemy: the LDP', *The Diplomat*, 14 April 2014, http://thediplomat.com/2014/04/shinzo-abes-biggest-enemy-the-ldp/.
73 Memorably, Abe's first stint in office in 2006–7 was cut short because of this larger agenda. Tabuchi, 'With Shrine Visit, Leader Asserts Japan's Track from Pacifism'.
74 Quoted in Jeremy Au Yong, 'Japan Gets a Rare Rebuke from its Close Ally US', *The Straits Times*, 28 December 2013, p. A8.
75 Bosco, 'Entrapment and Abandonment in Asia'.
76 Ulises Granados, *US Involvement in the Sino-Japanese Diayu/Senkaku Conflict: Finding Solutions for Stability in the East China Sea*, prepared for 2013 East Asia

Security Symposium and Conference (Robina, QLD: East Asia Security Centre, Bond University, 2014), p. 5. As a *New York Times* editorial has tersely noted, 'Japan's military adventures are only possible with American support; the United States needs to make it clear that Mr. Abe's agenda is not in the region's interest'. The Editorial Board, 'Editorial: Risky Nationalism in Japan', *The New York Times*, 26 December 2013.

77  Another analyst compared Abe's visit to a visit by a German chancellor to Auschwitz or Buchenwald in the midst of some disagreement with Israel: 'There is almost nothing a Japanese prime minister could have done that would have inflamed tempers more along the Japan–China–South Korea–US axis than to make this visit'. Michael J. Green and James Fallows, respectively, quoted in The Editorial Board, 'Editorial: Risky Nationalism in Japan'.

78  Prime Minister Takeo Fukuda famously pledged that Japan will never become a military power.

79  Shinzo Abe, 'The Bounty of the Open Seas: Five New Principles for Japanese Foreign Policy', *Prime Minister of Japan and his Cabinet*, 18 January 2013 www.kantei.go.jp/foreign/96_abe/statement/201301/18speech_e.html.

80  'Editorial: Abe Should Pursue Universal Values in Diplomacy with ASEAN', *The Asahi Shimbun*, 16 December 2013.

81  Ken Jimbo, 'Japan and Southeast Asia: Three Pillars of a New Strategic Relationship', The Tokyo Foundation, 30 May 2013, www.tokyofoundation.org/en/articles/2013/japan-and-southeast-asia.

82  Jimbo, 'Japan and Southeast Asia'.

83  Hannah Beech, 'Return of the Samurai', *Time*, 7 October 2013.

84  In this regard, Abe offered what seemed a somewhat dubious explanation for his recent shrine visit: he felt Japan's ties with China and South Korea could not get any worse than they already were. Kwan Weng Kin, 'Worsening Ties Embolden Abe to Make Shrine Visit', *The Straits Times*, 28 December 2013, www.straitstimes.com/st/print/1892198.

85  Terada, 'Directional Leadership in Institution-Building'.

86  'Keynote Address by Shinzo Abe, Prime Minister of Japan'.

87  Joshua Meltzer, Takuji Okubo, Brian Jackson and Jack Sheehan, 'TPP: What's at Stake with the Trade Deal?', *BBC News*, 22 April 2014, www.bbc.com/news/business-27107349.

88  'Japan Must Engage China, Freeze the Senkaku Debate: An Interview with Former Japanese Ambassador to China Niwa Uichirō', *Nippon.com*, 29 October 2013, www.nippon.com/en/people/e00050/.

89  Jimbo et al., *Japan's Security Strategy toward China*.

90  Stephen Grenville, 'The Trans-Pacific Partnership: Where Economics and Geopolitics Meet', *The Lowy Interpreter*, 4 March 2014, www.lowyinterpreter.org/post/2014/03/04/Trans-Pacific-Partnership-Where-economics-and-geopolitics-meet.aspx?COLLCC=3559796430&.

91  'U.S.–Japan Joint Statement: The United States and Japan: Shaping the Future of the Asia-Pacific and Beyond', *The White House: Office of the Press Secretary*, 25 April 2014, www.whitehouse.gov/the-press-office/2014/04/25/us-japan-joint-statement-united-states-and-japan-shaping-future-asia-pac.

92  Shannon Tiezzi, 'China's Response to the US Cyber Espionage Charges', *The Diplomat*, 21 May 2014 http://thediplomat.com/2014/05/chinas-response-to-the-us-cyber-espionage-charges/.

93  Patrick M. Cronin, Ely Ratner, Elbridge Coby, Zachary M. Hosford and Alexander Sullivan, *Tailored Coercion: Competition and Risk in Maritime Asia* (Washington, D.C.: Center for New American Security, 2014).

94  Leszek Buszynski and Christopher B. Roberts, *The South China Sea: Stabilization and Resolution*, Occasional Paper (Canberra, ACT: National Security College, Australian National University, 2013); Hugh White, 'Japanese Collective Self-Defense: Abe's

Changes Won't Help', *The Lowy Interpreter*, 4 July 2014, www.lowyinterpreter.org/post/2014/07/04/Japan-collective-self-defence-abe.aspx.

95 Rizal Sukma, 'Insight: East Asia Needs a Steering Committee', *The Jakarta Post*, 4 September 2014, www.thejakartapost.com/news/2012/09/04/insight-east-asia-needs-a-steering-committee.html.

96 Yuen Foong Khong, 'Coping with Strategic Uncertainty: The Role of Institutions and Soft Balancing in Southeast Asia's Post-Cold War Strategy', in J. J. Suh, Peter J. Katzenstein and Alan Carlson, eds., *Rethinking Security in East Asia: Identity, Power, and Efficiency* (Stanford, CA: Stanford University Press, 2004), pp. 172–298; T. J. Pempel, 'Soft Balancing, Hedging, and Institutional Darwinism: The Economic-Security Nexus and East Asian Regionalism', *Journal of East Asian Studies*, Vol. 10, No. 2 (2010), pp. 209–38.

97 Hughes, *Japan's Re-emergence as a 'Normal' Military Power*.

98 Edström, *Japan and Human Security*; Lam, 'Japan's Human Security Role in Southeast Asia'.

99 Tomotaka Shoji, 'Japan's Perspective on Security Environment in the Asia Pacific and Its Approach toward Multilateral Cooperation: Contradictory or Consistent?', Paper presented at the National Institute of Defense Studies (NIDS) International Symposium on Security, Tokyo, 12 November 2013, p. 2.

100 Hideshi Futori, 'Japan's Disaster Relief Diplomacy: Fostering Military Cooperation in Asia'. *Asia-Pacific Bulletin*, No. 213, 13 May 2013.

101 'New Year's Reflection by Prime Minister Shinzo Abe, January 1, 2015' (transcript provided by Japanese Embassy in Singapore, 7 January 2015).

# 6 China

To some, the notion of China rising might sound like a tired but by no means retired cliché. Far from having reached its full potential in terms of power and influence, China has in recent times served notice of its sense of assurance – or arrogance, for some – in its own clout. If Japan's foreign policy practice has evolved over the years from an indirect style to a more assertive one in conjunction with its normalization (as we saw in chapter 5), so too has China, it could be argued. For its part, China has evolved from the revolutionary state it had been under the ideological leadership of Mao Zedong, to a normal power under the pragmatic leadership of Deng Xiaoping and the leaders who succeeded him. By all indications, the question of China becoming a great and putatively responsible power, whether with Xi Jinping or a future Chinese leader as helmsman, is not one of 'if' but 'when'. From the 'keeping a low profile' orientation that had largely dominated Chinese foreign policy since Deng, China has in recent times exhibited a greater sense of self-confidence and diplomatic assertiveness in conjunction with its growing power and influence. Nowhere has this been more apparent than under the leadership of Xi, who, in a break from the tradition of secrecy adhered to by his predecessors, has shared publicly not only his nationalist vision of China's imminent rejuvenation as a great nation and power (the 'Chinese dream'[1]), but also his aims to double his country's gross domestic product (GDP) and per capita income and to establish a 'prosperous, strong, democratic, culturally advanced and harmonious' China by 2049 (the 'centenary goals'[2]). According to the noted China historian Jian Chen in 2008,

> China, in continuing its own course of development, found it necessary to establish an identity that would allow it to appear as an 'insider' in the US/West-dominated international system while, at the same time, emphasizing its unique contribution to the world's peace, stability and prosperity.[3]

Should Chinese grand strategy continue to hew to Chen's depiction – China's current position as the largest foreign holder of US Treasury debt (7.2 per cent in August 2014, with Japan second at 7.0 per cent[4]) is a likely indication of its continued support of the existing international system – it does and should not in any way connote obsequiousness on Beijing's part, if it did at all in the past.

Against that backdrop of China's growing power and prominence, this chapter considers China's participation in and contributions to multilateralism in Asia from the 1980s, when it began seriously to engage ASEAN, through to the present. China has evolved from a wary neophyte at multilateral diplomacy to a self-assured connoisseur and convenor of the practice. As a prominent China watcher has put it, 'China's perception of [multilateral] organizations [has] evolved from suspicion, to uncertainty, to supportiveness'.[5] On the one hand, the evolution of Chinese multilateral diplomacy in the post-Cold War years has been a sight to behold.[6] China's involvement in Asian multilateralism has not only provided it with a platform from which to promote if not protect its economic and security interests, but also, or so it is hoped, 'to calm regional concerns and reassure neighbours on how China will deploy its rising power and influence'.[7] The incentives for its near abroad are opportunities for increased trade and enhanced political ties with China and, further down the road, the collective formation of regional communities. The importance which the Chinese attach to outreach to their near abroad is clear in their multilateral commitments and conduct: strong, active and even creative in its near abroad, but decreasing steadily with distance away from China.[8] That many if not most Asian countries have sought to take advantage of economic cooperation with China is evidenced by the fact that China has supplanted Japan and/or the United States as their most important trading partner. This includes US allies such as Australia and Japan, which, as we have seen in the case of the Australian strategic community, has elicited public concern over a prospective costly dilemma for Australia should conflict between its key trading partner (China) and its key security ally (America) arise.[9]

In the diplomatic-strategic arena, Beijing has advanced, with relative success, the idea that its rise to power is an essentially 'peaceful' development that does not threaten others. It has patiently endured ('tolerated', according to the former head of CSCAP China) and benefited from US primacy and leadership in Asia, but of late has shown an increasing tendency to question that given the perceived decline in US power and influence in contrast to its own rising power and influence. In contrast to the United States and the former Soviet Union with their common emphasis on 'backyards', 'buffer zones' and 'spheres of influence', China, it has been argued, has avoided those strategies in favour of a regional 'community-building' approach.[10] Echoing his predecessors (going back as far as Deng the 'paramount leader'), Chinese President Xi Jinping has claimed that China would never seek 'hegemony or expansion' in the Asia-Pacific, even as it strengthens its diplomatic and military footprint in the region.[11] In the international economic arena, it has supported the World Trade Organization (WTO) and promoted unilateral and multilateral liberalization.[12] As an 'authoritarian capitalist' great power[13] – evolving and liberalizing in selective ways, to be sure, but with political power jealously guarded and maintained by the Chinese Community Party leadership – China has naturally sought to influence and shape its external security environment in ways that best benefit its nationalist ends. It has actively pursued engagement with the outside world and advocated regional integration with its near abroad. It has strong commercial ties with various African nations and has struck deals on trade facilitation, direct investment, cross-border infrastructure construction and development aid with the East African Community (EAC) and the Economic Community of West African States (ECOWAS) as well as contributing to the African Development Bank.[14] It has also reached out to the European region, particularly engaging central and eastern European states, through a 'one plus sixteen' strategy.[15]

On the other hand, the liberal supposition that multilateralism is a case of Lilliputians restraining Gulliver with institutional cords has shown itself idealistic if not overly simplistic in the context of Asia. If great powers as a rule do not make good multilateral players,[16] then China's involvement in Asia's regional arrangements has also highlighted the limits of socialization to institutional norms particularly as China has gone from strength to strength.[17] The idea that China's rise has been relatively peaceful, status quo-oriented, and a key pillar for a stable regional order has also received strong backing by noted scholars.[18] However, the perceptibly provocative actions taken by the Chinese in the East and South China Seas have fed regional circumspection over China's strategic intentions given the perceived gap between its words and deeds. In this regard, against the alleged crassness of some robustly realist interpretations with their ominous conclusions,[19] others have proposed that discrepancies between Beijing's assurances about its 'peaceful rise' or 'peaceful development' (as the Chinese call it), on the one hand, and its perceived assertiveness over its maritime disputes on the other are better explained by recourse to identity-based considerations, where China's national security is closely tied to its nationalist insecurities.[20] To be sure, China seeks constructive relationships with the other great powers and tries to avoid confrontation with any of them – a condition which it deems necessary for its peaceful rise. But not every Asian country is persuaded that a China-centric order in Asia is a good thing.[21]

## China and Asian multilateralism

Getting the People's Republic in from the revolutionary cold and into the regional fold, as it were, has long been the regional 'game plan' of ASEAN (certainly Indonesia's, as we shall see in chapter 8). The strategy (to the extent that it could be so called) has essentially involved extending the ASEAN model of regional security – the ASEAN *modus operandi* of soft regionalism and process-driven institutionalism – to the wider Asia-Pacific region, and providing great and regional powers with a stake in the preservation and promotion of the peace and prosperity of Asia. ASEAN's regionalist approach to engaging China has been partly informed by the collective historical experience of the ASEAN member states in engaging post-*konfrontasi* (confrontation) Indonesia. In this regard, the Association's model of security regionalism can be understood as a historically tried-and-tested strategy that committed New Order Indonesia to the region through an ASEAN framework that not only provided Jakarta with a regional leadership role but concomitantly assured recognition of sovereignty and non-interference for the other member nations. In like fashion, the ASEAN model would permit the endorsement of China as a status quo leader – though not ahead of America in the power hierarchy necessarily – and responsible power/stakeholder of the web of regional institutions and ties within which it is enmeshed.[22] It is likely that ASEAN's complex yet provisional engagement of China has had a part to play in facilitating China's successive permutations from revolutionary regime to normal state to, if only embryonic, responsible great power (although it should be said that this contention – qualified at best – does not insist that ontological priority be granted ASEAN as the causal agent of change).

Reciprocity played a significant part as both parties learned to accommodate one another. By the 1970s onwards China had, in fits and starts, volitionally begun its incremental shift away from ideology and towards pragmatism in its conduct of international affairs. This transition has more or less continued throughout the post-Cold War period to the present. In theoretical terms, it could be said that the evolution of Chinese foreign policy through successive political leaderships – from that of Mao Zedong, Deng Xiaopeng, Jiang Zemin, Hu Jintao and now Xi Jinping – reflects a China in transition from a quasi-expansionist state, at least in terms of its ideological support for communist movements throughout Southeast Asia during the Cold War, to a 'security seeker' rather than an 'offensive realist' aggrandizer.[23] Arguably, ASEAN's 'China policy' – at times robust and concerted, at other times ambivalent and disjointed – played a relatively significant role in assuaging the latter's concerns over perceived risks about its assimilation into the post-Cold War regional order. To be sure, other factors are equally important, not least China's changing assessment, under Deng's leadership, that nuclear war with America was not inevitable, and its pragmatic emphasis on national economic development, which essentially denoted a growing reliance upon and support for the US-led liberal international economic order.[24] Indeed, other than occasional hints of bellicosity where the Taiwan Straits in the 1990s and, in more recent times, the East and South China Seas are concerned, China has continually prized the stability and prosperity of the region, and to that extent has largely supported the regional status quo.

## Coming in from the cold

It bears reminding that when ASEAN was formed in 1967, China branded the organization as an anti-Chinese, anti-communist alliance.[25] Be that as it may, Beijing's engagement with ASEAN began during the Cold War years in the context of the Cambodian conflict.[26] That Indonesia under Sukarno was one of the first countries officially to recognize the newly established People's Republic of China in 1950 probably facilitated ties, despite Indonesia's troubles with communism in the mid-1960s and Suharto's eventual normalization of ties with Beijing in 1990. Despite the pervasive concern with the prospect of Beijing's ideological influence upon internal communist subversion within Southeast Asian societies – especially Indonesia, Malaysia and Singapore – the Third Indochina War, which lasted throughout the 1980s, saw a cementing of the China–ASEAN political relationship as a consequence of China's need for ASEAN's diplomatic backing against China's main Cold War adversaries,

Vietnam and the Soviet Union, and ASEAN's commensurate reliance on Chinese support in its diplomatic effort to prevent non-communist Southeast Asia from falling into Vietnamese hands.[27]

Moreover, the Sino-Soviet split during the late 1960s and Sino-US rapprochement of the early 1970s probably contributed, if only indirectly, to ameliorating concerns among ASEAN states regarding collaboration with China. In rejoinder to Washington's attempt at rapprochement, Beijing apparently surprised the United States – and probably the ASEAN countries – by insisting it had always been Chinese policy 'to maintain friendly relations with all states, regardless of social system, on the basis of the Five Principles of Peaceful Coexistence'.[28] This proved a crucial gesture signalled China's intent for rapprochement and cooperation. In a manner of speaking, Beijing also signalled its tacit acceptance of Washington's policy of geopolitical triangulation, and its readiness to play this game to enhance both its and Washington's strategic interests at Moscow's expense.[29] Following the Vietnamese invasion of Cambodia in late December 1978, the Chinese conveyed their willingness to cooperate with ASEAN, with the latter reciprocating in kind. Mutual reassurance arguably provided a basis for China–ASEAN cooperation against a perceived common threat. Indeed, more than reassurance alone, China actively sought ASEAN's involvement, as evidenced by repeated Vietnamese warnings against Chinese efforts at 'promoting confrontation' between the ASEAN states and Vietnam. Indeed, Hanoi insisted that rather than pressure Vietnam, ASEAN should pressure China to find a solution to the Cambodian question.[30] In this respect, *de facto* China–ASEAN cooperation against Vietnam emerged as a function of mutual expedience. Nevertheless, that very basis for cooperation was removed following the termination of the Cold War and the settlement of the Cambodian conflict.

From as early as 1989, China, it could be said, morphed from a strategic partner of ASEAN to a strategic competitor of sorts with the dissolution of the Soviet-Vietnamese threat. That said, China was less a competitor, if by this we mean a countervailing power, than a rising hegemonic presence for the considerably weaker ASEAN states – particularly the Indochinese countries as they respectively assumed ASEAN membership in the 1990s – whose relations with China principally focused on managing their respective vulnerabilities and dependencies *vis-à-vis* the latter.[31] If anything, the sheer enormity of the Chinese presence in the region is something that could neither be ignored nor, for that matter, refused by China's considerably smaller and/or weaker regional counterparts. And no amount of protestations to the effect that China's rise in the post-Cold War period is inherently 'peaceful' would likely convince all Southeast Asians to be completely reassured about Chinese intentions, not least when China's prodigious growth might (or, for some, has already) come at the ASEAN region's expense where the (perceived) competition over foreign direct investments have been concerned.[32]

China began its involvement in the initial manifestations of Asia's new regionalisms, APEC and the ARF, with a fair bit of suspicion about the true intent behind such 'new regionalisms' and concerned over their possible use by the United States and others to constrain China's rise. As Jing-dong Yuan has observed:

China is strongly opposed to establishing any institutionalized mechanisms for dealing with regional security issues since the countries in the region are vastly different in terms of history, culture, political and social systems, and different visions of national security and priorities. An OSCE-type institutional arrangement not only will not be able to deal with the complexity of issues but also likely falls under the control of certain powers. Indeed, Chinese analysts assert that a direct transplant of the CSCE model to the Asia-Pacific region is impractical and may even be counterproductive.[33]

But while the existence of balancing dynamics within Asia's multilateral institutions is undeniable, the architects of the APEC and the ARF (as we have seen with the ASEAN, Australia, Indonesia and Japan chapters in this book) also envisioned their creations as institutional platforms to engage deeply a post-revolutionary China and help socialize its evolution towards becoming a 'normal' and 'responsible' power.[34] Following Asia's financial crisis of 1997–8, China's reputation as a regional stakeholder and putative provider of regional public goods benefited indirectly from the perceived highhandedness of the United States and the International Monetary Fund (IMF), which not only imposed on ailing East Asian economies stringent structural conditions but effectively squashed Japan's proposal for an Asian Monetary Fund (see chapter 5).[35] In the light of the bitter pill East Asians were forced to swallow at a time when they most needed America's and the IMF's support, China's readiness to advance a form of regionalism that excludes the United States paved the way to the formation of the APT and a currency swap arrangement, the Chiang Mai Initiative (CMI).[36] China also began placing a great deal of emphasis on its engagement with Southeast Asia. Although the Master Plan in ASEAN Connectivity (MPAC) unveiled in 2010 drew attention to the issue of China–ASEAN 'connectivity', infrastructural links between China and the ASEAN region effectively began in the 1990s with China's southern provinces, especially Yunnan and Guangxi, as key nodes within those infrastructural corridors.

Paradoxically, the burnishing of China's growing reputation as the region's friend in a time of dire need did not transfer easily over to the security dimension. In security terms, China consistently advanced its principles of peaceful coexistence and, since 1996–7, promoted a 'new security concept' that emphasizes equality, mutual trust, respect and cooperation, consensus through consultation and the peace settlement of disputes.[37] And although Chinese intellectual and policy contributions to the concept and practice of non-traditional security (NTS) did not systematically develop until 2003 in the wake of the SARS crisis, it is fair to say that its initial ruminations about non-traditional concerns had their origins in the new security concept.[38] The early 1990s also witnessed China's initial involvements in United Nations-led peacekeeping, which by 2012 had grown to nearly 2,000 Chinese peacekeepers participating in nine UN peace missions around the world.[39] But few, not least other claimant states over the South China Sea, were convinced that China's rise was entirely peaceful. Indeed, so acute was the threat perception that China apparently posed to ASEAN states in the immediate post-Cold War period – indeed, as early as 1991 if not earlier – that the prospect of China resorting to direct military coercion in support of its maritime claims could not be discounted.[40] In this respect, instances of China's territorial disputes with several ASEAN states – with the Philippines over Mischief Reef and Scarborough Shoal and with Vietnam over land and sea borders in the 1990s – have since become, for the Southeast Asian claimant states, a stark warning against unwarranted presumptions about China's goodwill. If anything, Chinese actions in the South China Sea, correctly or otherwise, have given credence to regional worries that Beijing's strategic objective for China is to turn the entire South China Sea into a Chinese lake.[41] This thinking has clearly not gone away. For example, it has been argued that Chinese strategic thinkers are predisposed to regard the South China Sea, seen through the lens of the American naval strategist Mahan, 'as a preserve where commercial and political imperatives demand dominant [Chinese] naval power'; in short, China views the South China Sea as its own 'Caribbean'.[42] A difficulty complicating Chinese attempts to reassure their neighbours has to do with China's lack of transparency concerning its security policy, which hampered attempts by ASEAN security planners at forming assessments of Chinese intentions and likely actions. More crucial than prospects for potential conflict, however, is the fact that all sides have by and large sought to avoid tensions and promote an atmosphere of mutual respect and cooperation.[43] Elsewhere, it has been argued that the South China Sea has remained primarily a political rather than military consideration due to China's desire to accommodate the concerns of the ASEAN states and the limited naval capabilities of the various claimants[44] (a situation obviously complicated in the late 2000s by the US and Japanese efforts to strengthen the maritime capacities of some of the claimant states, such as Japan's supply of patrol boats to enhance the Philippine Coast Guard's maritime surveillance capabilities in the disputed waters[45]).

Remarkably, it is against this backdrop of strategic asymmetry and pervasive regional circumspection about China's strategic intentions, on the one hand, and initial Chinese reservations about participating in ASEAN-centred institutions on the other that a marked improvement in China's ties with ASEAN during the 1990s nevertheless occurred. It reflected the growing agreement on questions of regional peace, prosperity and security and the ways those questions are best approached. Yet such progress was best measured not in terms of 'headline-making cooperative ventures' but by a process of gradualism or 'mundane accomplishments', that is, various minor achievements in the minutiae of functional cooperation.[46] A variety of parallel frameworks for dialogue emerged within the decade. Beginning in 1991, when Chinese foreign minister Qian Qichen was invited to attend the opening ceremony of that year's ASEAN ministerial meeting, China became a consultative partner in 1992, joined the ARF as a founding member in 1994, and 'graduated' to become official dialogue partner of ASEAN in 1996. In 1997, the first ever China–ASEAN summit was conducted in Malaysia, where President Jiang and his ASEAN counterparts issued a joint statement on the collective decision to establish a partnership of good neighbourliness and mutual trust between the two parties, thereby providing the groundwork for the 'strategic partnership for peace and prosperity' announced in 2003. What conceivably led the Chinese to set aside their initial reservations about joining and participating in the myriad regional arrangements, particularly the ARF, could be partly attributed to the process-oriented ASEAN Way, whose holistic emphasis on the common search for new areas of agreement rather than a contractually driven form of cooperation probably persuaded Beijing that its interests would not discounted.[47] The very principles of the ASEAN Way have clearly resonated well with China. As Alice Ba has argued, ASEAN's pursuit of 'complex engagement' – 'informal, non-confrontational, open-ended and mutual' – probably swayed China to reconsider its relations with ASEAN, to view ASEAN more positively, and to be more responsive to ASEAN's concerns.[48] The readiness to grant China a say – an overly huge say, some critics would probably suggest – was clearly apparent, for instance, when the ARF acceded to China's demand that the third phase of regional security cooperation as envisaged in the 1995 ARF Concept Paper – 'conflict resolution' – be amended to 'the elaboration of approaches to conflict'.[49]

That China shares in the so-called illiberal values held by a number of ASEAN countries probably worked in the latter's favour.[50] In this regard, it is possible that the controversial 'Asian values' debate of the 1990s sparked by European criticisms of ASEAN and the rejoinders to that by some of Asia's political leaders and public intellectuals – several from Singapore alone[51] – aided ASEAN's engagement effort, not least by proving to China that ASEAN was no lackey of the West. On its part, China's growing involvement in and enthusiasm for ASEAN-based regionalisms could also be viewed as indications of its willingness for cooperation and the exercise of strategic restraint. According to an analyst, 'Beijing's move to involve itself in ASEAN activities since the early 1990s was part of the country's "good-neighbourliness" policy [*mulin zhengce*] that aimed at strengthening its ties with the neighbouring countries in the wake of the Tiananmen Incident in 1989', rather than a new orientation in the conduct of Chinese foreign policy.[52] Whether the Indonesian precedent (as we shall see in Chapter 8) influenced Chinese behaviour towards Southeast Asia is uncertain. But what seemed clear enough at that point was ASEAN's apparent belief that the Chinese penchant for good neighbourliness and strategic restraint deserved strong encouragement and reinforcement, with the promise of regional recognition of China's proper place as a regional leader, but one very much within an ASEAN-centred framework. It amounted to an invitation to China to assume its place in the regional order as a responsible stakeholder on ASEAN's terms.

## From charming to offensive

Much of the first decade of this present century was marked by the intensification in China's ties with the ASEAN region that built upon the developments of the 1990s. In 2002, Chinese goodwill led to the establishment of joint declarations on cooperation in non-traditional security issues as well as on the South China Sea. In the latter instance, the DOC was not quite an actual regional code of conduct as some ASEAN countries had hoped for, but constituted a step in the right direction.[53] In 2003, China became the first extra-regional power to sign the Treaty of Amity and Cooperation. Following a period of inactivity – a lost opportunity in the view of many analysts – both sides subsequently agreed at their 2007 bilateral summit to expedite progress towards the establishment of a regional code of conduct. The other crucial development of 2002 was the agreement to establish a free trade agreement between China and ASEAN. The FTA deal clearly caught the Japanese unawares and led to Tokyo's attempt to catch up with the Chinese in 2005 in negotiating its own FTA with ASEAN. Further, as noted, China inked a strategic partnership with ASEAN in 2003. To the extent that Chinese reassurance succeeded in its aims, East Asian countries for the most part found China in the early to mid-2000s 'a good neighbour, a constructive partner, a careful listener, and a non-threatening regional power'.[54] To be sure, Chinese disappointment over opposition to its vision for the EAS as naturally comprising only the membership of the APT caused a division of sorts between those who supported the EAS and those who favoured the APT as the appropriate regional vehicle to establish the proposed East Asia Community (EAC).[55] China strongly supported an EAS that went beyond the APT's membership because it viewed the proposed summit as the logical evolution of the APT from a ministerial-level forum to a leaders-led gathering. As we saw in chapter 5, Beijing's understanding clashed, however, with Tokyo's vision of an EAC that would include Australia and New Zealand with the ten APT countries, and Singapore's insistence that India should also be included in such an arrangement.[56] But there have been indications that, beyond the rhetoric, Beijing is prepared to countenance the EAS as a possible framework for regional economic integration notwithstanding its preferences.[57]

Notwithstanding its differences with ASEAN over the shape and substance of East Asian regionalism, China nonetheless played an indirect but no less key role in thwarting the Australian leader Kevin Rudd's APC proposal. As noted in chapter 4, the Chinese, for quite different reasons, joined with the Americans in not supporting Rudd's idea, presumably because the Australian defence white paper of 2009 which the Rudd government published made no bones about the strategic threat that China purportedly posed to Australia even if the document offered no specifics but referred only to a 'major military adversary'. In 2012, it was revealed that the Rudd government conducted a secret assessment on the risks of a Chinese attack and made detailed plans for possible military action against China.[58] Whether the Chinese had prior knowledge of that development was in a sense immaterial as the notion of sharing power in co-managing Asia in a concert-like arrangement that would marginalize ASEAN – as envisaged in subsequent iterations of the APC idea – was presumably something to which the Chinese would not be particularly favourable.

Beyond East Asia, China's part in the formation of the Shanghai Cooperation Organization (SCO) in 2001 has partly been attributed to its experiences in the ARF and the like.[59] Currently limited to six members (China, Russia, Kazakhstan, Kyrgyzstan, Tajikistan and Uzbekistan), the SCO has hitherto kept its focus on security issues, namely, counterterrorism cooperation. With the SCO seeking to add new members – of the eight countries that presently enjoy observer and/or dialogue partner status in the SCO, India, Iran and Pakistan are touted as the most likely to become members in the foreseeable future – as well as broaden its remit to include intramural economic integration, China and SCO counterparts are likely to focus their collective efforts in 2015 on establishing a legal basis to accommodate those intended activities.[60] It bears reminding, however, that the goal of economic integration did not originate with the SCO but with its predecessor arrangement, the Shanghai Five, which was formed in 1996 by current SCO states with the exception of Uzbekistan. But the fulfilment of this initial ambition would be thwarted by a combination of the Shanghai Five's failure to implement its own economic vision, Deng's emphasis on China's eastern coastal regions as the preferred zones for the country's economic modernization and Deng's penchant for China to maintain a low profile.[61] China's pressing need today to find new export markets and, more crucially, close the developmental and wealth gaps between the well-developed eastern seaboard of China and its economically depressed (and security-challenged) western provinces is behind China's 'one belt, one road' notion. In this regard, the SCO, as the successor to the Shanghai Five, is seen as the logical regional vehicle to implement that envisaged economic belt, or at least to provide the overarching framework for bottom-up processes of integration.[62] Furthermore, the argument could be made that under Chinese leadership, the SCO has demonstrated a strong potential for rule-based regionalism should Beijing and its counterparts collectively decide to institutionalize their organization. For instance, it has been suggested that Russia's failure in August 2008 to obtain the SCO's endorsement of its push to blame Georgia for their short war over South Ossetia – and, subsequently and more crucially, Russia's *acceptance* of the SCO's decision – indicated the relative institutional stoutness of the SCO.[63] On the other hand, Russian acquiescence on that occasion could have been implicit acknowledgement of China's *de facto* position as the dominant actor within the SCO (just as Russia is the undisputed dominant actor within the Collective Security Treaty Organization).

By 2009, Beijing's charm offensive towards the East Asian region had more or less ended. On 7 May that year, China submitted its infamous nine-dashed lines map – the original was an eleven-dashed lines map issued by China's Kuomintang government in 1947 – which looked to claim the entire South China Sea as part of its maritime territory. The Chinese action was probably provoked by the Malaysian and Vietnamese submissions the day before (on 6 May 2009) to the Commission on the Limits of the Continental Shelf of the UNCLOS (United Nations Convention on the Law of the Sea). A hardening in Chinese strategy arose putatively in response to the US rebalancing strategy, which prompted the gravitation to the United States by some regional states that had benefited from a decade of Chinese goodwill – arguably a costly act of signalling by China that failed to secure Southeast Asian loyalties where it mattered most.[64] By December, China, fairly or otherwise, would gain international notoriety for its purported intransigence and obduracy at the Copenhagen climate change conference, which prevented any deal from emerging.[65] Perceived Chinese provocations in the East and South

China Seas and robust responses by the United States led to the ARF becoming an arena for heated Sino-US debates – such as the exchange between Yang Jiechi and Hillary Clinton at the 2010 ARF meeting and that between Wang Yi and John Kerry at the 2014 ARF meeting – to the consternation of ASEAN. It clearly had an impact on ASEAN's intramural cohesion as the organization's failure to produce a communiqué at the end of its ministerial meeting in Phnom Penh in July 2012 – courtesy of Cambodia's actions as the chair of ASEAN in 2012, presumably out of concern for China's interests – implied.[66]

China has also demonstrated its readiness to employ sanctions against those whom it deems are opposing it, as it did with the Philippines in 2012 over Scarborough Shoal.[67] Moreover, China's use of gunboat diplomacy – albeit mostly with the use of Chinese coastguard 'white hulls' and (as a Japanese diplomat once put it) 'militant fishermen' – in the East and South China Seas, otherwise calibrated to avoid direct military confrontation with the United States, runs the risk of provoking rather than mitigating conflict despite its express intent to ensure regional stability. While ASEAN's apparent inability to broker solutions to those big power disagreements has been seen by some as reflective of the organization's effeteness as a regional leader, that the ARF – more by accident rather than design – has evolved into a multilateral mechanism for serious debate instead of vacuous platitudes might not necessarily be a bad thing. For example, in March 1996, China's military exercises aimed at intimidating Taiwan and influencing the outcome of its presidential election led to a US deployment of two carrier squadrons to deter further Chinese actions. It has been argued that the ARF at the time furnished a convenient vehicle for the Chinese and the Americans to engage in mutual crisis management, which led to the eventual de-escalation of the crisis.[68] Not all that China did in 2009 troubled the region, however. Together with its APT counterparts at a gathering of East Asian finance ministers and central bank governors in February, China agreed to establish the Chiang Mai Initiative Multilateralization (CMIM), a US$120 billion reserve currency pool of which the Chinese would be one of its largest contributors. In 2012, the pool was doubled to US$240 billion.

Whether the effective conclusion of the charm offensive had to do with the rise of Xi Jinping to the vice-presidency in 2008 is debatable. It has been suggested that relative to its past history, the 'newly assertive' brand of Chinese diplomacy which purportedly emerged in 2009 was neither new nor assertive, even though there was no question where Chinese words and deeds in response to the South China Sea were concerned.[69] What could have spurred Beijing's diplomatic assertiveness was its abiding concern over perceived US interference in the maritime disputes issue at a time when China needed the regional strategic environment to remain relatively calm and stable in order to facilitate a smooth transition for its top leadership between 2012 (when Xi was due to take over the reins of the Chinese Community Party and the Central Military Commission) and 2013 (when Xi would become president).[70] That being said, the case could be made that with leadership transition also comes a policy transition, where Beijing no longer feels the need to keep a low profile as it did during the Deng years. This would naturally include the perception that China no longer has to accept wholesale rules rendered by other big powers. Indeed, so careful had China been in downplaying its ascendance in the past that it assiduously avoided trumpeting its soft power policy for fear that it could be used paradoxically by Western critics as indirect evidence to support the purported existence of a 'China threat' and the perceived need to camouflage that.[71] With China having come into its own, such obsequiousness would no longer be necessary. Nowhere was this more evident than at the Sunnylands summit between Xi Jinping and Barack Obama in June 2013. President Xi outlined China's two key wishes: one, for respect from the United States, and two, for 'a new relationship among major powers' to be forged between the two countries. While President Obama acknowledged the need for a 'new model of cooperation', he reportedly avoided use of the Chinese phraseology of a 'new model of major country relationships',[72] hinting perhaps that, in Washington's view, China as a power is neither responsible nor major just yet. Whatever America's perception of China, it has not prevented the latter from an ambitious effort to re-engage the Asian region, including through the new multilateral ideas and innovations.

## China's 'new normal'?

The absence of Obama at both the APEC and EAS summits in Bali, Indonesia in October 2013 as a consequence of the federal shutdown in the United States coincided with a Chinese 'charm offensive 2.0', which saw both Xi and Premier Li Keqiang making the rounds in Southeast Asia, which both used to effect in promoting China's 'maritime Silk Road' vision. As conceived, the maritime Silk Road is an economic waterway and trade route that would link the Indian and Pacific Oceans. The still vague idea of the maritime Silk Road has hitherto attracted prospective discussions on 'connectivity' involving environmental protection, fisheries and trade cooperation; at the same time, it has also evoked concerns over how this proposal relates to China's aspiration to become a great maritime power.[73] Originally mooted in the early 1990s by Chinese leaders in the wake of the collapse of the Soviet Union, the concept marked an attempt by Beijing to strengthen cooperation with the newly formed states of the post-Soviet era. However, as noted, China's early outreach to its west and south did not really take root owing to a combination of the slowness of the Shanghai Five arrangement. While a number of South and Southeast Asian states have indicated interest in the idea, others see in the maritime Silk Road a potentially uneasy correspondence with the so-called 'string of pearls', that is, China's network of maritime facilities in the Pacific and Indian Oceans.[74]

But while most Chinese commentators have tended to emphasize the maritime Silk Road as a new driving force for the prosperity of the entire East Asian region, others wary of Chinese intentions have drawn links to the military connotation associated with the 'string of pearls' – a notion that did not originate with the Chinese but was introduced courtesy of a 2004 report by the US defence contractor, Booze Allen Hamilton[75] – and the vision, advanced first by Hu Jintao, to build

China into a maritime power that would 'resolutely safeguard China's maritime rights and interests'.[76] Much as the Chinese tend to see US rebalancing as principally a military policy despite the Obama administration's incessant efforts to explain otherwise, the same probably holds true for the maritime Silk Road/string of pearls vision, which China's wary neighbours may see, fairly or otherwise, as a Chinese ploy to gain strategic control of the Indo-Pacific waterways. Much as America's efforts at economic engagement with Asia via the TPP have been viewed by Beijing, fairly or otherwise, as part of Washington's alleged containment effort against China's continued rise, China's own attempts at providing leadership in regional security have been viewed as excluding the United States. This perception has been indirectly aided by Beijing's inopportunely labelled 'anti-access/ anti-denial' (A2/AD) strategy, which refers to Chinese military capabilities and tactics aimed at preventing US forces from entering into a theatre of operations (anti-access) and, failing that, preventing their freedom of action in the more narrow confines of the area under China's direct control (area-denial).[77]

Also featured in October 2013 was a worrying trend in Chinese behaviour towards its fellow maritime disputants. For example, China's relations with Vietnam, on the mend following Li's visit to Hanoi in October which produced agreements to enhance bilateral cooperation in several issue areas, have since been severely undermined by China's deployment of an oil rig in a maritime boundary area not far from Vietnam's shoreline, which elicited anti-Chinese violence in Vietnam and the forced evacuation of thousands of Chinese citizens from Vietnam.[78] Much of international media coverage has hitherto asserted the illegality of the Chinese move; others however have suggested that the effective occupation and administration by China of Woody Island – 'Phú Lâm' to the Vietnamese and 'Yongxing' to the Chinese – barely eighty nautical miles from the oil rig's location, could benefit China more than Vietnam should a legal solution through the International Tribunal for the Law of the Sea (ITLOS) be sought.[79] That said, what has mystified many observers is why China did what it did at the expense of its rapprochement with Vietnam. Beijing's apparent willingness to subvert its reconciliation efforts with other claimants has raised questions about its strategic aims and the seemingly contradictory approaches it has adopted to achieving them.

In many ways, 2014 marked China's emergence as not only an active and assertive global power but one that seeks to prove its responsibility as a provider of global public goods. Nowhere has this been more apparent than in Chinese putative achievements in Asian multilateralism, both those chaired by China and those in which it participated. At the APEC summit in Beijing in November, China demonstrated economic leadership in calling for the creation of a Free Trade Area of the Asia-Pacific (FTAAP) – a vision which APEC members readily embrace, despite America's reservations, and to which the Chinese have committed a 'Silk Road' fund worth $40 billion for infrastructure-related investments. Also in 2014, Beijing's successful conclusion of free trade pacts with Australia and South Korea has only added to China's lustre. China will reportedly invest US$1.25 trillion abroad over the next ten years, and import more than US$10 trillion in goods in the next five years.[80] 'As its overall national strength grows', as President Xi noted in his address to the APEC CEO Summit in November, 'China will be both capable and willing to provide more public goods for the Asia-Pacific and the world, especially new initiatives and visions for enhancing regional cooperation'. In language reminiscent of his 'Chinese dream', Xi told his audience in Beijing, 'We are duty-bound to create and fulfil an Asia-Pacific dream for our people'.[81] That said, according to Alan Bollard, executive director of the APEC secretariat, 'None of the economies want to start negotiating on the FTAAP. It is far too early to do that'.[82]

In October of that same year, Beijing launched its controversial idea for an international development bank, the Asian Infrastructure Investment Bank (AIIB), which twenty-one countries have hitherto joined.[83] The AIIB was set up with the aim of building a US$100 billion fund – with the Chinese pledging to contribute half of that amount in initial capital – to finance infrastructure projects in developing parts of Asia. There is no question that the Asian region is hungry for infrastructure financing. For example, the Asian Development Bank (ADB), whose own portfolio stands at US$165 million and whose largest and most influential funders are the Americans and the Japanese, has estimated that developing countries in Asia require US$800 billion in infrastructure funding on an annual basis – and, arguably, as much as US$8 trillion by 2020 – although its loans for 2013 totalled a mere US$21 billion.[84] But while the AIIB has been welcomed by developing countries (which, in any case, would logically comprise its key beneficiaries) it has nonetheless been viewed by others in the region – certainly by the ADB, hitherto Asia's sole regional development bank, although Beijing reportedly has bigger plans for the AIIB than just positioning it as a regional bank[85] – as a bald attempt on Beijing's part to compete with the United States, Europe and Japan as the development lenders of first resort. Be that as it may, China had evidently hoped to attract support from so-called the region's 'marquee lenders' – particularly its fellow major contributor to the CMIM, South Korea (with Japan, as a key pillar of the ADB, opposed to the AIIB), as well as Australia and some European nations – but to no avail given the quiet but aggressive lobbying by the United States against the AIIB idea.[86]

China is also a founding member of the RCEP, the sixteen-party free trade agreement (FTA) comprising ASEAN countries and the regional grouping's FTA partners (Australia, India, Japan, Korea, New Zealand and of course China), which was formally introduced in November 2011 and whose negotiations began on the margins of the EAS in November 2012. Although based on existing 'ASEAN plus one' FTAs between ASEAN and those six dialogue partners, its proposed rules of origin (ROOs) differ from the former in that the RCEP aims to harmonize the extant ROOs of the six FTAs in question.[87] At the same time, China has indicated it would keep its options open regarding the TPP.[88] At the Conference on Interaction and Confidence-Building Measures in Asia (CICA) held in Shanghai in May 2014, Xi pledged that China would stick to peaceful methods to resolve its disputes over territory.[89] Echoing his predecessors, Xi has claimed that China would never seek 'hegemony or expansion' in the Asia-Pacific, even as it strengthens its diplomatic and military footprint in the region.[90] The logic undergirding Xi's pledge, according to analysts, is a new security paradigm' that China wishes to promote, where elements such as mutual respect and understanding and the search for common ground while shelving differences would provide the basis for Asian security to 'be handled in the Asian way'.[91] As another of Xi's initiatives, the CICA could in a sense be regarded as the security counterpart of the AIIB and the New Silk Road initiatives. Finally, the Chinese People's Liberation Army (PLA) has been a committed participant in regional joint exercises in humanitarian assistance and disaster relief (HADR) and military medicine conducted under the aegis of the ADMM-Plus process. At the first HADR exercise in Bandar Seri Begawan, Brunei in June 2013, the PLA dispatched over a hundred troops (including engineer and medical detachments) as well as the Peace Ark, a PLA Navy hospital ship.[92]

## Conclusion

Under Deng Xiaoping, there was considerably less effort by China to pursue comprehensive engagement with the outside world as Beijing's focus then was very much on China's internal social and economic development with outreach limited to the quest for foreign markets for Chinese exports.[93] Following the Tiananmen incident in June 1989, Beijing also sought to 'keep a low profile' and avoid unwarranted attention.[94] As China under Jiang Xemin and subsequently Hu Jintao began to engage more deeply with the outside world, it arguably evolved as a mere 'norm-taker' to, under Xi Jinping, an embryonic 'norm-entrepreneur' or 'norm-socializer', albeit one driven by instrumental rather than normative reasons.[95] In that regard, China's ostensible attractiveness as an economic model could arguably be considered as another aspect of its ideational contribution, if only an indirect one, to Asian multilateralism. As a former 'follower goose' – according to the 'flying geese' model popular during the 1950s and 1960s, with Japan as the 'lead goose'[96] – China's spectacular growth has in the view of some rendered it the 'leading dragon' whose model of industrialization has become one developing economies and lower-income countries are seeking to emulate.[97] While Japan led the way as Asia's growth engine for much of the latter part of the twentieth century, the post-Cold War era has all been about 'Factory Asia' with China leading the way in riding global supply and value chains.[98] Possibly more salient than global chains, however, are regional supply and value chains and regional trade agreements that criss-cross Asia.[99] In recent years, intraregional trade and investment patterns have grown substantially, with China at their centre.[100] And while the so-called 'Beijing Consensus' remains as ambiguous an idea as ever, the fact that China is now the world's second largest economy after the United States and that it has seemingly escaped the problems that have preoccupied the post-crisis West – fiscal cliffs, high unemployment, political gridlock – has added to its lustre even if democracies are likely to find China's communist-capitalist-Confucian system unacceptable on ideological and pragmatic grounds.[101]

Whether Chinese-led economic integration has decreased the propensity for war in Asia remains unclear, even if most analysts do not seem to think major war in Asia is likely.[102] While the benefits China accrues from strong economic ties with Japan are likely to trump its desire to raise the stakes on their islands dispute, the wildcard probably remains China's concern over the prospect of America's military entry into the fray on Japan's behalf should the East China Sea dispute significantly escalate between the Chinese and the Japanese.[103] The rub for Beijing appears to be the perceived lack of gratitude and reciprocity from Asian beneficiaries of Chinese goodwill and largesse as well as their evident distrust of China's strategic intentions. China's commitment to regional security and stability has been questioned. Moreover, China's obduracy, particularly its resistance against any attempt to 'internationalize' disputes over territory or to adopt multilateral approaches to their resolution, has long been seen as a key impediment against the ARF's ability to progress from informal confidence-building to preventive diplomacy even though such an anticipated evolution has long formed part of the ARF's security road map.[104] Chinese dominance of the APT has been viewed with concern by its fellow APT members for whom China's overwhelming size, economic heft and military power are a source of constant worry even as they have benefited from their ties with the Chinese.[105] As we have seen, the shared anxiety over Chinese primacy in East Asian regionalism led to visible tensions in the lead-up to the creation of the EAS in December 2005. The ensuing tension drew attention to the inevitable involvement by APT members in balance of power politics in order to constrain China's influence.[106]

The challenge confronting China today has to do with its management of the tension between its desire to be acknowledged by the international community as a responsible great power, on the one hand, and its propensity to assert its power and influence in increasingly provocative ways in East Asia on the other.[107] Chinese leaders, it has been argued, have purportedly embraced the notion of China as a responsible great power with its attendant normative meanings and ramifications,[108] even as allegations about its free riding and perceived reluctance to contribute to global governance and the cause of world stability more broadly continue to abound.[109] But it has also been pointed out that Chinese leaders view external attempts to define China as a responsible international actor – former US official Robert Zoellick's notion of 'responsible stakeholder' is an oft-cited example – as a normative constraint which they are still reluctant to accept, in the belief that it holds China to behavioural standards to which it may not be ready to live up.[110] The perception that China has not received the international respect it believes it rightly deserves and that its rise to greatness is being unfairly constrained by others have led to mounting frustration and dissatisfaction among the Chinese.[111] Yet as this discussion has also shown, China has sought increasingly, if still selectively and instrumentally, to contribute meaningfully and substantively to Asian multilateralism and in ways it deems appropriate. In all likelihood, China will be a responsible great power and stakeholder, but probably a complicated and difficult one.

## Notes

1 Laurie Burkitt, 'The Chinese Dream vs. the American Dream', *The Wall Street Journal*, 8 May 2014, http://blogs.wsj.com/chinarealtime/2014/05/08/the-chinese-dream-vs-the-american-dream-in-4-charts/; 'Chasing the Chinese Dream', *The Economist*, 4 May 2013, www.economist.com/news/briefing/21577063-chinas-new-leader-has-been-quick-consolidate-his-power-what-does-he-now-want-his.
2 'Xi Eyes More Enabling Int'l Environment for China's Peaceful Development', *Xinhua*, 30 November 2014, http://news.xinhuanet.com/english/china/2014-11/30/c_133822694_2.htm.
3 Jian Chen, 'China and the Bandung Conference', in See Seng Tan and Amitav Acharya, eds., *Bandung Revisited: The Legacy of the 1955 Asian-African Conference for International Order* (Singapore: National University of Singapore Press, 2008), pp. 132–59, on pp. 148–9. Also see, Ian Storey, 'China's Missteps in Southeast Asia: Less Charm, More Offensive', *China Brief*, Vol. 10, No. 25 (17 December 2010), www.jamestown.org/single/?tx_ttnews%5Btt_news%5D=37294&no_cache=1#.VLOJ301xmM8
4 Mike Patton, 'Who Owns the Most U.S. Debt?', *Forbes*, 28 October 2014, www.forbes.com/sites/mikepatton/2014/10/28/who-owns-the-most-u-s-debt/; Cedric Muhammad, 'So What if China Has $1.32 Trillion in U.S. Treasuries? It Still Can't Crash America's Economy', *Forbes*, 16 January 2014, www.forbes.com/sites/cedricmuhammad/2014/01/16/so-what-if-china-has-1-32-trillion-in-u-s-treasuries-it-still-cant-crash-americas-economy/.
5 David Shambaugh, cited in Shogo Suzuki, 'Effective Multilateralism and Sino-Japanese Reconciliation', in Jochen Prantl, ed., *Effective Multilateralism: Through the Looking Glass of East Asia* (London: Palgrave Macmillan, 2013), pp. 153–76, on p. 153.
6 Guoguang Wu, 'Multiple Levels of Multilateralism: The Rising China in the Turbulent World', in Guoguang Wu and Helen Landsdowne, eds., *China Turns to Multilateralism: Foreign Policy and Regional Security* (Abingdon: Routledge, 2008), pp. 267–89; Hongying Wang and Erik French, 'China's Participation in Global Governance from a Comparative Perspective', *Asia Policy*, No. 15 (2013), pp. 89–114.
7 Chien-peng Chung, *China's Multilateral Cooperation in Asia and the Pacific: Institutionalizing Beijing's 'Good Neighbour Policy'* (Abingdon: Routledge, 2010), p. 3
8 Wu, 'Multiple Levels of Multilateralism', p. 267.
9 Hugh White, 'Power Shift: Rethinking Australia's Place in the Asian Century', *Australian Journal of International Affairs*, Vol. 65, No. 1 (2011), pp. 81–93.
10 Yugang Chen, 'Community-Building or Rebalancing? China and the United States in Southeast Asia', in Mingjiang Li and Dongmin Lee, eds., *China and East Asian Strategic Dynamics: The Shaping of a New Regional Order* (Lanham, MD: Lexington Books, 2011), pp. 3–18; Zhang Xiaoming, 'The Rise of China and Community Building in East Asia', *Asian Perspective*, Vol. 30, No. 3 (2006), pp. 129–48.
11 Jeremy Blum, 'Former Foreign Minister Says "China Will Never Seek to Become a Hegemonic Power"', *South China Morning Post*, 18 September 2013; Patrick Donahue and Brian Parkin, 'Xi Says China's Military Expansion Not Aimed at Asian Hegemony', *Bloomberg News*, 29 March 2014, www.bloomberg.com/news/2014-03-28/xi-says-china-s-military-expansion-not-aimed-at-asian-hegemony.html.
12 Razeen Sally, 'Free Trade Agreements and the Prospects for Regional Integration in East Asia', *Asian Economic Policy Review*, Vol. 1, No. 2 (2006), pp. 306–21.
13 Azur Gat, 'The Return of Authoritarian Great Powers', *Foreign Affairs*, Vol. 86, No. 4 (2007), pp. 59–69.
14 Larry Hanauer and Lyle J. Morris, *Chinese Engagement in Africa: Drivers, Reactions, and Implications for US Policy* (Santa Monica, CA: RAND Corporation, 2014); Sarah Raine, *China's Africa Challenges*, The Adelphi Papers, No. 49 (404–05) (Abingdon: Routledge for International Institute for Strategic Studies, 2009); Yun Sun, 'China's Aid

to Africa: Monster or Messiah?', *Brookings East Asia Commentary*, No. 75, February 2014, www.brookings.edu/research/opinions/2014/02/07-china-aid-to-africa-sun. China has also increased its ties with the Latin American region – and with it, raised questions about the strategic ramifications for the United States. Patricia Rey Mellén, 'Latin America Increases Relations with China: What Does That Mean for the US?', *International Business Times*, 28 June 2013, www.ibtimes.com/latin-america-increases-relations-china-what-does-mean-us-1317981; Mark Weisbrot, 'U.S. Foreign Policy in Latin America Leaves an Open Door for China', *The Guardian*, 31 January 2014.

15 Shannon Tiezzi, 'China "Marches West" — to Europe', *The Diplomat*, 27 November 2013, http://thediplomat.com/2013/11/china-marches-west-to-europe/.

16 Steven Holloway, 'US Unilateralism at the UN: Why Great Powers Do Not Make Great Multilateralists', *Global Governance*, Vol. 6, No. 3 (2000), pp. 361–81.

17 Hongying Wang, 'Multilateralism in Chinese Foreign Policy: The Limits of Socialization', *Asian Survey*, Vol. 40, No. 3 (2000), pp. 475–91.

18 David C. Kang, 'Getting Asia Wrong: The Need for New Analytical Frameworks', *International Security*, Vol. 27, No. 4 (2003), pp. 57–85, on p. 66. Also see Alastair Iain Johnston, 'Is China a Status Quo Power?', *International Security*, Vol. 27, No. 4 (2003), pp. 5–56; Alastair Iain Johnston, *Social States: China in International Institutions, 1980–2000* (Princeton, NJ: Princeton University Press, 2008).

19 Aaron L. Friedberg, *A Contest for Supremacy: China, America, and the Struggle for Mastery in Asia* (New York: W. W. Norton and Co, 2012).

20 William A. Callahan, *China: The Pessoptimist Nation* (Oxford: Oxford University Press, 2012).

21 Amitav Acharya, 'Will Asia's Past Be Its Future?', *International Security*, Vol. 28, No. 3 (2003/4), pp. 149–64.

22 Rosemary Foot, 'Chinese Strategies in a US-Hegemonic Global Order: Accommodating and Hedging', *International Affairs*, Vol. 82, No. 1 (2006), pp. 77–94.

23 Nan Li, 'The Evolving Chinese Conception of Security and Security Approaches', in See Seng Tan and Amitav Acharya, eds., *Asia-Pacific Security Cooperation: National Interests and Regional Order* (Armonk, NY: M. E. Sharpe, 2004), pp. 53–70; Tang Shiping, *From Offensive Realism to Defensive Realism: A Social Evolutionary Interpretation of China's Security Strategy*, State of Security and International Studies No. 3 (Singapore: S. Rajaratnam School of International Studies, 2007).

24 Cher, 'China and the Bandung Conference'.

25 Vincent K. Pollard, 'ASA and ASEAN, 1961–1967: Southeast Asian Regionalism', *Asian Survey*, Vol. 10, No. 3 (1970), pp. 244–55.

26 William S. Turley and Jeffrey Race, 'The Third Indochina War', *Foreign Policy*, No. 38 (1980), pp. 92–116; Donald E. Weatherbee, Ralf Emmers, Mari Pangestu, Leonard C. Sebastian, 'The Third Indochina War', in *International Relations in Southeast Asia: The Struggle for Autonomy* (Lanham, MD: Rowman and Littlefield, 2005), pp. 75–82.

27 Alice D. Ba, 'Who's Socializing Whom? Complex Engagement in China–ASEAN Relations', *The Pacific Review*, Vol. 19, No. 2 (2006), pp. 157–79, on p. 162. Amitav Acharya, 'ASEAN and Conditional Engagement', in James Shinn, ed., *Weaving the Net: Conditional Engagement with China* (New York: Council on Foreign Relations, 1996), pp. 220–48.

28 John H. Holdridge, *Crossing the Divide: An Insider's Account of Normalization of US–China Relations* (Lanham, MD: Rowman and Littlefield, 1997), p. 25.

29 Robert L. Biesner, 'History and Henry Kissinger', *Diplomatic History*, Vol. 14, No. 4 (2007), pp. 511–28.

30 Chang Pao-min, *Kampuchea between China and Vietnam* (Singapore: Singapore University Press, 1985), p. 141.

31 Alice D. Ba, 'Southeast Asia and China', in Evelyn Goh, ed., *Betwixt and Between: Southeast Asian Strategic Relations with the U.S. and China* (Singapore: Institute of Defence and Strategic Studies, 2005), pp. 93–108.

32 Yukon Huang, 'China's Rise: Opportunity or Threat for East Asia?', *East Asia Forum*, 20 May 2012, www.eastasiaforum.org/2012/05/20/chinas-economic-rise-opportunity-or-threat-for-east-asia/; Friedrich Wu, Poa Tiong Siaw, Yeo Han Sia and Puah Kok Keong, 'Foreign Direct Investments to China and Southeast Asia: Has ASEAN Been Losing Out?', *Economic Survey of Singapore 2002* (Third Quarter), pp. 96–115. For a contrarian view arguing that the ASEAN region's apparent loss of economic investment to China is grossly exaggerated, see John Ravenhill, 'Is China an Economic Threat to Southeast Asia?', *Asian Survey*, Vol. 46, No. 5 (2006), pp. 653–74.
33 Jing-dong Yuan, *Asia-Pacific Security: China's Conditional Multilateralism and Great Power Entente* (Carlisle, PA: Strategic Studies Institute, US Army War College, 2000), p. 7.
34 Jusuf Wanandi, 'ASEAN's China Strategy: Towards Deeper Engagement', *Survival*, Vol. 38, No. 2 (1996), pp. 117–28. There are, to be sure, limits to socialization; see, Wang, 'Multilateralism in Chinese Foreign Policy'.
35 Phillip Y. Lipscy, 'Japan's Asian Monetary Fund Proposal', *Stanford Journal of East Asian Affairs*, Vol. 3, No. 1 (2003), pp. 93–104.
36 Mark Beeson, 'ASEAN Plus Three and the Rise of Reactionary Regionalism', *Contemporary Southeast Asia*, Vol. 25, No. 2 (2003), pp. 251–68.
37 David Capie and Paul Evans, *The Asia-Pacific Security Lexicon*, 2nd edn (Singapore: Institute of Southeast Asian Studies, 2007), pp. 169–72.
38 Pak K. Lee and Lai-Ha Chan, 'Non-traditional Security Threats in China: Challenges of Energy Shortage and Infectious Diseases', in Joseph Y. S. Cheng, ed., *Challenges and Policy Programmes of China's New Leadership* (Hong Kong: City University of Hong Kong Press, 2007), pp. 297–336.
39 Bates Gill and Chin-hao Huang, *China's Expanding Role in Peacekeeping: Prospects and Policy Implications*, SIPRI Policy Paper, No. 25 (Stockholm: Stockholm Institute for International Peace Research, 2009).
40 Michael Leifer, 'The Maritime Regime and Regional Security in East Asia', *The Pacific Review*, Vol. 4, No. 2 (1991), pp. 126–36.
41 James R. Holmes, 'The South China Sea: "Lake Beijing"', *The Diplomat*, 7 January 2013, www.thediplomat.com/2013/01/the-south-china-sea-lake-beijing/.
42 James R. Holmes and Toshi Yoshihara, 'China's "Caribbean" in the South China Sea', *SAIS Review of International Affairs*, Vol. 26, No. 1 (2006), pp. 79–92.
43 Lai To Lee, 'East Asian Assessments of China's Security Policy', *International Affairs*, Vol. 73, No. 2 (1997), pp. 251–62, on p. 251.
44 Ralf Emmers, *Maritime Disputes in the South China Sea: Strategic and Diplomatic Status Quo*, Working Paper No. 87 (Singapore: Institute of Defence and Strategic Studies, 2005).
45 Ian Storey, 'Japan's Evolving Security Concerns in Maritime Southeast Asia: From Safety of Navigation to "Lake Beijing"', in Takashi Shiraishi and Takaaki Kojima, eds., *ASEAN–Japan Relations* (Singapore: Institute of Southeast Asian Studies, 2013), pp. 114–34, on p. 129.
46 Ba, 'Who's Socializing Whom?', p. 160; Yuen Foong Khong, 'Review Article: Making Bricks without Straw in the Asia Pacific?', *The Pacific Review*, Vol. 10, No. 2 (1997), pp. 289–300, on p. 291.
47 Alastair Iain Johnston and Robert S. Ross, eds., *Engaging China: The Management of an Emerging Power* (London: Routledge, 1999).
48 Ba, 'Who's Socializing Whom?', p. 160.
49 In all this, ASEAN second-track diplomacy has arguably facilitated the building of mutual confidence and the dissemination and socialization of regional conventions and norms. Hiro Katsumata, 'The Role of ASEAN Institutes of Strategic and International Studies in Developing Security Cooperation in the Asia-Pacific Region', *Asian Journal of Political Science*, Vol. 11, No. 1 (2003), pp. 93–111.

50 Fareed Zakaria, 'The Rise of Illiberal Democracy', *Foreign Affairs*, Vol. 76, No. 6 (1997), pp. 22–43.
51 Eric Jones, 'Asia's Fate', *The National Interest*, No. 35 (2004), pp. 18–28. In this respect, ASEAN involvement in that debate – which quietly dissipated by 1997 thanks to the Asian financial crisis – arguably served as a costly signal of sorts from ASEAN to China regarding the Association's 'credibility'. That said, not all ASEAN member states probably agreed to the concept of Asian values, not least the Philippines.
52 Kuik Cheng-Chwee, 'Multilateralism in China's ASEAN Policy: Its Evolution, Characteristics, and Aspiration', *Contemporary Southeast Asia*, Vol. 27, No. 1 (2005), pp. 102–22, on p. 102.
53 Leszek Buszynski, 'ASEAN, the Declaration of Conduct, and the South China Sea', *Contemporary Southeast Asia*, Vol. 25, No. 3 (2003), pp. 343–62; Carlyle A. Thayer, 'ASEAN, China and the Code of Conduct in the South China Sea', *SAIS Review of International Affairs*, Vol. 33, No. 2 (2013), pp. 75–84.
54 David Shambaugh, 'China Engages Asia: Reshaping the Regional Order', *International Security*, Vol. 29, No. 3 (2004/5), pp. 64–99, on p. 64.
55 Masahiro Kawai and Ganeshan Wignaraja, *ASEAN+3 or ASEAN+6: Which Way Forward?*, ADB Institute Discussion Paper No. 77 (Tokyo: Asian Development Bank Institute, 2007); Mohan Malik, 'The East Asia Summit: More Discord than Accord', *YaleGlobal*, 20 December 2005, http://yaleglobal.yale.edu/display.article?id=6645.
56 Ralf Emmers, Joseph Chinyong Liow and See Seng Tan, *The East Asia Summit and the Regional Security Architecture*, Maryland Series in Contemporary Asian Studies, No. 3-2010 (202) (College Park, MD: University of Maryland, 2011).
57 Author's personal communications with leading Chinese international relations experts Su Hao and Cai Penghong, Singapore, January 2008. Even then, some Chinese pundits continue to insist on the greater wisdom and performance of the APT in economic integration. Zhong Sheng, 'ASEAN Plus Three cooperation is driving force for East Asia', *People's Daily Online*, 16 August 2011, http://english.peopledaily.com.cn/90780/91343/7571027.html.
58 Adam Taylor, 'The Australian Government Made a Secret Plan for War with China in 2009', *Business Insider*, 1 June 2012, www.businessinsider.com/australia-china-kevin-rudd-2009-2012-6#ixzz3OgDgBZ2L.
59 Mely Caballero-Anthony, 'Regional Security Institutions in Asia: Some Insights on Asian Regionalism', Background Paper No. 6 for the Asian Development Bank's Study Finalization Workshop on Institutions for Regionalism in Asia and the Pacific, Shanghai, 2–3 December 2009.
60 Shannon Tiezzi, 'The New, Improved Shanghai Cooperation Organization', *The Diplomat*, 13 September 2014, http://thediplomat.com/2014/09/the-new-improved-shanghai-cooperation-organization/.
61 Pradumna B. Rana and Chia Wai-Mun, *The Revival of the Silk Roads (Land Connectivity) in Asia*, RSIS Working Paper, No. 274, 12 May (Singapore: S. Rajaratnam School of International Studies, 2013).
62 Raffaello Pantucci and Li Lifan, 'Shanghai Cooperation Organization: Not Quite the New Silk Road', *The Diplomat*, 12 September 2013, http://thediplomat.com/2013/09/shanghai-cooperation-organization-not-quite-the-new-silk-road-2/.
63 Matthew Sussex, 'The Shanghai Cooperation Organization: A Future Balancing Coalition in Asia?', in Peter Shearman, ed., *Power Transition and International Order in Asia: Issues and Challenges* (Abingdon: Routledge, 2014), pp. 69–85, on p. 77.
64 See Seng Tan, 'The Perils and Prospects of Dragon Riding: Reassurance and "Costly Signals" in China–ASEAN Relations', in Ron Huisken, ed., *Rising China: Power and Reassurance* (Canberra: Australian National University E-Press, 2009), pp. 165–84. Also see Yuen Foong Khong, 'Primacy or World Order? The United States and China's Rise: A Review Essay', *International Security*, Vol. 38, No. 3 (2013/14), pp. 153–75.

65 Mark Lynas, 'How Do I Know China Wrecked the Copenhagen Deal? I Was in the Room', *The Guardian*, 22 December 2009, www.theguardian.com/environment/2009/dec/22/copenhagen-climate-change-mark-lynas.
66 Don Emmerson, 'ASEAN Stumbles in Phnom Penh', *PacNet*, No. 45, 19 July 2012, csis.org/files/publication/Pac1245.pdf. Also see William W. Keller and Thomas G. Rawski, eds., *China's Rise and the Balance of Influence in Asia* (Pittsburgh, PA: University of Pittsburgh Press, 2007).
67 Andrew Higgins, 'In Philippines, Banana Growers Feel Effect of South China Sea Dispute', *The Washington Post*, 11 June 2012, www.washingtonpost.com/world/asia_pacific/in-philippines-banana-growers-feel-effect-of-south-china-sea-dispute/2012/06/10/gJQA47WVTV_story.html.
68 Ralf Emmers and See Seng Tan, 'The ASEAN Regional Forum and Preventive Diplomacy: Built to Fail?', *Asian Security*, Vol. 7, No. 1 (2011), pp. 44–60, on p. 50.
69 Alastair Iain Johnston, 'How New and Assertive Is China's New Assertiveness?', *International Security*, Vol. 37, No. 4 (Spring 2013), pp. 7–48.
70 Thus understood, Beijing had 'no choice' but to respond forcefully to what it might have regarded as a possible US effort to unsettle its leadership transition. Author's interviews at various Chinese think tanks in Beijing, 2–6 July 2012.
71 Li Mingjiang, *Soft Power in Chinese Discourse: Popularity and Prospect*, Working Paper No. 165 (Singapore: S. Rajaratnam School of International Studies, Nanyang Technological University, 2008), p. 23.
72 Elizabeth Economy, 'The Xi-Obama Summit: As Good as Expected – and Maybe Even Better', *The Atlantic*, 11 June 2013, www.theatlantic.com/china/archive/2013/06/the-xi-obama-summit-as-good-as-expected-and-maybe-even-better/276733/.
73 C. Raja Mohan, 'Will India Join China's Maritime Silk Road?', *The Indian Express*, 15 February 2014, http://indianexpress.com/article/opinion/columns/will-india-join-chinas-maritime-silk-road/.
74 Shannon Tiezzi, 'The Maritime Silk Road vs. The String of Pearls', *The Diplomat*, 13 February 2014, http://thediplomat.com/2014/02/the-maritime-silk-road-vs-the-string-of-pearls/; Keith Johnson, 'Rough Ride on the New Silk Road', *Foreign Policy*, 1 May 2014, www.foreignpolicy.com/articles/2014/05/01/rough_ride_on_the_silk_road.
75 Juli A. MacDonald, Amy Donahue, Bethany Danyluk and Booz Allen Hamilton, *Energy Futures in Asia: Final Report* (McLean, VA: Booz-Allen & Hamilton, 2004).
76 Kathrin Hille, 'Hu Calls for China to be a "Maritime Power"', *The Financial Times*, 8 November 2012, www.ft.com/cms/s/0/ebd9b4ae-296f-11e2-a604-00144feabdc0.html#axzz35wwM4q4p.
77 Dean Cheng, 'China's ADIZ as Area Denial', *The National Interest*, 4 December 2013, http://nationalinterest.org/commentary/chinas-adiz-area-denial-9492; Zachary Keck, 'The Political Utility of China's A2/AD Challenge', *The Diplomat*, 19 March 2014, http://thediplomat.com/2014/03/the-political-utility-of-chinas-a2ad-challenge/; Andrew Krepinevich, Barry Watts and Robert Work, *Meeting the Anti-Access and Area-Denial Challenge* (Washington, D.C.: Center for Strategic and Budgetary Assessments, 2003).
78 Per Liljas, 'Two Ships Have Arrived in Vietnam to Evacuate Chinese Nationals', *Time*, 19 May 2014, http://time.com/#104284/chinese-ships-arrive-in-vietnam-to-evacuate-nationals-vung-ang/.
79 Sam Bateman, 'New Tensions in the South China Sea: Whose Sovereignty over Paracels?', *RSIS Commentaries* 088/2014, 14 May 2014, www.rsis.edu.sg/publications/Perspective/RSIS0882014.pdf.
80 Dexter Roberts, 'Obama and Xi Spar over Rival Free-Trade Pacts at APEC Forum', *Bloomberg Businessweek*, 10 November 2014, www.businessweek.com/articles/2014-11-10/obama-and-xi-spar-over-rival-free-trade-pacts-at-apec-forum.
81 'Chinese President Proposes Asia-Pacific Dream', *China Daily*, 9 November 2014, www.chinadaily.com.cn/china/2014-11/09/content_18889698.htm.

82 Shannon Tiezzi, 'China's Push for an Asia-Pacific Free Trade Agreement', *The Diplomat*, 30 October 2014, http://thediplomat.com/2014/10/chinas-push-for-an-asia-pacific-free-trade-agreement/.
83 Dingding Chen, 'China's "Marshall Plan" Is Much More', *The Diplomat*, 10 November 2014, http://thediplomat.com/2014/11/chinas-marshall-plan-is-much-more/.
84 Rachel Cheng, 'AIIB: China Needs to Win Over Naysayers', *The Straits Times*, 4 November 2014, www.straitstimes.com/news/opinion/eye-the-economy/story/aiib-china-needs-win-over-naysayers-20141104; Jane Perlez, 'US Opposing China's Answer to World Bank', *The New York Times*, 9 October 2014.
85 Zachary Keck, 'Why the US is Trying to Squash China's New Development Bank', *The Diplomat*, 10 October 2014, http://thediplomat.com/2014/10/why-the-us-is-trying-to-squash-chinas-new-development-bank/.
86 Jamil Anderlini, 'Big nations Snub Beijing Bank Launch after US Lobbying', *Financial Times*, 22 October 2014, www.ft.com/intl/cms/s/0/41c3c0a0-59cd-11e4-9787-00144feab7de.html#axzz3VBgz8Xz2.
87 Jayant Menon, 'The Challenge Facing Asia's Regional Comprehensive Economic Partnership', *East Asia Forum*, 23 June 2013, www.eastasiaforum.org/2013/06/23/the-challenge-facing-asias-regional-comprehensive-economic-partnership/.
88 Zhao Hong, 'China's Evolving Views on the TPP and the RCEP', *ISEAS Perspective*, No. 28, 8 May 2014, pp. 5–6, www.iseas.edu.sg/documents/publication/iseas_perspective_2014_28_china_evolving_views_on_the_tpp_and_the_rcep.pdf.
89 John Ruwitch, 'China's Xi Issues Veiled Warning to Asia over Military Alliances', *Reuters*, 21 May 2014, http://news.yahoo.com/chinas-xi-says-committed-peacefully-resolving-territorial-disputes-024633860.html.
90 Jeremy Blum, 'Former Foreign Minister Says "China Will Never Seek to become a Hegemonic Power"', *South China Morning Post*, 18 September 2013, www.scmp.com/news/china-insider/article/1312346/former-foreign-minister-says-china-will-never-seek-become; Patrick Donahue and Brian Parkin, 'Xi Says China's Military Expansion Not Aimed at Asian Hegemony', *Bloomberg News*, 29 March 2014, www.bloomberg.com/news/2014-03-28/xi-says-china-s-military-expansion-not-aimed-at-asian-hegemony.html.
91 Kor Kian Beng, 'China Puts Low-Key Summit in Spotlight', *The Straits Times*, 10 May 2014, p. A18, www.stasiareport.com/the-big-story/asia-report/china/story/china-puts-low-key-summit-spotlight-20140510.
92 'Chinese Hospital Ship Makes Port Call, Joins Drill in Brunei', *Global Times*, 16 June 2013, www.globaltimes.cn/content/789169.shtml.
93 Y. Y. Kueh, *China's New Industrialization Strategy: Was Chairman Mao Really Necessary?* (Cheltenham: Edward Elgar, 2008).
94 Justyna Szczudlik-Tatar, *China's New Silk Road Diplomacy*, PISM Policy Paper 34 (82) (Warsaw: Polish Institute of International Affairs, 2013), p. 2.
95 Emilian Kavalski, 'The Struggle for Recognition of Normative Powers: Normative Power Europe and Normative Power China in Context', *Cooperation and Conflict*, Vol. 48, No. 2 (2013), pp. 247–67; Martha Finnemore and Kathryn Sikkink, 'International Norm Dynamics and Political Change', *International Organization*, Vol. 52, No. 4 (1998), pp. 887–917; Tomoyuki Kojima, 'China's "Omnidirectional Diplomacy": Cooperation with All, Emphasis on Major Powers', *Asia-Pacific Review*, Vol. 8, No. 2 (2001), pp. 81–95.
96 Pekka Korhonen, 'The Theory of the Flying Geese Pattern of Development and Its Interpretations', *Journal of Peace Research*, Vol. 31, No. 1 (1994), pp. 93–108.
97 Justin Yifu Lin, *From Flying Geese to Leading Dragons: New Opportunities and Strategies for Structural Transformation in Developing Countries*, Policy Research Working Paper, No. 5702 (Washington, D.C.: The World Bank, 2011).

98 Richard Baldwin, 'By Invitation: Supply Chains Changed the Growth Model', *The Economist*, 15 August 2012, www.economist.com/economics/by-invitation/guest-contributions/supply-chains-changed-growth-model.
99 Zhi Wang, William Powers, and Shang-Jin Wei, *Value Chains in East Asian Production Networks: An International Input-Output Model Based Analysis*, Office of Economics Working Paper, No. 2009-10-C (Washington, D.C.: US International Trade Commission, 2009).
100 John Wong, *East Asian Economic Cooperation: Lessons for South American Regionalism*, EAI Working Paper, No. 160 (Singapore: East Asian Institute, National University of Singapore, 2012), p. 5.
101 Katrin Bennhold, 'What Is the Beijing Consensus?', *The New York Times*, 28 January 2011, http://dealbook.nytimes.com/2011/01/28/what-is-the-beijing-consensus/?_r=0.
102 Richard Bitzinger and Barry Desker, 'Why East Asian War is Unlikely', *Survival*, Vol. 50, No. 6 (2008), pp. 105–28.
103 Justin McCurry, 'Why Will Japan and China Avoid Conflict? They Need Each Other', *Christian Science Monitor*, 5 February 2014.
104 Emmers and Tan, 'The ASEAN Regional Forum and Preventive Diplomacy'.
105 Denny Roy, *Return of the Dragon: Rising China and Regional Security* (New York: Columbia University Press, 2013), ch. 3.
106 Christopher W. Hughes, 'Japan's Response to China's Rise: Regional Engagement, Global Containment, Dangers of Collision', *International Affairs*, Vol. 85, No. 4 (2009), pp. 837–56; Takashi Terada, 'Forming an East Asian Community: A Site for Japan–China Power Struggles', *Japanese Studies*, Vol. 26, No. 1 (2006), pp. 5–17.
107 Yukon Huang, 'China's Road to Becoming a "Responsible" World Power', *Financial Times*, 26 March 2013; Carlyle A. Thayer, 'Chinese Assertiveness in the South China Sea and Southeast Asian Responses', *Journal of Current Southeast Asian Affairs*, Vol. 30, No. 2 (2011), pp. 77–104; Xia Liping, 'China: A Responsible Great Power', *Journal of Contemporary China*, Vol. 10, No. 26 (2001), pp. 17–25.
108 Tiang Boon Hoo, 'A Responsible Great Power: The Anatomy of China's Proclaimed Identity', DPhil thesis, University of Oxford, 2013.
109 Stephanie T. Kleine-Ahlbrandt, 'Beijing, Global Free-Rider', *Foreign Policy*, 12 November 2009, www.foreignpolicy.com/articles/2009/11/12/beijing_global_free_rider; Stewart Patrick, 'Irresponsible Stakeholders? The Difficulty of Integrating Rising Powers', *Foreign Affairs*, Vol. 89, No. 6 (2010), pp. 44–53.
110 Kai He, 'A Tale of Three Fears: Why China Does Not Want To Be No. 1', *RSIS Commentaries* 104/2014, 2 June 2014, www.rsis.edu.sg/rsis-publication/idss/a-tale-of-three-fears-why-china-does-not-want-to-be-no-1/#.VQ-1nU39mM8.
111 Shaun Breslin, 'China's Emerging Global Role: Dissatisfied Responsible Great Power', *Politics*, Vol. 30, No. 1 (2010), pp. 52–62; Michael T. Klare, 'Containing China: The US's Real Objective', *Asia Times Online*, 20 April 2006, www.atimes.com/atimes/China/HD20Ad01.html.

# 7 United States

This chapter looks at the contributions the United States of America have rendered to the shape and substance of Asia's multilateral architecture, its content and its conventions. More than any of the other key external stakeholders, America did not particularly favour Asia's 'multilateral turn' primarily because it read that as an either/or proposition at the plausible expense of the longstanding security architecture of alliances and other collective defence arrangements that it had built during the Cold War and has sustained to the present. America relented only when it realized its Asian allies and partners continue to value their security ties with it. By and large, the United States has been a strong supporter of Asian multilateralism, albeit not as much as countries like Australia and Japan. While Washington has chafed at times over the lack of substantive progress in regional cooperation, it nonetheless has persisted in supporting and legitimizing ASEAN's centrality and leadership in Asian multilateralism even when other non-ASEAN stakeholders criticized and dismissed ASEAN's relevance.

There can be no question over the vital importance of the United States to Asian multilateralism, even when its focus on the Asian region, already uneven at the best of times, has waxed and waned over the years. Despite its long and deep historical engagement with Asia, the United States has proved ambivalent in its disposition and policy towards the region – an unfortunate yet understandable situation for the only global power, one preoccupied at times with developments in other parts of the world. For instance, while Washington's post-Vietnam orientation towards Southeast Asia throughout the remainder of the Cold War era could not really be termed as isolationist – even though Nixon warned against such a prospect back in 1971[1] – its general approach to Southeast Asia has been described as an inadvertent policy of 'benign neglect and missed opportunities' and/or 'systemic neglect'.[2] Yet no other great power has ever received from Asians the resounding pleas for attention which America gets whenever regional countries – presumably with the exception of a more assertive China in recent times – feel they are being ignored by the Americans. On the other hand, there have been times when American attention on the region has had the opposite impact not least because of its destabilizing effects real or imagined.

Against that backdrop, this chapter will survey and examine US involvement in Asia and in Asian multilateral institutions from the Cold War period to the present.

It compares the dispositions and policies of succeeding US administrations towards Asia and Asian multilateralism to that of the Obama administration in the light of President Obama's claim to be his nation's first 'Pacific president' and his ardent advocacy of a US role in multilateralism.[3] Discounting differences in presidential and foreign policy leadership styles as well as expected policy variations between Democratic and Republican administrations – obviously by no means insignificant – it could be argued that there is a fairly consistent trend in how the United States has engaged the Asian region and, specifically for our purposes, the post-Cold War emergence and evolution of Asian multilateralism, whose shape and substance have been and continue to be affected by America's attitude and actions. Ultimately, Washington's approach to multilateralism, both internationally and most certainly in Asia, has remained steadfastly selective and utilitarian in orientation, and looks to stay that way for the foreseeable future.

## America and/in Asia

As a Pacific power and the 'hub' of the post-war San Francisco system of bilateral alliances with a number of Asia-Asian countries – such as Australia, Japan, the Philippines, South Korea, Taiwan and Thailand – and a key partner of the arrangements like the Australia, New Zealand, United States Security Treaty (ANZUS) as well as the now defunct Southeast Asia Treaty Organization (SEATO), the United States consistently rejected proposals and discouraged initiatives for multilateral institution-building in Cold War Asia. In the 1980s, the United States rejected Soviet leader Mikhail Gorbachev's proposal for an Asia-wide security forum along the lines of the Conference for Security Cooperation in Europe (CSCE) – an idea at the core of Gorbachev's comprehensive 'Asia-Pacific agenda' – because it revived suspicions reserved for Leonid Brezhnev's proposal in 1969 for a system of collective security in Asia.[4]

Yet the American disposition against the idea of an Asian multilateralism did not connote an absolute rejection of multilateralism as Washington's first mover role in Europe's post-war multilateral framework saw the former taking the lead to build formal multilateral arrangements – the United Nations (UN), the North Atlantic Treaty Organization (NATO), and the Bretton Woods monetary system undergirded by the International Monetary Fund (IMF) and the World Bank – that would contribute to not only Europe's reconstruction (in conjunction with the Marshall Plan) but indeed global governance itself.[5] But much as America's self-imposed isolation from Europe between the two world wars differed markedly from its deep and extensive engagement in the Asia-Pacific during that same period,[6] so too its reliance on a multilateral strategy towards Cold War Europe differed markedly from its dependence on bilateralism in Cold War Asia. America's engagement with Cold War Asia emphasized a foundation of strong bilateral ties, one supplemented in the post-Cold War period by loose multilateral arrangements.[7] This had as much to do with the form and substance of America's long uneven engagement with the Asia-Pacific region since the late nineteenth century as anything else. Without the vacillation between internationalism and isolationism which characterized its European engagement in the twentieth century, America has treated Asia as its own stomping ground during the first half of the last century – forcibly colonizing the Philippines, putting down the Boxer revolt in China, maintaining its military posture in the region, and resisting Japan's demands for parity[8] – and, in the wake of the Pacific War, taking the lead to establish a 'hub and spokes' model of bilateral alliances that has lasted from 1951 to the present.[9]

Between the 1950s and the 1970s, America would fight hot wars in both Northeast Asia (Korea) and Southeast Asia (Vietnam) and, with the drawdown of its armed forces in Southeast Asia in the wake of the Vietnam War, witness the folding of a troubled investment in multilateral collective defence, the SEATO – which Indonesian president Sukarno openly criticized given his opprobrium for western collective defence arrangements.[10] The Eisenhower administration's policy towards Asia has been praised by its revisionist champions while pilloried by its post-revisionist critics. While discord and harmony coexisted in equal measure in the United States' relations with its allies, particularly Great Britain, over the process of decolonization in the region, it is safe to say that the Eisenhower administration's record was neither as successful as its champions made it out to be nor as disastrous as its critics would have it.[11] The US involvement in the region during the Vietnam War years has received a great deal of attention and need not be rehearsed here, other than to note the pervasive influence of the domino theory which to a large extent shaped the policies of the Kennedy and Johnson administrations toward the region. Richard Nixon famously set aside ideology in favour of a pragmatic foreign policy in normalizing ties with communist China in 1972, a policy continued by Gerald Ford – the link between the two administrations' policies being Henry Kissinger – as the United States sought closer cooperation with China against the Soviet Union. Similarly uninterested in Southeast Asia (at least initially), the Carter administration also sought closer ties with China and supported ASEAN following Vietnam's invasion of Cambodia in late 1978. This prompted the then Singaporean foreign minister Sinnathamby Rajaratnam to assure President Carter that ASEAN was firmly 'on the American side',[12] thereby making the organization 'the hallmark' of Carter's Southeast Asia policy in the view of some.[13] Likewise, Cyrus Vance, Carter's Secretary of State, has noted that a building block of the Carter administration's post-Vietnam policy 'was support of regional economic or political organizations that could bear an increasing role in maintaining stability in the world' – and ASEAN, in Vance's view, constituted 'the outstanding example of such an organization'.[14] While Ronald Reagan considered ASEAN a model for regional cooperation and resilience, and even declared his administration's support for ASEAN to be the keystone of US policy in Southeast Asia, it did not translate into sustained high-level interest in the area, however.[15] As Terry Deibel has noted, 'Reagan's reflexive anticommunism and Cold War mentality caused him to view developing countries in East and Southeast Asia as irrelevant to US policy except as battlegrounds in the East–West struggle'.[16] But at a rhetorical level, Reagan would go as far as to insist that 'support for and cooperation with ASEAN is a linchpin of American Pacific policy'.[17]

If ASEAN's quest for institutional legitimacy precluded an overly and overtly intimate partnership with the United States during the Cold War out of concern that that would only confirm Vietnam's suspicions that ASEAN was nothing more than a US-sponsored bloc,[18] the end of the Cold War removed any such inhibition particularly in the wake of the forced closure of US military bases in the Philippines in the early 1990s, thanks to the serendipitous confluence of a nationalistic Philippine Senate and the extensive damage wrought to Clark Airbase (located about forty miles from Metro Manila) by the eruption of Mount Pinatubo. Urged to clarify its commitment to the region, the George H. W. Bush administration promoted the United States as an 'Asian power' and identified its key post-Cold War goal for Asia as securing American access to Asian markets – reflected in part by Bush's support for US participation in the inaugural meeting of the APEC in Canberra in 1989 – where a continued American military presence would ensure regional stability, the precondition for the region's economic prosperity. As Richard Solomon, US Assistant Secretary of State for East Asia and the Pacific from 1989 to 1992, argued in August 1991, 'Our adaptation to new circumstances must not be interpreted as withdrawal. America's destiny lies across the Pacific [and] our engagement in the region is here to stay'.[19] The self-image of the United States as an Asian power would continue under the Clinton presidency, as evidenced by language contained in two subsequent East Asia Strategy Reports of 1995 and 1997.[20] Along with the global war on terrorism (GWOT) relegating conventional strategic competition for the time being during the first decade of the twenty-first century, Southeast Asia became identified as the 'second front' of the GWOT, courtesy of incidents such as the foiling of a terrorist plot in Singapore in December 2001, bomb attacks in Bali, Indonesia in October 2002, and the like.[21] Perceptions that the region was being neglected by the administration of George W. Bush, due not only to the apparent militarization of US foreign policy as a result of the GWOT but also because of high-profile absences by the US Secretary of State Condoleeza Rice at the ARF in 2005 and 2007, generated consternation and disgruntlement among Asians, especially Southeast Asians.[22] This arguably prompted assurances such as those from Colin Powell, Rice's immediate predecessor, to the effect that the United States 'is a Pacific power and we will not yield our strategic position in Asia'.[23]

Not unlike his predecessors in the White House, Barack Obama came to power with the promise to make Asia a key feature of his foreign policy. For example, in an address to a Tokyo audience in November 2009, President Obama referred to himself as 'America's first Pacific President', promising his listeners that the United States would 'strengthen and sustain our leadership in this vitally important part of the world'.[24] Assuming leadership when the wars in Afghanistan and Iraq were winding down even as concern over Iran's apparent quest to develop nuclear weapons was growing, the Obama administration chose instead to focus its policy attention on Asia in the light of China's fast-growing power and influence, underscored in part by its overtaking Japan on two counts, first as the world's second largest economy between 2010 and 2011, and second as the world's second largest stock market.[25] 'In Asia', then US Secretary of State Hillary Clinton wrote in 2011 at the launch of Obama's pivot/rebalancing to Asia strategy, they ask whether we are really there to stay, whether we are likely to be distracted again by events elsewhere, whether we can make – and keep – credible economic and strategic commitments, and whether we can back those commitments with action. The answer is: We can, and we will.[26]

As Kurt Campbell, one of the architects of Obama's pivot, has rightly argued, the use of the pivot or rebalancing terminology should not foster the erroneous impression that the United States withdrew from the Asia-Pacific. Instead, what the pivot ostensibly represents is 'a vast and dynamic increase in US focus and depth of engagement in the region'.[27] But precisely how extensive, deep and dynamic an engagement has the United States initiated, and can it be sustained?

However, since Obama formally announced the pivot before the Australian Parliament in late 2011, its objectives and the ostensible strategic intention driving it have been questioned, not least by the Chinese who believe the initiative is aimed at constraining China's rise – a perception bolstered by the Pentagon's preoccupation with its AirSea Battle strategy as the plausible antidote to China's anti-access/area denial (A2/AD) strategy[28] – but also by America's Asian allies and partners. While this latter group more or less welcomes the pivot, they worry whether their American friends have the stomach to see it through in the face of serious fiscal constraints, political uncertainties and diplomatic distractions dogging the United States.[29] For that matter, the general lack of reference to the pivot in Obama's 2014 State of the Union address – it was mentioned in one short paragraph, but ironically received less attention than Afghanistan, the issue it was meant to replace – has led a number of observers to suggest that the Asia-Pacific has effectively dimmed in importance for the Obama administration.[30] There are to be sure concrete manifestations of the pivot here and there, such as the arrival in Singapore in December 2014 of the *USS Fort Worth*, the second Freedom-class littoral combat ship to be deployed to the region. Be that as it may, it is not entirely clear how truly 'Pacific' a president Barack Obama is or would be, when the pivot is measured against the history of past US engagement with Asia. At the time of writing, Obama has undertaken (in April 2014) a four-nation visit to the region with the reassurance that the pivot 'is real', whilst his defence secretary has argued that America 'is a Pacific Power for many years' and seeks to continue 'building those relationships and those partnerships [in the region] as we go forward'.[31]

In November 2014, the Obama administration found itself reeling in the wake of a Republican victory at the mid-term congressional elections and a damning US Senate report on the Central Intelligence Agency's use of harsh interrogation methods during its counterterrorism campaign. A visit to Beijing for the APEC summit – Obama's attendances at the APEC and the EAS (in Naypidaw) constituted a success of sorts given his no-shows at both summits in 2013 as a consequence of the federal shutdown brought about by the US government's inability to resolve its fiscal cliff crisis – produced, on the margins of APEC 2014, a landmark climate change agreement with China that specifies a timetable for emission reduction. However, Obama's international reputation appeared visibly diminished among the Chinese; for example, a conservative Chinese periodical dismissed the US president's leadership as 'insipid' – a far cry from 2009 during Obama's first presidential visit to China where he reportedly dazzled a student audience at a town hall-style meeting in Shanghai.[32] It remains to be seen whether he can persuade sceptical partners, including those in Southeast Asia who – in the light of Washington's reorientation to the Middle East because of the emergence in Iraq and Syria in 2013 of the Islamic State insurgency – see a shrinking US military footprint in the region, lack of progress in realizing the TPP trade pact, and a potential 'lame duck' presidency even though Obama still has two more years in the White House.[33]

## America and/in Asian multilateralism

If America's engagement with Asia has been relatively uneven in concrete terms despite its incessant descriptions of itself as a Pacific power, then its participation in Asia's multilateral institutions has proved just as spotty. That said, there is no question that the support of the United States for ASEAN (of which it is a dialogue partner), of the regional architecture ASEAN has sought to establish together with its partners, and ASEAN's so-called 'centrality' in that architecture – the last a condition Americans, much as other non-ASEAN stakeholders, have increasingly felt is unsustainable but nonetheless continue publicly to support because few if any feasible alternatives exist – has been crucial to the establishment and instantiation of regional multilateral cooperation in Asia. To be sure, America's support in this regard has not simply been for ASEAN but equally importantly for its allies – especially Australia, Japan, New Zealand, the Philippines, South Korea and Thailand – that are keen participants in the ASEAN-led architecture. America's significance has also mattered in another way, namely, as the global power whose strategic presence in and long-term commitment to Asia many if not most regional countries have actively sought to deepen through, among other ways, ensuring that America becomes a member of Asia's multilateral arrangements or, if it is already a part of such, continues as a member. However, as the following discussion seeks to show, notwithstanding the wax and wane of US commitment to Asian multilateralism, Washington has shown that its influence on the region's institutions has not always been merely implicit and indirect, but in fact extensive and deep.

In fairness to the Americans, it should be said there was precious little in Asia during the Cold War years to suggest that multilateral institutions and strategies stood a chance of succeeding in that volatile region. Better known as the Bandung Conference, the Afro-Asian Conference of 1955, despite the illusion of trans-regional unity promoted by its founders, has received a fair bit of positive attention in recent years for its putative significance as a model of diplomatic-security conventions – a sort of 'cognitive prior', if you will – that influenced the subsequent adoption by the postcolonial states of Asia of international norms and principles.[34] If so, it arguably explains why no robust multilateral forms – certainly no supranational entities – have taken root in Asia, not least because the norms that mattered most at the Bandung Conference, like national sovereignty and non-interventionism/non-interference, continue to enjoy primacy in contemporary Asia. While the relative success of ASEAN as a regional multilateral organization and the regional architecture comprising various Asia-wide institutional spinoffs which ASEAN helped spawn is an important counterpoint, its key regional convention, the so-called 'ASEAN Way', has long stood out as a paean to sovereignty norms, informal practices, intergovernmental regionalism and institutional minimalism.[35] Absent US advocacy and leadership of and in multilateralism in Asia, on the one hand, and regional political conditions conducive to the hosting and husbanding of an ambitious multilateralism in the region, on the other, it stands to reason why the multilateral enterprise in Asia was a late development and why it evolved the way it did.

## *From Bush to Bush*

With such reservations against US participation in multilateral diplomacy in post-Cold War Asia, the United States relented only when it realized its regional counterparts had no intention of severing their bilateral security alliances and economic ties with the United States, but regarded the emerging regional architecture as a supplementary structure that would ideally complement the existing bilateral structures and the broader balance of power system, rather than replace them.[36] Historically, there is a discernible pattern where America would show initial distrust of multilateral experiments in the region, but would subsequently support them once it has confirmed its participation. Ironically, Washington's scepticism did not prevent it from complaining about its perceived exclusion from such processes. For example, James Baker, as Secretary of State for George H. W. Bush, reportedly reacted angrily to Australia's initial proposal for the APEC, which did not include the United States.[37] It was President Bill Clinton who invited heads of government to the APEC meeting in Seattle in 1993, which eventuated in the upgrading of the trade forum from a gathering of economic ministers to a summit. 'We have to develop new institutional arrangements that support our national economic and security interests internationally', as Clinton noted in 1993. 'We're working to build a prosperous and peaceful Asia Pacific region through our work here in APEC'.[38] However, a US federal government shutdown in 1995 forced Clinton to miss the APEC meeting that year, which Clinton's press secretary would later lament as an episode that 'blew a hole in our Asia outreach strategy'.[39] Though the relatively modest agenda of APEC contributed to 'business facilitation', Asian anger at the International Monetary Fund (IMF) and the United States for their non-negotiable insistence on tough structural adjustments for Asian economies in the wake of the 1997 financial crisis led however to a weakening in East Asian commitment to the APEC. As discussed in the chapter on Japan, the Clinton administration was quick to quash the Hashimoto government's proposed Asian Monetary Fund (AMF) idea, whose widespread support in East Asia did little to change Washington's mind. Fair or otherwise, such experiences fostered the perception that the United States cared for little else in Asia other than its own interests. Indeed, even prior to the 1997 crisis, there was already regional apprehension over the APEC as 'a tool for US regional domination'.[40]

Be that as it may, while the subsequent formation of the APT and the Chiang Mai Initiative (CMI) currency swap arrangement for addressing short-term liquidity problems constituted East Asia's brand of 'reactionary regionalism' against the IMF and Washington, it ultimately did not represent a rejection as such of the 'Washington consensus' because the CMI swap arrangement relied (and continue to rely) on conditionality set forth by the IMF.[41] The fact that the CMI has never been activated, not even once, since its implementation in 2000 – it assumed a multilateral character in 2010 and was renamed the CMI Multilateralization (CMIM) – reflected Asia's abiding fidelity to world bodies and global-level mechanisms rather than regional ones.[42] Driven by perceived lack of American sensitivity towards and support for an ailing region, the formation of the APT and CMI/CMIM can therefore be understood as an expression of exclusive regionalism that arose in reaction to the United States; in other words, it was an ad hoc reaction to crisis rather than a creation born of indigenous strategic design and forethought. More than anything else, the Clinton administration's actions made it clear in no uncertain terms to Asians that America's preference for Asian regionalism is that it stays open and inclusive, rather than exclusive. All said, as the emergence of the TPP and the RCEP visions have shown, much as the problems of the Doha Round of world trade talks have contributed to the regional shift towards the formation of preferential trade agreements, so too, it should be said, has regional disenchantment with the APEC acted as a driving force.[43]

The sense of American insensitivity towards the region would persist into the first decade of the twenty-first century. With the onset of George W. Bush's presidency and the emergence of the US-led GWOT in the post-9/11 era, counterterrorism came to dominate the agendas of regional arrangements. While China responded with initial scepticism (especially when the APEC met in Shanghai in October 2001),[44] counterterrorism cooperation between China and the United States – the symbolism as much as, if not more than, the reality of it, since by most accounts actual bilateral cooperation was limited at best[45] – provided the basis for a tacit agreement between the two big powers that allowed both to pursue their respective security agendas with relatively little interference from each other. Meanwhile, Condoleeza Rice's uneven attendance at ARF meetings and her counterpart at Defense Donald Rumsfeld's express preference for a mission-oriented 'coalition of the willing' approach generated untold consternation among America's Asian security partners over the George W. Bush administration's apparent lack of support for Asia multilateralism.[46] However, it could be argued, where the region is concerned, that the Bush administration did not quite follow the same script of foreign policy unilateralism it drew up for the Middle East. Rather, efforts were made to seek and secure international collaboration as far as possible. To that end, in its prosecution of the GWOT, the United States has 'sought to engage and cooperate with nations whose governments share [its] values', as a senior US State Department official explained in 2003. 'The United States has scores of partners across the globe [including in Asia] in the war on terrorism …

Ninety countries have expressed support for the global war on terrorism'.[47] And while the antipathy of the neoconservative element during Bush's first presidential term toward large-scale standing multilateral institutions – or multilateralism with big numbers, as Kahler has put it[48] – was well known, Bush did however regard (or came to regard) particular functional arrangements – ad hoc coalitions of the willing and likeminded[49] – as useful for enhancing trade with the region and for cobbling together cooperative initiatives in support of the GWOT.

Moreover, the Bush administration strongly supported the APEC and the vision to create an Asia-Pacific free trade area. The idea here was to invest in trans-Pacific trade partnerships in view of the formation in late 2005 of the EAS (of which the United States, at that time, was not yet a member), which would presumably have provided the overarching framework for an East Asian trade area that excluded the United States. Crucially, beginning in 2005, Bush seized the opportunity provided by the APEC summits to engage in annual multilateral meetings with his counterparts from the ASEAN countries. These sessions laid the groundwork for the ASEAN-US Enhanced Partnership (2006–2011) and subsequently the ASEAN-US Leaders' Meeting. The Bush administration also played an instrumental role in initiating a host of other agreements with ASEAN, including the ASEAN Cooperation Plan (2002), the Enterprise for ASEAN Initiative (2002) and the ASEAN-US Trade and Investment Framework Agreement (2006).[50] Furthermore, the Bush administration began unofficially to engage Myanmar through the ASEAN–US Dialogue process and, following the waiver in November 2005 of remaining legislative restrictions on military assistance to Indonesia, resumed its policy of providing military aid to the Indonesians.[51] Finally, it played a key part in enhancing ASEAN–US relations – *inter alia* it was the first ASEAN dialogue partner to appoint an ambassador to ASEAN in April 2008 – without which the ASEAN–US Leaders' Meeting would probably not have been conceivable.[52]

### *Obama*

Barack Obama came to office in 2009 promising a foreign policy aimed at 'the restoration of multilateral diplomacy'.[53] In contrast to his predecessor George W. Bush's apparent disregard for multilateral institutions and conventions (especially during the first half of his presidency) – what international relations theorists have referred to as unilateralism[54] – Obama's persistent stress on the need for agreement among nations and strong international institutions in order to co-manage global and regional security challenges reflects his advocacy of what an analyst calls 'multilateralism with teeth'.[55] Obama's belief in multilateralism, it has further been proposed, is behind his administration's strong support for and active participation in Asia's regional economic and security institutions. As the president himself has put it:

> In addition to our bilateral relations, we also believe that the growth of multilateral organizations can advance the security and prosperity of this region. I know that the United States has been disengaged from many of these

organizations in recent years. So let me be clear: Those days have passed. As a [sic] Asia-Pacific nation, the United States expects to be involved in the discussions that shape the future of this region, and to participate fully in appropriate organizations as they are established and evolve.[56]

His first Secretary of State, Hillary Clinton, wrote in 2011:

> At a time when the [Asian] region is building a more mature security and economic architecture to promote stability and prosperity, US commitment there is essential. It will help build that architecture and pay dividends for continued American leadership well into this century, just as our post-World War II commitment to building a comprehensive and lasting transatlantic network of institutions and relationships has paid off many times over – and continues to do so. The time has come for the United States to make similar investments as a Pacific power, a strategic course set by President Barack Obama from the outset of his administration and one that is already yielding benefits.[57]

Support for multilateralism is one among a number of elements that make up Obama's pivot. As Kurt Campbell has put it, continued engagement with Asia's multilateral institutions stands alongside US alliances in Asia, relations with great and emerging regional powers in the region, economic statecraft, defence engagement and advocacy and support for democratization and human rights promotion in the region as Washington's key policy priorities for the Asia Pacific.[58] Carefully managed, the pivot could help the United States, long accustomed to being the region's strategic guarantor on its own, gradually to reduce the burdens and expectations heaped on it as an overextended global power through getting allies and partners involved.[59] In the view of one analyst, the Obama administration's strategy of 'repositioning' Washington's attention to Asia has been to utilize Asia's multilateral frameworks 'to convince China to make the rules with their neighbors in this region and play by these rules'.[60]

Obama, as noted, sees himself as the Pacific president America allegedly never had. More than any other region in the world, Asia would be the place where both a Pacific-oriented and multilateralist America are supposed to merge seamlessly in the form of the pivot/rebalance. It is safe to say that both these ideas have not yet been fully realized; indeed, there are good reasons to suggest they are likely to stay underdeveloped for the remainder of Obama's presidency. Against insinuations regarding the purported novelty of Obama's declared Asia-oriented focus and support of multilateral diplomacy, his policy as hitherto implemented has not substantively altered the broad strategic thrust pursued by the United States toward Asia throughout the post-Cold War period – neither in terms of America's enduring but ambivalent engagement with the region nor in terms of its equally ambivalent involvement in the region's multilateral processes (strange as this may sound in view of Obama's advocacy of multilateralism). Generally speaking, the ends being sought by way of his Asia pivot are not in question here; they are, as declared in another setting, 'as American as apple pie'.[61] To be sure, the Obama administration has expressed interest in engaging more deeply with Southeast Asia, which his predecessors' respective policies toward the Asia Pacific arguably lacked following America's involvement in the Vietnam War. There were good reasons behind Washington's past strategic disinterest over Southeast Asia, due not least to its post-Vietnam War fatigue, its greater concern over a new cold war with the Soviet Union, persistent worries over the Middle East, the forced closure of its military bases in the Philippines in the 1991–2 period, and the like. But even here it remains to be seen just how substantive Obama's engagement with Southeast Asia would be relative to efforts by past US presidents. The depth and extent of Obama's support for multilateral diplomacy are also questionable when viewed against the broader history of US engagement with Asian multilateralism in the post-Cold War years. The United States has long preferred to invest in its bilateral alliances with Asia-Pacific countries rather than rely on the region's multilateral arrangements, which, while not ignored by Washington, are at best seen by most Americans (and Asians alike) as adjunct or secondary to its alliance system.[62] Yet this has not prevented efforts by all US presidents in the post-Cold War period, both Democratic and Republican, to engage to varying extents with multilateralism – or, more accurately, with some multilateral arrangements and initiatives but not others – in Asia. Indeed, some of the security issues which the United States and its allies had previously managed together on a bilateral basis were subsequently handled multilaterally well before Obama assumed the presidency.[63]

This is not to imply Obama has been all empty talk. Under him, the United States acceded to the Treaty of Amity and Cooperation in Southeast Asia (TAC) in July 2009 – something his immediate predecessor in the White House was reluctant to do – and took part in the inaugural ASEAN–US Leaders' Meeting in Singapore in November 2009 – developments which, according to an official ASEAN account, led to a 'seismic change' in ASEAN–US relations.[64] His administration pursued the prospect of participation in the EAS with enthusiasm, and the United States, together with Russia, officially joined the summit in 2011. American participation in the EAS is important as the summit brings together all the great powers of the Asia-Pacific within a single setting (India, currently not a part of the APEC, is represented in the EAS), potentially strengthening the 'ASEAN plus eight' configuration – also reflected in the ADMM-Plus process – as 'a crucial pattern for regional cooperation'.[65] As two analysts have argued:

> The EAS has become surprisingly prominent largely as a consequence of the United States seeking to reengage or 'pivot' back to the region. Whatever one thinks of the merits of or necessity for such a policy, that these institutions are seen by the Obama administration as potentially important ways of exerting influence is significant and in marked contrast to the Bush era. The principal attractions of the EAS for the United States are: first, it is a member and so are key allies like Australia and, second, it potentially offers a way of curbing China's influence.[66]

Washington's emphasis on the EAS also underscores its continued commitment to a regional security architecture centred on ASEAN. In her October 2010 speech, Hillary Clinton referred to ASEAN as a 'fulcrum for the region's emerging regional architecture' and declared America's intentions to 'sustain and strengthen America's leadership in the Asia Pacific region'.[67] While this might have partially assuaged regional angst over whether the United States would continue its support of ASEAN centrality in Asian regionalism, it also raised expectations regarding the regional architecture's ability to 'produce results', as Clinton had emphasized in her speech.[68] As Donald Emmerson, describing Clinton's dictum that 'showing up is half of diplomacy', has suggested, the unsaid other half in Clinton's formulation of diplomacy is likely to be performance or at least the expectation of it.[69] For a brand of multilateralism that has principally favoured process over progress, the Obama administration's focus on results is a litmus test, especially for an ASEAN given increasingly to division and disunity, as highlighted by the fiasco caused by differences between Cambodia and its fellow ASEAN members at the ASEAN ministerial meeting in Phnom Penh in July 2012.

Further, the Obama administration has shown a willingness to use Asia's multilateral security mechanisms to raise objections against perceived provocations by other members. An obvious case in point is China's apparent assertiveness in the East and South China Seas against other territorial claimants. In this regard, the ARF, presumably to the consternation of ASEAN, has increasingly become an arena of sorts for heated exchanges between the United States and China over China's purported use of 'tailored coercion'.[70] At the 2010 ARF, the foreign ministers of the United States and China, Clinton and Yang Jiechi respectively, jousted verbally over perceived Chinese actions in the South China Sea, with the American side insistent that ensuring a peaceful resolution to the competing sovereignty claims therein constituted a US 'national interest' and the Chinese side objecting to the US position as 'an attack on China'.[71] Similarly, at the 2014 ARF, Clinton's successor John Kerry implicitly took the Chinese to task for provocative-cum-revisionist actions in the South China Sea and urged that a moratorium on provocation be observed – a charge his Chinese counterpart, Wang Yi, expectantly denied and roundly rejected.

Moreover, the likelihood that the United States would want to enlarge the EAS's remit – originally restricted to finance, education, avian flu, disaster management, and climate change as the priority areas for cooperation – to include security issues could face resistance from countries – China concerning its territorial claims, for example – that would rather keep those off the summit agenda. There is also concern among ASEAN states that the EAS, despite clear evidence of ASEAN's 'convening power', could end up being hijacked by heightened Sino-US rivalry and/or collaboration,[72] should the latter lead to the formation of an exclusive 'G2' comprising the world's two most powerful nations – an unlikely proposition – at the expense of the rest.[73] On the other hand, Obama's absences at both the APEC and EAS meetings in Bali, Indonesia in 2013, as with Rice's no-shows at the ARF, evoked similar sentiments from ASEAN leaders even as they commiserated with the US president over the fiscal and political problems he faced back in Washington. Referring to Obama's absence at the Bali meetings as 'a very big disappointment', the prime minister of Singapore stated, 'Obviously we prefer a US government that is working to one that is not. And we prefer a US president who is able to travel and fulfil his international duties to one who is preoccupied with national domestic preoccupations'.[74] And while Obama's attendances at both APEC and EAS meetings in 2014 in themselves represent a victory of sorts for US diplomacy, there was, at least at the APEC summit in Beijing, a sense, despite pulling off a landmark climate change agreement with China that specifies a timetable for emission reduction, that the United States had been upstaged by China, whose bold call for renewed efforts to establish the Asia-Pacific free trade area (a clear snub against the US-backed TPP) grand vision for the revival of the Silk Road, and formation of the Asian Infrastructure Investment Bank (AIIB) reflected Beijing's pushback against the Obama pivot.

## Conclusion: America's *à la carte* multilateralism

This chapter has sought to understand America's complex relationship with the Asian region particularly through Washington's contributions, in ways direct and less so, to multilateral architecture and diplomacy in Asia. It has shown that the history of US engagement with the region, and Southeast Asia in particular, has been marked by periods of ambivalence and occasional absenteeism, which ASEAN, especially in the wake of the Vietnam War, has done well to exploit and use to promote its own regional agency.[75] Moreover, there are reasons to suspect that Obama's pivot could well be subject to a similar fate.

What is multilateralism to Americans? According to the noted pundit Robert Kagan, US-style multilateralism amounts to 'getting a few important allies on board'[76] – a viewpoint his fellow Americans might identify more with the former president George W. Bush's version of multilateral engagement. Arguably, there is a distinct difference in the way Americans and Europeans comprehend multilateralism, which has led to public disagreements between the two groups in the post-Cold War era.[77] Interestingly, criticisms of the prominent academic-practitioner Joseph Nye's influential writings on soft power and smart power respectively,[78] which collectively provide the foundation to the Obama administration's emphasis on the imperative of smart power in its foreign policy, have highlighted Nye's alleged tendency to conflate multilateralism's focus on collective burden-sharing and the need for unequal contributions by stakeholders, on the one hand, with what Nye regards uncritically as the United States' given right to lead and to control multilateral institutions on the other.[79] What this implies is that when the United States faces opposition to its presumed right to lead, it might be tempted to defect from multilateralism or to avoid it altogether – as did a neoconservative-led Bush foreign policy with its rejection of the Kyoto protocol on global warming in 2001, its abrogation of the anti-ballistic missile treaty in 2002, and its prosecution of the Iraq war in 2003. And if American liberal internationalists are reportedly as willing as their neoconservative counterparts to ride roughshod over international law – the key difference being liberals 'feel sort of bad about it and wish they didn't have to do it'[80] – then it could conceivably explain why, apart from stylistic nuances, significant as they might have been, the substance of America's engagement with Asian multilateralism has varied little from president to president.[81] Echoing the unevenness of its long engagement with Asia, America's involvement in the region's multilateral diplomacy and its institutions has, at best, equally been an ambivalent exercise.[82]

The question of how truly committed Obama is to multilateralism has generated considerable interest ever since his presidency began. The foregoing analysis points to a pattern, since Asian multilateralism began in earnest in the post-Cold War period, of relatively active US involvement in Asian regional institutions. While George W. Bush's Asia policy has been singled out for criticism, it is clear that his Democrat counterparts, who may have publicly favoured multilateralism, did not fare very much better than Bush in this regard. Indeed, even Bill Clinton, who famously advocated 'assertive multilateralism',[83] proved equally unilateral in his policy over the Balkans, so much so that it provoked America's European allies to accuse the Clinton administration of overbearing behaviour.[84] Debating whether US foreign policy in the post-Cold War era has been unilateral or multilateral in approach has only been partially helpful where US policy towards the Asia Pacific is concerned.[85] The real challenge confronting Obama, the avowed multilateral diplomatist, could well be to avoid making the false choices between formal institutions and functional coalitions which he, like his predecessors, has equally embraced. As Stewart Patrick has contended, Obama would need to 'draw on both the legitimacy and capacity of standing institutions as well as the flexibility and agility of ad hoc coalitions'.[86]

Ultimately, America's missed opportunities to engage more deeply with the Asian region highlight the gap in words and deeds: between verbal declarations and protestations of US support for its Asia-Pacific allies and for ASEAN, on the one hand, and the reality of America's benign neglect of its regional partners on the other. To be sure, Washington did not completely abandon the ASEAN states but furnished them with economic, humanitarian and other forms of assistance during this period.[87] That said, contrary to the popular contention that the Asian region has largely been defined by great power designs and dynamics,[88] American neglect of the region arguably furnished the requisite geopolitical space for ASEAN to emerge as a regional political force in its own right.[89] Thus understood, rather than reading them merely as vacuous 'diplomatic speak', the aforementioned statements by US leaders in support of ASEAN could also be regarded as a reflection of Washington's endorsement of the regional organization as the key bulwark against the spread of communism in Southeast Asia during the Cold War, and a key partner of the United States in the contemporary era. In much the same vein, American ambivalence towards Asia and Asian multilateralism, perhaps more a function of its role as the only global power than anything else, has facilitated the emergence of regional powers, most notably China, leading to what some see as a shift in not only the region's balance of power but equally its influence.[90] Whether this shift – heavily contested by America, in the view of some – would lead to a power sharing arrangement between America and China advocated by analysts such as Hugh White remains to be seen.[91] As a recent Chatham House report has concluded:

> Over the long-term, America will continue to play a central role in the region, but not indefinitely as the lead actor. It will be looking in Asia, as elsewhere, to share the burdens of leadership. In the next 15 years, Asians may well have to get used to a situation with which Europeans are only just coming to terms – a United States that is a very important regional actor, but not always the first or principal port of call for ensuring security.[92]

This could well be the United States', and Asia's, shared future.

## Notes

1 John Lamberton Harper, *The Cold War* (Oxford: Oxford University Press, 2011), p. 166.
2 'Nixon Warns of Hard Choices', *Daytona Beach Morning Journal*, 26 February 1971, www.news.google.com/newspapers?nid=1873&dat=19710226&id=-00fAAAAIBAJ &sjid=mdEEAAAAIBAJ&pg=4570,7013521. On the other hand, a recent analysis of US behaviour in Southeast Asia during the global war on terror period has argued that a form of strategic benignity has its uses as well: 'While the "war on terror" depicted the centrality of the United States, it subsequently became apparent that Washington could only guarantee its place in the hierarchy if it projected itself as a benign hegemon'. Charmaine G. Misalucha, 'Southeast Asia–US Relations: Hegemony or Hierarchy?', *Contemporary Southeast Asia*, Vol. 33, No. 2 (2011), pp. 209–28, on p. 209. Also see Alice Ba, 'Systemic Neglect? A Reconsideration of US-Southeast Asia Policy', *Contemporary Southeast Asia*, Vol. 31, No. 3 (2009), pp. 369–98.
3 Parts of this chapter draw from See Seng Tan, 'Change and Continuity in America's Asia Pivot: US Engagement with Multilateralism in the Asia Pacific', in Hugo Meier, ed., *Origins and Evolution of the US Rebalance toward Asia: Diplomatic, Military and Economic Dimensions* (Houndmills, Basingstoke: Palgrave Macmillan, 2015), (in press).
4 Leszek Buszynski, 'Russia and the Asia-Pacific Region', *Pacific Affairs*, Vol. 65, No. 4 (1992–3), pp. 486–509; Tom J. Farer, 'The Role of Regional Collective Security Arrangements', in Thomas G. Weiss, ed., *Collective Security in a Changing World* (Boulder, CO: Lynne Rienner, 1993), pp. 153–89, on p. 180; Arnold L. Horelick, 'The Soviet Union's Asian Collective Security Proposal: A Club in Search of Members', *Pacific Affairs*, Vol. 47, No. 3 (1974), pp. 269–85.
5 G. John Ikenberry, *After Victory: Institutions, Strategic Restraint, and the Rebuilding of Order after Major Wars* (Princeton, NJ: Princeton University Press, 2001). On NATO, see, Frank Schimmelfennig, 'Multilateralism in Post-Cold War NATO: Functional Form, Identity-Driven Cooperation', Paper for AUEB International Conference on 'Assessing Multilateralism in the Security Domain', Delphi, Greece, 3–5 June 2005.
6 Philip Zelikow, 'American Engagement in Asia', in Robert D. Blackwill and Paul Dibb, eds., *America's Asian Alliances* (Cambridge, MA: MIT Press, 2000), pp. 19–30.
7 G. John Ikenberry, 'Power and Liberal Order: America's Postwar World Order in Transition', *International Relations of the Asia Pacific*, Vol. 5, No. 2 (2005), pp. 133–52, on p. 134.
8 Philip Zelikow, 'American Engagement in Asia', in Robert D. Blackwill and Paul Dibb, eds., *America's Asian Alliances* (Cambridge, MA: MIT Press, 2000). pp. 19–30.
9 Victor D. Cha, 'Powerplay: Origins of the US Alliance System in Asia', *International Security*, Vol. 34, No. 3 (2009/10), pp. 158–96.

*United States* 125

10 Anthony L. Smith, *Strategic Centrality: Indonesia's Changing Role in ASEAN* (Singapore: Institute of Southeast Asian Studies, 2000), p. 10.
11 Joey S. R. Long, *Safe for Decolonization: The Eisenhower Administration, Great Britain, and Singapore* (Kent, OH: Kent State University Press, 2011).
12 Russell H. Fifield, *National and Regional Interests in ASEAN: Competition and Cooperation in International Politics*, Occasional Paper, No. 57 (Singapore: Institute of Southeast Asian Studies, 1979), p. 70.
13 Robert J. McMahon, 'The US, and South and Southeast Asia, 1975–2000', in Robert D. Schulzinger, ed., *A Companion to American Foreign Relations* (Malden, MA: Blackwell Publishing, 2003), p. 442.
14 Cyrus R. Vance, *Hard Choices: Critical Years in America's Foreign Policy* (New York: Simon and Schuster, 1983), p. 125.
15 Robert J. McMahon, *The Limits of Empire: The United States and Southeast Asia Since World War II* (New York: Columbia University Press, 1999), pp. 197–8.
16 Terry L. Deibel, 'Reagan's Mixed Legacy', *Foreign Policy*, No. 75 (1989), pp. 34–55, at p. 38, cited in Diane K. Mauzy and Brian L. Job, 'US Policy in Southeast Asia: Limited Re-engagement after Years of Benign Neglect', *Asian Survey*, Vol. 47, No. 4 (2007), pp. 622–41, on p. 624.
17 McMahon, *The Limits of Empire*, p. 198.
18 Amitav Acharya and See Seng Tan, 'Betwixt Balance and Community: America, ASEAN, and the Security of Southeast Asia', *International Relations of the Asia-Pacific*, Vol. 6, No. 1 (2006), pp. 37–59, on p. 47.
19 'US Wants Fully Restored Relationship with New Zealand', US Assistant Secretary of State Richard Solomon's address to the American Chamber of Commerce in Auckland, New Zealand, 6 August 1999, http://newzealand.usembassy.gov/uploads/DK/E4/DKE4vNH3fqaXhev0GuHWqQ/full.pdf.
20 Michael McDevitt, 'US Security Strategy in East Asia', 6 November 2002, http://web.mit.edu/ssp/seminars/wed_archives02fall/mcdevitt.htm.
21 John Gershman, 'Is Southeast Asia the Second Front?', *Foreign Affairs*, Vol. 81, No. 4 (2003), pp. 60–74; Amitav Acharya and Arabinda Acharya, 'The Myth of the Second Front: Localizing the "War on Terror" in Southeast Asia', *The Washington Quarterly*, Vol. 3, No. 4 (2007), pp. 75–90; Kumar Ramakrishna and See Seng Tan, eds., *After Bali: The Threat of Terrorism in Southeast Asia* (Singapore: World Scientific, 2003).
22 Chong Guan Kwa and See Seng Tan, 'The Keystone of World Order', *The Washington Quarterly*, Vol. 24, No. 3 (2001), pp. 95–103.
23 Former US Secretary of State Colin Powell, in June 2002. Powell's director for policy planning in the State Department, Mitchell Reiss, likewise stated that 'America is a Pacific power, firmly rooted in this region. We are determined to play a vital role in the Asia of tomorrow that is taking shape today'. Both cited in M. Taylor Fravel and Richard J. Samuels, 'The United States as an Asian Power: Realism or Conceit?', *Audit of the Conventional Wisdom*, No. 05-2 (Cambridge, MA: MIT Center for International Studies, 2005), p. 2.
24 'Remarks by President Barack Obama at Suntory Hall', *The White House: Office of the Press Secretary*, 14 November 2009, www.whitehouse.gov/the-press-office/remarks-president-barack-obama-suntory-hall.
25 Andrew Monahan, 'China Overtakes Japan as World's No. 2 Economy', *The Wall Street Journal*, 14 February 2011; 'China Overtakes Japan as World's Second-Biggest Stock Market', *Bloomberg News*, 28 November 2014, www.bloomberg.com/news/2014-11-27/china-surpasses-japan-as-world-s-second-biggest-equity-market.html.
26 Hillary Clinton, 'America's Pacific Century', *Foreign Policy*, 11 October 2011, www.foreignpolicy.com/articles/2011/10/11/americas_pacific_century?page=full.
27 According to Campbell and Andrews, 'Some have mistakenly described the rebalance as a "return" to Asia – nothing could be further from the truth because, in reality, the

United States had never left'. Kurt Campbell and Brian Andrews, 'Explaining the US "Pivot" to Asia', *Americas 2013/01* (London: Chatham House/Royal Institute of International Affairs, 2013), p. 2.
28. Michael D. Swaine, 'America's Asia Pivot Threatens Regional Stability', *The National Interest*, 7 December 2011, http://nationalinterest.org/commentary/washington-destabilizes-sino-american-relations-6211?page=1; Harry Kazianis, 'America's AirSea Battle vs. China's A2/AD: Who Wins?', *The Diplomat*, 19 July 2013, http://thediplomat.com/2013/07/americas-airsea-battle-vs-chinas-a2ad-who-wins/.
29. William Kyle, 'The US Navy and the Pivot: Less Means Less', *The Diplomat*, 31 March 2014, http://thediplomat.com/2014/03/the-us-navy-and-the-pivot-less-means-less/.
30. Max Boot, 'Obama's Disappearing Pacific Pivot', *Commentary*, 29 January 2014, www.commentarymagazine.com/2014/01/29/obamas-disappearing-pacific-pivot-state-of-the-union/; Shannon Tiezzi, 'Has Obama Abandoned the Pivot to Asia?', *The Diplomat*, 20 January 2014, http://thediplomat.com/2014/01/has-obama-abandoned-the-pivot-to-asia/.
31. US Secretary of Defense Chuck Hagel in April 2014, cited in Zachary Keck, 'US Swears Asia Pivot Isn't Dead', *The Diplomat*, 2 April 2014, http://thediplomat.com/2014/04/us-swears-asia-pivot-isnt-dead/.
32. Matt Schiavenza, 'The "Insipid" Mr. Obama Goes to China', *The Atlantic*, 6 November 2014, www.theatlantic.com/international/archive/2014/11/obama-visits-china-global-times/382435/. The Chinese commentary in question is from 'Midterm Result Will Further Thwart Obama', *Global Times*, 5 November 2014. www.globaltimes.cn/content/890056.shtml.
33. Steve Coll, 'Two More Years: Can Obama Duck Lame-Duck Syndrome?', *The New Yorker*, 17 November 2014, www.newyorker.com/magazine/2014/11/17/two-years-2; Philip Ewing, 'Obama's Asia Pivot: A Work in Progress', *Politico*, 20 April 2014, www.politico.com/story/2014/04/barack-obama-asia-pivot-105842.html; Isabel Reynolds and Maiko Takahashi, 'US–Japan Remain Divided on TPP Deal Weeks Before Obama Visit', *Bloomberg*, 10 April 2014, www.bloomberg.com/news/2014-04-10/u-s-japan-remain-divided-on-tpp-deal-weeks-before-obama-visit.html.
34. Amitav Acharya, *Whose Ideas Matter? Agency and Power in Asian Regionalism* (Ithaca, NY: Cornell University Press, 2009); See Seng Tan and Amitav Acharya, eds., *Bandung Revisited: The Legacy of the 1955 Asian-African Conference for International Order* (Singapore: NUS Press, 2008).
35. Amitav Acharya, 'Ideas, Identity, and Institution-Building: From the "ASEAN Way" to the "Asia-Pacific Way"?', *The Pacific Review*, Vol. 10, No. 3 (1997). pp. 319–46.
36. See Seng Tan, 'Spectres of Leifer: Insights on Regional Order and Security for Southeast Asia Today', *Contemporary Southeast Asia*, Vol. 34, No. 3 (2012), pp. 309–37, on p. 323.
37. Michael Wesley, 'The Dog That Didn't Bark: The Bush Administration and East Asian Regionalism', in Mark Beeson, ed., *Bush and Asia: America's Evolving Relations with East Asia* (London: Routledge, 2006), p. 69.
38. Cited in Frank Langdon and Brian L. Job, 'APEC Beyond Economics: The Politics of APEC', Working Paper 243 (Notre Dame, IN: The Helen Kellogg Institute for International Studies, 1997), p. 3.
39. Zachary Keck, 'Shutdown Forces Obama to Cancel Malaysia Trip, APEC May Be Next', *The Diplomat*, 2 October 2013, http://thediplomat.com/2013/10/shutdown-forces-obama-to-cancel-malaysia-trip-apec-may-be-next/.
40. Helen Nesadurai, 'APEC: A Tool for US Regional Domination?', *The Pacific Review*, Vol. 9, No. 1 (2006), pp. 31–57. Also see Mark Beeson, 'American Hegemony: The View from Australia', *SAIS Review of International Affairs*, Vol. 23, No. 2 (2003), pp. 113–31.
41. Mark Beeson, 'ASEAN Plus Three and the Rise of Reactionary Regionalism', *Contemporary Southeast Asia*, Vol. 25, No. 2 (2003), pp. 251–68.

42 Hall Hill and Jayant Menon, 'Asia's New Financial Safety Net: Is the Chiang Mai Initiative Designed Not To Be Used?', *Vox*, 25 July 2012, www.voxeu.org/article/chiang-mai-initiative-designed-not-be-used.
43 Edward J. Lincoln, 'Taking APEC Seriously', *Brookings Policy Brief Series* No. 92 (Washington, D.C.: Brookings Institution, 2001), www.brookings.edu/research/papers/2001/12/japan-lincoln.
44 'China's Disappointment: The Fight against Terrorism Will Dominate the APEC meeting', *The Economist*, 18 October 2001, www.economist.com/node/825358.
45 Shirley A. Kan, 'US–China Counterterrorism Cooperation: Issues for US Policy', *Congressional Research Service*, 15 July 2010, www.fas.org/sgp/crs/terror/RL33001.pdf.
46 Stewart Patrick, '"The Mission Determines the Coalition": The United States and Multilateral Cooperation after 9/11', in Bruce D. Jones, Shepard Forman and Richard Gowan, eds., *Cooperating for Peace and Security: Evolving Institutions and Arrangements in a Context of Changing US Security Policy* (Cambridge: Cambridge University Press, 2010), pp. 20–44, on p. 32; Emma-Kate Symons, 'ASEAN Anger at Snub by Rice', *The Australian*, 28 July 2007, www.theaustralian.com.au/archive/news/asean-anger-at-snub-by-rice/story-e6frg6t6-1111114037879; Edward J. Lincoln, 'The Bush Second Term and East Asian Economic Regionalism', *JCER* (Japan Center for Economic Research), undated, www.jcer.or.jp/eng/pdf/EJ.Lincoln0503.pdf.
47 Paula J. Dobriansky, 'Unilateralism and US Foreign Policy', Remarks to Woodrow Wilson School of International and Public Affairs, Princeton University, Princeton, NJ, 5 December 2003, www.2001-2009.state.gov/g/rls/rm/2003/27418.htm.
48 Miles Kahler, 'Multilateralism with Small and Large Numbers', *International Organization*, Vol. 46, No. 3 (1992), pp. 681–708.
49 Amitav Acharya and See Seng Tan, 'Introduction', in See Seng Tan and Amitav Acharya, eds., *Asia-Pacific Security Cooperation: National Interests and Regional Order* (Armonk, NY: M. E. Sharpe, 2004), pp. xxvi–xxix.
50 With the Enterprise for ASEAN Initiative, which furnished a roadmap for upgrading largely consultation-based bilateral trade and investment framework agreements (TIFAs) to more binding free trade agreements (FTAs), as the basis, the Bush administration negotiated FTAs with various ASEAN countries with whom the United States had bilateral TIFAs, but succeeded in some instances (e.g. Singapore) but not in others (e.g. Malaysia, Thailand), at least back in 2007. Robert G. Sutter, *The United States in Asia* (Lanham, MD: Rowman and Littlefield, 2009), p. 114.
51 'US to Resume Select Military Assistance to Indonesia', *usinfo.state.gov*, 25 November 2005, www.fas.org/asmp/resources/govern/109th/MilAidIndonesia22Nov05.htm.
52 Jürgen Haacke, 'Playing Catch-Up: The United States and Southeast Asia', *LSE IDEAS Special Report (SR) 003: Obama Nation? US Foreign Policy One Year On* (2010), pp. 28–33, on p. 28.
53 Richard Gowan and Bruce Jones, 'Mr. Obama Goes to New York: The President and the Restoration of Multilateral Diplomacy', *Brookings Report*, 17 September 2009 (Washington, D.C.: Brookings Institution, 2009), www.brookings.edu/research/reports/2009/09/obama-united-nations-jones.
54 David M. Malone and Yuen Foong Khong, eds., *Unilateralism and US Foreign Policy: International Perspectives* (Boulder, CO: Lynne Rienner, 2003).
55 Chris Good, 'The Obama Doctrine: Multilateralism with Teeth', *The Atlantic*, 10 December 2009, www.theatlantic.com/politics/archive/2009/12/the-obama-doctrine-multilateralism-with-teeth/31655/.
56 'Remarks by President Barack Obama at Suntory Hall'.
57 Clinton, 'America's Pacific Century'.
58 Campbell and Andrews, 'Explaining the US "Pivot" to Asia'.
59 Ba, 'Systemic Neglect?', p. 369.

60 Ernest Bower of Washington-based CSIS, cited in Jay Newton-Small, 'Burma's Thein Sein Visits Washington', *Time*, 20 May 2013, http://swampland.time.com/2013/05/20/burmas-thein-sein-visits-washington/.
61 Francis Fukuyama, 'After Neoconservatism', *The New York Times*, 19 February 2006, www.nytimes.com/2006/02/19/magazine/neo.html?pagewanted=print&_r=0.
62 Bates Gill, Michael Green, Kiyoto Tsuji and William Watts, *Strategic Views on Asian Regionalism: Survey Results and Analysis* (Washington, D.C.: Center for Strategic and International Studies, 2009).
63 Elliot S. Krauss and T. J. Pempel, eds., *Beyond Bilateralism: US–Japan Relations in the New Asia Pacific* (Stanford, CA: Stanford University Press, 2004).
64 'Overview of ASEAN–US Dialogue Relations', *www.asean.org*, undated, www.asean.org/news/item/overview-of-asean-us-dialogue-relations.
65 David Capie and Amitav Acharya, 'The United States and the East Asia Summit: A New Beginning?', *PacNet*, No. 64, 14 November 2011. On the ADMM+8, see See Seng Tan, '"Talking Their Walk"? The Evolution of Defence Regionalism in Southeast Asia', *Asian Security*, Vol. 8, No. 3 (2012), pp. 232–50.
66 Mark Beeson and Diane Stone, 'Patterns of Leadership in the Asia-Pacific: A Symposium', *The Pacific Review*, Vol. 27, No. 4 (2014), pp. 505–22, on p. 516.
67 Aaron Sirila, 'Clinton: Renewed American Leadership in Asia', *Asia Matters for America* (East–West Center), 4 November 2010, www.asiamattersforamerica.org/asia/clinton-renewed-american-leadership-in-asia.
68 As Hillary Clinton has argued, 'It's more important to have organizations that produce results, rather than simply producing new organizations'. Cited in See Seng Tan, 'Competing Visions: EAS in the Regional Architecture Debate', *East Asia Forum*, 15 November 2011, www.eastasiaforum.org/2011/11/15/competing-visions-eas-in-the-regional-architecture-debate/.
69 Donald K. Emmerson, *Asian Regionalism and US Policy: The Case for Creative Adaptation*, RSIS Working Paper, No. 193 (Singapore: S. Rajaratnam School of International Studies, 2010), p. 24.
70 Patrick M. Cronin, Ely Ratner, Elbridge Colby, Zachary M. Hosford and Alexander Sullivan, *Tailored Coercion: Competition and Risk in Maritime Asia* (Washington, D.C.: Center for New American Security, 2014).
71 Gordon C. Chang, 'Hillary Clinton Changes America's China Policy', *Forbes*, 28 July 2010, www.forbes.com/2010/07/28/china-beijing-asia-hillary-clinton-opinions-columnists-gordon-g-chang.html.
72 See Seng Tan, *Facilitating China–US Relations in the Age of Rebalancing: ASEAN's 'Middle Power' Diplomacy*, EAI MPDI Working Paper No. 1 (Seoul: East Asia Institute, 18 October 2013); Yang Razali Kassim, 'East Asia Summit 2012: Asia's Power Game Unfolds', *East Asia Forum*, 12 December 2012, www.eastasiaforum.org/2012/12/12/east-asia-summit-2012-asias-power-game-unfolds/.
73 Richard C. Bush, 'The United States and China: A G-2 in the Making?', *Brookings*, 11 October 2011, www.brookings.edu/research/articles/2011/10/11-chira-us-g2-bush; Elizabeth C. Economy and Adam Segal, 'The G-2 Mirage: Why the United States and China Are Not Ready to Upgrade Ties', *Foreign Affairs*, Vol. 88, No. 3 (2009), pp. 14–23; Ramon Pacheco Pardo, 'Return of the G2: Can US and China Run the World?, *The Telegraph*, 12 November 2014.
74 'Apec 2013: US Shutdown Fears Perturb Apec Summit', *The Straits Times*, 6 October 2013, www.straitstimes.com/the-big-story/asia-report/indonesia/story/apec-2013-us-shutdown-fears-perturb-apec-summit-20131006.
75 Amitav Acharya, 'Review Article: The Emerging Regional Architecture of World Politics', *World Politics*, Vol. 59, No. 4 (2007), pp. 629–52.

76 Robert Kagan, 'Multilateralism, American Style', *The Washington Post*, 13 September 2002, http://carnegieendowment.org/2002/09/13/multilateralism-american-style/2poj?reloadFlag=1.
77 Bruce Jones, 'The Coming Clash? Europe and US Multilateralism under Obama', in Alvaro de Vasconcelos and Marcin Zaborowski, eds., *The Obama Moment: European and American Perspectives* (Paris: European Union Institute for Security Studies, 2010), pp. 63–77.
78 Joseph S. Nye, *Soft Power: The Means to Success in World Politics* (New York: Public Affairs, 2004); Joseph S. Nye, 'Public Diplomacy and Soft Power', *Annals of the American Academy of Political and Social Science*, No. 616 (2008), pp. 94–109; and, Joseph S. Nye, 'Security and Smart Power', *American Behavioral Scientist*, Vol. 51, No. 9 (2008), pp. 1351–6.
79 Paul Cammack, 'Smart Power and US Leadership: A Critique of Joseph Nye', *49th Parallel*, No. 22 (2008), pp. 4–20. As the title of one of Nye's books has it, the United States is 'bound to lead'. See, Joseph S. Nye, *Bound to Lead: The Changing Nature of American Power* (New York: Basic Books, 1990).
80 David Bosco, 'What Divides Neocons and Liberal Interventionists', *Foreign Policy*, 9 April 2012, http://bosco.foreignpolicy.com/posts/2012/04/09/what_divides_neocons_and_liberal_interventionists.
81 Ba, 'Systemic Neglect?'.
82 Stewart Patrick and Shepard Forman, eds., *Multilateralism and US Foreign Policy: Ambivalent Engagement* (Boulder, CO: Lynne Rienner, 2002).
83 Commenting on Clinton's 'assertive multilateralism', Stewart Patrick argues that the United States 'has demonstrated a growing willingness to act alone and to opt out of multilateral initiatives'. Stewart Patrick, 'America's Retreat from Multilateral Engagement', *Current History*, Vol. 99 (December 2000), pp. 430–39, on p. 437.
84 François Heisbourg, 'American Hegemony? Perceptions of the US Abroad', *Survival*, Vol. 41, No. 4 (1999–2000), pp. 5–19.
85 Frederick Tsai, 'The False Binary Choice between Unilateralism and Multilateralism', *SAIS Review of International Affairs*, Vol. 28, No. 2 (2008), pp. 45–8.
86 Stewart Patrick, 'Prix Fixe *and* à la Carte: Avoiding False Multilateral Choices', *The Washington Quarterly*, Vol. 32, No. 4 (2009), pp. 77–95, see p. 83.
87 Mauzy and Job, 'US Policy in Southeast Asia', p. 624.
88 The argument is made most forcefully in Barry Buzan and Ole Wæver, *Regions and Powers: The Structure of International Security* (Cambridge: Cambridge University Press, 2003); and Peter J. Katzenstein, *A World of Regions: Asia and Europe in the American Imperium* (Ithaca, NY: Cornell University Press, 2005).
89 Acharya and Tan, 'Betwixt Balance and Community'.
90 William W. Keller and Thomas G. Rawski, eds., *China's Rise and the Balance of Influence in Asia* (Pittsburgh, PA: University of Pittsburgh Press, 2007).
91 Aaron L. Friedberg, *A Contest for Supremacy: China, America, and the Struggle for Mastery in Asia* (New York: W. W. Norton, 2012); Hugh White, *The China Choice: Why America Should Share Power* (Collingwood, VIC: Black Inc., 2013). Also see Yuen Foong Khong, 'Primacy or World Order? The United States and China's Rise – A Review Essay', *International Security*, Vol. 38, No. 3 (2013/14), pp. 153–75.
92 Xenia Dormandy with Rory Kinane, *Asia-Pacific Security: A Changing Role for the United States*, Chatham House Report (London: Chatham House/Royal Institute of International Affairs, 2014), p. viii.

# 8   Indonesia

While this book has focused on the material and ideational contributions of non-ASEAN powers and stakeholders of the regional multilateral architecture of Asia – in particular, Australia, Japan, China and the United States – it is nonetheless useful to compare their involvement and impact in and on Asian multilateralism with that of the *de facto* leader of ASEAN, Indonesia. If the historical approaches adopted by Japan and China towards Asia had been to 'lead from behind' (see chapters 5 and 6), the same could also be said of post-Sukarno Indonesia. This has certainly been true of the presidential tenure of Suharto. Yet it was also in this period that Indonesia's leadership of ASEAN and the shaping of the emerging regional architecture proved most productive, not least because of the relative willingness of the other ASEAN member countries to accede to Indonesia's lead. The abrupt downfall of Suharto coincided with – indeed, was partly brought about by – the Asian financial crisis of 1997, and the ensuing few years proved difficult for ASEAN and Asian multilateralism more generally as Indonesia's continued ability and will to provide regional leadership was questioned as the nation sought to consolidate its fledging democratization while, at the same time, struggling with religious militancy and terrorism throughout the 2000s up to the present. Yet that same period has also witnessed democratic Indonesia's leadership in security and in the promotion of democracy and human rights in the region.

Be that as it may, with the economic rise and growing diplomatic prominence of Indonesia has come growing frustration among many Indonesians over the perception that their country's long-standing practice of treating ASEAN as the 'cornerstone' of its foreign policy is in fact an unwarranted hindrance to Indonesia's continued rise. Although the path towards power and prosperity is by no means given, extant achievements such as Indonesia's membership in the Group of Twenty (G20) and the new presidency of Joko Widodo furnish hope that the country's long-held aspiration towards greatness might be realized sooner than later.

Against this backdrop, this chapter examines four interrelated issues. The first is the persistent problem that has long plagued Indonesia, namely, its grand ambition of becoming a great nation – at the very least, a thriving 'middle power' – and hitherto an inability to fulfil its putative destiny due to a chronic lack of capacity. For Indonesia, the compromise solution, and a historically profitable one, has been to focus on ASEAN as the centrepiece of its foreign policy. The second issue involves Indonesia's contributions, in and through ASEAN, to moulding the shape and substance of Asian multilateralism. The third concern has to do with the feature of Asian multilateralism to which Indonesia, perhaps more than any other country and 'stakeholder' in Asia's ensemble of regional arrangements, has furnished leadership, namely, the engagement and socialization of China towards norms of regional responsibility (a process whose 'success' has understandably been questioned in recent times). Finally, the chapter asks whether there is any merit in the argument, often heard throughout Indonesia, concerning the increasing irrelevance of ASEAN to Indonesia's interests. Should Jakarta, whether during the tenure of President Widodo or a future leader, decide to significantly downgrade ASEAN as a priority concern – or, for that matter, sever its ties with ASEAN altogether – the repercussions for ASEAN and Asian multilateralism would be serious, possibly (and ironically) to Indonesia's detriment.

## Aspiration without ability

As one of the Third World's largest countries and key actor in the Non-Aligned Movement (NAM) and the first Afro-Asian Conference (better known as the Bandung Conference) in 1955 – as well as being the world's most populous Muslim-majority nation – modern Indonesia, whose nationalists have consistently traced their national lineage to the historical empires of Srivijaya and Majapahit – presumably the latter more so than the former given Java-centred Majapahit's domination over Sumatra-centred Srivijaya via a putdown of the rebellion in Palembang in 1377[1] – has long maintained a belief in its inherent right to regional hegemony and leadership in Southeast Asia and a putative role in world affairs. Where modern Indonesia is concerned, there was no question by the early 1960s of Sukarno's pretentions about Indonesia's putative place at the centre of his dream of a pan-Malay 'Indonesia Raya' (Greater Indonesia).[2] And despite his obvious differences with his predecessor in terms of policy and personality, Suharto nonetheless held the same belief that Indonesia should play a wider regional and ultimately global role. Yet both leaders sought to realize this same desired end through different means, with the former adopting a bellicose approach through his policy of *konfrontasi* (confrontation) and the latter a considerably more constructive, even cooperative, approach through ASEAN regionalism. (Indeed, *konfrontasi* would prove costly to Indonesia where its international reputation was concerned since it raised the spectre that Indonesia, a darling of the Third World and the NAM, seemed bent on pursuing regional hegemony through aggrandizement and belligerence. The perceived hypocrisy has been described by Dewi Fortuna Anwar: 'While claiming to be a champion of the oppressed peoples in Asia and Africa, Indonesia, in fact, appeared to be aggressive and expansionist'.[3]) Hitherto, that ambition to greatness has been consistently frustrated by its persistent inadequacies. 'Indonesia has aspirations to play a leading role in the Southeast Asian region and yet there is some dissonance between this intention and the capacity to achieve regional leadership', as Anthony L. Smith has observed. 'Modern reality is that Indonesia's ability to get involved in regional affairs is significantly hampered, but this does not change Jakarta's long-term outlook'.[4]

More than anything, it is the incessant attempt to reconcile aspiration with the glaring lack in ability and capacity that has led Indonesia to look towards ASEAN and rendering it 'the cornerstone' of Indonesian foreign policy since the founding of that organization in 1967. In return (and arguably much in the same way as other middle powers like Australia and South Korea), the growing international influence of ASEAN and its convening power have furnished Indonesia with a regional and global reach otherwise unachievable on its own. To that end, Indonesia has been ASEAN's most ardent supporter and its political epicentre rolled into one, and in a sense, the pivot nation of Asia's multilateral architecture through the ASEAN Way, whose social convention of decision by consultation (or deliberation) and consensus – that is, *musyawarah* and *mufakat* – stems in part from traditional Javanese ideas and practices.[5] On the other hand, the tension between the ideal and the real for Indonesia in terms of its centrality in and leadership of ASEAN serves equally as a microcosm of that organization's putative centrality in and leadership of the broader project of Asian multilateralism. That Indonesia has sought to lead ASEAN is not in question. Ralf Emmers, for example, has persuasively argued that Indonesia's leadership in regional security, in concrete terms, can be seen in three broad areas, namely, its effort to establish Southeast Asia as a stable – and, critically, autonomous – region, its work in conflict mediation in the Cambodian conflict during the 1980s and over the South China Sea disputes especially in the 1990s, and its promotion of democracy, security and human rights in the region through developing institutional and consultative mechanisms.[6] Be that as it may, there have been phases in its post-Suharto years where Jakarta seemed distracted, as happened in the period of domestic economic, social and political crisis in the wake of Suharto's downfall in May 1998, or in more recent times where key pundits at home have publicly questioned the rationale for keeping ASEAN as the cornerstone of its foreign policy.

In that regard, Indonesia's regional leadership has been constrained by a number of related factors. Externally, despite the relative acceptance of Indonesia by its fellow ASEAN members as *primus inter pares* within the institution, Jakarta's regional leadership has been limited due in part to resistance from some Southeast Asian states, whether those which view Jakarta's preference for regional autonomy as an expedient rationale for its long-standing aspiration to achieve regional hegemony, on the one hand, or those which see post-Suharto Indonesia's promotion of democracy and human rights as a threat to their political systems on the other.[7] Jakarta has held firmly to the notion that the management of regional order in Southeast Asia is best left to the region's countries themselves. 'The nations of Southeast Asia should consciously work toward the day when security in their own region will be the primary responsibility of the Southeast Asian nations themselves', as Adam Malik, the former Indonesian foreign minister, noted in 1971. 'Not through big power alignments, not through the building of contending military pacts or military arsenals but through strengthening the state of respective endurance, through effective regional cooperation with other states sharing this basic view on world affairs'.[8] In other words, regional security is to be achieved through intramural cooperation within ASEAN rather than through dependence on external powers. At the same time, the realization of such an approach to regional security – 'regional solutions to regional problems', as the mantra goes[9] – has always been subject to the competing preferences of individual Southeast Asian countries, on the one hand, and the limits of national capacity on the other.[10]

Internally, Indonesia has long struggled to satisfy even the most basic requirements of regional economic integration, failing more often than succeeding. In 1994 – two years after the ASEAN Free Trade Area (AFTA) had ostensibly been formed in 1992 – Dewi Fortuna Anwar, one of Indonesia's foremost security analysts, underscored succinctly the paradox confronting Indonesia's leadership of ASEAN:

> Among the puzzles that need to be answered are the seeming contradictions in Indonesian policy towards ASEAN. Indonesia's support for the association has often been seen as one of the keys for ASEAN's success, yet the former has also been blamed for the latter's lack of progress, particularly in the economic field.[11]

With 2015 now being referred to as 'a milestone on the slow and long journey towards the AEC' rather than the promised deadline of its completion,[12] the finger of blame has not only been pointed at the usual suspects, the CLMV (Cambodia, Laos, Myanmar and Vietnam) economies, but equally at Indonesia. Its strong economic performance in recent years has done little to assuage domestic concerns over what a more advanced form of integration could mean for Indonesia. As an analyst observed in 2011, 'Indonesia was particularly wary of even the smallest efforts to create a common market. Even today there is the fear that the home market could be flooded with cheaper imported goods'.[13]

Arguably, this problem has worsened in the light of recent difficulties facing the Indonesian economy.[14] ASEAN's own slow progress towards forming the AEC – Surin Pitsuwan, the former secretary general of ASEAN, has conceded that ASEAN's aim to establish the AEC by 2015 is probably far-fetched in the light of numerous constraints and impediments still in place[15] – is arguably the consequence of the collective anxieties of ASEAN economies, including Indonesia's, over the risks posed by intra-ASEAN flows of cheap labour and even cheaper commodities to their domestic markets and indigenous industries. For Indonesia, the ASEAN–China free trade agreement (FTA) has proved particularly challenging where dealing with the influx of inexpensive goods from China into the Indonesian market is concerned. According to a survey conducted by the Indonesian government in 2011, since the ASEAN–China FTA came into force in January 2010, China has reportedly 'dumped' nearly forty different products in Indonesia, prompting Hatta Radjasa, Indonesia's Coordinating Minister for Economic Affairs, to insist that the FTA could be reassessed if the Chinese were to continue their unfair trade practices.[16] However, while Chinese dumping practices are clearly a legitimate concern, the reality is that Indonesia has yet to remove domestic labour laws and trade restrictions – the so-called 'behind the border' barriers – that stand in the way of the AEC's formation.[17] Nor has Indonesia's own proclivity towards protectionism – such as its failure to ratify the ASEAN Multilateral Agreement for Full Liberalization of Air Freight Services (MAFLAFS) in order to protect its domestic aviation industry from regional competition –invited criticism that ASEAN's very leader stands in the way of the realization of the AEC.[18] While it looks like the Jokowi administration could be distracted from regional affairs by its dire need to prioritize managing the domestic economy, the fact that the first major decision Jokowi and his team rendered was to make good on his electoral promise to reduce state energy subsidies in an effort to free up funds for development plans is a good early sign of the new president's resolve.[19]

Against this litany of impediments towards realization of the AEC stand the incontrovertible positive contributions of Indonesia to regional security. As elaborated in greater detail in the following section, Indonesia's post-*konfrontasi* show of strategic restraint through President Suharto's 'good neighbour' policy made it possible for ASEAN to be formed in 1967, whilst its robust advocacy of deep constructive engagement of China in the post-Cold War period, despite its own long-standing reservations about the Chinese, furnished Asian multilateralism with a key feature of its broader *raison d'être*, namely, the socialization of a post-revolutionary China and accommodation of the latter's 'peaceful rise'. Further, Indonesia's long-standing efforts to enhance the region's collective understanding of issues pertinent to the South China Sea disputes – and, presumably, to develop an epistemic community that could contribute policy solutions to those challenges – through initiating a series of dialogical workshops (discussed below) have been acknowledged. In 2003, Indonesia took advantage of its turn as chair of ASEAN and, together with its fellow members, successfully launched the second ASEAN (or Bali) Concord and the plan to form the ASEAN Community, whose security pillar, the ASEAN Security Community (later renamed the ASEAN Political-Security Community), was conceptualized by the Indonesians. In 2007, together with Singapore and other like-minded members, Indonesia successfully convinced reluctant CLMV countries to endorse the proposed ASEAN Charter – albeit a considerably diluted version of the one Jakarta and other pro-charter members might have hoped for.[20] In 2012, the frantic shuttle diplomacy conducted by Indonesian foreign minister Marty Natalegawa in the wake of the apparent disharmony among the ASEAN member states at the annual meeting of foreign ministers in Phnom Penh in July, which produced the so-called 'six-point consensus', underscored the salience ASEAN still holds for Indonesia.[21] Prior to the Phnom Penh fiasco, Indonesia had also served as mediator (and, subsequently, agreed to serve as monitor) when hostilities broke out between Cambodia and Thailand in February 2011 over the Preah Vihear promontory.[22] These and other security contributions not only burnish Indonesia's deserved reputation as a regional conciliator but enhance its moral authority as a regional security actor.

There is possibly a third constraining factor – Indonesia's enduring aspiration towards regional and international prominence could also have played a role to restrain Indonesia from throwing in its lot with ASEAN. 'While ASEAN was only possible with Indonesia's involvement, in many ways this is a two-edged sword', as Anthony Smith has opined.

> Small powers are more likely to seek the protection of regional and international organizations, but Indonesia's greater aspirations of future status (and memory of its former Srivijaya and Majapahit empires) have at times proved to be a 'brake' on greater integration.[23]

While recent debate has focused on the appeals among some Indonesian strategic thinkers for a 'post-ASEAN foreign policy' (an issue elaborated below), their frustration over perceived constraints placed on their nation's regional aspirations through being tethered to a divided and ineffective ASEAN is by no means new. Commenting on the contrast between Indonesia's regional vision and its limited role as 'regional spectator', Michael Leifer wrote in the 1980s about Indonesia's sense of frustration at 'not being able to influence events in the region [which has been] reinforced by the fact that individual members went their own way in foreign policy', which led President Suharto to 'express disappointment at ASEAN's limited progress'.[24] Indeed, Suharto's emphasis on ASEAN regionalism as the ostensible cornerstone of Indonesia's foreign policy earned him the ire of some of his own countrymen for having perceptibly held Indonesia back from playing a larger global role. Whether the mandala-based world-view reportedly held by Suharto[25] – where domestic affairs form the innermost circle and neighbourly and regional relations form the next circle – played a role is debatable. Clearly, pragmatism necessitated such an approach as well since Indonesia's relative lack of capacity effectively limited it to a fairly modest foreign policy. Given such constraints, focusing on ASEAN therefore made good sense. As Anwar has noted:

> Suharto's foreign policy was more pragmatic and low profile, and aimed at ensuring a safe and stable regional environment within which Indonesia could develop, while also gaining international support in the form of access to other markets, foreign investment and technical assistance. Suharto's focus was on south east Asia and relations with the United States, Japan and key European countries. He came in for criticism internally, though, for betraying the spirit of the preamble to the 1945 Indonesian Constitution, which exhorts Indonesia to play an active role in fostering world peace.[26]

Yet the latent desire to transcend the region probably led to a relatively uneven and even half-hearted embrace by Jakarta of ASEAN regionalism, cornerstone or otherwise.

Whether Indonesia today can finally fulfil its ambition remains to be seen. That the country is being courted by and included among the world's most economically and diplomatically influential powers has only exacerbated Indonesia's sense that its fellow ASEAN states neither acknowledge its regional leadership nor appreciate its contributions to regional conflict management sufficiently. In recent times a gush of compliments have flowed from pundits about the prospects of Indonesia, 'Asia's third giant' according to a recently released anthology on Indonesia,[27] as a rising economic and diplomatic power.[28] As the only Southeast Asian country granted membership in the G20, a member of the 'BRICS' club of emerging economic titans (Brazil, Russia, India, China and South Africa, with Indonesia named as a plausible candidate),[29] and Indonesia appears to be on the cusp of assuming a prominent place not only in Asia but indeed in the world at large.[30]

## Shaping Asian multilateralism

For Indonesian strategic thinkers, the key strategic issue confronting Asia in the early to mid-1990s concerned the appropriate conditions under which a multilateral security arrangement would emerge and flourish in the region. Nowhere was this more evident than in the thinking of Indonesia's leading policy intellectual, Jusuf Wanandi, who in the 1990s argued for the emergence of multilateralism in Asia owing to three factors: one, the unlikelihood of major war in the region; two, growing regional economic integration and the attendant emergence of common interests, ideals and objectives towards a 'cooperative regionalism'; and three, existing relations and networks that render the region more interdependent than ever.[31] Unlike the 2008 Australian proposal for a revamped and streamlined regional architecture, or the 2009 Japanese proposal for a European Union-like institution for East Asia,[32] Indonesia has relied on – indeed, contributed significantly to – an *ad hoc* formation of various regional arrangements whose *raison d'être* was the furnishing of 'meeting places'[33] wherein the great powers and regional countries can interact according to ASEAN's terms.[34] According to Jakarta's reasoning, a single institution servicing East Asia could open the entire region up to excessive great power influence, whereas 'a looser and more pluralistic arrangement ... will not be under the sway of one or more powers, and so will continue to let ASEAN to play the key role of convenor'.[35] 'ASEAN is viewed as indispensable for managing relations with major powers', as Dewi Fortuna Anwar has argued.

> Policymakers in Jakarta believe that the bloc should be ambitious about spreading its code of conduct eschewing force to resolve conflicts to [sic] countries outside the region, and that ASEAN should be the primary driver in regional architecture initiatives in East Asia.[36]

Crucially, what critics of ASEAN see as its confusing ecosystem of not particularly efficient regional arrangements is not only Indonesia's and other ASEAN states' way of creating institutional arenas for counterbalancing, but equally relatively 'neutral', spaces where regional powers can manage and hopefully resolve their mutual security dilemmas. What critics dismiss as a wasteful oversupply of institutions is seen by ASEAN as its provision of a multiplicity of venues from which contending states can opt to continue their deliberations should negotiations become deadlocked in any one institutional setting.[37] Indonesia's adamant stance on the centrality of ASEAN in the regional architecture stems equally from a concern highlighted in the preceding section, namely, its worry that, as during the Cold War where the region was arguably reduced to a mere geopolitical front for Soviet–US rivalry, contemporary East Asia could suffer a similar fate should the region come to be viewed primarily through the lens of Sino-US competition and/or cooperation. Indeed, it is safe to say that to the extent ASEAN centrality has been treated by ASEAN as non-negotiable, it has been Indonesia more than any single ASEAN member that has done most to ensure that. This was clear enough from their distinct views in the immediate post-Cold War period despite their shared perspective on the need for an Asia-wide security institution. While Malaysia was anxious to get such a project started, Indonesia's foreign minister Ali Alatas worried over the possibility of ASEAN losing its place and identity within a larger institutional entity that would include the great powers.[38] Indeed, Alatas's concern was even more basic than the prospect of the proposed institution adopting a multilateral vision stemming from outside the ASEAN region, such as those advanced by Australia, Canada or going further back, the Soviet Union.[39] His concern was mollified by the decision taken at the ASEAN ministerial meeting in July 1993 to use the ASEAN–PMC as the foundation for what would become the ARF. Further, that the ASEAN Way, with its consensual and consultative style of decision-making bequeathed by Indonesia, would also serve as the diplomatic-security model for the ARF also underscored the influence Indonesia had on that facet of Asian multilateralism.[40]

It is significant that Indonesian disdain towards collective defence systems did not prevent Jakarta from actively participating in the ARF, whose membership includes external major powers. If anything, Indonesia's support for the ARF is, as Rizal Sukma has argued, an indication of its willingness to accommodate the legitimate security interests of extra-regional powers in regional affairs.[41] Indeed, 1994, the year of the inauguration of the ARF, would also mark Jakarta's broader effort openly to engage the international community through a renewed involvement in the NAM and, more crucially, its hosting and chairmanship of the APEC summit in Bogor, Indonesia. Nor, for that matter, did Indonesia's aspiration for regional autonomy prevent it from engaging, where it deemed necessary, in bilateral security relationships with select external powers. In that regard, Indonesia has pursued security ties with the United States since 1951 – except during Washington's suspension of the International Military Education and Training (IMET) programme for much of the 1990s into the first half of the 2000s in protest against human rights abuses perpetrated by the Indonesian military[42] – and with Australia since the 1990s. And while historical ties with China have in the past been complicated by Jakarta's fears over Beijing's ostensible links with the Indonesian communist element (even though the Indonesian Communist Party (PKI) was primarily affiliated with the Soviet Union) and its political and ideological influence on Indonesia's Chinese minority – indeed, the project of regional reconciliation, post-*konfrontasi*, through ASEAN was arguably embraced by Indonesia as a prospective bulwark against the apparent threat posed to itself by China[43] – bilateral relations have significantly improved since 1998 (even though Indonesia normalized ties with China in 1990).[44]

Remarkably, for all its flaws, ASEAN has continued to enjoy the support of major and regional powers, which regard ASEAN-based arrangements like the EAS, despite persistent complaints about their inefficacy, as useful frameworks for regional dialogue and interaction. If anything, such regional cooperative frameworks enable Indonesia to pursue and conceivably realize its goal of dynamic equilibrium. Granted, Indonesia's recent exertions at preventing meltdowns in ASEAN unity have no doubt frustrated Jakarta, but they also highlight the considerable lengths to which Indonesia is prepared to go to redeem the embattled organization.

## Engaging China through Asian multilateralism

In order to understand Indonesian strategic thinking on the reliance of Asian multilateral arrangements as platforms through which to engage with as well as balance and hedge against China and the other great powers, it is useful to recall Indonesia's own formative experience in regionalism through ASEAN.[45] According to this strategy, ASEAN would furnish the institutional framework in which Indonesia would be recognized by its fellow entrants in return for Jakarta's acknowledgement of their rightful existence as sovereign states.[46] Through ASEAN, the other members would engage in political counterbalancing and presumably discourage Indonesia's hegemonic tendencies. Although such a strategy had as its inspiration the Concert of Europe's balance of power system, the challenge for the architects of ASEAN was how exactly to devise such a system without explicit reference to its European origins. For an Indonesia that professed non-alignment and which aspired to a regionally autonomous structure of order under its guidance, the balance of power was clearly anathema.[47]

Whether by dint of the indirect style of communication evidently favoured by the Javanese or of Suharto's own personality,[48] the only conceivable way forward, it seemed, would be for Indonesia volitionally to adopt a non-assertive posture and exercise a 'leading from behind' brand of regional leadership that fundamentally did not threaten its neighbours. Again, according to Leifer, 'President Suharto well understood that one way to restore regional confidence and stability would be to lock Indonesia into a structure of multilateral partnership and constraint' – furnished by ASEAN – 'that would be seen as a rejection of hegemonic pretensions'.[49] As Lee Kuan Yew, Singapore's first prime minister, has put it, 'Indonesia wanted to reassure Malaysia and Singapore that, with the end of the Sukarno era, its intentions were peaceful and it had abandoned Sukarno's aggressive policies'.[50] Persuading his fellow ASEAN states regarding Indonesia's pacific intentions required a 'good neighbour policy', which for Suharto comprised three things: one, the pursuit of cordial bilateral relations; two, the commitment to regional reconciliation and unification; and three, the settlement of regional conflicts.[51] For Lee Kuan Yew, nowhere were Suharto's good intentions more pronounced than when his New Order government appealed for calm and assured Singapore that Indonesia had no wish to retaliate against its execution of two Indonesian marine commandos for terrorist actions in Singapore committed during the *konfrontasi* campaign.[52]

That Indonesia was effectively prepared to exercise strategic restraint and commit its fortunes to an embryonic regionalism via an untested ASEAN – to the extent of making it its foreign policy 'cornerstone' – cannot be overstated in terms of its significance for the future shape and substance of Asian multilateralism. As Leifer has suggested, 'The extent to which Indonesia's example of political self-denial in the interest of regional order may be emulated within the wider Asia-Pacific is central to any parallel between ASEAN and the ASEAN Regional Forum'.[53] In short, ASEAN's subsequent socialization of China probably has its inspiration and model in this historical socialization of Indonesia. As we have seen in chapter 2, today it has become conventional wisdom to assume the significance of ASEAN's contribution in encouraging and facilitating China's involvement in Asia's regional institutions. This said, so successful has China's integration in Asian regionalism been that some analysts wonder at the influence China has over the region, including the ASEAN states.[54] Indeed, where regional security discourse is concerned, few if any instances of ASEAN countries identifying China as a strategic *threat* against them appear to exist.[55] Yet they also differed in their perceptions about China.

Accordingly, cooperative regionalism would mean Beijing's support for ASEAN-led regionalism because 'China needs ASEAN for a peaceful environment to continue with her modernization' – and, in early appreciation of Chinese strategic considerations in the immediate post-Cold War period, 'to prevent any possibility of encirclement to contain her in the future'.[56] In this respect, the persistent advocacy of the region's diplomatic engagement of China, rather than its containment – captured vividly by former Indonesian president Susilo Bambang Yudhoyono's 'a million friends and zero enemies' maxim[57] – has been and remains a hallmark of Indonesian strategic thought. To that end, Indonesian security intellectuals have long urged that Chinese sensitivities be taken into consideration by key bilateral alliances in Asia, especially the Japan–US relationship, whose policies and activities could benefit with greater coordination so as to avoid unnecessarily antagonizing China.[58] At the same time, they worried over the prospect of US fixation on China to the detriment of the former's ties with other countries. As an analyst has noted, 'From Jakarta's perspective, the importance Washington attaches to Indonesia and ASEAN should not simply be derivative of China's rise but instead be based on the intrinsic value of the country and sub-region'.[59] In that regard, multilateral processes like the APEC, ARF and APT – including, it should be said, second-track multilateral processes such as the CSCAP and PECC[60] – were deemed as particularly important because they could 'help China integrate peacefully into East Asia'.[61] Not unlike their Southeast Asian counterparts, many Indonesians see the ARF (certainly at the time of its establishment) as a core piece of the regional security architecture, whose success must necessarily require the commitment and participation of all the great powers because a 'pluralism of power' within the context of ASEAN-based cooperative security arrangements engenders political-diplomatic spaces within which ASEAN countries can more flexibly manoeuvre.[62] Accordingly, the key to regional peace and stability in the post-Cold War period boils down to two interests: on the one hand, ASEAN's desire for a new regional order in contemporary Asia; on the other hand, the effort to secure the clear commitment to and pacific participation of the major powers – China, to be sure, but so too the United States, Japan and others – in that regional order.

More likely than not, Indonesia will continue to hedge against the major powers, especially China and the United States. Jakarta's perdurable concern that its regional environment should stay as secure and stable as possible – in short, conditions most suited for developing an Indonesia that is 'sovereign, independent, just and prosperous'[63] and, it might be added, democratic – has remained fundamentally unchanged. Natalegawa's concept of 'dynamic equilibrium',[64] which urges peaceful coexistence among the great powers in Asia, is the most recent expression of that long-standing aspiration. Nor, as a consequence of its contemporary transformation, has Indonesia's enduring predilection for strategic hedging been replaced by an explicit policy to ally with or to balance against particular powers.[65] It has been argued that Indonesia's strategic partnerships with extra-regional countries such as Australia, India, Japan and South Korea are a reflection of its desire to see that the emerging regional order would not be dominated only by the United States and China.[66] Elsewhere, it has also been argued that 'Indonesia does not want to be tied to a US or China dominated security web. It wants an independent middle-power role to assert itself both regionally and globally'.[67] From Jakarta's vantage point, there is a very real risk of regional concerns being reduced purely to, say, the rise of China or the rebalance by the United States. As one analyst has put it, 'The big picture of China and the regional balance of power needs to be filled in with the detail of the other countries and their many different stories'.[68] This implies that Indonesia's long-held aim of having a 'free and active' (*bebas-aktif*) foreign policy, first articulated by Vice President Mohammad Hatta in a speech in September 1948 and originally designed to mitigate persistent domestic tensions between secular nationalism and religious nationalism,[69] continues to guide the country's approach to its external relations despite its democratic transition in the post-Suharto period.

Crucially, Indonesian efforts to engage China multilaterally did not take place in the absence of Indonesian concerns about rising Chinese power and influence. In September 1996, following Ali Alatas's visit to Beijing in July 1995 – four months after the Chinese occupation of Mischief Reef in the Spratly islands – to discuss China's apparent inclusion of the purportedly oil-rich Natuna islands (which Indonesia claims as its territories) in a map detailing its South China Sea claims, Alatas registered national concerns about Chinese maritime assertiveness before the Indonesian parliament whilst expressing hope that the ARF would exert a moderating influence over China.[70] Thus understood, Indonesia's opposition in 2005 to the idea of an East Asian Community (EAC) comprising only the members of the APT – the ten ASEAN members together with China, Japan and South Korea – is therefore not a surprise. In this, Indonesia shared

Japan's concern that perceived Chinese dominance in the APT would not make for a stable regional order in East Asia, much less for the anticipated EAC.[71] Rather, Jakarta's preference for the more inclusive EAS underscored its aspiration to engage the great and regional powers and – crucially – to do it principally through ASEAN.[72] This suggested that Indonesia had no interest in seeing the Southeast Asian region, much less the Indonesian archipelago, become a theatre of great power competition.

Despite such reservations over Chinese intentions and actions regarding the South China Sea, Indonesia, much like its ASEAN counterparts, persisted in the shared belief that 'constructive engagement' remained the best and most productive way of dealing with China.[73] For Wanandi, Asian multilateralism through the ARF, APT, EAS and so forth remained the key to facilitating China's post-Cold War 'normalization' – its transition – still ongoing, it could be said – from Cold War revolutionary regime to a great and responsible power. In his view, China had evolved into a 'prudent regional power, more traditional and conservative, a pro status quo power and one which is starting to link up with the region more intensely and responsibly'; as such, Chinese engagements with the region's institutions, he argued, were 'real'.[74] In the early 2000s, he further posited that China could be considered a status quo power given its accession to the WTO and support for the US-led coalition against global terrorism.[75] To be sure, engaging the Chinese is not a strategy unique to Wanandi and other Indonesian strategic thinkers who share his ideas. What perhaps makes his appeal especially compelling is the consistency and vigour with which he has promoted this position. Writing as far back in 1978, Wanandi was already arguing that the ASEAN countries were not unaware that China, as a power in the Asia-Pacific region, '[needed] to be included in the structure of international relations so that it [would] abide by the rules of the international community which acknowledge the sovereignty and freedom of all countries of the world'.[76] China's present-day participation in Asian multilateralism is as much the outcome of the vigorous sustained efforts by various norm entrepreneurs of whom Wanandi has few if any equals.

Another key contribution by Indonesia to Asian multilateralism has been in its long-standing effort to establish an informal multilateral dialogue process among regional countries regarding the South China Sea. Over twenty informal workshops on the South China Sea have been conducted since Indonesia initiated the first one in 1989, with the focus in the latest efforts geared understandably towards the pursuit of full implementation of the Declaration on the Conduct of Parties in the South China Sea (DOC) and the early conclusion of the Code of Conduct (COC) negotiations. The veteran Indonesian diplomat Hasjim Djalal, long lauded for his leadership of the process since its genesis, explained what motivated his initiative:

> When I took the initiative to launch the workshop process on Managing Potential Conflicts in the South China Sea in 1989, endorsed by the Indonesian Minister of Foreign Affairs and financially supported by Canada, Indonesia and I had no ulterior motive except to promote peace, stability and cooperation in the South China Sea. We saw this as important for the development of the

region as a whole, including Indonesia. I was therefore motivated by the conviction that everyone in the region should be guided by the principle that the promotion of regional peace, stability and cooperation in the South China Sea is part of the national interest of the respective countries, and that cooperation is preferable and better than confrontation. My perception was largely shared by the countries in the region.[77]

It is not uncommon today to hear it argued that China's diplomatic assertiveness and use of aggressive tactics in the East and South China Seas had their start in 2008–9, presumably in reaction to the perceived failure of its 'charm offensive' through most of the 2000s. But as Alastair Iain Johnston has persuasively shown, Chinese intentions and behaviour in this respect – notwithstanding the 'tailored coercion' and 'maritime militancy' that has been attributed, correctly, to the Chinese (including their 'special forces' fishermen!)[78] – have neither been particularly novel nor aggressive when measured against its past practices.[79] If so, despite the rise in interstate tensions over those maritime disputes and the snail-paced progress made in the COC negotiations, it is fair to say that the workshops inspired by Djalal and the Indonesians – and subsequent others modelled after them – have facilitated the region's improved understanding of the issues at hand and their plausible solutions even as early as the 1990s.[80] Although China initially refused to participate in the workshops started by Indonesia, it subsequently did so following Beijing's normalization of ties with Jakarta in 1990. Arguably, China's charm offensive towards Southeast Asia in the 2000s, marked by milestones like the DOC signed with ASEAN in 2002 and its accession to the ASEAN Treaty of Amity and Cooperation (TAC) in 2003, might not have been possible without the exercises in mutual confidence furnished by Indonesia's South China Sea workshops.

## Will Indonesia go beyond ASEAN?

In recent times there again has emerged within Indonesia's strategic circles a growing perception (and with it, a sense of frustration) over ASEAN as an impediment to Indonesia's evolution from a regional power to becoming a major player in global affairs.[81] With episodes like the Cambodian–Thai border dispute and ASEAN's fiasco at Phnom Penh in July 2012 denting ASEAN's internal cohesion and hampering the organization's efforts to become 'political-security community' by 2015, Indonesia has worked valiantly, if at times in vain, to mediate between the offending parties and salvage the organization's reputation. Yet such experiences have led Indonesians to question the viability of their country's long-standing regional policy, not least when it seems as if Jakarta's position as the *de facto* leader of ASEAN is no longer accepted, in practice at least, by some recalcitrant members. In a different way, membership in the G20, a marker of Indonesia's emerging economic and diplomatic power, has raised public awareness and pride in the nation's global prominence and led to questions over why Indonesia should allow itself to be constrained by ASEAN. The most common complaints revolve around the perceived growing irrelevance of ASEAN as the cornerstone of

Indonesian foreign policy in the light of the inability and seeming reluctance of its member states to preserve the cohesion and solidarity of the institution despite their differences.[82] And even though Indonesia is keen to position itself as a mouthpiece for ASEAN countries and as a representative of developing nations within the G20,[83] it is not immediately apparent that other ASEAN member states, given the long-standing mutual distrust some of them have shared with Indonesia, believe that the latter could be relied on to represent their interests in the G20.[84]

Conceding the importance which membership in ASEAN had for Indonesia during the early years of regional reconciliation, Jusuf Wanandi, echoing a popular sentiment within Indonesia, argues that ASEAN has become the proverbial albatross around Jakarta's neck and should henceforth be discarded:

> If ASEAN cannot move beyond its lowest common denominator, as defined by Laos or Myanmar, it is likely that Indonesia will seek to become more independent from ASEAN. In the last 40 years, Indonesia has become too dependent on ASEAN as the instrument of its foreign policy, and has constrained its freedom of action and use of other vehicles to implement its free and independent foreign policy. This was right in the first decades of ASEAN, to enable Indonesia to get the trust back from its neighbours. And Indonesia has achieved that.[85]

As an Indonesian insider has explained,

> Indonesia's activist foreign policy is supply-driven, with domestic opinion demanding that Jakarta stand up and be counted in the region and beyond; it is also demand-driven as Indonesia's partners are asking that it take on greater regional and even global responsibilities.[86]

For his part, Rizal Sukma, who heads the Jakarta-based Centre for Strategic and International Studies, had this to say:

> If other ASEAN countries do not share Indonesia's passion for and commitment to ASEAN, then it is indeed time for us to start another round of debate on the merits of a post-ASEAN foreign policy. We have many other important foreign policy agendas to attend to other than just whining and agonizing over ASEAN's failures.[87]

Against this ambivalent backdrop, it is not immediately apparent that the enthusiasm of some of Indonesia's most prominent strategic thinkers for a post-ASEAN foreign policy is necessarily shared by those within *Kemlu*, the Indonesian foreign ministry, or indeed by the executive branch of the Indonesian government. Arguably, it is not only instrumental reasons that matter to Indonesia but equally ideational ones as well, not least Indonesia's role as a founding member of ASEAN.[88] Hitherto, *Kemlu*'s official refrain emphasizes Indonesia's continued commitment to ASEAN. 'Our involvement in ASEAN is not optional', noted a *Kemlu* official in 2010.[89] Likewise, Yudhoyono rejected the suggestion that Indonesia's G20 membership might cause Jakarta to downgrade its commitment to ASEAN or quit the organization altogether and instead argued the continuing importance of ASEAN to his country.[90]

Indonesia's self-awareness of its growing importance has led it to pursue what one pundit has termed 'confidence diplomacy', as embodied in its enhanced role in ASEAN, increased engagement with the great powers, active use of multilateral diplomacy, and embrace of peace and democracy as values worth pursing and advocating.[91] Jakarta's heightened awareness and considerably broadened perspective of its place and role beyond Southeast Asia was already evident during the Yudhoyono presidency, in the form of Natalegawa's call for a more expansive understanding of the region in which Indonesia is located – specifically, the 'Indo-Pacific' – and the establishment of 'an Indo-Pacific wide treaty of friendship and cooperation' (not unlike the TAC) as a code of interstate conduct for the proposed Indo-Pacific region.[92] Indeed, the leading role played by Indonesia in the Indian Ocean Rim Association for Regional Cooperation (IOR-ARC) has spurred one analyst to opine that 'Southeast Asia no longer remains perhaps the appropriate analytical geopolitical category to capture appropriately the evolving dynamics of Indonesia's relations with major powers of the region'.[93] As for the Jokowi administration, it has been suggested that it would avoid investing time in foreign relations that do not benefit Indonesia. However, there are early hints that Indonesia under Jokowi might not be as fixated with ASEAN as his predecessors had been. Going beyond the 'Indo-Pacific' idea advanced by Natalegawa, the Jokowi administration's vision for Indonesia is as a global maritime fulcrum connecting the Indian and Pacific Oceans.[94] Known as 'PACINDO', the area of engagement envisioned here is ostensibly geographically more extensive than the Indo-Pacific region the Yudhoyono administration had in mind. To that end, India and the Gulf states have been identified as countries with whom Jokowi would engage more deeply. As a foreign policy adviser to Jokowi has declared: 'We used to say ASEAN is *the* cornerstone of our foreign policy. Now we change it to *a* cornerstone of our foreign policy'.[95]

Be that as it may, Indonesian foreign policy has never been ASEAN-centric to the exclusion of other pathways and pillars. In this regard, the appeal for a post-ASEAN foreign policy, though useful for clarifying Indonesia's strategic interests and the appropriate modalities through which to achieve its interests, is however in a sense misleading since Indonesia's foreign policy, strictly speaking, has never been centred primarily on ASEAN. To be sure, the received wisdom has long presupposed, with good reason, the centrality of ASEAN to Indonesia's foreign policy. In this regard, when Wanandi argued that Indonesia need no longer rely solely on ASEAN, but should in the future 'pursue its own national interests, on top of its loyalty and solidarity with ASEAN',[96] we could read his argument less as an appeal for a post-ASEAN foreign policy than an implicit affirmation for what the conduct of Indonesian foreign policy has all along been about, namely, a calculated appropriation of a number of diplomatic instruments and security strategies of which ASEAN regionalism is but one.

Nowhere is this sort of pragmatic reliance on multiple approaches more legitimated – ironically – than within ASEAN itself. ASEAN's very success as a diplomatic community has long been predicated on its achieving the limited aim of ensuring the respect of member nations for one another's sovereignty through their mutual adherence to the principle of non-interference. Put differently, the organization's *raison d'être*, defined in this minimalist way, effectively legitimated member countries' resorts to their own devices – via the nebulous doctrine of 'national resilience' (*ketahanan nasional*) conceived by Indonesia – so long as their actions did not affect their fellow members' national security and sovereignty in adverse ways. To that extent, the very formation of ASEAN in 1967 was made possible as a consequence of Indonesia's assurance to the other founding member countries of the organization that they would be able to pursue their foreign policy goals in their own ways without interference from Indonesia, with each effectively minding its own business.[97] With ASEAN regionalism treated by its participants as little more than a sort of insurance policy in the event of their preferred strategies failing, most of the ASEAN member countries have looked to a combination of self-help, alliance with the United States or collective defence arrangements (such as the Five Powers Defence Arrangements), and world bodies (such as the United Nations) to guarantee their security.[98]

Not unlike its fellow ASEAN member states, Indonesia has long relied on permutations comprising unilateral, bilateral as well as multilateral strategies to its security, and has assiduously avoided putting all its eggs in the regional basket. To be sure, lingering Indonesian anger at the International Court of Justice's (ICJ) awarding of Ligitan and Sipadan islands to Malaysia has raised questions about whether Jakarta would ever use the ICJ or other international tribunals to settle its territorial disputes.[99] Arguably, any hint of ASEAN-centricity in Indonesia's past behaviour, if indeed such existed, probably reflected its lack of national capacity, rather than will, for a more ambitious and expansive internationalism. It is for these reasons that commentators such as van der Kroef have argued that Indonesia's ASEAN membership has in fact been an insignificant concern for Jakarta.[100] Going further, Donald McCloud has suggested that, historically, Indonesia's regional actions did not reflect any 'grand design [Indonesia might have had] for working through ASEAN to gain control of a broad segment of the region'.[101] The academic debate over the importance of ASEAN to Indonesian foreign policy implies that Indonesia, despite its own political discourse about the centrality of ASEAN in Jakarta's regional affairs, probably advanced – or at least sought to do so – its foreign policy goals through a number of strategies, of which ASEAN was but one. True, ASEAN has been important to Indonesia, but never singularly and unequivocally so, as the contemporary debate about a post-ASEAN foreign policy for Indonesia has unwittingly sought to portray.

There are obviously no guarantees that a path that takes Indonesia away from ASEAN would be any better or less worse for Indonesia. As we have seen, Indonesia is determined to play not just a role in regional leadership but it aspires to be 'an increasingly vocal player in global issues'.[102] This has coincided with the country's democratic transition – a difficult one, by most counts – in the post-Suharto era.[103] Ironically, the very elements which render Indonesia today an attractive force for emulation worldwide – namely, its blend of Islam, democracy and modernity – are complicating Indonesian leaders' formulation and implementation of their nation's foreign policy. While Indonesian foreign policy in the post-Suharto years has generally exhibited greater religiosity, it has done so in a relatively moderate fashion, however. In that respect, Habibie's foreign policy, to the extent it has assumed an Islamic character, has done so only in form rather than substance.[104] Far from alarmist, Indonesia's foreign policy under Abdurrahman Wahid (popularly known as 'Gus Dur') has proved more orthodox than some of his earlier rhetoric might have indicated. While the issue of East Timor continued to be a bone of contention between Jakarta and some Western capitals, the foreign policy focus of Gus Dur did not deviate much from that of his predecessors.[105]

That said, foreign policymaking in Indonesia today is no longer the exclusive preserve of the foreign policy establishment in Jakarta, but is subject increasingly to inputs, welcomed or otherwise, from society at large, the political parties, and religious mass organizations.[106] This situation differs markedly from the 1980s, when the Indonesian government would probably not have lost much sleep over the interests of domestic actors, as Jörn Dosch has noted. However, with Indonesia's democratization following Suharto's abrupt departure in 1999, the policy process has

> opened up to the extent that groups from outside the executive branch have forced [the Indonesian government] to pay more prominent attention to issues such as human rights and environmental matters in foreign affairs and blocked or significantly reshaped governmental initiatives toward other countries.[107]

As Michael Leifer noted in 1983, 'They have sought to avoid incautious engagement in international issues which might be exploited either to advance claims presented by Muslim groups or to enhance the political standing of Islam in the Republic'.[108] However, as has often been observed, Indonesia's traditional reputation for religious tolerance is today being undermined by the growing clout of Muslim extremists in Indonesia as well as the general perception that Indonesia, despite being the world's largest Muslim-majority nation, lies at the periphery of the Islamic world.[109] It is this concern that has put at risk the hopes pinned on Indonesia, as a country where Islam, democracy and modernity conceivably go hand in hand could serve as the alternative face of Islam amidst global patterns of Islamist extremism and terrorism.[110]

## Conclusion

What Indonesia's relationship with ASEAN in the coming years will be and how that might affect Asian multilateralism in the foreseeable future is difficult to say. Naturally, given Indonesia's long-standing role and place as *de facto* leader of ASEAN, the relegation of the organization in Jakarta's policy priorities, deliberate or otherwise, is likely to have significant ramifications for ASEAN as well as its centrality in the regional architecture in Asia. Yet if Indonesia aspires to a middle-power role in international affairs commensurate with its rising power and influence,[111] then it makes sense for Jakarta to continue to see ASEAN and its wider complex of region-wide institutions as ready platforms through which Indonesia can fulfil its ambitions. More often than not, middle powers rely on multilateral diplomacy to achieve their foreign policy goals,[112] and there is little to suggest that Indonesia will deviate from the norm. To that end, ASEAN and its wider complex of institutions will arguably remain relevant to Indonesia's efforts to engage with the great powers.[113] As an analyst has put it, 'A turbulent and weakened ASEAN will allow a vacuum leading to great power collision thereby leaving Indonesia on its own and vulnerable'.[114] If Indonesia is indeed intent on life beyond ASEAN, the road it must take could prove a long and complex one, not least because of its own enduring limitations, which could take a considerably longer time to overcome, if at all.

## Notes

1 Donald K. Emmerson, 'What is Indonesia?', in John Bresnan, ed., *Indonesia: The Great Transition* (Lanham, MD: Rowman and Littlefield, 2005), pp. 7–73, on p. 22.
2 Marshall Clark and Juliet Pietsch, *Indonesia–Malaysia Relations: Cultural Heritage, Politics and Labour Migration* (Abingdon: Routledge, 2014), ch. 1. Also see Michael Yahuda, *The International Politics of Asia-Pacific, 1945–1995* (Abingdon: Routledge, 2005), p. 73.
3 Dewi Fortuna Anwar, *Indonesia in ASEAN: Foreign Policy and Regionalism* (Singapore: Institute of Southeast Asian Studies, 1994), p. 27.
4 Anthony L. Smith, *Strategic Centrality: Indonesia's Changing Role in ASEAN*, Pacific Strategic Papers, No. 10 (Singapore: Institute of Southeast Asian Studies, 2000), pp. 2–3, 8.
5 Koichi Kawamura, *Consensus and Democracy in Indonesia: Musyawarah-Mufakat Revisited*, IDE Discussion Paper, No. 308 (Tokyo: Institute of Developing Economies, JETRO, 2011).
6 Ralf Emmers, 'Indonesia's Role in ASEAN: A Case of Incomplete and Sectorial Leadership', *The Pacific Review*, Vol. 27, No. 4 (2014), pp. 543–62.
7 Emmers, 'Indonesia's Role in ASEAN'.
8 Cited in Michael Leifer, *Indonesia's Foreign Policy* (London: Allen and Unwin, 1983), pp. 148–9.
9 Michael Leifer, 'Regional Solutions to Regional Problems?', in Gerald Segal and David S. G. Goodman, eds., *Towards Recovery in Pacific Asia* (London: Routledge, 2000), pp. 108–18.
10 Rizal Sukma, 'Indonesia and Regional Security: The Quest for Cooperative Security', in See Seng Tan and Amitav Acharya, eds., *Asia-Pacific Security Cooperation: National Interests and Regional Order* (Armonk, NY: M. E. Sharpe, 2004), p. 71.
11 Anwar, *Indonesia in ASEAN*, p. 7.
12 Jayant Menon, 'Moving Too Slowly Towards an ASEAN Economic Community', *East Asia Forum*, 14 October 2014, www/eastasiaforum.org/2014/10/14/moving-too-slowly-towards-an-asean-economic-community/.
13 Winfried Weck, 'ASEAN and G20: Indonesia's Foreign Policy Objectives', *KAS (Konrad-Adenauer-Stiftung) International Reports*, No. 2 (2011), p. 24.
14 As Stephen Norris has argued, with national elections in 2014, policymakers are unlikely to take the tough fiscal and regulatory decisions needed to put the economy

back on track. Stephen Norris, 'Just Getting By: The Outlook for Indonesia's Economy', *Global Asia*, Vol. 8, No. 4 (2013), www.globalasia.org/article/just-getting-by-the-outlook-for-indonesias-economy/.
15 Yang Razali Kassim, 'ASEAN Community: Losing Grip over Vision 2015?', *RSIS Commentaries*, No. 87/2011, 2 June 2011.
16 Esther Samboh, 'Chinese Goods Hurt Local Producers', *The Jakarta Post*, 12 April.
17 Maria Monica Wihardja, 'Second-Generation Reform in Asia', *East Asia Forum*, 18 August 2011, www.eastasiaforum.org/2011/08/18/second-generation-reforms-the-key-to-deeper-regional-cooperation/; 'Splitting Stitches: China's Textile Industry Is Moving Abroad, but Politics Prevent Indonesia from fully Reaping the Benefits', *China Economic Review*, 1 May 2011, www.chinaeconomicreview.com/content/splitting-stitches.
18 Ji Xianbai, 'Why the ASEAN Economic Community Will Struggle', *The Diplomat*, 24 September 2014, http://thediplomat.com/2014/09/why-the-asean-economic-community-will-struggle/.
19 Rieka Rahadiana, Agus Suhana and Herdaru Purnomo, 'Bank Indonesia Raises Key Rate after Fuel-Price Increase', *Bloomberg*, 18 November 2014, www.bloomberg.com/news/2014-11-17/indonesia-s-widodo-increases-subsidized-gasoline-diesel-prices.html.
20 See Seng Tan, 'Herding Cats: The Role of Persuasion in Political Change and Continuity in the Association of Southeast Asian Nations (ASEAN)', *International Relations of the Asia-Pacific*, Vol. 13, No. 2 (2013), pp. 233–65, on pp. 244–53.
21 Donald K. Emmerson, 'Beyond the Six Points: How Far Will Indonesia Go?', *East Asia Forum*, 29 July 2011, www.eastasiaforum.org/2012/07/29/beyond-the-six-points-how-far-will-indonesia-go/; Don Emmerson, 'ASEAN Stumbles in Phnom Penh', *PacNet*, No. 45, 19 July 2012.
22 See, International Crisis Group, 'Waging Peace: ASEAN and the Thai–Cambodian Border Conflict', *Crisis Group Asia Report*, No. 215, 6 December 2011, www.crisisgroup.org/~/media/Files/asia/south-east-asia/thailand/215%20Waging%20Peace%20-%20ASEAN%20and%20the%20Thai-Cambodian%20Border%20Conflict.pdf.
23 Smith, *Strategic Centrality*, p. 8.
24 Michael Leifer, quoted in Anwar, *Indonesia in ASEAN*, p. 9.
25 Amitav Acharya and Barry Buzan, 'Conclusion: On the Possibility of a Non-Western International Relations Theory', in Amitav Acharya and Barry Buzan, eds., *Non-Western International Relations Theory: Perspectives on and beyond Asia* (Abingdon: Routledge, 2009), pp. 221–38, on p. 228.
26 Dewi Fortuna Anwar, 'Indonesia's Wary Thinking on Foreign Policy', *Europe's World*, 1 June 2013, www.europesworld.org/2013/06/01/indonesias-wary-thinking-on-foreign-policy/#.UsYcxY_2NMs.
27 Anthony Reid, ed., *Indonesia Rising: The Repositioning of Asia's Third Giant* (Singapore: Institute of Southeast Asian Studies, 2012); 'Indonesia – the Other Asian Giant', Ditchley Foundation, 21–23 March www.ditchley.co.uk/conferences/past-programme/2010-2019/2013/indonesia.
28 Santo Darmosumarto, 'Indonesia: A New "Middle Power"', *The Jakarta Post*, 11 November 2012, www.thejakartapost.com/news/2009/10/30/indonesia-a-new-middle-power039.html; Richard Dobbs, Fraser Thompson and Arief Budiman, '5 Reasons to Believe in the Indonesian Miracle: Why This Amazing Archipelago is on Track to be the World's Seventh Largest Economy', *Foreign Policy*, 21 September 2012, www.foreignpolicy.com/articles/2012/09/21/5_reasons_to_believe_in_the_indonesian_miracle?page=full; 'Everybody's Friend: Indonesia Deserves a Better Image', *The Economist*, 11 September 2009; Hugh White, 'Indonesia's Rise is the Big Story We're Missing', *The Age*, 29 May 2012, www.theage.com.au/it-pro/indonesias-rise-is-the-big-story-were-missing-20120528-1zf72.html.

29  Eva Pereira, 'World Bank: The Rise of the BRIICS a Harbinger of a New World Economic Order', *Forbes*, 17 May 2011, www.forbes.com/sites/evapereira/2011/05/17/world-bank-the-rise-of-the-briics-a-harbinger-of-a-new-world-economic-order/.
30  As has been argued, Indonesia may interest investors for its economic growth, while its globally oriented foreign policy and role as an international consensus-builder has often been overlooked by analysts. Dewi Fortuna Anwar, 'Indonesia: Building Norms and Consensus on the World Stage', *Global Asia*, Vol. 8, No. 4 (2013), www.globalasia.org/article/indonesia-building-norms-and-consensus-on-the-world-stage/.
31  Jusuf Wanandi, 'ASEAN's China Strategy: Towards Deeper Engagement', *Survival*, Vol. 38, No. 2 (1996), pp. 117–28; Jusuf Wanandi, 'The Need and the Challenge for an East Asian Multilateral Regional Institution', *Asian Affairs*, No. 6 (2005), pp. 91–102.
32  Tan See Seng, 'Visions at War? EAS in the Regional Architecture Debate', *The Straits Times*, 12 November 2011.
33  The term is used in Evelyn Goh and Amitav Acharya, 'The ASEAN Regional Forum and US–China Relations: Comparing Chinese and American Positions', paper for the Fifth China-ASEAN Research Institutes Roundtable on Regionalism and Community Building in East Asia (Hong Kong: University of Hong Kong, 2002).
34  Tan, *Facilitating China–U.S. Relations in the Age of Rebalancing: ASEAN's 'Middle Power' Diplomacy*, EAI MPD Working Paper No. 1 (Seoul: East Asia Institute, 2013).
35  Anwar, 'Indonesia's Wary Thinking on Foreign Policy'.
36  Anwar, 'Indonesia's Wary Thinking on Foreign Policy'.
37  This argument is also made in Victor D. Cha, 'Complex Patchworks: U.S. Alliances as Part of Asia's Regional Architecture', *Asia Policy*, No. 11 (2011), pp. 27–50.
38  Leszek Buszynski, *Asia Pacific Security: Values and Identity* (London: Routledge, 2004), pp. 136–63.
39  Amitav Acharya, 'How Ideas Spread: Whose Norms Matter? Norm Localization and Institutional Change in Asian Regionalism', *International Organization*, Vol. 58, No. 2 (2004), pp. 239–75, on p. 256.
40  Amitav Acharya, 'Ideas, Identity, and Institution-Building: From the "ASEAN Way" to the "Asia-Pacific Way"?', *The Pacific Review*, Vol. 10, No. 3 (1997), pp. 319–46; Leifer, *The ASEAN Regional Forum*.
41  Sukma, 'Indonesia and Regional Security', p. 72
42  Fabiola Desy Unidjaja, 'Indonesia Looks Forward to Reinstatement of IMET Program', *The Jakarta Post*, 30 November 2002.
43  Scholars such as Bernard K. Gordon and Sheldon W. Simon, among others, have emphasized this point.
44  Rizal Sukma, 'Indonesia–China Relations: The Politics of Re-engagement', *Asian Survey*, Vol. 49, No. 4 (2009), pp. 591–608.
45  Part of the discussion in this section draws from Tan, 'Herding Cats'.
46  Michael Leifer, *The ASEAN Regional Forum: Extending ASEAN's Model of Regional Security*, Adelphi Papers, No. 32 (London: Oxford University Press for the International Institute for Strategic Studies, 1996), p. 13.
47  Michael Leifer, *ASEAN and the Security of South-East Asia* (London: Routledge, 1989), pp. 5–6; also see Michael Leifer, 'Regional Solutions to Regional Problems?', in Gerald Segal and David S. G. Goodman, eds., *Towards Recovery in Pacific Asia* (London: Routledge, 2000), pp. 108–18.
48  Retnowati Abdulgani-Knapp, *Soeharto: The Life and Legacy of Indonesia's Second President: An Authorized Biography* (Singapore: Marshall Cavendish, 2007), p. 279.
49  Leifer, *The ASEAN Regional Forum*, p. 13.
50  Lee Kuan Yew, *From Third World to First: The Singapore Story: 1965–2000* (Singapore: Times Editions, 2000), p. 369.
51  Lau Teik Soon, 'ASEAN Diplomacy: National Interest and Regionalism', in Ashok Kapur, ed., *Diplomatic Ideas and Practices of Asian States* (Leiden: E. J. Brill),

pp. 114–26, on p. 115. Hedley Bull has written of a similar approach evidently adopted by US President Franklin D. Roosevelt towards Latin American states that arguably proved a more benign expression of the Monroe Doctrine:

> Is it the case that a state which finds itself in a position of preponderant power will always use it to 'lay down the law to others'? Will a locally preponderant state always be a menace to the independence of its neighbours, and a generally preponderant state to the survival of the system of states? The proposition is implicitly denied by the leaders of powerful states, who see sufficient safeguard of the rights of others in their own virtue and good intentions. Franklin Roosevelt saw the safeguard of Latin America's rights in United States adherence to the 'good-neighbour' policy.

Hedley Bull, *The Anarchical Society: A Study of Order in World Politics* (London: Macmillan, 1977), p. 110.

52 Lee, *From Third World to First*, p. 297.
53 Leifer, *The ASEAN Regional Forum*, p. 13.
54 See, David C. Kang, 'Getting Asia Wrong: The Need for New Analytical Frameworks', *International Security*, Vol. 27, No. 4 (2003), pp. 57–85; Alice D. Ba, 'Who's Socializing Whom? Complex Engagement in Sino-ASEAN Relations', *The Pacific Review*, Vol. 19, No. 2 (2006), pp. 157–79.
55 Evelyn Goh, 'Introduction', in Evelyn Goh, ed., *Betwixt and Between. Southeast Asian Strategic Relations with the US and China* (Singapore: Institute of Defence and Strategic Studies, Nanyang Technological University, 2005), pp. 1–8.
56 Jusuf Wanandi, 'The Effects of Leadership Changes in East Asia (Part 1 of 2)', *The Jakarta Post*, 27 January 2004. As Wanandi has put it,

> ASEAN will not adopt a strategy of containing China lightly. For ASEAN, a good relationship with China is vital. As the emerging superpower in the region, China plays a crucial role in regional peace and stability, a prerequisite for maintaining the region's existing economic growth and dynamics. At the same time, ASEAN members – small- and medium-size countries – have the greatest stake in establishing a regional order that is supported by the great powers, including China.

Wanandi, 'ASEAN's China Strategy', p. 117.
57 'SBY: Indonesia Has "A Million Friends and Zero Enemies"', *The Jakarta Globe*, 20 October 2009, http://thejakartaglobe.beritasatu.com/archive/sby-indonesia-has-a-million-friends-and-zero-enemies/.
58 Jusuf Wanandi, Gerald Segal, Yukio Satoh and Jin-hyun Park, 'The Security Setting Part 1: Thinking Strategically about Security in Pacific Asia', in Hanns Maull, Gerald Segal and Jusuf Wanandi, eds., *Europe and the Asia-Pacific* (New York: Routledge, 1998), pp. 207–34, on p. 117. Also see Jusuf Wanandi, 'ASEAN and China Form Strategic Partnership', *The Indonesian Quarterly*, Vol. 33, No. 4 (2005), pp. 328–31, on p. 329.
59 Dewi Fortuna Anwar, 'An Indonesian Perspective on the US Rebalancing Effort towards Asia', *NBR Commentary*, 26 February 2013, p. 3, www.thejakartapost.com/news/2006/11/02/importance-onechina-policy.html.
60 Wanandi, 'ASEAN's China Strategy', p. 117. For Wanandi, a key part of deeper engagement with China would involve acknowledgement and acceptance by ASEAN of the 'one-China' policy. Jusuf Wanandi, 'The Importance of the One-China Policy', *The Jakarta Post*, 2 November 2006.
61 Jusuf Wanandi, 'East Asia, Terrorism and New Global Rules', in Frank-Jürgen Richter and Pamela C. M. Mar, eds., *Recreating Asia: Visions for a New Century* (Singapore: John Wiley and Sons, 2002), pp. 22–33, on p. 31.

Indonesia 151

62 Wanandi, 'ASEAN's China Strategy', p. 127.
63 Mohammad Hatta, 'Indonesia's Foreign Policy', *Foreign Affairs*, Vol. 31, No. 3 (1953), pp. 441–52.
64 '"Dynamic Equilibrium" in the Asia Pacific: Interview with Marty Natalegawa, Indonesia's Foreign Affairs Minister', *Australia Network*, 23 February 2012, http://australianetwork.com/focus/s3440427.htm.
65 See, Evelyn Goh, 'Great Powers and Hierarchical Order in Southeast Asia: Analyzing Regional Security Strategies', *International Security*, Vol. 32, No. 3 (2007/8), pp. 113–57; Jeongseok Lee, 'Hedging against Uncertain Future: The Response of East Asian Secondary Powers to Rising China', prepared for the International Political Science Association XXII World Congress of Political Science, Madrid, 8-12 July 2012.
66 Rizal Sukma, 'Regional Security Order in Southeast Asia: An Indonesian View', paper for the Asia-Pacific Roundtable (APR), 28–30 May 2012, p. 5.
67 Leonard Sebastian, 'Indonesia's Regional Diplomacy: Imperative to Maintain ASEAN Cohesion', *RSIS Commentaries*, No. 132/2012, 23 July 2012.
68 Dewi Fortuna Anwar, 'A Problem of Mixed Messages: An Indonesian Insider's View of the Australian Relationship', *The Asialink Essays 2012*, Vol. 4. No. 6 (August 2012), p. 3.
69 Anak Agung Bany Perwita, *Indonesia and the Muslim World: Islam and Secularism in the Foreign Policy of Soeharto and Beyond* (Copenhagen: NIAS Press, 2007); Rizal Sukma, *Islam in Indonesia's Foreign Policy* (London: RoutledgeCurzon, 2003).
70 Michael Leifer, 'Indonesia's Encounters with China and the Dilemmas of Engagement', in Alastair Iain Johnston and Robert Ross, eds., *Engaging China: The Management of an Emerging Power* (London: Routledge, 2005), pp. 89–110, on p. 106.
71 Richard J. Samuels, *Securing Japan: Tokyo's Grand Strategy and the Future of East Asia* (Ithaca, NY: Cornell University Press, 2007), p. 166.
72 Anwar, 'Indonesia's Wary Thinking on Foreign Policy'.
73 Lai To Lee, *China and the South China Sea Dialogues* (Santa Barbara, CA: Greenwood, 1999), p. 71.
74 Jusuf Wanandi, 'China after the Communist Party's 16th Congress', *The Jakarta Post*, 21 November 2002.
75 Wanandi, 'East Asia, Terrorism and New Global Rules'. The argument has also been made by Alastair Iain Johnston, 'Is China a Status Quo Power?', *International Security*, Vol. 27, No. 4 (2003), pp. 5–56.
76 Jusuf Wanandi, 'Security in the Asia-Pacific Region: An Indonesian Observation', *Asian Survey*, Vol. 18, No. 2 (1978), pp. 1209–20, on p. 1219.
77 Hasjim Djalal, 'Managing Potential Conflicts in the South China Sea: Lessons Learned', in Mark J. Valencia, ed., *Maritime Regime Building* (London: Kluwer Law International, 2001), pp. 87–92, on p. 89.
78 Patrick M. Cronin, Ely Ratner, Elbridge Colby, Zachary M. Hosford and Alexander Sullivan, *Tailored Coercion: Competition and Risk in Maritime Asia* (Washington, D.C.: Center for New American Security, 2014); Alan Dupont and Christopher G. Baker, 'East Asia's Maritime Disputes: Fishing in Troubled Waters', *The Washington Quarterly*, Vol. 37, No. 1 (2014), pp. 79–98.
79 Alastair Iain Johnston, 'How New and Assertive Is China's New Assertiveness?', *International Security*, Vol. 37, No. 4 (2013), pp. 7–48.
80 The following appeal suggests the solutions are not unknown, but whether China and other claimants are prepared to do what is necessary remains the key challenge:

> We must honour the spirit of the [DOC]. We must press ahead seriously with direct negotiations and consultations among the countries involved. We must promote cooperation and joint development in a concrete manner, and only

address the disputes through peaceful means. Only then can we transform the South China Sea into a sea of friendship and cooperation.

Wu Shicun, 'Preface', in Wu Shicun and Nong Hong, eds., *Recent Developments in the South China Sea Dispute: The Prospect of a Joint Development Regime* (Abingdon: Routledge, 2014), pp. xv–xvi, on p. xvi.

81 This section draws from See Seng Tan, 'Indonesia Among the Powers: Will ASEAN Still Matter to Indonesia?', in Christopher B. Roberts, Ahmad D. Habir and Leonard C. Sebastian, eds., *Indonesia's Ascent: Power, Leadership and Asia's Security Order* (Houndmills, Basingstoke: Palgrave Macmillan, 2015), pp. 287–307.
82 Andi Lolo, University of Hasanuddin (Makasar), quoted in Lilian Budianto, 'Benefit from ASEAN or Leave It, Experts Say', *The Jakarta Post*, 24 February 2010, www.thejakartapost.com/news/2010/02/24/benefit-from%C2%A0asean-or-leave-it-experts-say%C2%A0.html.
83 Weck, 'ASEAN and G20', p. 22.
84 As Jörn Dosch has acknowledged, 'Not all Asean member states trust each other, as there is a strong sense of nationalism'. Quoted in 'The Reality of the State of the Asean Economic Community', *Monash University Malaysia*, undated, www.monash.edu.my/news/researchers-say/the-reality-of-the-state-of-the-asean-economic-community.
85 Wanandi, 'Indonesia's Foreign Policy and the Meaning of ASEAN'.
86 Anwar, 'Indonesia's Wary Thinking on Foreign Policy'.
87 Rizal Sukma, 'Insight: Without Unity, No Centrality', *The Jakarta Post*, 17 July 2012, www.thejakartapost.com/news/2012/07/17/insight-without-urity-no-centrality.html. Also see Rizal Sukma, 'Indonesia Needs a post-ASEAN Foreign Policy', *The Jakarta Post*, 30 June 2009, www.thejakartapost.com/news/2009/10/05/a-postasean-foreign-policy-a-postg8-world.html; Rizal Sukma, 'A Post-ASEAN Foreign Policy for a Post-G8 World', *The Jakarta Post*, 5 October, 2009, www.thejakartapost.com/news/2009/10/05/a-postasean-foreign-policy-a-postg8-world.html; and, Jusuf Wanandi, 'Indonesia's Foreign Policy and the Meaning of ASEAN', *PacNet*, No. 27, 15 May 2008. http://csis.org/files/media/csis/pubs/pac0827.pdf.
88 As an analyst has observed,

> For Indonesia, 'ASEAN solidarity above all' could inhibit its own aspiration for an independent foreign policy course. Indonesia's commitment to ASEAN has always forced it to compromise its own foreign policy interests. Yet, ASEAN has failed to provide an effective dispute-settling mechanism for Indonesia when it is needed most, such as over Sipadan-Ligitan The territorial dispute was brought to the International Court of Justice instead. Nevertheless, any move away from ASEAN will cause a backlash to the idealist nature of Indonesia as one of the founders of the organisation, and as the anchor of unity of ASEAN. Therefore, another pertinent foreign policy priority for Indonesia is how to pursue its own foreign policy agenda without decreasing its commitments to ASEAN.

Emirza Adi Syailendra, 'Indonesia's Foreign Policy Outlook: Challenges of 2013 and Beyond', *RSIS Commentaries*, No. 019/2013, 4 February 2013.
89 Djauhari Oratmangun, director-general of ASEAN affairs, Ministry of Foreign Affairs, Indonesia. Quoted in Budianto, 'Benefit from ASEAN or Leave It, Experts Say'.
90 President Susilo Bambang Yudhoyono of Indonesia, quoted in 'President: RI Will Never Leave Asean', *Antaranews.com*, 26 October 2009, www.antaranews.com/en/news/1256525105/president-ri-will-never-leave-asean. At the launch of a new Indonesian policy journal in New York in September 2012, President Yudhoyono took pains to highlight the ostensible achievements of the ASEAN-based regional architecture:

to further consolidate the stability and prosperity of the Asia-Pacific, a regional architecture that is conducive to peace has to be built. We in ASEAN have been building that regional architecture, making use of building blocks that ASEAN developed over the decades. These include the ASEAN Plus processes between the regional organization and its individual dialogue partners, the [APT] process that brings together all the ten ASEAN members with the more mature economies of northeast Asia. A recent high-point in ASEAN's network building is the expansion of the [EAS] to include not only the ASEAN members and their northeast Asian partners, as well as Australia, India and New Zealand, but also two great Pacific powers, Russia and the United States.

'Keynote Speech by H.E. Dr. Susilo Bambang Yudhoyono, President of the Republic of Indonesia, at the Launching of the *Strategic Review Journal*', New York, 26 September 2012, p. 4.

91 Those elements are discussed in Jiang Zhida, 'Indonesia's "Confidence" Diplomacy under the Yudhoyono Government', *CIIS (China Institute of International Studies)*, 31 December 2012, www.ciis.org.cn/english/2012-12/31/content_5638110.htm.
92 'An Indonesian Perspective on the Indo-Pacific', Keynote Address by H.E. Dr. R.M. Marty M. Natalegawa, Foreign Minister, Republic of Indonesia, at the Conference on Indonesia, Washington, D.C., 16 May 2013, p. 4.
93 Vibhanshu Shekhar, *Rising Indonesia and Indo-Pacific World*, ICWA (Indian Council of World Affairs) Issue Brief, 26 September 2012, p. 2.
94 Rendi A. Witular, 'Jokowi Launches Maritime Doctrine to the World', *The Jakarta Post*, 13 November 2014, www.thejakartapost.com/news/2014/11/13/jokowi-launches-maritime-doctrine-world.html.
95 Rizal Sukma at a public conference in Washington in December 2014, emphasis added. Cited in Prashanth Parameswaran, 'Is Indonesia Turning Away From ASEAN Under Jokowi?', *The Diplomat*, 18 December 2014, http://thediplomat.com/2014/12/is-indonesia-turning-away-from-asean-under-jokowi/.
96 Wanandi, 'Indonesia's Foreign Policy and the Meaning of ASEAN'.
97 The argument is made in Tan, 'Herding Cats'.
98 See, Muthiah Alagappa, ed., *Asian Security Practice: Material and Ideational Influences* (Stanford, CA: Stanford University Press, 1998); and, Muthiah Alagappa, ed., *Asian Security Order: Instrumental and Normative Features* (Stanford, CA: Stanford University Press, 2003).
99 Donald E. Weatherbee, *International Relations in Southeast Asia: The Struggle for Autonomy*, 2nd edn (Lanham, MD: Rowman and Littlefield, 2009), pp. 39–40.
100 Justus Maria van der Kroef, *Indonesia after Sukarno* (Vancouver, BC: University of British Columbia Press, 1971).
101 Donald G. McCloud, *System and Process in Southeast Asia: The Evolution of a Region* (Boulder, CO: Westview Press, 1986).
102 Avery Poole, 'A "Democratic" Process? Change and Continuity in Foreign Policymaking in Indonesia', paper for the Australian Political Science Association annual conference 2013, p. 2.
103 See, for example, Edward Aspinall and Marcus Mietzner, eds., *Problems of Democratization in Indonesia: Elections, Institutions and Society* (Singapore: Institute of Southeast Asian Studies, 2012).
104 Sukma, *Islam in Indonesia's Foreign Policy*, p. 92.
105 Anthony L. Smith, 'Indonesia's Foreign Policy under Abdurrahman Wahid: Radical or Status Quo State?', *Contemporary Southeast Asia*, Vol. 22, No. 3 (2000), pp. 498–526.
106 Iisgindarsah, *Indonesia's Democratic Politics and Foreign Policy-Making: A Case Study of Iranian Nuclear Issue, 2007–2008*, RSIS Working Paper, No. 236, April 19 (Singapore: S. Rajaratnam School of International Studies, Nanyang Technological University, 2012), p. ii.

107 Jörn Dosch, 'The Impact of Democratization on the Making of Foreign Policy in Indonesia, Thailand and the Philippines', *Südostasien aktuell*, Vol. 5 (2006), p. 48.
108 Michael Leifer, *Indonesia's Foreign Policy* (London: Allen and Unwin, 1983), p. xvi.
109 Syed Farid Alatas, 'Is Religious Intolerance Going Mainstream in Indonesia?', *Global Asia*, Vol. 8, No. 4 (Winter 2013), www.globalasia.org/article/is-religious-intolerance-going-mainstream-in-indonesia/; Giora Eliraz, *Islam in Indonesia: Modernism, Radicalism, and the Middle East Dimension* (Brighton: Sussex Academic Press, 2004), p. vii.
110 Dewi Fortuna Anwar, 'Foreign Policy, Islam and Democracy in Indonesia', *Journal of Indonesian Social Sciences and Humanities*, Vol. 3 (2010), pp. 37–54, on p. 37.
111 Anwar, 'Foreign Policy, Islam and Democracy in Indonesia'.
112 The link between middle power diplomacy and the appropriation of multilateral institutions and initiatives through which to achieve its aims is often acknowledged. See, Sook-Jong Lee, *South Korea as a New Middle Power: Seeking Complex Diplomacy*, EAI Asia Security Initiative Working Paper (Seoul: East Asia Institute, 2012); Mark Beeson, 'Can Australia Save the World? The Limits and Possibilities of Middle Power Diplomacy', *Australian Journal of International Affairs*, Vol. 65, No. 5 (2011), pp. 563–77.
113 Ralf Emmers and See Seng Tan, 'The ASEAN Regional Forum and Preventive Diplomacy: Built to Fail?', *Asian Security*, Vol. 7, No. 1 (2011), pp. 44–60.
114 Sebastian, 'Indonesia's Regional Diplomacy'.

# 9 Conclusion

The puzzle that motivated the writing of this book had to do with the apparent lack of attention, in the literature on ASEAN and Asian multilateralism, given to the roles and contributions – significant in their respective ways, as this study has sought to show – by various non-ASEAN countries that participate in multilateralism in Asia and specifically in Asia's regional architecture. Naturally, ASEAN-centric literature would focus on ASEAN's contributions and its ostensible centrality in Asian regionalism and the architecture that supports and services it. In fairness to that literature and the scholars who contribute to it, the contributions of non-ASEAN countries and stakeholders are acknowledged in their writings. Yet there is an intriguing and persistent tendency nonetheless therein to view ASEAN as the actor primarily responsible for the origins and state of Asia's evolving regional architecture – whether good and bad, and of late, more bad than good. But as the preceding chapters have shown, a number of non-ASEAN states have not been mere takers of a given architecture and its norms which ASEAN has presumably constructed and maintained. Rather, together with ASEAN – in both cooperative as well as competitive ways, it should be said – those non-ASEAN powers and stakeholders have in fact actively influenced the shape and substance of Asian multilateralism for their own purposes and interests.

As the book's analysis of the vigorous regional debate on what Asia's regional architecture ought to look like and what it should achieve has highlighted, there is discontent among the stakeholders of Asian multilateralism over what they perceive as the ineffectiveness and inefficiency of the existing architecture – and, by implication, what some stakeholders see as the relative ineptitude of ASEAN as the custodian of that architecture – in delivering the peace and prosperity dividends collectively desired by the region's inhabitants. As we shall see in the final section of this concluding chapter, what many have deemed the overabundance of regional institutions, all formed in ad hoc fashion and judged by many as subpar in performance, have led some regional stakeholders – Australia under Rudd, for example – to urge for the overhaul of Asia's architecture and the creation of an apex arrangement whose membership would be handpicked on the basis of efficacy rather than equity. On the other hand, more pragmatically minded countries – the United States and increasingly Japan under Shinzo Abe's leadership

156  *Conclusion*

– urge not the dismantling of underperforming institutions but the greater enablement and empowerment of existing arrangements, especially the EAS.

## One broth, many cooks

However, as the cross-national, comparative qualitative analysis of the material and ideational contributions of Australia, China, Japan and the United States to Asia's evolving architecture undertaken here has demonstrated, all four countries have at various points and for extended periods contributed actively to making and keeping that architecture the way it is in order to promote and protect their respective interests. A fifth case, Indonesia, was included given that country's increasingly complicated position – on the one hand, as the *de facto* leader of ASEAN and whose foreign policy has long privileged ASEAN as its 'cornerstone', but on the other hand, as a nation whose rising power and prominence and growing frustration with its less cooperative ASEAN fellows have encouraged a domestic chorus calling for Indonesia to pursue a 'post-ASEAN foreign policy' – within ASEAN. Notwithstanding Indonesia's long history as an unapologetic champion of the ASEAN Way and for the centrality of ASEAN in Asian multilateralism, it too stands less as a counterpoint to the other stakeholders than as one which has increasingly though informally questioned the relevance of ASEAN to Indonesian interests. To be sure, with the possible exception of China, the other countries examined here – Australia, Japan, the United States, and increasingly Indonesia in its post-New Order incarnations – have sought to varying extents to deepen the institutionalization of Asia's architecture beyond the ASEAN Way of consensus, consultation and informality. So too, it could be argued, has ASEAN in a limited fashion through its establishment of a charter and its ongoing efforts – slow and painful, to be sure – towards developing a regional economic and political security community. But as this book has shown, Asia's still evolving multi-multilateral architecture – with its lack of coherence, variable geometries, overlapping compositions and potentially competing agendas and interests, and incessant hedging, balancing and coalition-building among its participants – is neither the outcome of the effort of ASEAN alone nor is it the sole responsibility of ASEAN. Indeed, from its very genesis, its non-stakeholder countries, including and perhaps especially the five studied here, have each proactively and variously sought, in the same ad hoc fashion typically ascribed to ASEAN, to influence the shape and substance of that architecture and its component parts – and their respective agendas – into what they are today.

As this book's chapters make clear, the initial formation of the APEC involved crucial roles by Australia and Japan, while the upgrade of APEC from a ministerial to a summit was the work of the United States, known ironically for its long opposition to multilateralism in Asia despite its commitment to the same in post-war Europe. And while ASEAN was not the first mover in the case of the APEC, its subsequent impact in shaping the trade forum was clearly felt through its influence on the APEC agenda and the collective decision to host the APEC meeting every other year in an ASEAN state. In the case of the ARF, it is not entirely clear whether there would have been an Asia-wide security institution had ASEAN been left to its own devices. There were distinct pressures stemming from different countries – Australia and Japan, as well as (not considered in this book) Canada and the former Soviet Union shortly because its dissolution[1] – for such an institution. While the existence of ASEAN's post-ministerial conference (PMC) process furnished a ready foundation which eventuated in the ARF, it was equally if not more likely the part played by Indonesia to ensure that ASEAN would not be marginalized by any new and larger institution which helped secure ASEAN its position in the 'driving seat' of the ARF. And as the above chapters have also shown, the difficult legwork and other prosaic but no less important investments put in by a number of middle powers in persuading the major powers – say, the role of Japan in convincing the United States or the part played by Canada and others in convincing China,[2] both of whom were sceptical and suspicious of the prospect of Asian multilateralism in their own ways – to participate in APEC and the ARF are all reflective of the proactivity of non-ASEAN stakeholders.

Similarly, it is uncertain whether the APT, whose emergence had much to do with East Asia's (temporary) disillusionment with the United States and the IMF over their harsh treatment of the region during the 1997 Asian financial crisis, would have been possible were it not for the strong support shown by China and Japan as well as their subsequent contributions, which led to the creation of the Chiang Mai Initiative (CMI). With the growing dominance by China in the APT, Japan's counterbalancing move via Koizumi's EAC idea, which led to the hotly contested formation of the EAS as a consequence of fundamentally different visions held by the Chinese and the Japanese respectively regarding what the EAS ought to represent and who should properly constitute its membership, was the symptom of a shared uneasiness among many East Asian countries regarding China's felt power and influence in the region. Indeed, as discussed in chapter 5, the fact that the sixteen-country RCEP ('Regional Comprehensive Economic Partnership') plan advanced by ASEAN bears a striking resemblance in both membership and name to Japan's 2006 proposal for the CEPEA ('Comprehensive Economic Partnership for East Asia') – a direct counter to the EAFTA (East Asia Free Trade Area) idea championed by China – is perhaps an indication that not only did the Japanese vision win out, but that such economic agreements are fundamentally *political* in nature. That some Chinese analysts are ambivalent about the RCEP despite talk about it being ASEAN's attempt to engage a China worried over America's purported containment of China's continued ascendance through the TPP and other instruments implies that the Chinese have not completely forgotten much less forgiven ASEAN for having formed the EAS despite China's misgivings.[3] Nor did that mark the end of the EAS story. Australia under Kevin Rudd's premiership would push unsuccessfully for the dismantlement of the ARF in favour of a new and more comprehensive regional institution, the 'Asia-Pacific Community' (APC). But while that endeavour ended unhappily for Australia – both in terms of its failure to reshape Asian multilateralism and as a temporary loss of political capital and goodwill with its ASEAN friends – the subsequent expansion of the EAS to include Russia and the United States has been attributed by some to the impact caused by the APC debate. More recently, the call to institutionalize the EAS and empower it with 'steering capacity' over the entire regional architecture – and the potential challenge this could pose to ASEAN's centrality in Asian multilateralism – has been driven by Japanese and American efforts, among others.

At this juncture, it is worth pausing for a moment to consider what Europe's contributions to Asian multilateralism – after all, the EU is a member of the ARF – have been or could be. Much as countries like Australia, Canada, Japan and other non-ASEAN stakeholders sought to provide security ideas and security models which post-Cold War Asia could consider and perhaps emulate, their inspiration has been the Helsinki Process, the Conference (later Organization) of Security Cooperation in Europe (CSCE/OSCE) and the concepts of cooperative and common security which stemmed from those processes.[4] On the other hand, European criticisms of Asia's human rights record and the ensuing 'Asian values' debate in the 1990s, in conjunction with the growing view that European integration and regionalism, despite being the 'gold standard' of multilateralism worldwide, were in fact *sui generis*, ensured that formal Asian multilateralism would develop largely independently of European influence despite EU involvement in the ARF. Moreover, the Asia–Europe Meeting (ASEM) process, which has seen very slow progress – some have even described it as moribund – has not been particularly encouraging.[5] Nonetheless, while the brand of cooperative security and/or confidence-building which eventually took root in the ARF would differ significantly from the way they are implemented in the EU and the OSCE, the fact that their very development in the ARF is indebted, if only indirectly, to European experiences is not to be discounted.[6] More pointedly, the establishment of the ASEAN Charter in 2007 and the broader ongoing project to build the ASEAN Community have been explained as having obtained their collective inspiration from the earlier phases of European integration.[7]

## Competing visions for Asia's evolving architecture

This book is not complete without considering what Asian multilateralism might become and where it might end up in the foreseeable future. Much as non-ASEAN stakeholders, in ways as deep and extensive as their ASEAN counterparts if not more, have impacted the formation and evolution of Asia's regional architecture, it is fair to assume they will continue to do so, or try to do so, in the future.

Foremost on some observers' minds is the perceived incoherence of the region's existing architecture and whether it can deliver the peace and prosperity dividends its stakeholders seek for themselves and the region as a whole.[8] Proposals for architectural reform introduced in the last few years, including those by the former prime ministers of Australia and Japan, in their respective ways question the presumed primacy of ASEAN in Asian multilateralism. As discussed in chapter 3, despite incessant affirmations of 'ASEAN centrality' by ARF or EAS members, many critics see ASEAN centrality, fairly or otherwise, as a sure recipe for institutional inefficacy and ineffectiveness. And while the former US Secretary of

State Hillary Clinton had taken pains to praise ASEAN as 'a fulcrum' of the Asian security architecture, its insistence on a results-oriented architecture has heaped pressure on ASEAN to deliver.[9] Even China, which hitherto has been an enthusiastic supporter of an ASEAN-centred architecture for its own strategic preferences, could conceivably grow weary and wary of ASEAN countries' persistent strategic hedging.[10]

At risk of oversimplifying things, there are at least three broad visions or 'schools of thought' regarding what Asian multilateralism might or should look like. Borrowing from economics terminology, they are referred to below as three ideal types of multilateralism, namely, 'command', 'laissez faire' and 'functional'. A command or control economy is a centrally planned economy of the sort that characterized Leninist regimes. For present purposes, *command multilateralism* refers to a coherent architecture designed to facilitate top-down management of the region. By contrast, a laissez faire economy is one that operates (relatively) free of state intervention. As such, *laissez faire multilateralism* refers to a fairly loose architecture, probably with disjointed components. To the extent that Asia's existing architecture is perceptibly loose, incoherent and disjointed, laissez-faire regionalism is in effect status quo regionalism. Finally, *functional multilateralism*, as understood here, refers to a results-oriented approach to regional cooperation and integration, with neither particular preference for either the top down emphasis of command multilateralism nor the bottom up emphasis of laissez faire multilateralism. In a sense, it is not unlike a mixed economy where features of both command and laissez faire economies are combined. Needless to say, each perspective comes with its own loose set of assumptions and prescriptions. All three perspectives concur that Asia's security architecture is messy, disjointed and potentially incongruent as a consequence of the ad hoc way in which they have arisen. To an extent, they agree that the existing structures and conventions – the common characteristics of Asian security institutions identified and discussed in the preceding section – have hitherto served, more or less, the interests of their member countries. Beyond that, they disagree over how Asia should proceed from henceforth. Importantly, the perspectives do not denote actual situations but are ideal categories that serve as useful entry points to our discussion.

## *Command multilateralism*

This first perspective presupposes that the existing architecture in Asia is largely ineffective for enhancing the peace and security of the region. A survey of Asian policymakers, practitioners and intellectuals conducted by a Washington-based think tank in 2009 suggests that the region's security intellectuals and practitioners seem to think so as well; their preference, according to the report, is to rely on national strategies and global bodies rather than regional institutions to ensure the region's security.[11] As a solution, proponents of command regionalism favour the creation of an overarching or 'super' institution (or at least a lead institution that is authorized to guide if not to drive all the other arrangements within the regional architecture) that has hitherto been lacking in Asia, which, its proponents contend, the region desperately needs.[12] In their view, Asia's economic and political-strategic future, the argument continues, can only be secured if an overarching arrangement – a kind of 'one stop shop' for all things Asia, as it were – exists that could provide governance oversight of the existing architecture. In this case, multilateralism in Asia is of a command or control variety insofar as it denotes regional governance that works in a top-down fashion with a supporting architecture that facilitates that style of management. Accordingly, the absence of an apex institution is seen as an architectural deficit/defect that arguably reflects the concomitant absence of any strategic vision, rationale and leadership in East Asian regionalism. As the eminent economist Richard Baldwin once pointedly noted about Asian economic integration, 'Factory Asia' lacks a 'top level management' that could make the key economic decisions for the region as a whole and steer its economic policy.[13] Likewise, the assumption here is that multilateral cooperation in Asia similarly requires its own top-level management that could lead and oversee the process. Without an overarching framework, the region, it is believed, stands to suffer as a consequence of the lack of overall direction, common purpose and regional leadership, not least when the existing ASEAN-based architecture has had to endure persistent questions (and endless jokes) over who precisely occupies the 'driving seat' in regionalism. Crucially, if only indirectly, this perspective questions ASEAN's default role as at the centre of the region's multilateral architecture.

But other proponents of this perspective have also questioned the utility of the existing architecture and urged for it to be streamlined. 'The Asia Pacific region has too many organizations, yet they still cannot do all the things we require of them', in the view of an eminent Australian academic-practitioner. 'Instead of focusing on what we've got, we should look at what we need'.[14] Accordingly, irrelevant arrangements – the ARF in particular has been in the gun sights of command multilateralists – should be discarded, whereas viable ones could be further enhanced through the integrative pull of the super institution. In the same vein, the special envoy tasked to promote Kevin Rudd's APC vision has claimed regarding the ARF: 'many believe it is too large and has made insufficient progress since its inception'.[15] In place of the ARF, the super institution envisaged would boast a comprehensive agenda that covers security as well as economic and other pertinent regional issues. Another plausible vision of command multilateralism was former Japanese premier Yukio Hatoyama's version of the EAC (quite distinct from that of his predecessor, Junichiro Koizumi), which appeared to be based on the EU.[16] And much as the EU is anchored by the Franco-German condominium, the Japanese proposal envisioned a future East Asian Community anchored by a putative Sino-Japanese condominium, without which no region-wide community is likely to be possible.[17] However, it is improbable that an East Asian version of the Élysée Treaty, or a substantive rapprochement between the two East Asian giants, would materialize any time soon.

As discussed in chapters 4 and 5, neither the Australian nor the Japanese proposals fared well for various reasons. Both disappeared as soon as their respective champions left political office. For the ASEAN countries, what was

## Conclusion    161

especially unsettling about the Rudd proposal was its prescription (at least in an early version of it) for regional order through a kind of concert of powers arrangement, with the big powers China and the United States accompanied by a tier of middle powers (Australia, Japan, Indonesia, and the like).[18] In short, a concentric circles approach with the envisaged power concert as the inner ring and other Asia-Pacific countries in the outer rings. As noted, members of the inner circle are often the agenda setters who define and decide the state of play of regional cooperation. If realized, the Rudd proposal, as some Southeast Asian countries understood it, would have effectively relegated ASEAN to the margins of regional affairs (see chapter 4).[19] Interestingly enough, neither China nor the United States supported the proposal, not publicly at least. When member nations of the EAS agreed in Hanoi in April 2010 to enlarge its membership from sixteen to eighteen countries by including Russia and the United States, it was suggested by some that EAS expansion is the culmination of the regional debate initiated by Rudd's APC idea.[20] On the other hand, this suggestion has been robustly rejected by many others.[21]

That said, some analysts have been tempted nonetheless to see the newly expanded EAS, a leaders-led forum, as the logical overarching institution under which the ARF, ADMM-Plus, and other ministerial processes could come. The idea that the EAS should be empowered with the capacity to 'steer' the various regional arrangements appears to have garnered growing support among a number of strategic thinkers. Mindful of the problems Rudd's APC idea caused, Rizal Sukma, known to have advised President Joko Widodo of Indonesia on foreign policy matters, has argued:

> [T]he EAS should function as a sort of steering committee for the Asia-Pacific region in two inter-related ways. First, it should be allowed to function as a steering committee for coordinating various regional institutions in the region such as the [APT], the [ARF], the [ADMM-Plus], and the [APEC]. Second, there is also the need for the EAS members of the G20 to form an informal caucus to coordinate their policies and interests at the global level.[22]

It is debatable whether other ASEAN states – with the possible exception of Indonesia, the only Southeast Asian member of the G20 – would accept the preceding idea. As the following chapters will show, the challenge for Japan, the United States and other powers would be to ensure, in the collective quest to enhance the EAS, that the concerns and interests of the smaller players are not ignored. Notwithstanding these affirmations of the EAS's putative relevance, a nagging concern for ASEAN and its member states would be what such inordinate focus on the EAS could mean for their part and place in Asian multilateralism.

### Functional multilateralism

The second 'school of thought' on the regional architecture shares the command multilateralist's conclusion that the existing architecture is incoherent and ineffectual and hence requires reform. Functionalism multilateralism is very much results oriented. This is not to imply that command multilateralism is any less concerned with outcomes. Proponents of functional multilateralism also argue for a new and inclusive structure, but do not necessarily presuppose the need for an apex institution with oversight responsibilities for the whole architecture. Rather, their primary concern has to do with building a regional architecture that would ensure that arrangements both existing and emerging are functioning not as they *are* but as they *should*. The emphasis here is on an institutional efficacy and relevance that, in all of its existing variable geometric glory or in spite of it, could nonetheless deliver the desired results. Unlike command multilateralists, who may be prepared to dismiss and even discard existing arrangements which they deem woefully ineffective and irrelevant, functional multilateralists argue for improving and enhancing the efficiency of underperforming institutions. As Hillary Clinton has noted, 'It's more important to have organizations that produce results, rather than simply producing new organizations'.[23] The concern here is for multilateral institutions to do precisely that for which they were created.

Easier said than done for Asian regionalism, where vision far outstrips reality. For example, as a trade and investment body, APEC is expected to deliver on its Bogor Goals (achieving free and open trade and investment in the Asia Pacific by 2010 for industrialized economies and by 2020 for developing economies) of 1994. The official statement offered by the APEC Leaders' Meeting in Yokohama in November 2010 was as follows: 'It is a fair statement to say that the 2010 economies have some way to go to achieve free and open trade in the region. APEC challenges in pursuing free and open trade and investment continues'.[24] Likewise, as a political-security forum, ARF should facilitate better management of the security challenges facing the Asia-Pacific region. However, the ARF's long inability or reluctance to move beyond informal confidence-building – there is now a formal acceptance of preventive diplomacy in the ARF but its implementation has remained painfully slow[25] – has led many to doubt the collective commitment of its members to fulfil plans proposed as far back as 1995 with the publication of the ARF Concept Paper.

A second related concern for the functional multilateralist perspective has to do with the perceived incoherence of the present architecture, where no formal division of labour exists. As a consequence, Asian institutions have tended to involve themselves in matters unrelated to their original remits (though this in itself is unsurprising given the need for them to respond to the quite protean international and regional environments in which they operate). Institutional agendas widen to include emerging issues which arguably have some bearing on their primary concerns. For example, APEC, at the behest of the United States and with the region-wide consensus and support given the Americans,[26] expanded its agenda to include anti-terrorism in the wake of the 9/11 attacks. In a sense, this reflects the nexus between economics and security in the Asian context. But with APEC's involvement in antiterrorism – including recent interest in de-radicalization and social resilience – or the lack of clarity over the APT or the EAS as the appropriate regional vehicle for economic integration, the likelihood of architectural incoherence and inefficacy rises as mandates, agendas and interests overlap and institutions potentially compete with one another over finite resources and the short attention spans of policymakers.[27]

Third, the preoccupation over the need for a distinct differentiation of responsibilities and/or division of labour among institutions implies that an instrumentalism underlies the functional approach to Asian multilateralism. In other words, rather than the concentric circles of command multilateralism, it is the logic of variable geometries – institutions or coalitions of like-minded states within institutions collaborating on specific issues and shared interests – that undergirds functional multilateralism. Again, as Hillary Clinton reportedly noted in her oft-cited 2010 address on Asian regionalism, the regional architecture is to be complemented by effective and practical groupings of countries around specific issues or interests, citing the results oriented work done responding to the tsunamis that struck the Indian Ocean littoral in December 2004.[28] This also underscores the American penchant for ad hoc, issue-specific initiatives like 'mini-laterals' and/or 'pluri-laterals'.[29] The Trilateral Strategic Dialogue (involving Australia, Japan and the United States), a security initiative aimed at 'rimming' the Australian and Japanese 'spokes', so to speak, and transforming America's alliances with its allies into a trilateral relationship, is one example.[30] So too the TPP and the RCEP, both multilateral free trade agreements comprising different yet overlapping groupings of regional states. Understandably, variable geometry is anathema to command regionalism, not least because it complicates the regional architecture with a myriad of arrangements with distinct memberships. Put differently, functional multilateralists seem relatively unperturbed by the complexity and inelegance of 'patchwork' regionalisms, so long as they produce the peace and/or prosperity dividends hoped for by their 'shareholders'.[31]

Fourth, functional multilateralists appear less elitist than command multilateralists in their prescriptions. For instance, the Rudd vision's emphasis on a concert-like arrangement as the hard core of the proposed APC – a non-communitarian, certainly hierarchical, 'community' of 'haves' and 'have-nots'[32] – could lead to ASEAN being marginalized even though Indonesia gets a seat at the high table, so to speak. In contrast, functional multilateralists envisage an inclusive structure that comprises the key Asian powers but that would not be dominated by any one country. Nor do they necessarily seek to challenge the idea of ASEAN centrality in the regional architecture; for example, commenting on Secretary Clinton's Honolulu speech on Asia's architecture, a team of US analysts concluded that Washington acknowledges 'a strong ASEAN is the vital core of a balanced and peaceful Asian architecture'.[33]

## *Laissez faire multilateralism*

Clearly, advocates of the two preceding perspectives do not think that the extant institutional architecture of Asia is able to satisfy the region's increasing demands. Hence their respective appeals to various architectural reforms and more broadly innovations to enhance Asia's ability to address regional challenges. In harmony with command and functional multilateralisms, laissez faire multilateralism does not dismiss the severity of existing and emerging challenges confronting Asia today.[34] Nor does it disagree with the conventional wisdom about Asia's security architecture as largely ad hoc, loose, incoherent and disjointed. In contrast to their counterparts, however, laissez faire regionalists for the most part do not think that all this amounts to a fundamentally flawed architecture. As a prominent Singaporean diplomat known for his robust advocacy of multilateralism once reportedly argued, there is, in his view, 'nothing wrong with the region's current multi-layered or "multiplex" system'.[35] Certainly, they are prepared to accept that aspects of that architecture may require reform, but by and large, there is minimal urgency among them to seek institutional change, not least when the structures and conventions do not constrain states' efforts to promote and advance their respective interests. Not surprisingly, the proponents of laissez faire multilateralism are mostly to be found among the ASEAN states and especially China, for whom maintenance of the regional status quo best suits their policy goals in the short to medium terms (see chapters 3 and 6, respectively).[36] On the other hand, stakeholders who may not openly support laissez faire multilateralism have – as we saw in the case of Japan – nonetheless actively participated in constructing and maintaining such an architecture in Asia to suit their own interests at specific historical junctures, even if they seem intent at present to reform that architecture (see chapter 5).

Laissez faire multilateralists welcome a looser architecture wherein other institutions could furnish states with alternative venues for dialogue and conflict management should they encounter gridlock, or worse deadlock, in one institution.[37] Needless to say, smaller and weaker states do not want to be limited by a fixed hierarchal architecture controlled by the big powers. For that reason, they would prefer a looser structure as well in order to enjoy greater manoeuvrability. Further, it is not entirely clear if China would support such an empowered EAS. Granted, a concert of powers arrangement via the EAS would ensure a significant place and role for Beijing in the co-management of East Asia. But Chinese strategic ambitions could prove more grandiose than mere power-sharing; moreover, China could see the EAS as a potential constraint on its freedom.[38]

## Conclusion

It remains an open question whether the evolving regional security architecture of Asia will move towards developing a hierarchy of arrangements with an apex institution, be it the EAS or something other, at the top. Granted, with the appropriate political conditions, the remit of the EAS could, over time, be expanded to include managerial and/or coordinating functions, but this development is likely to be evolutionary and incremental rather than sudden. The aim of enhancing the efficiency and effectiveness of institutions, which functional multilateralists call for albeit without the sort of architectural overhaul and overarching institution insisted by command multilateralists, could move faster than critics who have written Asian regionalism off might allow. It is a process which ASEAN, in fits and starts, has begun and is likely to spread to affect the Asia-wide arrangements. Whether the express pursuit of institutional efficacy and effectiveness would satisfy the functionalist requirement of a neat and strict division of labour – APEC handling trade and investment matters, the ARF taking care of broad security concerns, ADMM-Plus managing operational issues, and the like – could prove more complicated, however.

This book has shown that ASEAN is not the only decider and definer of the shape and substance of regionalism and architecture in Asia. From the inception of multilateralism in post-Cold War Asia to its present, non-ASEAN stakeholders have actively conceptualized, made, moulded, and, where conditions permitted, sought to revise architecture to suit their own purposes. While these non-ASEAN stakeholders have so far given way to ASEAN, their continued endorsements of 'ASEAN centrality' cannot hide their growing disenchantment over ASEAN's ineffectiveness. Should ASEAN's ineffectiveness persist, the future possibility of defections from this norm cannot be ruled out. However, it is unlikely that external stakeholders will abandon the architecture they have helped to build. Rather, they are likely to seek ways to manage it themselves so long as a *modus vivendi* among them could be reached – a prospect possibly even more improbable than the idea of their abandoning ASEAN.

## Notes

1 Alastair Iain Johnston, 'Socialization in International Institutions: The ASEAN Way and International Relations Theory', in G. John Ikenberry and Michael Mastanduno, eds., *International Relations Theory and the Asia-Pacific* (New York: Columbia University Press, 2003), pp. 107–62, on p. 134.
2 See Seng Tan, 'Courting China: Track 2 Diplomacy and the Engagement of the People's Republic', in Hiro Katsumata and See Seng Tan, eds., *People's ASEAN and Governments' ASEAN*, RSIS Monograph, No. 11, (Singapore: S. Rajaratnam School of International Studies, Nanyang Technological University, 2007), pp. 134–42.
3 Yuzhu Wang, 'The RCEP Initiative and ASEAN "Centrality"', *China Institute of International Studies (CIIS)*, 6 December 2013, www.ciis.org.cn/english/2013-12/06/content_6518129.htm.
4 David B. Dewitt, 'Common, Comprehensive, and Cooperative Security', *The Pacific Review*, Vol. 7. No. 1 (1994), pp. 1–15.
5 David Camroux, *The Rise and Decline of the Asia-Europe Meeting (ASEM): Asymmetric Bilateralism and the Limitations of Interregionalism*, Les Cahiers européens de Sciences Po., No. 4 (Paris: Sciences Po, 2006); Sebastian Bersick, Wim Stokhof and Paul van der Velde, eds., *Multiregionalism and Multilateralism: Asian–European Relations in a Global Context* (Amsterdam: Amsterdam University Press, 2006); Wim Stokhof and Paul van der Velde, eds., *Asian-European Perspectives: Developing the ASEM Process* (Abingdon: Routledge, 2013).
6 Ralf Emmers, *Cooperative Security and the Balance of Power in ASEAN and the ARF* (London: Routledge, 2003).
7 Anja Jetschke and Philomena Murray, 'Diffusing Regional Integration: The EU and Southeast Asia', *West European Politics*, Vol. 35, No. 1 (2012), pp. 174–91.
8 William T. Tow and Brendan Taylor, 'What is Asian Security Architecture?', *Review of International Studies*, Vol. 36, No. 1 (2010), pp. 95–116.
9 Ernest Bower, '"After Hillary" Era Concerns Southeast Asia', *East Asia Forum*, 30 March 2011, www.eastasiaforum.org/2011/03/30/after-hillary-era-concerns-southeast-asia/.

10 Denny Roy, 'Southeast Asia and China: Balancing or Bandwagoning?', *Contemporary Southeast Asia*, Vol. 27, No. 2 (2005), pp. 305–22; Kuik Cheng-Chwee, 'The Essence of Hedging: Malaysia and Singapore's Response to a Rising China', *Contemporary Southeast Asia*, Vol. 30, No. 2 (2008), pp. 159–85; See Seng Tan, 'Faced with the Dragon: Perils and Prospects in Singapore's Ambivalent Relationship with China', *Chinese Journal of International Politics*, Vol. 5, No. 3 (2012), pp. 245–65.
11 Bates Gill, Michael Green, Kiyoto Tsuji and William Watts, *Strategic Views on Asian Regionalism: Survey Results and Analysis* (Washington, D.C.: Center for Strategic and International Studies, 2009).
12 Allan Gyngell, 'Design Faults: The Asia Pacific's Regional Architecture', *Lowy Institute Policy Brief*, 18 July (Sydney, NSW: Lowy Institute for International Policy, 2007); Hadi Soesastro, Allan Gyngell, Charles E. Morrison and Jusuf Wanandi, 'Report of Regional Task Force on Regional Institutional Architecture', report for the Pacific Economic Cooperation Council (PECC) Standing Committee, 2009; Rizal Sukma, 'Insight: East Asia needs a steering committee', *The Jakarta Post*, 4 September 2012; Tow and Taylor, 'What is Asian Security Architecture?'.
13 Richard E. Baldwin, *Managing the Noodle Bowl: The Fragility of East Asian Regionalism*, CEPR Discussion Paper Series No. 5561 (London: Centre for Economic Policy Research, 2006), p. 1.
14 Gyngell, 'Design Faults', p. 1.
15 Richard Woolcott, 'Towards an Asia Pacific Community', *The Asialink Essays*, No. 9 (Melbourne, VIC: Asialink, 2009), p. 3.
16 Aurelia Georg-Mulgan, 'Hatoyama's East Asian Community and Regional Leadership Rivalries', *East Asia Forum*, 13 October 2009, www.eastasiaforum.org/2009/10/13/hatoyamas-east-asian-community/.
17 You Ji, 'East Asian Community: A New Platform for Sino-Japanese Cooperation and Contention', *Japanese Studies*, Vol. 26, No.1 (2006), pp. 19–28.
18 See Seng Tan, 'Spectres of Leifer: Insights on Regional Order and Security for Southeast Asia Today', *Contemporary Southeast Asia*, Vol. 34, No. 3 (2012), pp. 309–37, on p. 316.
19 Tommy Koh, 'Rudd's Reckless Regional Rush', *The Australian*, 18 December 2009, www.theaustralian.com.au/opinion/rudds-reckless-regional-rush/story-e6frg6zo-1225811530050.
20 Thom Woodroofe, 'Is the East Asia Summit Rudd's Gift to the World?', *Australian Policy Outline*, 12 January 2012, http://apo.org.au/commentary/east-asia-summit-rudd%E2%80%99s-gift-world.
21 Aaron Connolly, 'Canberra's Clouseau Strategy', *Lowy Interpreter*, 5 January 2011, www.lowyinterpreter.org/post/2011/01/05/Canberras-Clouseau-strategy.aspx.
22 Sukma, 'Insight'.
23 US Secretary of State Hillary Clinton, 'Remarks on Regional Architecture in Asia: Principles and Priorities', East-West Center, Honolulu, 12 January 2010, www.state.gov/secretary/rm/2010/01/135090.htm.
24 Cited in Ippei Yamazawa, 'Has APEC Achieved Its Midterm Bogor Target?' www.pecc.org, 13 December 2010, www.pecc.org/blog/2010/12/13/has-apec-achieved-its-mid-term-bogor-target/#more-165.
25 Ralf Emmers and See Seng Tan, 'The ASEAN Regional Forum and Preventive Diplomacy: Built to Fail?', *Asian Security*, Vol. 7, No. 1 (2011), pp. 44–60.
26 In response to the 9/11 attacks, the French daily *Le Monde* famously ran a front-page headline, 'Nous sommes tous Américains' (We are all Americans).
27 See Seng Tan, 'Introduction', in See Seng Tan, ed., *Do Institutions Matter? Regional Institutions and Regionalism in East Asia*, RSIS Monograph No. 13 (Singapore: S. Rajaratnam School of International Studies, Nanyang Technological University, 2008), pp. 9–10.

28 Michael J. Green, Ernest Z. Bower, Victor Cha, Charles Freeman, 'Analysis of Secretary of State Clinton's Asia Architecture Speech', *csis.org*, 13 January 2010, http://csis.org/publication/analysis-secretary-state-clinton%E2%80%99s-asia-architecture-speech.
29 Miles Kahler, *International Institutions and the Political Economy of Integration* (Washington, D.C.: The Brookings Institution, 1995), p. 5.
30 William Tow, Michael Auslin, Rory Medcalf, Akihiko Tanaka, Zhu Feng and Sheldon Simon, *Assessing the Trilateral Strategic Dialogue*, NBR Special Report, No. 16 (Seattle, WA: National Bureau of Asian Research, 2008).
31 I borrow from Cha the idea of patchworks. Victor D. Cha, 'Complex Patchworks: U.S. Alliances as Part of Asia's Regional Architecture', *Asia Policy*, No. 11 (2011), pp. 27–50.
32 Amitav Acharya, 'Asia-Pacific Security: Community, Concert or What?', *PacNet*, No. 11, 12 March 2010.
33 Green et al., 'Analysis of Secretary of State Clinton's Asia Architecture Speech'.
34 This third perspective is pieced together from comments made by Bilahari Kausikan, the former permanent secretary of the Singapore Ministry of Foreign Affairs, at a couple of public speeches he gave in Singapore between 2011 and 2012.
35 Tommy Koh, cited in Amitav Acharya, 'Asia's Competing Communities and Why Asian Regionalism Matters', *amitavacharya.com*, pp. 3–4, www.amitavacharya.com/sites/default/files/Competing%20Communities.pdf.
36 Jing-dong Yuan, *Asia-Pacific Security: China's Conditional Multilateralism and Great Power Entente* (Carlisle, PA: Strategic Studies Institute, US Army War College, 2000), p. 7.
37 Cha, 'Complex Patchworks'.
38 Georg-Mulgan, 'Hatoyama's East Asian Community and Regional Leadership Rivalries'.

# Bibliography

Abdulgani-Knapp, Retnowati. 2007. *Soeharto: The Life and Legacy of Indonesia's Second President: An Authorized Biography*. Singapore: Marshall Cavendish.

Abe, Shinzo. 2013. 'The Bounty of the Open Seas: Five New Principles for Japanese Foreign Policy', *Prime Minister of Japan and his Cabinet*, 18 January, www.kantei.go.jp/foreign/96_abe/statement/201301/18speech_e.html.

Abe, Shinzo. 2014. 'Keynote Address by Shinzo Abe, Prime Minister of Japan', The Thirteenth IISS (International Institute for Strategic Studies) Asia Security Summit, the Shangri-La Dialogue, 30 May, www.iiss.org/en/events/shangri%20la%20dialogue/archive/2014-c20c/opening-remarks-and-keynote-address-b0b2/keynote-address-shinzo-abe-a787.

Abe, Shinzo. 2015. 'New Year's Reflection by Prime Minister Shinzo Abe, January 1, 2015'. Transcript provided by Japanese Embassy in Singapore, 7 January 2015.

Acharya, Amitav. Undated. 'Asia's Competing Communities and Why Asian Regionalism Matters', *amitavacharya.com*, www.amitavacharya.com/sites/default/files/Competing%20Communities.pdf.

Acharya, Amitav. 1996. 'ASEAN and Conditional Engagement', in James Shinn, ed., *Weaving the Net: Conditional Engagement with China*. New York: Council on Foreign Relations: 220–48.

Acharya, Amitav. 1997. 'Ideas, Identity and Institution-Building: From the "ASEAN Way" to the "Asia-Pacific Way?"', *The Pacific Review*, Vol. 10, No. 3: 319–46.

Acharya, Amitav. 2000. *Constructing a Security Community in Southeast Asia: ASEAN and the Problem of Regional Order*. London: Routledge.

Acharya, Amitav. 2003/4. 'Will Asia's Past Be Its Future?', *International Security*, Vol. 28, No. 3: 149–64.

Acharya, Amitav. 2004. 'How Ideas Spread: Whose Norms Matter? Norm Localization and Institutional Change in Asian Regionalism', *International Organization*, Vol. 58, No. 2: 239–75.

Acharya, Amitav. 2007. 'Review Article: The Emerging Regional Architecture of World Politics', *World Politics*, Vol. 59, No. 4: 629–52.

Acharya, Amitav. 2009. *Whose Ideas Matter? Agency and Power in Asian Regionalism*. Ithaca, NY: Cornell University Press.

Acharya, Amitav. 2010. 'Asia-Pacific Security: Community, Concert or What?', *PacNet*, No. 11, 12 March.

Acharya, Amitav. 2011. *Asian Regional Institutions and the Possibilities for Socializing the Behaviour of States*, ADB Working Paper Series on Regional Economic Integration, No. 82. Manila: Asian Development Bank.

Acharya, Amitav. 2012. 'The End of ASEAN Centrality?', *Asia Times Online*, 8 August, www.atimes.com/atimes/Southeast_Asia/NH08Ae03.html.
Acharya, Amitav. 2014. *The End of American World Order*. Oxford: Polity Press.
Acharya, Amitav, and Alastair Iain Johnston. 2007. 'Comparing Regional Institutions: An Introduction', in Amitav Acharya and Alastair Iain Johnston, eds., *Crafting Cooperation: Regional International Institutions in Comparative Perspective*. Cambridge: Cambridge University Press: 1–31.
Acharya, Amitav and Arabinda Acharya. 2007. 'The Myth of the Second Front: Localizing the "War on Terror" in Southeast Asia', *The Washington Quarterly*, Vol. 3, No. 4: 75–90.
Acharya, Amitav, and Barry Buzan. 2009. 'Conclusion: On the Possibility of a Non-Western International Relations Theory', in Amitav Acharya and Barry Buzan, eds., *Non-Western International Relations Theory: Perspectives on and beyond Asia*. Abingdon: Routledge: 221–38.
Acharya, Amitav, and See Seng Tan. 2004. 'Introduction', in See Seng Tan and Amitav Acharya, eds., *Asia-Pacific Security Cooperation: National Interests and Regional Order*. Armonk, NY: M. E. Sharpe: xxvi–xxix.
Acharya, Amitav, and See Seng Tan. 2006. 'Betwixt Balance and Community: America, ASEAN, and the Security of Southeast Asia', *International Relations of the Asia-Pacific*, Vol. 6, No. 1: 37–59.
ADB. 2014. *ASEAN 2030: Toward a Borderless Economic Community*. Tokyo: Asian Development Bank Institute.
Ahmed, Zahid Shahab. 2013. *Regionalism and Regional Security in South Asia: The Role of SAARC*. Farnham: Ashgate.
Alagappa, Muthiah, ed. 1998. *Asian Security Practice: Material and Ideational Influences*. Stanford, CA: Stanford University Press.
Alagappa, Muthiah, ed. 2003. *Asian Security Order: Instrumental and Normative Features*. Stanford, CA: Stanford University Press.
Alatas, Syed Farid. 2013. 'Is Religious Intolerance Going Mainstream in Indonesia?', *Global Asia*, Vol. 8, No. 4, www.globalasia.org/article/is-religious-intolerance-going-mainstream-in-indonesia/.
Anderlini, Jamil. 2014. 'Big Nations Snub Beijing Bank Launch after US Lobbying', *Financial Times*, 22 October, www.ft.com/intl/cms/s/0/41c3c0a0-59cd-11e4-9787-00144feab7de.html#axzz3VBgz8Xz2.
Antara News. 2009. 'President: RI Will Never Leave Asean', *Antaranews.com*, 26 October, www.antaranews.com/en/news/1256525105/president-ri-will-never-leave-asean.
Antara News. 2011. 'ASEAN Centrality Maintained, Says Yudhoyono', *AntaraNews.com*, 19 November, www.antaranews.com/en/news/77754/aseans-centrality-maintained--says-yudhoyono.
Anwar, Dewi Fortuna. 1994. *Indonesia in ASEAN: Foreign Policy and Regionalism*. Singapore: Institute of Southeast Asian Studies.
Anwar, Dewi Fortuna. 2010. 'Foreign Policy, Islam and Democracy in Indonesia', *Journal of Indonesian Social Sciences and Humanities*, Vol. 3: 37–54.
Anwar, Dewi Fortuna. 2012. 'A Problem of Mixed Messages: An Indonesian Insider's View of the Australian Relationship', *The Asialink Essays 2012*, Vol. 4. No. 6: 1–4.
Anwar, Dewi Fortuna. 2013. 'An Indonesian Perspective on the US Rebalancing Effort towards Asia', *NBR Commentary*, 26 February, www.thejakartapost.com/news/2006/11/02/importance-onechina-policy.html.

## Bibliography

Anwar, Dewi Fortuna. 2013. 'Indonesia's Wary Thinking on Foreign Policy', *Europe's World*, 1 June, http://europesworld.org/2013/06/01/indonesias-wary-thinking-on-foreign-policy/#.UsYcxY_2NMs.

Anwar, Dewi Fortuna. 2013. 'Indonesia: Building Norms and Consensus on the World Stage', *Global Asia*, Vol. 8, No. 4, www.globalasia.org/article/indonesia-building-norms-and-consensus-on-the-world-stage/.

Arner, Douglas W., Paul Lejot and Wang Wei. 2010. 'Governance and Financial Integration in East Asia', in Masahiro Kawai, Jong-Wha Lee and Peter A. Petri, eds., *Asian Regionalism in the World Economy: Engine for Dynamism and Stability*. Cheltenham: Edward Elgar: 209–48.

The Asahi Shimbun. 2013. 'Editorial: Abe Should Pursue Universal Values in Diplomacy with ASEAN', *The Asahi Shimbun*, 16 December.

ASEAN. Undated. 'Overview of ASEAN–US Dialogue Relations', www.asean.org, www.asean.org/news/item/overview-of-asean-us-dialogue-relations.

ASEAN. 2010. 'ASEAN Centrality and EAS Tops AMM Agenda Ha Noi, July 20, 2010', *Association of Southeast Asian Nations*, 20 July, www.asean.org/news/item/asean-centrality-and-eas-tops-amm-agenda-ha-noi-20-july-2010#.

Ashizawa, Kuniko. 2013. *Japan, the US, and Regional Institution-Building in the New Asia: When Identity Matters*. Houndmills, Basingstoke: Palgrave Macmillan.

Aspinall, Edward, and Marcus Mietzner, eds. 2012. *Problems of Democratization in Indonesia: Elections, Institutions and Society*. Singapore: Institute of Southeast Asian Studies.

Atkinson, Joel. 2010. *Australia and Taiwan: Bilateral Relations, China, the United States, and the South Pacific*. Leiden: Brill.

Atlantic Council. 2014. 'Obama Warns NATO Allies to Share Defence Burden: "We Can't Do It Alone"', *Atlantic Council*, 3 June, www.atlanticcouncil.org/blogs/natosource/obama-warns-nato-allies-to-share-defense-burden-we-can-t-do-it-alone.

Au Yong, Jeremy. 2013. 'Japan Gets a Rare Rebuke from Its Close Ally US', *The Straits Times*, 28 December.

Australia Network. 2012. '"Dynamic Equilibrium" in the Asia Pacific: Interview with Marty Natalegawa, Indonesia's Foreign Affairs Minister', *Australia Network*, 23 February, http://australianetwork.com/focus/s3440427.htm.

Ba, Alice D. 2005. 'Southeast Asia and China', in Evelyn Goh, ed., *Betwixt and Between: Southeast Asian Strategic Relations with the US and China*. Singapore: Institute of Defence and Strategic Studies, Nanyang Technological University: 93–108.

Ba, Alice D. 2006. 'Who's Socializing Whom? Complex Engagement in China–ASEAN Relations', *The Pacific Review*, Vol. 19, No. 2: 157–79.

Ba, Alice D. 2009. *(Re)Negotiating East and Southeast Asia: Region, Regionalism, and the Association of Southeast Asian Nations*. Stanford, CA: Stanford University Press.

Ba, Alice D. 2009. 'Systemic Neglect? A Reconsideration of US-Southeast Asia Policy', *Contemporary Southeast Asia*, Vol. 31, No. 3: 369–98.

Babbage, Ross. 2008. 'Learning to Walk amongst Giants: The New Defence White Paper', *Security Challenges*, Vol. 4, No. 1: 13–20.

Baier, Matthias, ed. 2013. *Social and Legal Norms: Towards a Socio-legal Understanding of Normativity*. Farnham: Ashgate.

Baker, Gerard, and Jacob M. Schlesinger. 2014. 'Abe's Strategy: Rearrange Region's Power Balance', *The Wall Street Journal*, 26 May, www.wsj.com/articles/SB10001424052702304811904579585702903470312.

Baker, Mark. 2002. 'Mahathir Advises Australia to Stop Giving Advice', *The Age*, 28 November 2002, www.theage.com.au/articles/2002/11/27/1038386202475.html.

Baldwin, Richard E. 2006. *Managing the Noodle Bowl: The Fragility of East Asian Regionalism*, CEPR Discussion Paper Series No. 5561. London: Centre for Economic Policy Research.

Baldwin, Richard E. 2012. 'By Invitation: Supply Chains Changed the Growth Model', *The Economist*, 15 August, www.economist.com/economics/by-invitation/guest-contributions/supply-chains-changed-growth-model.

Bateman, Sam. 2014. 'New Tensions in the South China Sea: Whose Sovereignty over Paracels?', *RSIS Commentaries*, No. 088/2014, 14 May, www.rsis.edu.sg/publications/Perspective/RSIS0882014.pdf.

Bateman, Sam, Anthony Bergin and Hayley Channer. 2013. *Terms of Engagement: Australia's Regional Defence Policy*, Strategy, July. Barton, ACT: Australian Strategic Policy Institute.

Baviera, Aileen S. P. 2012. 'South China Sea Disputes: Why ASEAN Must Unite', *East Asia Forum*, 26 July, www.eastasiaforum.org/2012/07/26/south-china-sea-disputes-why-asean-must-unite/.

Beech, Hannah. 2013. 'Return of the Samurai', *Time*, 7 October.

Beeson, Mark. 1999. *Competing Capitalisms: Australia, Japan and Economic Competition in the Asia Pacific*. London: Macmillan.

Beeson, Mark. 2003. 'American Hegemony: The View from Australia', *SAIS Review of International Affairs*, Vol. 23, No. 2: 113–31.

Beeson, Mark. 2003. 'ASEAN Plus Three and the Rise of Reactionary Regionalism', *Contemporary Southeast Asia*, Vol. 25, No. 2: 251–68.

Beeson, Mark. 2009. 'ASEAN's Ways: Still Fit for Purpose?', *Cambridge Review of International Affairs*, Vol. 22, No. 3: 333–43.

Beeson, Mark. 2009. *Institutions of the Asia-Pacific: ASEAN, APEC and Beyond*. Abingdon: Routledge.

Beeson, Mark. 2011. 'Can Australia Save the World? The Limits and Possibilities of Middle Power Diplomacy', *Australian Journal of International Affairs, Vol.* 65, No. 5: 563–77.

Beeson, Mark, and Iyanatul Islam. 2005. 'Neoliberalism and East Asia: Resisting the Washington Consensus', *The Journal of Development Studies*, Vol. 41, No. 2: 197–219.

Beeson, Mark, and Diane Stone. 2014. 'Patterns of Leadership in the Asia-Pacific: A Symposium', *The Pacific Review*, Vol. 27, No. 4: 505–22.

Bennhold, Katrin. 2011. 'What Is the Beijing Consensus?', *The New York Times*, 28 January, http://dealbook.nytimes.com/2011/01/28/what-is-the-beijing-consensus/?_r=0.

Berkofsky, Axel. 2012. *A Pacifist Constitution for an Armed Empire: Past and Present of the Japanese Security and Defence Policies*. Milan: FrancoAngeli.

Bersick, Sebastian, Wim Stokhof and Paul van der Velde, eds. 2006. *Multiregionalism and Multilateralism: Asian–European Relations in a Global Context*. Amsterdam: Amsterdam University Press.

Betts, Richard K. 1993/94. 'East Asia and the United States after the Cold War', *International Security*, Vol. 18, No. 3: 34–77.

Biesner, Robert L. 2007. 'History and Henry Kissinger', *Diplomatic History*, Vol. 14, No. 4: 511–28.

Bisley, Nick. 2012. 'No Hedging in Canberra: The Australia–US Alliance in the "Asian Century"', *Asia-Pacific Bulletin*, No. 157, 3 April. Honolulu, HI: East-West Center.

Bitzinger, Richard, and Barry Desker. 2008. 'Why East Asian War is Unlikely', *Survival*, Vol. 50, No. 6: 105–28.

Blaxland, John. 2012. 'The Australian Mindset in Asia', *Lowy Interpreter*, 30 October, www.lowyinterpreter.org/?d=D – Reactions to 'Australia in the Asian Century' White Paper.

Blomqvist, Hans C. 1993. 'ASEAN as a Model for Third World Regional Economic Cooperation?', *ASEAN Economic Bulletin*, Vol. 10, No. 1: 52–67.
Bloomberg News. 2014. 'China Overtakes Japan as World's Second-Biggest Stock Market', *Bloomberg News*, 28 November, www.bloomberg.com/news/2014-11-27/china-surpasses-japan-as-world-s-second-biggest-equity-market.html.
Blum, Jeremy. 2013. 'Former Foreign Minister Says "China Will Never Seek to Become a Hegemonic Power"', *South China Morning Post*, 18 September, www.scmp.com/news/china-insider/article/1312346/former-foreign-minister-says-china-will-never-seek-become.
Boot, Max. 2014. 'Obama's Disappearing Pacific Pivot', *Commentary*, 29 January, www.commentarymagazine.com/2014/01/29/obamas-disappearing-pacific-pivot-state-of-the-union/.
Börzel, Tanja A., and Thomas Risse. 2009. *Diffusing (Inter-)Regionalism: The EU as a Model of Regional Integration*, KFG Working Paper, No. 7. Berlin: Free University.
Bosco, David. 2012. 'What Divides Neocons and Liberal Interventionists', *Foreign Policy*, 9 April, http://bosco.foreignpolicy.com/posts/2012/04/09/what_divides_neocons_and_liberal_interventionists.
Bosco, Joseph A. 2013. 'Entrapment and Abandonment in Asia', *The National Interest*, 8 July, http://nationalinterest.org/commentary/entrapment-abandonment-asia-8697.
Bower, Ernest Z. 2011. '"After Hillary" Era Concerns Southeast Asia', *East Asia Forum*, 30 March, www.eastasiaforum.org/2011/03/30/after-hillary-era-concerns-southeast-asia/.
Bower, Ernest Z. 2011. 'The Quintessential Test of ASEAN Centrality: Changing the Paradigm in the South China Sea', *Center for Strategic and International Studies (CSIS)*, 21 June, http://csis.org/publication/quintessential-test-asean-centrality-changing-paradigm-south-china-sea.
Breslin, Shaun. 2010. 'China's Emerging Global Role: Dissatisfied Responsible Great Power', *Politics*, Vol. 30, No. 1: 52–62.
Breslin, Shaun. 2010. 'Comparative Theory, China, and the Future of East Asian Regionalism(s)', *Review of International Studies*, Vol. 36, No. 3: 709–29.
Breslin, Shaun, Christopher Hughes, Nicola Phillips and Ben Rosamond, eds. 2002. *New Regionalisms in the Global Political Economy: Theories and Cases*. London: Routledge.
Broinowski, Alison. 2003. *About Face: Asian Accounts of Australia*. Melbourne, VIC: Scribe.
Broinowski, Alison. 2009. 'Why Do We Want an Asia Pacific Community?', *East Asia Forum*, 2 May, www.eastasiaforum.org/2009/05/02/why-do-we-want-an-asia-pacific-community/.
Brooks, Stephen G., and William C. Wohlforth. 2005. 'Hard Times for Soft Balancing', *International Security*, Vol. 30, No. 1: 72–108.
Budianto, Lilian. 2010. 'Benefit from ASEAN or Leave It, Experts Say', *The Jakarta Post*, 24 February, www.thejakartapost.com/news/2010/02/24/benefit-from%C2%A0asean-or-leave-it-experts-say%C2%A0.html.
Bull, Hedley. 1977. *The Anarchical Society: A Study of Order in World Politics*. London: Macmillan.
Burkitt, Laurie. 2014. 'The Chinese Dream vs. the American Dream', *The Wall Street Journal*, 8 May, http://blogs.wsj.com/chinarealtime/2014/05/08/the-chinese-dream-vs-the-american-dream-in-4-charts/.
Bush, Richard C. 2011. 'The United States and China: A G-2 in the Making?', *Brookings*, 11 October, www.brookings.edu/research/articles/2011/10/11-china-us-g2-bush.
Buszynski, Leszek. 1992/93. 'Russia and the Asia-Pacific Region', *Pacific Affairs*, Vol. 65, No. 4: 486–509.
Buszynski, Leszek. 2003. 'ASEAN, the Declaration of Conduct, and the South China Sea', *Contemporary Southeast Asia*, Vol. 25, No. 3: 343–62.

Buszynski, Leszek. 2004. *Asia Pacific Security: Values and Identity*. London: Routledge.
Buszynski, Leszek, and Christopher B. Roberts. 2013. *The South China Sea: Stabilization and Resolution*, Occasional Paper. Canberra, ACT: National Security College, Australian National University.
Buzan, Barry, and Gerald Segal. 1994. 'Rethinking East Asian Security', *Survival*, Vol. 36, No. 2: 3–21.
Buzan, Barry, and Ole Wæver. 2003. *Regions and Powers: The Structure of International Security*. Cambridge: Cambridge University Press.
Caballero-Anthony, Mely. 2009. 'Regional Security Institutions in Asia: Some Insights on Asian Regionalism', Background Paper No. 6 for the Asian Development Bank's Study Finalization Workshop on Institutions for Regionalism in Asia and the Pacific, Shanghai, 2–3 December .
Caballero-Anthony, Mely. 2014. 'Understanding ASEAN's Centrality: Bases and Prospects in an Evolving Regional Architecture', *The Pacific Review*, Vol. 27, No. 4: 563–84.
Callahan, William A. 2012. *China: The Pessoptimist Nation*. Oxford: Oxford University Press.
Callen, Victor J. 1983. 'Anglo-Australian Attitudes toward Immigrants: A Review of Survey Evidence', *International Migration Review*, Vol. 17, No. 1: 120–37.
Camilleri, Joseph. 2005. 'East Asia's Emerging Regionalism: Tensions and Potential in Design and Architecture', *Global Change, Peace and Security*, Vol. 17, No. 3: 253–61.
Cammack, Paul. 2008. 'Smart Power and US Leadership: A Critique of Joseph Nye', *49th Parallel*, No. 22: 4–20.
Campbell, Kurt, and Brian Andrews. 2013. 'Explaining the US "Pivot" to Asia', *Americas 2013/01*. London: Chatham House/Royal Institute of International Affairs.
Camroux, David. 2006. *The Rise and Decline of the Asia-Europe Meeting (ASEM): Asymmetric Bilateralism and the Limitations of Interregionalism*, Les Cahiers européens de Sciences Po., No. 4. Paris: Sciences Po.
Camroux, David, and Christian Lechervy, 1996. 'Close Encounter of a Third Kind? The Inaugural Asia-Europe Meeting of March 1996', *The Pacific Review*, Vol. 9, No. 3: 442–53.
Capannelli, Giovanni. 2013. 'Time to Create an ASEAN Academy', *East Asia Forum*, 22 November, www.eastasiaforum.org/2013/11/22/time-to-create-an-asean-academy/.
Capie, David, and Amitav Acharya. 2011. 'The United States and the East Asia Summit: A New Beginning?' *PacNet*, No. 64, 14 November.
Capie, David, and Brendan Taylor. 2010. 'The Shangri-La Dialogue and the Institutionalization of Defence Diplomacy in Asia', *The Pacific Review*, Vol. 23, No. 3: 359–76.
Capie, David, and Paul Evans. 2007. *The Asia-Pacific Security Lexicon*, 2nd edn. Singapore: Institute of Southeast Asian Studies.
Carlson, Christine. 2006. 'Using Political Power to Convene', *National Civic Review*, Vol. 95, No. 3: 57–60.
Carlson, Christine, and Greg Wolf. 2005. 'The Power to Convene', *State News*, November/December. Lexington, KY: The Council of State Governments.
Carr, Bob. 2012. 'Transcript of Remarks by Senator the Hon Bob Carr, Minister for Foreign Affairs, Launch of the 40th Anniversary of Australia China Diplomatic Relations, Capital M, Beijing, May 15, 2012', www.china.embassy.gov.au/bjng/20120605Carrremarks-eng.html.
Caulder, Kent E., and Francis Fukuyama. 2008. 'Introduction', in Kent E. Caulder and Francis Fukuyama, eds., *East Asian Multilateralism: Prospects for Regional Stability*. Baltimore, MD: The Johns Hopkins University Press: 1–12.
Cayo, Dan. 2013. 'Opinion: B.C. Values Asia – We Just Don't Like It Much', *Vancouver Sun*, 30 May.

## Bibliography

Cha, Victor D. 2009/10. 'Powerplay: Origins of the US Alliance System in Asia', *International Security*, Vol. 34, No. 3: 158–96.

Cha, Victor D. 2011. 'Complex Patchworks: U.S. Alliances as Part of Asia's Regional Architecture', *Asia Policy*, No. 11: 27–50.

Chan, Man-jung Mignonne. 2009. 'APEC's Eye on the Prize: Participants, Modality, and Confidence-Building', in K. Kesavapany and Hank Lim, eds., *APEC at 20: Recall, Reflect, Remake*. Singapore: Institute of Southeast Asian Studies: 41–54.

Chang, C. Y. 1979. 'ASEAN's Proposed Neutrality: China's Response', *Contemporary Southeast Asia*, Vol. 1, No. 3: 249–67.

Chang, Gordon C. 2010. 'Hillary Clinton Changes America's China Policy', *Forbes*, 28 July, www.forbes.com/2010/07/28/china-beijing-asia-hillary-clinton-opinions-columnists-gordon-g-chang.html.

Chang, Pao-min. 1985. *Kampuchea between China and Vietnam*. Singapore: Singapore University Press.

Checkel, Jeff. 1993. 'Ideas, Institutions, and the Gorbachev Foreign Policy Revolution', *World Politics*, Vol. 45, No. 2: 271–300.

Chen, Dingding. 2014. 'China's "Marshall Plan" Is Much More', *The Diplomat*, 10 November, http://thediplomat.com/2014/11/chinas-marshall-plan-is-much-more/.

Chen, Jian. 2008. 'China and the Bandung Conference', in See Seng Tan and Amitav Acharya. eds., *Bandung Revisited: The Legacy of the 1955 Asian-African Conference for International Order*. Singapore: National University of Singapore Press: 132–59.

Chen, Yugang. 2011. 'Community-Building or Rebalancing? China and the United States in Southeast Asia', in Mingjiang Li and Dongmin Lee, eds., *China and East Asian Strategic Dynamics: The Shaping of a New Regional Order*. Lanham, MD: Lexington Books: 3–18.

Cheng, Dean. 2013. 'China's ADIZ as Area Denial', *The National Interest*, 4 December, http://nationalinterest.org/commentary/chinas-adiz-area-denial-9492.

Cheng, Rachel. 2014. 'AIIB: China Needs to Win Over Naysayers', *The Straits Times*, 4 November, www.straitstimes.com/news/opinion/eye-the-economy/story/aiib-china-needs-win-over-naysayers-20141104.

Chesterman, Simon, and Kishore Mahbubani. 2010. 'The Asian Way of Handling the World', *The Guardian*, 4 March, www.theguardian.com/commentisfree/2010/mar/04/global-problem-solving-asian-way.

China Daily. 2009. 'Japan's New Premier Pitches East Asia Union', *China Daily*, 29 September, www.chinadaily.com.cn/world/2009-09/23/content_8724372.htm.

China Daily. 2014. 'Chinese President Proposes Asia-Pacific Dream', *China Daily*, 9 November, www.chinadaily.com.cn/china/2014-11/09/content_18889698.htm.

Chinese Economic Review. 2011. 'Splitting Stitches: China's Textile Industry Is Moving Abroad, but Politics Prevent Indonesia from Fully Reaping the Benefits', *China Economic Review*, 1 May, www.chinaeconomicreview.com/content/splitting-stitches.

Chung, Chien-peng. 2010. *China's Multilateral Cooperation in Asia and the Pacific: Institutionalizing Beijing's 'Good Neighbour Policy'*. Abingdon: Routledge.

Clark, Marshall and Juliet Pietsch, 2014. *Indonesia–Malaysia Relations: Cultural Heritage, Politics and Labour Migration*. Abingdon: Routledge.

Claude, Inis L. 1989. 'The Balance of Power Revisited', *Review of International Studies*, Vol. 15, No. 2: 77–85.

Clements, Kevin P. 1983. 'Common Security in the Asia-Pacific Region: Problems and Prospects', *Alternatives: Global, Local, Political*, Vol. 14, No. 1: 49–76.

Clifford, S. 2011. 'Theory Talk #42: Amitav Acharya on the Relevance of Regions, ASEAN, and Western IR's False Universalisms', *Theory Talks*, 8 October, www.theorytalks.org/2011/08/theory-talk-42.htmlm.

Clifford, Tom. 2014. 'Abe and the Re-Militarization of Japan', *Counterpunch*, 1 April, www.counterpunch.org/2014/04/01/abe-and-the-re-militarization-of-japan/.

Clinton, Hillary. 2010. 'Remarks on Regional Architecture in Asia: Principles and Priorities', East-West Center, Honolulu, 12 January, www.state.gov/secretary/rm/2010/01/135090.htm.

Clinton, Hillary. 2010. 'Clinton's Speech on America's Engagement in the Asia-Pacific, October 2010', *Council on Foreign Relations*, 28 October, www.cfr.org/asia-and-pacific/clintons-speech-americas-engagement-asia-pacific-october-2010/p23280.

Clinton, Hillary. 2011. 'America's Pacific Century', *Foreign Policy*, 11 October, www.foreignpolicy.com/articles/2011/10/11/americas_pacific_century?page=full.

Clouse, Thomas. 2011. 'ASEAN Moves Closer to Political Cohesion', *Global Finance*, 29 August, www.gfmag.com/magazine/julyaugust-2011/asean-moves-closer-to-political-cohesion.

Cochrane, Liam. 2012. 'Kevin Rudd Claims Asia-Pacific Community Success', *Radio Australia*, 17 April, www.radioaustralia.net.au/international/radio/program/asia-pacific/kevin-rudd-claims-asiapacific-community-success/914668.

Colebatch, Tim. 2008. 'Rudd's Grand Vision for Asia-Pacific', *The Age*, 5 June, www.theage.com.au/national/rudds-grand-vision-for-asiapacific-20080604-2lw1.html.

Coll, Steve. 2014. 'Two More Years: Can Obama Duck Lame-Duck Syndrome?', *The New Yorker*, 17 November, www.newyorker.com/magazine/2014/11/17/two-years-2.

Collins, Alan. 2013. *Building a People-oriented Security Community the ASEAN Way*. Abingdon: Routledge.

Connolly, Aaron. 2011. 'Canberra's Clouseau Strategy', *Lowy Interpreter*, 5 January, www.lowyinterpreter.org/post/2011/01/05/Canberras-Clouseau-strategy.aspx.

Cook, Malcolm. 2011. *ASEAN's Triumph*, Policy Brief, No. 4. Adelaide, SA: Indo-Pacific Governance Research Centre, The University of Adelaide.

Cooney, Kevin J. 2002. *Japan's Foreign Policy Maturation: A Quest for Normalcy*. London: Routledge.

Cossa, Ralph A. 1994. *Multilateral Dialogue in Asia: Building on a Strong Bilateral Base*. Honolulu, HI: Pacific Forum CSIS.

Cronin, Patrick M., Ely Ratner, Elbridge Colby, Zachary M. Hosford and Alexander Sullivan. 2014. *Tailored Coercion: Competition and Risk in Maritime Asia*. Washington, D.C.: Center for New American Security.

CSIS. 2011. 'Concepts for the East Asia Summit: Connectivity, Security & ASEAN Centrality', *Center for Strategic and International Studies (CSIS)*, 20 May, http://csis.org/event/concepts-east-asia-summit.

Dae, Cheong Wa. 2009. 'President Announces "New Asia Initiative"', *Korea.net*, 8 March, www.korea.net/news/News/NewsView.asp?serial_no=20090308001&part=101&SearchDay=.

Damuri, Yose Rizal. 2012. 'East Asia Economic Integration and ASEAN Centrality', *The Jakarta Post*, 16 November.

Darmosumarto, Santo. 2012. 'Indonesia: A New "Middle Power"', *The Jakarta Post*, 11 November, www.thejakartapost.com/news/2009/10/30/indonesia-a-new-middle-power039.html.

Das, Sanchita Basu. 2013. 'The Trans-Pacific Partnership as a Tool to Contain China: Myth or Reality?', *East Asia Forum*, 8 June, www.eastasiaforum.org/2013/06/08/the-trans-pacific-partnership-as-a-tool-to-contain-china-myth-or-reality/.

Davidson, Paul J. 1997. *The Legal Framework for International Economic Relations: ASEAN and Canada*. Singapore: Institute of Southeast Asian Studies.

Daytona Morning Beach Journal. 1971. 'Nixon Warns of Hard Choices', *Daytona Beach Morning Journal*, 26 February, www.news.google.com/newspapers?nid=1873&dat=19710226&id=-00fAAAAIBAJ&sjid=mdEEAAAAIBAJ&pg=4570,7013521.

D'Cruz, Joseph V., and William Steele. 2003. *Australia's Ambivalence towards Asia: Politics, Neo/Post-Colonialism, and Fact/Fiction*. Melbourne, VIC: Monash Asia Institute, Monash University.

Deibel, Terry L. 1989. 'Reagan's Mixed Legacy', *Foreign Policy*, No. 75: 34–55.

Department of Defence. 2009. *Defending Australia in the Asia Pacific Century: Force 2030*, Defence White Paper 2009. Canberra, ACT: Commonwealth of Australia.

Department of Defence. 2013. *2013 Defence White Paper*. Canberra, ACT: Department of Defence, Commonwealth of Australia.

Desker, Barry. 2008. 'Is the ASEAN Charter Necessary?', *RSIS Commentaries*, No. 77/2008, 17 July.

Dewitt, David B. 1994. 'Common, Comprehensive, and Cooperative Security', *The Pacific Review*, Vol. 7, No. 1: 1–15.

Dibb, Paul. 1986. *Review of Australia's Defence Capabilities: Report to the Minister for Defence by Mr. Paul Dibb*. Canberra, ACT: Australian Government Publishing Service.

Ditchley Foundation. 2013. 'Indonesia: The Other Asian Giant', Ditchley Foundation, 21–23 March, www.ditchley.co.uk/conferences/past-programme/2010-2019/2013/indonesia.

Djalal, Hasjim. 2001. 'Managing Potential Conflicts in the South China Sea: Lessons Learned', in Mark J. Valencia, ed., *Maritime Regime Building*. London: Kluwer Law International: 87–92.

Dobbs, Richard, Fraser Thompson and Arief Budiman. 2012. '5 Reasons to Believe in the Indonesian Miracle: Why This Amazing Archipelago is on Track to be the World's Seventh Largest Economy', *Foreign Policy*, 21 September, www.foreignpolicy.com/articles/2012/09/21/5_reasons_to_believe_in_the_indonesian_miracle?page=full.

Dobell, Graeme. 2011. 'An Asia Pacific Concert by Another Name', *Lowy Interpreter*, 11 October, www.lowyinterpreter.org/post/2011/10/11/The-Asia-Pacific-concert-by-another-name.aspx?COLLCC=4060986791&.

Dobriansky, Paula J. 2003. 'Unilateralism and US Foreign Policy', Remarks to Woodrow Wilson School of International and Public Affairs, Princeton University, Princeton, NJ, 5 December, http://2001-2009.state.gov/g/rls/rm/2003/27418.htm.

Dobson, Wendy. 2011. 'Asia's Evolving Economic Institutions: Roles and Future Prospects', *East Asia Forum*, 21 August, www.eastasiaforum.org/2011/08/21/asia-s-evolving-economic-institutions-roles-and-future-prospects/.

Donahue, Patrick, and Brian Parkin. 2014. 'Xi Says China's Military Expansion Not Aimed at Asian Hegemony', *Bloomberg News*, 29 March, www.bloomberg.com/news/2014-03-28/xi-says-china-s-military-expansion-not-aimed-at-asian-hegemony.html.

Dorch, Jörn. 2006. 'The Impact of Democratization on the Making of Foreign Policy in Indonesia, Thailand and the Philippines', *Journal of Current Southeast Asian Affairs*, No. 5: 42–70.

Dormandy, Xenia, with Rory Kinane. 2014. *Asia-Pacific Security: A Changing Role for the United States*, Chatham House Report. London: Chatham House (Royal Institute of International Affairs).

Dosch, Jörn. 2006. 'The Impact of Democratization on the Making of Foreign Policy in Indonesia, Thailand and the Philippines', *Südostasien aktuell*, Vol. 5: 42–70.

Downer, Alexander. 2006. 'Should Australia Think Big or Small in Foreign Policy?', Address to the Centre for Independent Studies: The Policymakers Forum, Sydney, 10 July, www.foreignminister.gov.au/speeches/2006/060710_bigorsmall.html.
Drifte, Reinhard. 1998. *Japan's Foreign Policy for the 21st Century: From Economic Superpower to What Power?* Houndmills, Basingstoke: Palgrave Macmillan.
Drysdale, Peter. 1991. *Open Regionalism: A Key to East Asia's Economic Future*, Pacific Economic Papers, No. 197. Canberra, ACT: Australia–Japan Research Centre, Australian National University.
Drysdale, Peter. 2009. 'Rudd in Singapore on the Asia Pacific Community Idea', *East Asia Forum*, 31 May, www.eastasiaforum.org/2009/05/31/rudd-in-singapore-on-the-asia-pacific-community-idea/.
Drysdale, Peter, and Shiro Armstrong. 2009. 'Does APEC Matter?', *East Asia Forum*, 8 November, www.eastasiaforum.org/2009/11/08/does-apec-matter/.
Dunkel, Arthur. 1992. 'Don't Make "the Best Become Enemy of the Good"', Address delivered at the Pacific Economic Cooperation Council (PECC) IX, 25September, www.sunsonline.org/trade/process/during/uruguay/dunkel/09250092.htm.
Dupont, Alan. 2012. 'Inflection Point: the Australian Defence Force after Afghanistan', *Policy Brief*, March. Sydney, NSW: Lowy Institute for International Policy.
Dupont, Alan, and Christopher G. Baker. 2014. 'East Asia's Maritime Disputes: Fishing in Troubled Waters', *The Washington Quarterly*, Vol. 37, No. 1: 79–98.
Dyer, Geoff, and Daniel Dombey. 2010. 'Shadow Cast over Hopes for US–China "G2"', *Financial Times*, 14 January.
Ean, Peter Ho Hak. 1994. 'The ASEAN Regional Forum: The Way Forward', paper presented to the Third Workshop on ASEAN-UN Cooperation in Peace and Preventive Diplomacy, Bangkok, 17–18 February.
The Economist. 2001. 'China's disappointment: The Fight Against Terrorism Will Dominate the APEC Meeting', *The Economist*, 18 October, www.economist.com/node/825358.
The Economist. 2005. 'The Reluctant Deputy Sheriff' (Special Report: Australia), *The Economist*, 5 May.
The Economist. 2009. 'Everybody's Friend: Indonesia Deserves a Better Image', *The Economist*, 11 September.
The Economist. 2013. 'Chasing the Chinese dream', *The Economist*, 4 May, www.economist.com/news/briefing/21577063-chinas-new-leader-has-been-quick-consolidate-his-power-what-does-he-now-want-his.
Economy, Elizabeth. 2013. 'The Xi-Obama Summit: As Good as Expected – and Maybe Even Better', *The Atlantic*, 11 June, www.theatlantic.com/china/archive/2013/06/the-xi-obama-summit-as-good-as-expected-and-maybe-even-better/276733/.
Economy, Elizabeth C., and Adam Segal. 2009. 'The G-2 Mirage: Why the United States and China Are Not Ready to Upgrade Ties', *Foreign Affairs*, Vol. 88, No. 3: 14–23.
Edström, Bert. 2011. *Japan and Human Security: The Derailing of a Foreign Policy Vision*, Asia Paper, March. Stockholm: Institute for Security and Development Policy.
Eilstrup-Sangiovanni, Mette, and Daniel Verdier. 2005. 'European Integration as a Solution to War', *European Journal of International Relations*, Vol. 11, No. 1: 99–135.
Elek, Andrew. 2013. CAPS? 'APEC Paves the Way for Greater Regional Connectivity', *East Asia Forum*, 21 October, www.eastasiaforum.org/2013/10/21/apec-paves-the-way-for-greater-regional-connectivity/.
Eliraz, Giora. 2004. *Islam in Indonesia: Modernism, Radicalism, and the Middle East Dimension*. Brighton: Sussex Academic Press.

Emmers, Ralf. 2003. *Cooperative Security and the Balance of Power in ASEAN and the ARF*. London: Routledge.
Emmers, Ralf. 2005. *Maritime Disputes in the South China Sea: Strategic and Diplomatic Status Quo*, IDSS Working Paper No. 87. Singapore: Institute of Defence and Strategic Studies, Nanyang Technological University.
Emmers, Ralf. 2014. 'ASEAN's Search for Neutrality in the South China Sea', *Asian Journal of Peacebuilding*, Vol. 2, No. 1: 61–77.
Emmers, Ralf. 2014. 'Indonesia's Role in ASEAN: A Case of Incomplete and Sectorial Leadership', *The Pacific Review*, Vol. 27, No. 4: 543–62.
Emmers, Ralf, Joseph Chinyong Liow and See Seng Tan. 2011. *The East Asia Summit and the Regional Security Architecture*, Maryland Series in Contemporary Asian Studies No. 3-2010 (202). College Park, MD: University of Maryland.
Emmers, Ralf, and See Seng Tan. 2011. 'The ASEAN Regional Forum and Preventive Diplomacy: Built to Fail?', *Asian Security*, Vol. 7, No. 1: 44–60.
Emmerson, Donald K. 2005. 'What is Indonesia?', in John Bresnan, ed., *Indonesia: The Great Transition*. Lanham, MD: Rowman and Littlefield: 7–73.
Emmerson, Donald K. 2009. *Crisis and Consensus: American and ASEAN in a New Global Context*, Working Paper. Bangkok: American Studies Program, Chulalongkorn University.
Emmerson, Donald K. 2010. *Asian Regionalism and US Policy: The Case for Creative Adaptation*, RSIS Working Paper, No. 193. Singapore: S. Rajaratnam School of International Studies, Nanyang Technological University.
Emmerson, Donald K. 2012. 'ASEAN Stumbles in Phnom Penh', *PacNet*, No. 45, 19 July, csis.org/files/publication/Pac1245.pdf.
Emmerson, Donald K. 2012. 'Beyond the Six Points: How Far Will Indonesia Go?', *East Asia Forum*, 29 July, www.eastasiaforum.org/2012/07/29/beyond-the-six-points-how-far-will-indonesia-go/.
Evans, Gareth. 1992. 'Australia's Economic Engagement with Asia', Address by Senator Gareth Evans, Minister for Foreign Affairs and Trade, to the Australian Institute of Company Directors, 27 March, www.gevans.org/speeches/old/1992/270392_fm_auseconomicengage.pdf.
Evans, Gareth. 2012. 'No Power? No Influence? Australia's Middle Power Diplomacy in the Asian Century', 2012 Charteris Lecture by Professor the Hon Gareth Evans AO QC, to the Australian Institute of International Affairs (AIIA), New South Wales Branch, 6 June www.gevans.org/speeches/speech472.html.
Evans, Gareth, and Bruce Grant, 1995. *Australia's Foreign Relations: In the World of the 1990s*. 2nd edn. Melbourne, VIC: Melbourne University Press
Evans, Paul. 2005. 'Between Regionalism and Regionalization: Policy Networks and the Nascent East Asian Institutional Identity', in T. J. Pempel, ed., *Remapping East Asia: The Construction of a Region*. Ithaca, NY: Cornell University Press: 195–215.
Ewing, Philip. 2014. 'Obama's Asia Pivot: A Work in Progress', *Politico*, 20 April, www.politico.com/story/2014/04/barack-obama-asia-pivot-105842.html.
Ewing-Chow, Michael, and Hsien-Li Tan. 2013. *The Role of the Rule of Law in ASEAN Integration*, EUI Working Paper RSCAS 2013/16. Badia Fiesolana: European University Institute.
Farer, Tom J. 1993. 'The Role of Regional Collective Security Arrangements', in Thomas G. Weiss, ed., *Collective Security in a Changing World*. Boulder, CO: Lynne Rienner: 153–89.
Fifield, Russell H. 1979. *National and Regional Interests in ASEAN: Competition and Cooperation in International Politics*, Occasional Paper, No. 57. Singapore: Institute of Southeast Asian Studies.

Finnemore, Martha, and Kathryn Sikkink. 1998. 'International Norm Dynamics and Political Change', *International Organization*, Vol. 52, No. 4: 887–917.

Flitton, Daniel. 2011. 'My Dream of Asia is Here Now, Says Rudd', *The Sydney Morning Herald*, 24 July.

Foot, Rosemary. 2006. 'Chinese Strategies in a US-Hegemonic Global Order: Accommodating and Hedging', *International Affairs*, Vol. 82, No. 1: 77–94.

Ford, Michele. 2012. 'White Paper: Searching for Southeast Asia', *Lowy Interpreter*, 1 November, www.lowyinterpreter.org/?d=D - Reactions to 'Australia in the Asian Century' White Paper.

Fraser, Malcolm, with Cain Roberts. 2014. *Dangerous Allies*. Melbourne, VIC: Melbourne University Press.

Fravel, M. Taylor, and Richard J. Samuels. 2005. 'The United States as an Asian Power: Realism or Conceit?', *Audit of the Conventional Wisdom*, No. 05-2. Cambridge, MA: Center for International Studies, Massachusetts Institute of Technology.

Freeman, Lindon C. 1979. 'Centrality in Social Networks: Conceptual Clarification', *Social Networks*, Vol. 1: 215–39.

Friedberg, Aaron L. 1993/94. 'Ripe for Rivalry: Prospects for Peace in a Multipolar Asia', *International Security*, Vol. 18, No. 3: 5–33.

Friedberg, Aaron L. 2012. *A Contest for Supremacy: China, America, and the Struggle for Mastery in Asia*. New York: W. W. Norton.

Frost, Ellen L. 2008. *Asia's New Regionalism*. Boulder, CO: Lynne Rienner.

Frost, Frank. 1990. 'Introduction: ASEAN since 1967', in Alison Broinowski, ed., *ASEAN in the 1990s*. London: Macmillan: 1–31.

Frost, Frank. 2009. 'Australia's Proposal for an "Asia Pacific Community": Issues and Prospects', Parliamentary Library Research Paper, 1 December. Canberra, ACT: Department of Parliamentary Services, Parliament of Australia.

Fukuyama, Francis. 2006. 'After Neoconservatism', *The New York Times*, 19 February, www.nytimes.com/2006/02/19/magazine/neo.html?pagewanted=print&_r=0.

Fukuyama, Francis. 2007. *America at the Crossroads: Democracy, Power, and the Neoconservative Legacy*. New Haven, CT: Yale University Press.

Futori, Hideshi. 2013. 'Japan's Disaster Relief Diplomacy: Fostering Military Cooperation in Asia', *Asia-Pacific Bulletin*, No. 213, 13 May.

Ganjanakhundee, Supalak. 2013. 'Asean Must Unite on South China Sea: Kerry', *The Nation*, 29 September, www.nationmultimedia.com/national/Asean-must-unite-on-South-China-Sea-Kerry-30215874.html.

Garnaut, Ross. 1996. *Open Regionalism and Trade Liberalization: An Asia-Pacific Contribution to the World Trade System*. Singapore: Institute of Southeast Asian Studies, 1996.

Garrett, Geoffrey. 2010. 'Rudd's Chinese Whispers Will Have Been Heard Loud and Clear', *The Sydney Morning Herald*, 7 December, www.smh.com.au/federal-politics/political-opinion/rudds-chinese-whispers-will-have-been-heard-loud-and-clear-20101206-18mpa.html.

Gat, Azur. 2007. 'The Return of Authoritarian Great Powers', *Foreign Affairs*, Vol. 86, No. 4: 59–69.

Gaylord, Becky. 2001. 'In Optus Deal, Australians Ponder How to Trust Singapore', *The New York Times*, 13 August.

Gershman, John. 2003. 'Is Southeast Asia the Second Front?', *Foreign Affairs*, Vol. 81, No. 4: 60–74.

Gill, Bates, and Chin-hao Huang. 2009. *China's Expanding Role in Peacekeeping: Prospects and Policy Implications*, SIPRI Policy Paper, No. 25. Stockholm: Stockholm Institute for International Peace Research.

Gill, Bates, Michael Green, Kiyoto Tsuji and William Watts. 2009. *Strategic Views on Asian Regionalism: Survey Results and Analysis*. Washington, D.C.: Center for Strategic and International Studies.

Gilpin, Robert. 1997. 'APEC in a New International Order', in Donald C. Hellmann and Kenneth B. Pyle, eds., *From APEC to Xanadu: Creating a Viable Community in the Post-War Pacific*. Armonk, NY: M. E. Sharpe: 14–36.

Global Times. 2013. 'Chinese Hospital Ship Makes Port Call, Joins Drill in Brunei', *Global Times*, 16 June, www.globaltimes.cn/content/789169.shtml.

Global Times. 2014. 'Midterm Result Will Further Thwart Obama', *Global Times*, 5 November, www.globaltimes.cn/content/890056.shtml.

Goh, Evelyn. 2005. 'Introduction', in Evelyn Goh, ed., *Betwixt and Between: Southeast Asian Strategic Relations with the US and China*. Singapore: Institute of Defence and Strategic Studies, Nanyang Technological University: 1–8.

Goh, Evelyn. 2007/8. 'Great Powers and Hierarchical Order in Southeast Asia: Analyzing Regional Security Strategies', *International Security*, Vol. 32, No. 3: 113–57.

Goh, Evelyn. 2014. 'ASEAN-led Multilateralism and Regional Order: The Great Power Bargain Deficit', *The Asan Forum* (Special Forum), 23 May, www.theasanforum.org/asean-led-multilateralism-and-regional-order-the-great-power-bargain-deficit/.

Goh, Evelyn, and Amitav Acharya. 2002. 'The ASEAN Regional Forum and US–China Relations: Comparing Chinese and American Positions', paper for the Fifth China-ASEAN Research Institutes Roundtable on Regionalism and Community-Building in East Asia, Hong Kong: University of Hong Kong.

Goldberg, Jeffrey. 2005. 'Breaking Ranks: What Turned Brent Scowcroft against the Bush Administration?', *The New Yorker*, 31 October.

Goldstein, Judith, and Robert O. Keohane, eds. 1993. *Ideas and Foreign Policy: Beliefs, Institutions, and Political Change*. Ithaca, NY: Cornell University Press.

Good, Chris. 2009. 'The Obama Doctrine: Multilateralism with Teeth', *The Atlantic*, 10 December, www.theatlantic.com/politics/archive/2009/12/the-obama-doctrine-multilateralism-with-teeth/31655/.

Gowan, Richard, and Bruce Jones. 2009. 'Mr. Obama Goes to New York: The President and the Restoration of Multilateral Diplomacy', *Brookings Report*, 17 September. Washington, D.C.: Brookings Institution, www.brookings.edu/research/reports/2009/09/obama-united-nations-jones.

Granados, Ulises. 2014. *US Involvement in the Sino-Japanese Diayu/Senkaku Conflict: Finding Solutions for Stability in the East China Sea*, prepared for 2013 East Asia Security Symposium and Conference. Robina, QLD: East Asia Security Centre, Bond University.

Grant, Jeremy, Ben Bland and Gwen Robinson. 2012. 'South China Sea Issue Divides Asean', *Financial Times*, 16 July.

Green, Michael J. 2001. *Japan's Reluctant Realism*. Houndmills, Basingstoke: Palgrave Macmillan.

Green, Michael J., Ernest Z. Bower, Victor Cha, Charles Freeman, 'Analysis of Secretary of State Clinton's Asia Architecture Speech', *csis.org*, 13 January, http://csis.org/publication/analysis-secretary-state-clinton%E2%80%99s-asia-architecture-speech.

Grenville, Stephen. 2014. 'The Trans-Pacific Partnership: Where Economics and Geopolitics Meet', *Lowy Interpreter*, 4 March, www.lowyinterpreter.org/post/2014/03/04/Trans-Pacific-Partnership-Where-economics-and-geopolitics-meet.aspx?COLLCC=3559796430&.

Gyngell, Allan. 2007. 'Australia-Indonesia', in Brendan Taylor, ed., *Australia as an Asia Pacific Regional Power: Friendship in Flux*. Abingdon: Routledge: 97–115.

Gyngell, Allan. 2007. 'Design Faults: The Asia Pacific's Regional Architecture', *Lowy Institute Policy Brief*, 18 July. Sydney, NSW: Lowy Institute for International Policy.

Gyngell, Allan. 2012. 'What Happened to Diplomacy?', Address to the Australian Institute of International Affairs, ACT Branch, 7 May, www.ona.gov.au/media/39310/aiia-address_7-may-2012.pdf.

Haacke, Jürgen. 2010. 'Playing Catch-Up: The United States and Southeast Asia', *LSE IDEAS Special Report (SR) 003: Obama Nation? US Foreign Policy One Year On*, January: 28–33.

Haas, Michael. 1989. *The Asian Way to Peace: A Story of Regional Cooperation*. Portsmouth, NH: Greenwood Publishing Group.

Haggard, Stephen D. 2013. 'The Organizational Architecture of the Asia-Pacific: Insights from the New Institutionalism', in Miles Kahler and Andrew MacIntyre, eds., *Integrating Regions: Asia in Comparative Context*. Stanford, CA: Stanford University Press: 195–221.

Hall, John A., and Siniša Malešević, eds. 2013. *Nationalism and War*. Cambridge: Cambridge University Press.

Hall, Peter A. 1989. *The Political Power of Economic Ideas*. Princeton, NJ: Princeton University Press.

Hanauer, Larry, and Lyle J. Morris. 2014. *Chinese Engagement in Africa: Drivers, Reactions, and Implications for US Policy*. Santa Monica, CA: RAND Corporation.

Harding, Harry. 1994. 'Cooperative Security in the Asia-Pacific', in Janne E. Nolan, ed., *Global Engagement: Cooperation and Security in the 21st Century*. Washington, D.C.: The Brookings Institution Press: 419–46.

Harper, John Lamberton. 2011. *The Cold War*. Oxford: Oxford University Press.

Harrison, Matthew. 2013. 'What Role Does ASEAN Play in the US Pivot to Asia?', *Asia House*, 20 August, www.futureforeignpolicy.com/what-role-does-asean-play-in-the-us-pivot-to-asia-2/.

Hart, H. L. A. 1955. 'Are There any Natural Rights?', *Philosophical Review*, Vol. 64: 175–91.

Hartcher, Peter. 2008. Rudd Asia Plan Stirs Tensions with US, China', *Sydney Morning Herald*, 28 June, www.smh.com.au/news/national/rudd-asia-plan-stirs-tensions-with-us-china/2008/06/27/1214472770870.html.

Hatta, Mohammad. 1953. 'Indonesia's Foreign Policy', *Foreign Affairs*, Vol. 31, No. 3: 441–52.

Hayashi, Yuka. 2013. 'Abe Tells Obama Japan Will Boost Its Defence', *The Wall Street Journal*, 22 February, www.wsj.com/articles/SB10001424127887324503204578320640390164434.

Hayashi, Yuka. 2014. 'Abe's Military Push May Please U.S. but Rattle Neighbours', *The Wall Street Journal*, 22 April.

He, Baogang. 2011. 'The Awkwardness of Australian Engagement with Asia: The Dilemmas of Australian Idea of Regionalism', *Japanese Journal of Political Science*, Vol. 12, No. 2: 267–85.

He, Baogang. 2012. 'A Concert of Powers and Hybrid Regionalism in Asia', *Australian Journal of Political Science*, Vol. 47, No. 4: 677–90.

He, Kai. 2014. 'A Tale of Three Fears: Why China Does Not Want to Be No. 1', *RSIS Commentaries*, No. 104/2014, 2 June.

Heisbourg, François. 1999/2000. 'American Hegemony? Perceptions of the US Abroad', *Survival*, Vol. 41, No. 4: 5–19.

Hettne, Björn, and András Inotai, eds. 1994. *The New Regionalism: Implications for Global Development and International Security*. Helsinki: United Nations University/World Institute for Development Economics Research.

Hew, Denis. 2005. 'Introduction: Roadmap to an ASEAN Economic Community', in Denis Hew, ed., *Roadmap to an ASEAN Economic Community*. Singapore: Institute of Southeast Asian Studies: 1–12.

Hew, Denis. 2007. *Brick by Brick: The Building of an ASEAN Economic Community*. Singapore: Institute of Southeast Asian Studies.

Higgins, Andrew. 2012. 'In Philippines, Banana Growers Feel Effect of South China Sea Dispute', *The Washington Post*, 11 June, www.washingtonpost.com/world/asia_pacific/in-philippines-banana-growers-feel-effect-of-south-china-sea-dispute/2012/06/10/gJQA47WVTV_story.html.

Higgott, Richard. 1994. 'Introduction: Ideas, Interests and Identity in the Asia-Pacific' *The Pacific Review*, Vol. 7, No. 4: 367–79.

Hill, Hall, and Jayant Menon. 2012. 'Asia's New Financial Safety Net: Is the Chiang Mai Initiative Designed Not To Be Used?', *Vox*, 25 July, www.voxeu.org/article/chiang-mai-initiative-designed-not-be-used.

Hille, Kathrin. 2012. 'Hu calls for China to be a "Maritime Power"', *The Financial Times*, 8 November, www.ft.com/cms/s/0/ebd9b4ae-296f-11e2-a604-00144feabdc0.html#axzz35wwM4q4p.

Hirano, Ko. 2009. 'China Wary of Hatoyama's "East Asian Community"', *The Japan Times*, 3 October, www.japantimes.co.jp/news/2009/10/03/national/china-wary-of-hatoyamas-east-asian-community/#.VQ04XdGJjVI.

Hirose, Shunsuke. 2014. 'Shinzo Abe's Biggest Enemy: the LDP', *The Diplomat*, 14 April, http://thediplomat.com/2014/04/shinzo-abes-biggest-enemy-the-ldp/.

Ho, Benjamin. 2012. *ASEAN's Centrality in a Rising Asia*, RSIS Working Paper No. 249. Singapore: S. Rajaratnam School of International Studies, Nanyang Technological University.

Ho, Peter Hak Ean. 1994. 'The ASEAN Regional Forum: The Way Forward', paper for the Third Workshop on ASEAN-UN Cooperation in Peace and Preventive Diplomacy, Bangkok, 17–18 February.

Holdridge, John H. 1997. *Crossing the Divide: An Insider's Account of Normalization of US–China Relations*. Lanham, MD: Rowman and Littlefield.

Holloway, Steven. 2000. 'US Unilateralism at the UN: Why Great Powers Do Not Make Great Multilateralists', *Global Governance*, Vol. 6, No. 3: 361–81.

Holmes, James R. 2013. 'The South China Sea: "Lake Beijing"', *The Diplomat*, 7 January, http://thediplomat.com/2013/01/the-south-china-sea-lake-beijing/.

Holmes, James R., and Toshi Yoshihara. 2006. 'China's "Caribbean" in the South China Sea', *SAIS Review of International Affairs*, Vol. 26, No. 1: 79–92.

Hoo, Tiang Boon. 2013. 'A Responsible Great Power: The Anatomy of China's Proclaimed Identity', DPhil thesis, University of Oxford.

Hook, Glenn D. 1998. 'Japan and the ASEAN Regional Forum: Bilateralism, Multilateralism or Supplementalism?', *Japanstudien*, Vol. 10: 159–88.

Hook, Glenn D. 2009. 'Japan in the World', in William M. Tsutsui, ed., *A Companion to Japanese History*. Malden, MA: Blackwell: 333–47.

Hook, Glenn D., Julie Gilson, Christopher W. Hughes and Hugo Dobson. 2001. *Japan's International Relations: Politics, Economics, and Security*, 2nd edn. London and New York: Routledge.

Horelick, Arnold L. 1974. 'The Soviet Union's Asian Collective Security Proposal: A Club in Search of Members', *Pacific Affairs*, Vol. 47, No. 3: 269–85.
Huang, Yukon. 2012. 'China's Rise: Opportunity or Threat for East Asia?', *East Asia Forum*, 20 May, www.eastasiaforum.org/2012/05/20/chinas-economic-rise-opportunity-or-threat-for-east-asia/.
Huang, Yukon. 2013. 'China's Road to Becoming a "Responsible" World Power', *Financial Times*, 26 March.
Hughes, Christopher W. 2002. *Japan's Security Policy and the War on Terror: Steady Incrementalism or a Radical Leap?* CSGR Working Paper No. 104/02. Coventry: Centre for the Study of Globalization and Regionalization, Warwick University.
Hughes, Christopher W. 2004. *Japan's Security Agenda: Military, Economic, and Environmental Dimensions*. Boulder, CO: Lynne Rienner.
Hughes, Christopher W. 2007. *Japan's Re-emergence as a 'Normal' Military Power*, Adelphi Series No. 368–9. Abingdon: Routledge.
Hughes, Christopher W. 2009. 'Japan's Response to China's Rise: Regional Engagement, Global Containment, Dangers of Collision', *International Affairs*, Vol. 85, No. 4: 837–56.
Huisken, Ron. 2002. 'Civilizing the Anarchical Society: Multilateral Security Processes in the Asia-Pacific', *Contemporary Southeast Asia*, Vol. 24, No. 2: 187–202.
Hundt, David. 2012. 'Middle Powers and the Building of Regional Order: Australia and South Korea Compared', in Jehoon Park, T. J. Pempel, Geng Xiao, eds., *Asian Responses to the Global Financial Crisis: The Impact of Regionalism and the Role of the G20*. Cheltenham: Edward Elgar: 193–211.
Hunt, Luke. 2012. 'Can ASEAN Unite on South China Sea?', *The Diplomat*, 17 November, http://thediplomat.com/2012/11/can-asean-unite-on-south-china-sea/.
Huxley, Tim. 2012. 'Australian Defence Engagement with Southeast Asia', *Centre of Gravity* Series Paper, No. 2, November. Canberra, ACT: Strategic Defence Studies Centre, Australian National University.
Iisgindarsah. 2012. *Indonesia's Democratic Politics and Foreign Policy-Making: A Case Study of Iranian Nuclear Issue, 2007–2008*, RSIS Working Paper, No. 236. Singapore: S. Rajaratnam School of International Studies, Nanyang Technological University.
Ikenberry, G. John. 2001. *After Victory: Institutions, Strategic Restraint, and the Rebuilding of Order after Major Wars*. Princeton, NJ: Princeton University Press.
Ikenberry, G. John. 2005. 'Power and Liberal Order: America's Postwar World Order in Transition', *International Relations of the Asia Pacific*, Vol. 5 No. 2: 133–52.
Ikenberry, G. John, and Jitsuo Tsuchiyama. 2002. 'Between Balance of Power and Community: The Future of Multilateral Security Co-operation in the Asia-Pacific', *International Relations of the Asia-Pacific*, Vol. 2, No. 1: 69–94.
Iqbal, Muhammad Jamshed. 2006. 'SAARC: Origin, Growth, Potential and Achievements', *Pakistan Journal of History & Culture*, Vol. 26, No. 2: 127–40.
International Crisis Group. 2011. 'Waging Peace: ASEAN and the Thai–Cambodian Border Conflict', *Crisis Group Asia Report*, No. 215, 6 December, www.crisisgroup.org/~/media/Files/asia/south-east-asia/thailand/215%20Waging%20Peace%20--%20ASEAN%20and%20the%20Thai-Cambodian%20Border%20Conflict.pdf.
Jain, Pumendra Chandra. 2007. 'Australia's Attitude toward Asian Values and Regional Community Building', *Politics & Policy*, Vol. 35, No. 1: 26–41.
*The Jakarta Globe*. 2009. 'SBY: Indonesia Has "A Million Friends and Zero Enemies"', *The Jakarta Post*, 20 October, http://thejakartaglobe.beritasatu.com/archive/sby-indonesia-has-a-million-friends-and-zero-enemies/.

Jetschke, Anja, and Philomena Murray. 2012. 'Diffusing Regional Integration: The EU and Southeast Asia', *West European Politics*, Vol. 35, No. 1: 174–91.

Ji, Xianbai. 2014. 'Why the ASEAN Economic Community Will Struggle', *The Diplomat*, 24 September, http://thediplomat.com/2014/09/why-the-asean-economic-community-will-struggle/.

Jiang, Zhida. 2012. 'Indonesia's "Confidence" Diplomacy under the Yudhoyono Government', *CIIS (China Institute of International Studies)*, 31 December, www.ciis.org.cn/english/2012-12/31/content_5638110.htm.

Jimbo, Ken. 2013. 'Japan and Southeast Asia: Three Pillars of a New Strategic Relationship', The Tokyo Foundation, 30 May.

Jimbo, Ken, Ryo Sahashi, Sugio Takahashi, Yasuyo Sakata, Masayuki Masuda and Takeshi Yuzawa. 2011. *Japan's Security Strategy toward China: Integration, Balancing, and Deterrence in the Era of Power Shift*. Tokyo: The Tokyo Foundation.

Johnson, Carol, Paul Ahluwalia and Greg McCarthy. 2010. 'Australia's Ambivalent Re-imagining of Asia', *Australian Journal of Political Science*, Vol. 45, No. 1: 59–74.

Johnson, Keith. 2014. 'Rough Ride on the New Silk Road', *Foreign Policy*, 1 May, www.foreignpolicy.com/articles/2014/05/01/rough_ride_on_the_silk_road.

Johnston, Alastair Iain. 1999. 'The Myth of the ASEAN Way? Explaining the Evolution of the ASEAN Regional Forum', in Helga Haftendorn, Robert O. Keohane, and Celeste A. Wallander, eds., *Imperfect Unions: Security Institutions over Time and Space*. New York: Oxford University Press: 287–324.

Johnston, Alastair Iain. 2003. 'Socialization in International Institutions: The ASEAN Way and International Relations Theory', in G. John Ikenberry and Michael Mastanduno, eds., *International Relations Theory and the Asia-Pacific*. New York: Columbia University Press: 107–62.

Johnston, Alastair Iain. 2003. 'Is China a Status Quo Power?', *International Security*, Vol. 27, No. 4: 5–56.

Johnston, Alastair Iain. 2008. *Social States: China in International Institutions, 1980–2000*. Princeton, NJ: Princeton University Press.

Johnston, Alastair Iain. 2013. 'How New and Assertive Is China's New Assertiveness?', *International Security*, Vol. 37, No. 4: 7–48.

Johnston, Alastair Iain, and Paul Evans. 1999. 'China's Engagement with Multilateral Security Institutions', in Alastair Iain Johnston and Robert Ross, eds., *Engaging China*. London: Routledge: 235–72.

Jones, Bruce. 2010. 'The Coming Clash? Europe and US Multilateralism under Obama', in Alvaro de Vasconcelos and Marcin Zaborowski, eds., *The Obama Moment: European and American Perspectives*. Paris: European Union Institute for Security Studies: 63–77.

Jones, David Martin, and Michael L. R. Smith. 2001. 'The Changing Security Agenda in Southeast Asia: Globalization, New Terror, and the Delusions of Regionalism', *Studies in Conflict and Terrorism*, Vol. 24, No. 4: 271–88.

Jones, David Martin, and Michael L. R. Smith. 2007. 'Constructing Communities: The Curious Case of East Asian Regionalism', *Review of International Studies*, Vol. 33, No. 1: 165–86.

Jones, David Martin, and Michael L. R. Smith. 2007. 'Making Process, Not Progress: ASEAN and the Evolving East Asian Regional Order', *International Security*, Vol. 32, No. 1: 148–84.

Jones, David Martin, Michael L. R. Smith, and Nicholas Khoo. 2013. *Asian Security and the Rise of China: International Relations in an Age of Volatility*. Cheltenham: Edward Elgar.

Jones, Eric. 2004. 'Asia's Fate', *The National Interest*, No. 35: 18–28.
Jones, Lee. 2010. 'ASEAN's Unchanged Melody? The Theory and Practice of "Non-Interference" in Southeast Asia', *The Pacific Review*, Vol. 23, No. 4: 479–502.
Jones, Lee. 2010. 'Still in the "Drivers' Seat", But for How Long? ASEAN's Capacity for Leadership in East-Asian International Relations', *Journal of Current Southeast Asian Affairs*, Vol. 29, No. 3: 95–113.
Jones, Lee. 2011. *ASEAN, Sovereignty and Intervention in Southeast Asia*. London: Palgrave Macmillan.
Jupp, James. 1995. 'From "White Australia" to "Part of Asia": Recent Shifts in Australian Immigration Policy towards the Region', *International Migration Review*, Vol. 29, No. 1: 207–28.
Kagan, Robert. 2002. 'Multilateralism, American Style', *The Washington Post*, 13 September.
Kahler, Miles. 1992. 'Multilateralism with Small and Large Numbers', *International Organization*, Vol. 46, No. 3: 681–708.
Kahler, Miles. 1995. *International Institutions and the Political Economy of Integration*. Washington, D.C.: The Brookings Institution.
Kahler, Miles. 2000. 'Legalization as Strategy: The Asia-Pacific Case', *International Organization*, Vol. 54, No. 3: 549–71.
Kahler, Miles. 2009. *Networked Politics: Agency, Power, and Governance*. Ithaca, NY: Cornell University Press.
Kan, Shirley A. 2010. 'US–China Counterterrorism Cooperation: Issues for US Policy', *Congressional Research Service*, 15 July, www.fas.org/sgp/crs/terror/RL33001.pdf.
Kanaev, Yevgeny. 2010. 'The Driver's Seat Phenomenon', *International Affairs*, Special Issue: 29–36.
Kang, David C. 2003. 'Getting Asia Wrong: The Need for New Analytical Frameworks', *International Security*, Vol. 27, No. 4: 57–85.
Karp, Erika. 2012. 'The Power to Convene', *Forbes*, 10 December, www.forbes.com/sites/85broads/2012/12/10/the-power-to-convene/.
Kassim, Yang Razali. 2011. 'ASEAN Community: Losing Grip over Vision 2015?', *The Nation*, 6 June.
Kassim, Yang Razali. 2012. 'East Asia Summit 2012: Asia's Power Game Unfolds', *East Asia Forum*, 12 December, www.eastasiaforum.org/2012/12/12/east-asia-summit-2012-asias-power-game-unfolds/.
Katsumata, Hiro. 2003. 'The Role of ASEAN Institutes of Strategic and International Studies in Developing Security Cooperation in the Asia-Pacific Region', *Asian Journal of Political Science*, Vol. 11, No. 1: 93–111.
Katsumata, Hiro. 2010. *ASEAN's Cooperative Security Enterprise: Norms and Interests in the ASEAN Regional Forum*. London: Palgrave Macmillan.
Katsumata, Hiro. 2014. 'What Explains ASEAN's Leadership in East Asian Community Building?', *Pacific Affairs*, Vol. 87, No. 2: 247–64.
Katzenstein, Peter J. 2005. *A World of Regions: Asia and Europe in the American Imperium*. Ithaca, NY: Cornell University Press.
Kavalski, Emilian. 2013. 'The Struggle for Recognition of Normative Powers: Normative Power Europe and Normative Power China in Context', *Cooperation and Conflict*, Vol. 48, No. 2: 247–67.
Kawai, Masahiro, and Ganeshan Wignaraja. 2007. *ASEAN+3 or ASEAN+6: Which Way Forward?*, ADB Institute Discussion Paper No. 77. Tokyo: Asian Development Bank Institute.

Kawai, Masahiro, and Ganeshan Wignaraja. 2008. 'EAFTA or CEPEA', *ASEAN Economic Bulletin*, Vol. 25, No. 2: 113–39.

Kawamura, Koichi. 2011. *Consensus and Democracy in Indonesia: Musyawarah-Mufakat Revisited*, IDE Discussion Paper, No. 308. Tokyo: Institute of Developing Economies, JETRO.

Kazianis, Harry. 2013. 'America's AirSea Battle vs. China's A2/AD: Who Wins?', *The Diplomat*, 19 July, http://thediplomat.com/2013/07/americas-airsea-battle-vs-chinas-a2ad-who-wins/.

Keating, Paul. 2012. 'Asia in the New Order: Australia's Diminishing Sphere of Influence', The Keith Murdoch Oration, State Library of Victoria, 14 November.

Keck, Zachary. 2013. 'Shutdown Forces Obama to Cancel Malaysia Trip, APEC May Be Next', *The Diplomat*, 2 October, http://thediplomat.com/2013/10/shutdown-forces-obama-to-cancel-malaysia-trip-apec-may-be-next/.

Keck, Zachary. 2014. 'The Political Utility of China's A2/AD Challenge', *The Diplomat*, 19 March, http://thediplomat.com/2014/03/the-political-utility-of-chinas-a2ad-challenge/.

Keck, Zachary. 2014. 'US Swears Asia Pivot Isn't Dead', *The Diplomat*, 2 April, http://thediplomat.com/2014/04/us-swears-asia-pivot-isnt-dead/.

Keck, Zachary. 2014. 'Why the US is Trying to Squash China's New Development Bank', *The Diplomat*, 10 October, http://thediplomat.com/2014/10/why-the-us-is-trying-to-squash-chinas-new-development-bank/.

Keller, William W., and Thomas G. Rawski, eds. 2007. *China's Rise and the Balance of Influence in Asia*. Pittsburgh, PA: University of Pittsburgh Press.

Kesavapany, K. and Hank Lim, eds. 2007. *APEC at 20: Recall, Reflect, Remake*. Singapore: Institute of Southeast Asian Studies, 2009.

Khong, Yuen Foong. 1997. 'Review Article: Making Bricks without Straw in the Asia Pacific?', *The Pacific Review*, Vol. 10, No. 2: 289–300.

Khong, Yuen Foong. 2004. 'Coping with Strategic Uncertainty: The Role of Institutions and Soft Balancing in Southeast Asia's Post-Cold War Strategy', in J. J. Suh, Peter J. Katzenstein and Alan Carlson, eds., *Rethinking Security in East Asia: Identity, Power, and Efficiency*. Stanford, CA: Stanford University Press: 172–298.

Khong, Yuen Foong. 2013/14. 'Primacy or World Order? The United States and China's Rise: A Review Essay', *International Security*, Vol. 38, No. 3: 153–75.

Kim, Samuel S. 2004. 'Regionalization and Regionalism in East Asia', *Journal of East Asian Studies*, Vol. 4, No. 1: 39–68.

Klare, Michael T. 2006. 'Containing China: The US's Real Objective', *Asia Times Online*, 20 April, www.atimes.com/atimes/China/HD20Ad01.html.

Kleine-Ahlbrandt, Stephanie T. 2009. 'Beijing, Global Free-Rider', *Foreign Policy*, 12 November, www.foreignpolicy.com/articles/2009/11/12/beijing_global_free_rider.

Koh, Tommy. 2009. 'Rudd's Reckless Regional Rush', *The Australian*, 18 December, www.theaustralian.com.au/opinion/rudds-reckless-regional-rush/story-e6frg6zo-1225811530050.

Kojima, Tomoyuki. 2001. 'China's "Omnidirectional Diplomacy": Cooperation with All, Emphasis on Major Powers', *Asia-Pacific Review*, Vol. 8, No. 2: 81–95.

Komori, Yasumasa. 2009. 'Asia's Institutional Creation and Evolution', *Asian Perspective*, Vol. 33, No. 3: 151–82.

Kor, Kian Beng. 2014. 'China Puts Low-Key Summit in Spotlight', *The Straits Times*, 10 May, www.stasiareport.com/the-big-story/asia-report/china/story/china-puts-low-key-summit-spotlight-20140510.

Korhonen, Pekka. 1994. 'The Theory of the Flying Geese Pattern of Development and Its Interpretations', *Journal of Peace Research*, Vol. 31, No. 1: 93–108.

Koumura, Masahiko. 1999. 'Japan's Leadership for the Future of Asia', *Ministry of Foreign Affairs of Japan*, 3 June, www.mofa.go.jp/announce/fm/koumura/address9906.html.
Krauss, Elliot S., and T. J. Pempel, eds. 2004. *Beyond Bilateralism: US–Japan Relations in the New Asia Pacific*. Stanford, CA: Stanford University Press.
Krepinevich, Andrew, Barry Watts and Robert Work. 2003. *Meeting the Anti-Access and Area-Denial Challenge*. Washington, D.C.: Center for Strategic and Budgetary Assessments.
Kueh, Y. Y. 2008. *China's New Industrialization Strategy: Was Chairman Mao Really Necessary?* Cheltenham: Edward Elgar.
Kuik, Cheng-Chwee. 2005. 'Multilateralism in China's ASEAN Policy: Its Evolution, Characteristics, and Aspiration', *Contemporary Southeast Asia*, Vol. 27, No. 1: 102–22.
Kuik, Cheng-Chwee. 2008. 'The Essence of Hedging: Malaysia and Singapore's Response to a Rising China', *Contemporary Southeast Asia*, Vol. 30, No. 2: 159–85.
Kwa, Chong Guan, and See Seng Tan. 2001. 'The Keystone of World Order', *The Washington Quarterly*, Vol. 24, No. 3: 95–103.
Kwan Weng Kin. 2013. 'Worsening Ties Embolden Abe to Make Shrine Visit', *The Straits Times*, 28 December.
Kyle, William. 2014. 'The US Navy and the Pivot: Less Means Less', *The Diplomat*, 31 March, http://thediplomat.com/2014/03/the-us-navy-and-the-pivot-less-means-less/.
Lacy, James L. 1995. *Stonework or Sandcastle? Asia's Regional Security Forum*, IDA Paper No. P-3110, July. Alexandria, VA: Institute of Defense Analyses.
Lai, Yew Meng. 2014. *Nationalism and Power Politics in Japan's Relations with China: A Neoclassical Realist Interpretation*. Abingdon: Routledge.
Lake, David A., and Patrick M. Morgan, eds. 1997. *Regional Orders: Building Security in a New World*. University Park, PA: Pennsylvania State University Press.
Lam, Peng Er. 2006. 'Japan's Human Security Role in Southeast Asia', *Contemporary Southeast Asia*, Vol. 28, No. 1: 141–59.
Lam, Peng Er, ed. 2012. *Japan's Relations with Southeast Asia: The Fukuda Doctrine and Beyond*. Abingdon: Routledge.
Langdon, Frank, and Brian L. Job. 1997. 'APEC Beyond Economics: The Politics of APEC', Working Paper 243. Notre Dame, IN: The Helen Kellogg Institute for International Studies.
Lau, Teik Soon, 'ASEAN Diplomacy: National Interest and Regionalism', in Ashok Kapur, ed., *Diplomatic Ideas and Practices of Asian States*. Leiden: E. J. Brill: 114–26.
Lee, Jeongseok. 2012. 'Hedging against Uncertain Future: The Response of East Asian Secondary Powers to Rising China', paper for the International Political Science Association XXII World Congress of Political Science, Madrid, 8–12 July.
Lee, Kuan Yew. 2000. *From Third World to First: The Singapore Story: 1965–2000*. Singapore: Times Editions.
Lee, Lai To. 1997. 'East Asian Assessments of China's Security Policy', *International Affairs*, Vol. 73, No. 2: 251–62.
Lee, Lai To. 1999. *China and the South China Sea Dialogues*. Santa Barbara, CA: Greenwood.
Lee, Pak K., and Lai-Ha Chan. 2007. 'Non-traditional Security Threats in China: Challenges of Energy Shortage and Infectious Diseases', in Joseph Y. S. Cheng, ed., *Challenges and Policy Programmes of China's New Leadership*. Hong Kong: City University of Hong Kong Press: 297–336.
Lee, Sook-Jong. 2012. *South Korea as a New Middle Power: Seeking Complex Diplomacy*, EAI Asia Security Initiative Working Paper, September. Seoul: East Asia Institute.
Leifer, Michael. 1983. *Indonesia's Foreign Policy*. London: Allen and Unwin.

Leifer, Michael. 1987. *ASEAN's Search for Regional Order*. Singapore: Faculty of Arts and Social Sciences, National University of Singapore.
Leifer, Michael. 1989. *ASEAN and the Security of South-East Asia*. London: Routledge.
Leifer, Michael. 1991. 'The Maritime Regime and Regional Security in East Asia', *The Pacific Review*, Vol. 4, No. 2: 126–36.
Leifer, Michael. 1996. *The ASEAN Regional Forum: Extending ASEAN's Model of Regional Security*, Adelphi Paper, No. 302. Oxford: Oxford University Press for International Institute for Strategic Studies.
Leifer, Michael. 2000. 'Regional Solutions to Regional Problems?', in Gerald Segal and David S. G. Goodman, eds., *Towards Recovery in Pacific Asia*. London: Routledge: 108–18.
Leifer, Michael. 2005. 'Indonesia's Encounters with China and the Dilemmas of Engagement', in Alastair Iain Johnston and Robert Ross, eds., *Engaging China: The Management of an Emerging Power*. London: Routledge: 89–110.
Li, Mingjiang. 2008. *Soft Power in Chinese Discourse: Popularity and Prospect*, RSIS Working Paper No. 165. Singapore: S. Rajaratnam School of International Studies, Nanyang Technological University.
Li, Nan. 2004. 'The Evolving Chinese Conception of Security and Security Approaches', in See Seng Tan and Amitav Acharya, eds., *Asia-Pacific Security Cooperation: National Interests and Regional Order*. Armonk, NY: M. E. Sharpe: 53–70.
Liljas, Per. 2014. 'Two Ships Have Arrived in Vietnam to Evacuate Chinese Nationals', *Time*, 19 May, http://time.com/#104284/chinese-ships-arrive-in-vietnam-to-evacuate-nationals-vung-ang/.
Lim, Paul. 2003. 'ASEAN's Role in the ASEAN Regional Forum: Will ASEAN Remain in the Driver's Seat? A European Perspective', *Cooperation & Dialogue*, No. 2: 5–11.
Lim, Robyn. 1998. 'The ASEAN Regional Forum: Building on Sand', *Contemporary Southeast Asia*, Vol. 20, No. 2: 115–36.
Lin, Justin Yifu. 2011. *From Flying Geese to Leading Dragons: New Opportunities and Strategies for Structural Transformation in Developing Countries*, Policy Research Working Paper, No. 5702. Washington, D.C.: The World Bank.
Lincoln, Edward J. Undated. 'The Bush Second Term and East Asian Economic Regionalism', *JCER* (Japan Center for Economic Research), www.jcer.or.jp/eng/pdf/EJ.Lincoln0503.pdf.
Lincoln, Edward J. 2001. 'Taking APEC Seriously', *Brookings Policy Brief Series*, No. 92. Washington, D.C.: Brookings Institution, www.brookings.edu/research/papers/2001/12/japan-lincoln.
Lind, Jennifer M. 2004. 'Pacifism or Passing the Buck? Testing Theories of Japanese Security Policy', *International Security*, Vol. 29, No. 1: 92–121.
Lipscy, Phillip Y. 2003. 'Japan's Asian Monetary Fund Proposal', *Stanford Journal of East Asian Affairs*, Vol. 3, No. 1: 93–104.
Little, Richard. 1989. 'Deconstructing the Balance of Power: Two Traditions of Thought', *Review of International Studies*, Vol. 15, No. 2: 87–100.
Loder, Jeff, Jean Michel Montsion and Richard Stubbs. 2011. 'East Asian Regionalism and the European Experience', in Alex Warleigh-Lack, Nick Robinson and Ben Rosamond, eds., *New Regionalism and the European Union: Dialogues, Comparisons and New Research Directions*. Abingdon: Routledge: 80–96.
Long, Joey S. R. 2011. *Safe for Decolonization: The Eisenhower Administration, Great Britain, and Singapore*. Kent, OH: Kent State University Press.
Lynas, Mark. 2009. 'How Do I Know China Wrecked the Copenhagen Deal? I Was in the Room', *The Guardian*, 22 December, www.theguardian.com/environment/2009/dec/22/copenhagen-climate-change-mark-lynas.

Lyon, Rod. 2013. 'The Southeast Asian Emphasis in DWP2013', *The Strategist*, 21 June, www.aspistrategist.org.au/the-southeast-asian-emphasis-in-dwp2013/.
MacDonald, Juli A., Amy Donahue, Bethany Danyluk and Booz Allen Hamilton. 2004. *Energy Futures in Asia: Final Report*. McLean, VA: Booz-Allen & Hamilton.
Maher, Sid. 2013. 'China Deal the Cornerstone of Julia Gillard's Asian Century', *The Australian*, 10 April.
Mahoney, James. 2000. 'Path Dependence in Historical Sociology', *Theory and Society*, Vol. 29, No. 4: 507–48.
Malik, Mohan. 2005. 'The East Asia Summit: More Discord than Accord', *YaleGlobal*, 20 December, http://yaleglobal.yale.edu/display.article?id=6645.
Malik, Mohan. 2006. *China and the East Asia Summit: More Discord than Accord*, APCSS Working Paper. Honolulu, HI: Asia-Pacific Center for Security Studies.
Malone, David M., and Yuen Foong Khong. 2003. 'Unilateralism and US Foreign Policy: International Perspectives', in David M. Malone and Yuen Foong Khong, eds., *Unilateralism and US Foreign Policy*. Boulder, CO: Lynne Rienner: 1–19 .
Malone, Paul, ed. 2006. *Australian Department Heads under Howard: Career Paths and Practice*. Canberra, ACT: Australian National University E-Press, http://press.anu.edu.au/anzsog/dept_heads/mobile_devices/ch06.html.
Mauzy, Diane K., and Brian L. Job. 2007. 'US Policy in Southeast Asia: Limited Re-engagement after Years of Benign Neglect', *Asian Survey*, Vol. 47, No. 4: 622–41.
McCloud, Donald G. 1986. *System and Process in Southeast Asia: The Evolution of a Region*. Boulder, CO: Westview Press.
McCurry, Justin. 2014. 'Why Will Japan and China Avoid Conflict? They Need Each Other', *Christian Science Monitor*, 5 February.
McDevitt, Michael. 2002. 'US Security Strategy in East Asia', 6 November, http://web.mit.edu/ssp/seminars/wed_archives02fall/mcdevitt.htm.
McDougall, Derek. 2009. *Australian Foreign Relations: Entering the 21st Century*. FrenchsForest: Pearson.
McGeough, Paul. 2014. 'Australia Still at America's Beck and Call', *The Sydney Morning Herald*, 31 August, www.smh.com.au/federal-politics/political-opinion/australia-still-at-americas-beck-and-call-20140831-10albb.html.
McGregor, Jenny. 2013. 'An "Asia Capable" Australia for the Coming Century', *The Melbourne Review*, Marchwww.melbournereview.com.au/features/article/an-asia-capable-australia-for-the-coming-century-2012.
McKay, John. 2002. 'APEC: Successes, Weaknesses, and Future Prospects', in Daljit Singh and Anthony L. Smith, eds., *Southeast Asian Affairs 2002*. Singapore: Institute of Southeast Asian Affairs: 42–53.
McMahon, Robert J. 1999. *The Limits of Empire: The United States and Southeast Asia since World War II*. New York: Columbia University Press.
McMahon, Robert J. 2003. 'The US, and South and Southeast Asia, 1975–2000', in Robert D. Schulzinger, ed., *A Companion to American Foreign Relations*. Malden, MA: Blackwell Publishing: 000-000.
Medeiros, Evan S. 2005/6. 'Strategic Hedging and the Future of Asia-Pacific Stability', *The Washington Quarterly*, Vol. 29, No. 1: 145–67.
Mellén, Patricia Rey. 2013. 'Latin America Increases Relations with China: What Does That Mean for the US?', *International Business Times*, 28 June, www.ibtimes.com/latin-america-increases-relations-china-what-does-mean-us-1317981.
Meltzer, Joshua, Takuji Okubo, Brian Jackson and Jack Sheehan. 2014. 'TPP: What's at Stake with the Trade Deal?', *BBC News*, 22 April, www.bbc.com/news/business-27107349.

## Bibliography

Menon, Jayant. 2013. 'The Challenge Facing Asia's Regional Comprehensive Economic Partnership', *East Asia Forum*, 23 June, www.eastasiaforum.org/2013/06/23/the-challenge-facing-asias-regional-comprehensive-economic-partnership/.

Menon, Jayant. 2014. 'Moving Too Slowly Towards an ASEAN Economic Community', *East Asia Forum*, 14 October, www/eastasiaforum.org/2014/10/14/moving-too-slowly-towards-an-asean-economic-community/.

Merand, F., and S. Hofmann. 2011. 'Regional Institutions à la Carte: Mechanisms of Variable Geometry in Europe', paper presented at the annual meeting of the International Studies Association Annual Conference, Montreal, 16 March.

Midford, Paul. 2011. *Rethinking Japanese Public Opinion and Security: From Pacifism to Realism?* Stanford, CA: Stanford University Press.

Milner, Anthony. 2012. 'Think Again About ASEAN', *The Asialink Essays 2012*, Vol. 4, No. 2: 1–4.

Misalucha, Charmaine G. 2011. 'Southeast Asia–US Relations: Hegemony or Hierarchy?', *Contemporary Southeast Asia*, Vol. 33, No. 2: 209–28.

Mitton, Roger. 2011. 'The "Pacific Secretary" Needs to Ensure Her Regional Legacy', *The Phnom Penh Post*, 21 March.

Mohan, C. Raja. 2014. 'Will India Join China's Maritime Silk Road?', *The Indian Express*, 15 February, http://indianexpress.com/article/opinion/columns/will-india-join-chinas-maritime-silk-road/.

Monahan, Andrew. 2011. 'China Overtakes Japan as World's No. 2 Economy', *The Wall Street Journal*, 14 February.

Monash University Malaysia. Undated. 'The Reality of the State of the Asean Economic Community', *Monash University Malaysia*, www.monash.edu.my/news/researchers-say/the-reality-of-the-state-of-the-asean-economic-community.

Morrison, Charles E., and Eduardo Pedrosa, eds. 2007. *An APEC Trade Agenda? The Political Economy of a Free Trade Area of the Asia-Pacific*. Singapore: Institute of Southeast Asian Studies.

Muhammad, Cedric. 2014. 'So What if China Has $1.32 Trillion in U.S. Treasuries? It Still Can't Crash America's Economy', *Forbes*, 16 January, www.forbes.com/sites/cedricmuhammad/2014/01/16/so-what-if-china-has-1-32-trillion-in-u-s-treasuries-it-still-cant-crash-americas-economy/.

Mulgan, Aurelia George. 2009. 'Hatoyama's East Asia Community and Regional Leadership Rivalries', *East Asia Forum*, 13 October, www.eastasiaforum.org/2009/10/13/hatoyamas-east-asia-community/.

Munakata, Naoko. 2006. *Transforming East Asia: The Evolution of Regional Economic Integration*. Washington, D.C.: The Brookings Institution.

Nagara, Bunn. 2013. 'Misunderstanding the "Asean Way"', *The Jakarta Post*, 2 December, www.thejakartapost.com/news/2013/12/02/misunderstanding-asean-way.html.

Naím, Moisés. 2009. 'Minilateralism: The Magic Number to Get Real International Action', *Foreign Policy*, 22 June, www.foreignpolicy.com/articles/2009/06/18/minilateralism.

Narine, Shaun. 1997. 'ASEAN and the ARF: The Limits of the "ASEAN Way"', *Asian Survey*, Vol. 37, No. 10: 961–78.

Narine, Shaun. 2013. 'The English School and ASEAN', in Amitav Acharya and Richard Stubbs, ed., *Theorizing Southeast Asian Relations: Emerging Debates*. Abingdon: Routledge: 71–89.

Narjoko, Dionisius. 2014. 'Why Indonesia Needs to Lead in Economic Integration', *East Asia Forum*, 3 March, www.eastasiaforum.org/2014/03/03/why-indonesia-needs-to-lead-in-economic-integration/.

Natalegawa, Marty. 2011. 'Aggressively Waging Peace: ASEAN and the Asia-Pacific', *Strategic Review: The Indonesian Journal of Leadership, Policy and World Affairs*, Vol. 1, No. 2: 40–6.

Natalegawa, Marty. 2013. 'An Indonesian Perspective on the Indo-Pacific', Keynote Address by H.E. Dr. R.M. Marty M. Natalegawa, Foreign Minister, Republic of Indonesia, at the Conference on Indonesia, Washington, D.C., 16 May .

Nesadurai, Helen. 2006. 'APEC: A Tool for US Regional Domination?', *The Pacific Review*, Vol. 9, No. 1: 31–57.

*The New York Times*. 2013. 'Editorial: Risky Nationalism in Japan', *The New York Times*, 26 December.

Newton-Small, Jay. 2013. 'Burma's Thein Sein Visits Washington', *Time*, 20 May, http://swampland.time.com/2013/05/20/burmas-thein-sein-visits-washington/.

Nippon. 2013. 'Japan Must Engage China, Freeze the Senkaku Debate: An Interview with Former Japanese Ambassador to China Niwa Uichirō', *Nippon.com*, 29 October, www.nippon.com/en/people/e00050/.

Norris, Stephen. 2013. 'Just Getting By: The Outlook for Indonesia's Economy', *Global Asia*, Vol. 8, No. 4, www.globalasia.org/article/just-getting-by-the-outlook-for-indonesias-economy/.

Nozick, Robert. 1974. *Anarchy, the State, and Utopia*. New York: Basic Books.

Nye, Joseph S. 1990. *Bound to Lead: The Changing Nature of American Power*. New York: Basic Books.

Nye, Joseph S. 2004. *Soft Power: The Means to Success in World Politics*. New York: Public Affairs.

Nye, Joseph S. 2008. 'Public Diplomacy and Soft Power', *Annals of the American Academy of Political and Social Science*, No. 616: 94–109.

Nye, Joseph S. 2008. 'Security and Smart Power', *American Behavioral Scientist*, Vol. 51, No. 9: 1351–6.

Obama, Barack. 2009. 'Remarks by President Barack Obama at Suntory Hall', *The White House: Office of the Press Secretary*, 14 November, www.whitehouse.gov/the-press-office/remarks-president-barack-obama-suntory-hall.

Odell, John S. 1982. *U.S. International Monetary Policy: Markets, Power, and Ideas as Sources of Change*. Princeton, NJ: Princeton University Press.

Okawara, Nobuo, and Peter J. Katzenstein. 2001. 'Japan and Asia-Pacific Security: Regionalization, Entrenched Bilateralism, and Incipient Multilateralism', *The Pacific Review*, Vol. 14, No. 2: 165–94.

Ong Keng Yong. 2010. 'Asian Economies Now Providing More Aid and Development Assistance: The Case of Singapore', Keynote Address at the International Volunteer Cooperation Organization (IVCO), 4 October, www.spp.nus.edu.sg/ips/docs/enewsletter/Dec2010/OKY_Asian%20Economies%20Now%20Providing%20More%20Aid_011210.pdf.

Pakpahan, Beginda. 2012. 'Will RCEP Compete with the TPP? *East Asia Forum*, 28 November, www.eastasiaforum.org/2012/11/28/will-rcep-compete-with-the-tpp/.

Paltridge, Shane. 1965. 'Australia and the Defence of Southeast Asia', *Foreign Affairs*, Vol. 49: 49–61.

Pantucci, Raffaello, and Li Lifan. 2013. 'Shanghai Cooperation Organization: Not Quite the New Silk Road', *The Diplomat*, 12 September, http://thediplomat.com/2013/09/shanghai-cooperation-organization-not-quite-the-new-silk-road-2/.

Pape, Robert A. 2005. 'Soft Balancing against the United States', *International Security*, Vol. 30, No. 1: 7–45.

Parameswaran, Prashanth. 2014. 'Is Indonesia Turning Away From ASEAN Under Jokowi?', *The Diplomat*, 18 December, http://thediplomat.com/2014/12/is-indonesia-turning-away-from-asean-under-jokowi/.

Pardo, Ramon Pacheco. 2014. 'Return of the G2: Can US and China Run the World?', *The Telegraph*, 12 November.

Park, Yung Chul, and Inkyo Cheong. 2008. 'The Proliferation of FTAs and Prospects for Trade Liberalization in East Asia', in Barry Eichengreen, Yung Chul Park and Charles Wyplosz, eds., *China, Asia, and the New World Economy*. Oxford: Oxford University Press: 87–112.

Patrick, Stewart. 2000. 'America's Retreat from Multilateral Engagement', *Current History*, Vol. 99: 430–39.

Patrick, Stewart. 2009. 'Prix Fixe *and* à la Carte: Avoiding False Multilateral Choices', *The Washington Quarterly*, Vol. 32, No. 4: 77–95.

Patrick, Stewart. 2010. 'Irresponsible Stakeholders? The Difficulty of Integrating Rising Powers', *Foreign Affairs*, Vol. 89, No. 6: 44–53.

Patrick, Stewart. 2010. '"The Mission Determines the Coalition": The United States and Multilateral Cooperation after 9/11', in Bruce D. Jones, Shepard Forman and Richard Gowan, eds., *Cooperating for Peace and Security: Evolving Institutions and Arrangements in a Context of Changing US Security Policy*. Cambridge: Cambridge University Press: 20–44.

Patrick, Stewart, and Shepard Forman, eds. 2002. *Multilateralism and US Foreign Policy: Ambivalent Engagement*. Boulder, CO: Lynne Rienner.

Patton, Mike. 2014. 'Who Owns the Most U.S. Debt?', *Forbes*, 28 October, www.forbes.com/sites/mikepatton/2014/10/28/who-owns-the-most-u-s-debt/.

Paul, T. V. 2005. 'Soft Balancing in the Age of US Primacy', *International Security*, Vol. 30, No. 1: 46–71.

Pempel, T. J. 2010. 'Soft Balancing, Hedging, and Institutional Darwinism: The Economic-Security Nexus and East Asian Regionalism', *Journal of East Asian Studies*, Vol. 10, No. 2: 209–38.

Pereira, Eva. 2011. 'World Bank: The Rise of the BRIICS a Harbinger of a New World Economic Order', *Forbes*, 17 May, www.forbes.com/sites/evapereira/2011/05/17/world-bank-the-rise-of-the-briics-a-harbinger-of-a-new-world-economic-order/.

Perlez, Jane. 2014. 'US Opposing China's Answer to World Bank', *The New York Times*, 9 October.

Perwita, Anak Agung Banyu. 2007. *Indonesia and the Muslim World: Islam and Secularism in the Foreign Policy of Soeharto and Beyond*. Copenhagen: NIAS Press.

Petri, Peter A., and Michael G. Plummer. 2013. *ASEAN Centrality and the ASEAN–US Economic Relationship*, Advance Copy of Policy Studies No. 69. Honolulu, HI: East-West Center.

Pietsch, Juliet, and Hadyn Aarons. 2012. 'Australian Engagement with Asia: Towards Closer Political, Economic and Cultural Ties', in Juliet Pietsch and Hadyn Aarons, eds., *Australia: Identity, Fear and Governance in the 21st Century*. Canberra, ACT: ANU E-Press: 33–46.

Pollard, Vincent K. 1970. 'ASA and ASEAN, 1961–1967: Southeast Asian Regionalism', *Asian Survey*, Vol. 10, No. 3: 244–55.

Poole, Avery. 2013. 'A "Democratic" Process? Change and Continuity in Foreign Policymaking in Indonesia', paper for the Australian Political Science Association (APSA) Conference, Perth, 30 September–2 October.

Potter, Andrew. 2008. 'Two Concepts of Legitimacy', *MacLean's*, 3 December, www.macleans.ca/general/two-concepts-of-legitimacy/.

Pushpanathan, S. 2010. 'Opinion: No Place for Passive Regionalism in ASEAN', *The Jakarta Post*, 7 April, www.thejakartapost.com/news/2010/04/07/no-place-passive-regionalism-asean.html.

Quinn, Noel. 2013. '600 million reasons to invest in Asean', *South China Morning Post*, 7 October.

Radio Australia. 2002. 'Travel Warnings Cause Tension with Malaysia', *Radio Australia*, 6 November, www.radioaustralia.net.au/international/2002-11-06/travel-warnings-cause-tension-with-malaysia/599076.

Rahadiana, Rieka, Agus Suhana and Herdaru Purnomo. 2014. 'Bank Indonesia Raises Key Rate after Fuel-Price Increase', *Bloomberg News*, 18 November, www.bloomberg.com/news/2014-11-17/indonesia-s-widodo-increases-subsidized-gasoline-diesel-prices.html.

Raine, Sarah. 2009. *China's Africa Challenges*, The Adelphi Papers, No. 49 (404–05). Abingdon: Routledge for International Institute for Strategic Studies.

Ramakrishna, Kumar, and See Seng Tan, eds. 2003. *After Bali: The Threat of Terrorism in Southeast Asia*. Singapore: World Scientific.

Rana, Pradumna B., and Chia Wai-Mun. 2013. *The Revival of the Silk Roads (Land Connectivity) in Asia*, RSIS Working Paper, No. 274. Singapore: S. Rajaratnam School of International Studies, Nanyang Technological University.

Rathus, Joel. 2009. 'Squaring the Japanese and Australia Proposals for an East Asian and Asia Pacific Community: Is America In or Out?', *East Asia Forum*, 4 November, www.eastasiaforum.org/2009/11/04/squaring-the-japanese-and-australia-proposals-for-an-east-asian-and-asia-pacific-community-is-america-in-or-out/.

Ravenhill, John. 2002. *APEC and the Construction of Pacific Rim Regionalism*. Cambridge: Cambridge University Press.

Rawls, John. 1971. *A Theory of Justice*. Cambridge, MA: Harvard University Press.

Regnier, Philippe, and Daniel Warner, eds. 2001. *Japan and Multilateral Diplomacy*. Farnham: Ashgate.

Reid, Anthony Reid, ed. 2012. *Indonesia Rising: The Repositioning of Asia's Third Giant*. Singapore: Institute of Southeast Asian Studies.

Reuters. 2013. 'Malaysia summons Singapore envoy over Spying Reports', *Reuters*, 25 November, www.reuters.com/article/2013/11/26/us-malaysia-singapore-spying-idUSBRE9AP03P20131126.

Reynolds, Isabel, and Maiko Takahashi. 2014. 'US–Japan Remain Divided on TPP Deal Weeks Before Obama Visit', *Bloomberg News*, 10 April, www.bloomberg.com/news/2014-04-10/u-s-japan-remain-divided-on-tpp-deal-weeks-before-obama-visit.html.

Rix, Alan. 1993. 'Japan and the Region: Leading from Behind', in Richard Higgott, Richard Leaver and John Ravenhill, eds., *Pacific Economic Relations in the 1990s: Cooperation or Conflict?* Boulder, CO: Lynne Rienner: 62–82.

Roberts, Christopher. 2010. *ASEAN's Myanmar Crisis: Challenges to the Pursuit of a Security Community*. Singapore: Institute of Southeast Asian Studies.

Roberts, Dexter. 2014. 'Obama and Xi Spar over Rival Free-Trade Pacts at APEC Forum', *Bloomberg Businessweek*, 10 November, www.businessweek.com/articles/2014-11-10/obama-and-xi-spar-over-rival-free-trade-pacts-at-apec-forum.

Rodan, Garry, and Kevin Hewison, eds. 2006. *Neoliberalism and Conflict in Asia after 9/11*. London and New York: Routledge.

Roy, Denny. 2005. 'Southeast Asia and China: Balancing or Bandwagoning?', *Contemporary Southeast Asia*, Vol. 27, No. 2: 305–22.

Roy, Denny. 2013. *Return of the Dragon: Rising China and Regional Security*. New York: Columbia University Press.

Rudd, Kevin. 2008. 'The Singapore Lecture: Building on ASEAN's Success – Towards an Asia Pacific Century', 12 August, www.pm.gov.au/media/Speech/2008/speech_0419.cfm.

Rüland, Jürgen. 2014. The Limits of Democratizing Interest Representation: ASEAN's Regional Corporatism and Normative Challenges', *European Journal of International Relations*, Vol. 20, No. 1: 237–61.

Rüland, Jürgen, and Karsten Bechle. 2014. 'Defending State-Centric Regionalism through Mimicry and Localization: Regional Parliamentary Bodies in the Association of Southeast Asian Nations (ASEAN) and Mercosur', *Journal of International Relations and Development*, Vol. 17, No. 1: 61–88.

Rumley, Dennis. 1999. *The Geopolitics of Australia's Regional Relations*. New York: Springer.

Ruwitch, John. 2014. 'China's Xi Issues Veiled Warning to Asia over Military Alliances', *Reuters*, 21 May, http://news.yahoo.com/chinas-xi-says-committed-peacefully-resolving-territorial-disputes-024633860.html.

Sainsbury, Michael and Cameron Stewart. 2009. 'China a "Peaceful Force" in Beijing's Response to Defence Paper', *The Australian*, 6 May, www.theaustralian.com.au/news/nation/china-a-peaceful-force/story-e6frg6nf-1225710310338?nk=24297064718cd878e720eac78a4d6b65.

Sally, Razeen. 2006. 'Free Trade Agreements and the Prospects for Regional Integration in East Asia', *Asian Economic Policy Review*, Vol. 1, No. 2: 306–21.

Samboh, Esther. 2011. 'Chinese Goods Hurt Local Producers', *The Jakarta Post*, 12 April.

Samuels, Richard J. 2006. 'Japan's Goldilocks Strategy', *The Washington Quarterly*, Vol. 29, No. 4: 111–27.

Samuels, Richard J. 2007. *Securing Japan: Tokyo's Grand Strategy and the Future of East Asia*. Ithaca, NY: Cornell University Press.

Satoh, Yukio. 2012. 'Foreward', in Lam Peng Er, ed., *Japan's Relations with Southeast Asia: The Fukuda Doctrine and Beyond* (Abingdon: Routledge, 2012), pp. xv–xvi.

Schimmelfennig, Frank. 2005. 'Multilateralism in Post-Cold War NATO: Functional Form, Identity-Driven Cooperation', Paper for AUEB International Conference on 'Assessing Multilateralism in the Security Domain', Delphi, Greece, 3–5 June.

Schreer, Benjamin. 2013. 'Walking among Giants: Australia and Indonesia between the US and China', *The Strategist*, 24 May, www.aspistrategist.org.au/walking-among-giants-australia-and-indonesia-between-the-us-and-china/.

Schwab, Susan C. 2011. 'After Doha: Why the Negotiations Are Doomed and What We Should Do About It', *Foreign Affairs*, Vol. 90, No. 3: 104–77.

Sebastian, Leonard. 2012. 'Indonesia's Regional Diplomacy: Imperative to Maintain ASEAN Cohesion', *RSIS Commentaries*, No. 132/2012, 23 July.

Severino, Rodolfo C. 2006. *Southeast Asia in Search of an ASEAN Community: Insights from the Former ASEAN Secretary-General*. Singapore: Institute of Southeast Asian Studies.

Severino, Rodolfo C. 2009. *The ASEAN Regional Forum*. Singapore: Institute of Southeast Asian Studies.

Severino, Rodolfo C. 2009. 'Regional Institutions in Southeast Asia: The First Movers and Their Challenges', Background Paper, No. 24, Asian Development Bank Study Finalization Workshop on Institutions for Regionalism in Asia and the Pacific, Shanghai, 2–3 December.

Shambaugh, David. 2004/5. 'China Engages Asia: Reshaping the Regional Order', *International Security*, Vol. 29, No. 3: 64–99.

Shekhar, Vibhanshu. 2012. *Rising Indonesia and Indo-Pacific World*, ICWA (Indian Council of World Affairs) Issue Brief, 26 September.

Shiavenza, Matt. 2014. 'The "Insipid" Mr. Obama Goes to China', *The Atlantic*, 6 November, www.theatlantic.com/international/archive/2014/11/obama-visits-china-global-times/382435/.

Shoji, Tomotaka. 2013. 'Japan's Perspective on Security Environment in the Asia Pacific and Its Approach toward Multilateral Cooperation: Contradictory or Consistent?', paper presented at the National Institute of Defense Studies (NIDS) International Symposium on Security, Tokyo, 12 November.

Sieg, Linda, and Kiyoshi Takenaka. 2013. 'Japan to Bolster Military, Boost Asia Ties to Counter China', *Reuters*, 17 December, www.reuters.com/article/2013/12/17/us-japan-security-idUSBRE9BG02S20131217.

Sikkink, Kathryn. 1991. *Ideas and Institutions: Developmentalism in Brazil and Argentina*. Ithaca, NY: Cornell University Press.

Singh, Bhubhindar. 2013. *Japan's Security Identity: From a Peace State to an International State*. Abingdon: Routledge.

Sirila, Aaron. 2010. 'Clinton: 'Renewed American Leadership in Asia', *Asia Matters for America* (East–West Center), 4 November, http://asiamattersforamerica.org/asia/clinton-renewed-american-leadership-in-asia.

Smith, Anthony L. 2000. *Strategic Centrality: Indonesia's Changing Role in ASEAN*. Pacific Strategic Papers, No. 10, Singapore: Institute of Southeast Asian Studies.

Smith, Anthony L. 2000. 'Indonesia's Foreign Policy under Abdurrahman Wahid: Radical or Status Quo State?', *Contemporary Southeast Asia*, Vol. 22, No. 3: 498–526.

Smith, Anthony L. 2004. 'ASEAN's Ninth Summit: Solidifying Regional Cohesion, Advancing External Linkages', *Contemporary Southeast Asia*, Vol. 26, No. 3: 416–33.

Smith, Stephen. 2008. 'Australia, ASEAN and the Asia Pacific', 18 July, Lowy Institute, Sydney, www.foreignminister.gov.au/speeches/2008/080718_lowy.html.

Snyder, Glenn H. 2007. *Alliance Politics*. Ithaca, NY: Cornell University Press.

Soesastro, Hadi. 2001. 'Whither ASEAN Plus Three?', paper for the Pacific Economic Cooperation Council (PECC) Trade Policy Forum on Regional Trading Arrangements: Stocktake and Next Steps', Bangkok, 12–13 June.

Soesastro, Hadi, Allan Gyngell, Charles E. Morrison and Jusuf Wanandi. 2009. 'Report of Regional Task Force on Regional Institutional Architecture', report for the Pacific Economic Cooperation Council (PECC) Standing Committee.

Soeya, Yoshihide. 2010. 'An East Asian Community and Japan-China relations', *East Asia Forum*, 17 May, www.eastasiaforum.org/tag/eac/.

Soeya, Yoshihide. 2012. 'China, and Japan's Foreign Policy Posture', *East Asia Forum*, 8 April, www.eastasiaforum.org/2010/02/16/the-us-japan-alliance-beyond-futenma/.

Solingen, Etel. 1998. *Regional Orders at Century's Dawn: Global and Domestic Influences on Grand Strategy*. Princeton, NJ: Princeton University Press.

Solomon, Richard. 1999. 'US Wants Fully Restored Relationship with New Zealand', US Assistant Secretary of State Richard Solomon's address to the American Chamber of Commerce in Auckland, New Zealand, 6 August, http://newzealand.usembassy.gov/uploads/DK/E4/DKE4vNH3fqaXhev0GuHWqQ/full.pd.

South China Morning Post. 2014. 'China Urges Japan to Pursue Peace under New Defence Chief Gen Nakatani', *South China Morning Post*, 27 December.

Spitzer, Kirk. 2013. 'Why Japan Wants to Break Free of its Pacifist Past', *Time*, 22 October, http://world.time.com/2013/10/22/why-tokyo-wants-to-break-free-of-its-pacifist-past/.

Stokhof, Wim, and Paul van der Velde, eds. 2013. *Asian-European Perspectives: Developing the ASEM Process*. Abingdon: Routledge.

Storey, Ian. 2010. 'China's Missteps in Southeast Asia: Less Charm, More Offensive', *China Brief*, Vol. 10, No. 25, 17 December, www.jamestown.org/single/?tx_ttnews%5Btt_news%5D=37294&no_cache=1#.VLOJ301xmM8.

Storey, Ian. 2013. 'Japan's Evolving Security Concerns in Maritime Southeast Asia: From Safety of Navigation to "Lake Beijing"', in Takashi Shiraishi and Takaaki Kojima, eds., *ASEAN–Japan Relations*. Singapore: Institute of Southeast Asian Studies: 114–34.

The Straits Times. 2013. 'Apec 2013: US Shutdown Fears Perturb Apec Summit', *The Straits Times*, 6 October, www.straitstimes.com/the-big-story/asia-report/indonesia/story/apec-2013-us-shutdown-fears-perturb-apec-summit-20131006.

The Straits Times. 2014. 'China Demands Asean Neutrality over South China Sea', *The Straits Times*, 19 May.

Stubbs, Richard. 2002. 'ASEAN Plus Three: Emerging East Asian Regionalism?', *Asian Survey*, Vol. 42, No. 3: 440–55.

Stubbs, Richard. 2014. 'ASEAN's Leadership in East Asian Region-Building: Strength in Weakness', *The Pacific Review*, Vol. 27, No. 4: 523–41.

Sudo, Sueo. 1992. *The Fukuda Doctrine and ASEAN: New Dimensions in Japanese Foreign Policy*. Singapore: Institute of Southeast Asian Studies.

Sukma, Rizal. 2003. *Islam in Indonesia's Foreign Policy*. London: RoutledgeCurzon.

Sukma, Rizal. 2004. 'Indonesia and Regional Security: The Quest for Cooperative Security', in See Seng Tan and Amitav Acharya, eds., *Asia-Pacific Security Cooperation: National Interests and Regional Order*. Armonk, NY: M. E. Sharpe: 71–87.

Sukma, Rizal. 2009. 'Indonesia–China Relations: The Politics of Re-engagement', *Asian Survey*, Vol. 49, No. 4: 591–608.

Sukma, Rizal. 2009. 'Indonesia Needs a Post-ASEAN Foreign Policy', *The Jakarta Post*, 30 June, www.thejakartapost.com/news/2009/10/05/a-postasean-foreign-policy-a-postg8-world.html.

Sukma, Rizal. 2009. 'A Post-ASEAN Foreign Policy for a Post-G8 World', *The Jakarta Post*, 5 October, www.thejakartapost.com/news/2009/10/05/a-postasean-foreign-policy-a-postg8-world.html.

Sukma, Rizal. 2010. 'The Accidental Driver: ASEAN in the ASEAN Regional Forum', in Jürgen Haacke and Noel M. Morada, eds., *Cooperative Security in the Asia-Pacific: The ASEAN Regional Forum*. Abingdon: Routledge: 111–23.

Sukma, Rizal. 2012. 'Regional Security Order in Southeast Asia: An Indonesian View', paper for the Asia-Pacific Roundtable (APR), Kuala Lumpur, 28–30 May.

Sukma, Rizal. 2012. 'Insight: Without Unity, No Centrality', *The Jakarta Post*, 17 July, www.thejakartapost.com/news/2012/07/17/insight-without-unity-no-centrality.html.

Sukma, Rizal. 2014. 'Insight: East Asia Needs a Steering Committee', *The Jakarta Post*, 4 September, www.thejakartapost.com/news/2012/09/04/insight-east-asia-needs-a-steering-committee.html.

Sun, Yun. 2014. 'China's Aid to Africa: Monster or Messiah?', *Brookings East Asia Commentary*, No. 75, www.brookings.edu/research/opinions/2014/02/07-china-aid-to-africa-sun.

The Sunday Times. 2014. 'Editorial: Asean's Neutrality is its Strength', *The Sunday Times*, 23 May.

Sussex, Matthew. 2014. 'The Shanghai Cooperation Organization: A Future Balancing Coalition in Asia?', in Peter Shearman, ed., *Power Transition and International Order in Asia: Issues and Challenges*. Abingdon: Routledge: 69–85.

Sutter, Robert G. 2009. *The United States in Asia*. Lanham, MD: Rowman and Littlefield.

## Bibliography    197

Suzuki, Shogo. 2013. 'Effective Multilateralism and Sino-Japanese Reconciliation', in Jochen Prantl, ed., *Effective Multilateralism: Through the Looking Glass of East Asia*. London: Palgrave Macmillan: 153–76.

Swaine, Michael D. 2011. 'America's Asia Pivot Threatens Regional Stability', *The National Interest*, 7 December, http://nationalinterest.org/commentary/washington-destabilizes-sino-american-relations-6211?page=1.

Syailendra, Emirza Adi. 2013. 'Indonesia's Foreign Policy Outlook: Challenges of 2013 and Beyond', *RSIS Commentaries*, No. 019/2013, 4 February.

Symonds, Peter. 2010. 'WikiLeaks Cables Expose US Hostility to Rudd's Asia Pacific Community plan', *World Socialist Web Site*, 31 December, www.wsws.org/en/articles/2010/12/rudd-d31.html.

Symons, Emma-Kate. 2007. 'ASEAN Anger at Snub by Rice', *The Australian*, 28 July, www.theaustralian.com.au/archive/news/asean-anger-at-snub-by-rice/story-e6frg6t6-1111114037879.

Szczudlik-Tatar, Justyna. 2013. *China's New Silk Road Diplomacy*, PISM Policy Paper 34 (82). Warsaw: Polish Institute of International Affairs.

Tabuchi, Hiroko. 2013. 'With Shrine Visit, Leader Asserts Japan's Track from Pacifism', *The New York Times*, 26 December, www.nytimes.com/2013/12/27/world/asia/japanese-premier-visits-contentious-war-shrine.html?_r=0.

Tan, See Seng. 2007. 'Courting China: Track 2 Diplomacy and the Engagement of the People's Republic', in Hiro Katsumata and See Seng Tan, eds., *People's ASEAN and Governments' ASEAN*, RSIS Monograph, No. 11. Singapore: S. Rajaratnam School of International Studies, Nanyang Technological University: 134–42.

Tan, See Seng. 2008. 'Introduction', in See Seng Tan, ed., *Do Institutions Matter? Regional Institutions and Regionalism in East Asia*, RSIS Monograph No. 13. Singapore: S. Rajaratnam School of International Studies, Nanyang Technological University: 1–18.

Tan, See Seng, ed. 2009. *Regionalism in Asia Vol. 3: Regional Order and Architecture*. Abingdon: Routledge.

Tan, See Seng. 2009. 'The Perils and Prospects of Dragon Riding: Reassurance and "Costly Signals" in China–ASEAN Relations', in Ron Huisken, ed., *Rising China: Power and Reassurance*. Canberra: Australian National University E-Press: 165–84.

Tan, See Seng. 2011. 'Competing Visions: EAS in the regional architecture debate', *East Asia Forum*, 15 November, www.eastasiaforum.org/2011/11/15/competing-visions-eas-in-the-regional-architecture-debate/.

Tan, See Seng. 2011. 'Is Asia-Pacific Regionalism Outgrowing ASEAN?', *The RUSI Journal*, Vol. 156, No. 1: 58–62.

Tan, See Seng. 2011. 'Visions at War? EAS in the Regional Architecture Debate', *The Straits Times*, 12 November.

Tan, See Seng. 2012. 'ASEAN Centrality', in Desmond Ball, Anthony Milner, Rizal Sukma and Yusuf Wanandi, eds., *CSCAP Regional Security Outlook 2013*. Singapore: Booksmith Productions for Council for Security Cooperation in the Asia-Pacific: 26–9.

Tan, See Seng. 2012. 'Faced with the Dragon: Perils and Prospects in Singapore's Ambivalent Relationship with China', *Chinese Journal of International Politics*, Vol. 5, No. 3: 245–65.

Tan, See Seng. 2012. 'Spectres of Leifer: Insights on Regional Order and Security for Southeast Asia Today', *Contemporary Southeast Asia*, Vol. 34, No. 3: 309–37.

Tan, See Seng. 2012. '"Talking Their Walk"? The Evolution of Defence Regionalism in Southeast Asia', *Asian Security*, Vol. 8, No. 3: 232–50.

198  Bibliography

Tan, See Seng. 2013. *Facilitating China–U.S. Relations in the Age of Rebalancing: ASEAN's 'Middle Power' Diplomacy*, EAI MPD Working Paper No. 1. Seoul: East Asia Institute, 18 October.

Tan, See Seng. 2013. 'Herding Cats: The Role of Persuasion in Political Change and Continuity in the Association of Southeast Asian Nations (ASEAN)', *International Relations of the Asia-Pacific*, Vol. 13, No. 2: 233–65.

Tan, See Seng. 2013. 'Japan and Multilateralism in Asia', prepared for the Study Group on 'ASEAN-Japan Strategic Partnership on East Asian Community-Building', co-organized by the Centre for Strategic and International Studies (CSIS) Indonesia and the Japan Center for International Exchange (JCIE), Bali, 13–14 June.

Tan, See Seng. 2013. *The Making of the Asia Pacific: Knowledge Brokers and the Politics of Representation*. Amsterdam: Amsterdam University Press.

Tan, See Seng. 2014. 'Hobnobbing with Giants: Australia's Approach to Asian Regionalism', in Sally Percival Wood and Baogang He, eds., *The Australia-ASEAN Dialogue: Tracing 40 Years of Partnership*. New York: Palgrave Macmillan: 33–48.

Tan, See Seng. 2015. 'Change and Continuity in America's Asia Pivot: US Engagement with Multilateralism in the Asia Pacific', in Hugo Meier, ed., *Origins and Evolution of the US Rebalance toward Asia: Diplomatic, Military and Economic Dimensions*. Houndmills, Basingstoke: Palgrave Macmillan: 000–000.

Tan, See Seng. 2015. 'Indonesia Among the Powers: Will ASEAN Still Matter to Indonesia?', in Christopher B. Roberts, Ahmad D. Habir and Leonard C. Sebastian, eds., *Indonesia's Ascent: Power, Leadership and Asia's Security Order*. Houndmills, Basingstoke: Palgrave Macmillan: 287–307.

Tang Shiping. 2007. *From Offensive Realism to Defensive Realism: A Social Evolutionary Interpretation of China's Security Strategy*, State of Security and International Studies No. 3. Singapore: S. Rajaratnam School of International Studies, Nanyang Technological University.

Tang Siew Mun. 2007. 'Japan's Grand Strategic Shift from Yoshida to Koizumi: Reflections on Japan's Strategic Focus in the 21st Century', *Akademika*, No. 70: 117–36.

Tavola, Kaliopate, et al. 2006. *Reforming the Pacific Regional Institutional Framework*, SOPAC Paper, August, www.sopac.org/sopac/docs/RIF/07_RIF%20study,%20final_Tavola%20et%20al.pdf.

Tay, Simon. 2012. 'ASEAN, Neutral or Neutered?', *Today*, 17 July.

Taylor, Adam. 2012. 'The Australian Government Made a Secret Plan for War with China in 2009', *Business Insider*, 1 June, www.businessinsider.com/australia-china-kevin-rudd-2009-2012-6#ixzz3OgDgBZ2L.

Terada, Takashi. 1998. 'The Origins of Japan's APEC Policy: Foreign Minister Takeo Miki's Asia-Pacific Policy and Current Implications', *The Pacific Review*, Vol. 11, No. 3: 337–63.

Terada, Takashi. 1999. *The Japanese Origins of PAFTAD: The Beginning of an Asia Pacific Economic Community*, Pacific Economic Papers, No. 292. Canberra, ACT: Australia-Japan Research Centre, Australian National University.

Terada, Takashi. 1999. *The Genesis of APEC: Australia–Japan Political Initiatives*, Pacific Economic Papers, No. 298. Canberra, ACT: Australia–Japan Research Centre, Australian National University.

Terada, Takashi. 2001. 'Directional Leadership in Institution-Building: Japan's Approaches to ASEAN in the Establishment of PECC and APEC', *The Pacific Review*, Vol. 14, No. 2: 195–220.

Terada, Takashi. 2006. 'The Birth and Growth of ASEAN+3', in Bertrand Fort and Douglas Webber, eds., *Regional Integration in East Asia and Europe: Convergence or Divergence?* London: Routledge: 229–33.

Terada, Takashi. 2006. 'Forming an East Asian Community: A Site for Japan–China Power Struggles', *Japanese Studies*, Vol. 26, No. 1: 5–17.

Terada, Takashi. 2011. 'Security Partnership: Toward a Softer Triangle Alliance with the United States?', in G. John Ikenberry, Takashi Inoguchi, Yoichiro Sato, eds., *The U.S.–Japan Security Alliance: Regional Multilateralism*. Houndmills, Basingstoke: Palgrave Macmillan: 217–32.

Terrill, Ross. 2013. CAPS? 'We Shouldn't Be Marching to the Beat of Our New "Great and Powerful Friend"', *The Sydney Morning Herald*, 30 March.

Thakur, Ramesh. 2013. 'Is Australia Serious About Asia?', *Global Brief*, 5 March: 1–6, http://globalbrief.ca/blog/2013/03/05/is-australia-serious-about-asia/print/.

Thayer, Carlyle A. 2009. 'Kevin Rudd's Multi-layered Asia Pacific Community Initiative', *East Asia Forum*, 22 June, www.eastasiaforum.org/2009/06/22/kevin-rudds-multi-layered-asia-pacific-community-initiative/.

Thayer, Carlyle A. 2011. 'Chinese Assertiveness in the South China Sea and Southeast Asian Responses', *Journal of Current Southeast Asian Affairs*, Vol. 30, No. 2: 77–104.

Thayer, Carlyle A. 2013. 'ASEAN, China and the Code of Conduct in the South China Sea', *SAIS Review of International Affairs*, Vol. 33, No. 2: 75–84.

Thompson, Chuck. 2009. 'Interview: Bob Hawke and Gareth Evans, APEC architects', *CNN Global NewsView*, 12 November, http://travel.cnn.com/singapore/none/interview-bob-hawke-and-gareth-evans-apec-architects-295654.

Thomson, Mark. 2013. 'The Defence White Paper: Between the Lines', *The Strategist*, 14 May, www.aspistrategist.org.au/the-defence-white-paper-between-the-lines/.

Tiezzi, Shannon. 2013. 'China "Marches West" – to Europe', *The Diplomat*, 27 November, http://thediplomat.com/2013/11/china-marches-west-to-europe/.

Tiezzi, Shannon. 2014. 'Has Obama Abandoned the Pivot to Asia?', *The Diplomat*, 20 January, http://thediplomat.com/2014/01/has-obama-abandoned-the-pivot-to-asia/.

Tiezzi, Shannon. 2014. 'The Maritime Silk Road vs. The String of Pearls', *The Diplomat*, 13 February, http://thediplomat.com/2014/02/the-maritime-silk-road-vs-the-string-of-pearls/.

Tiezzi, Shannon. 2014. 'China's Response to the US Cyber Espionage Charges', *The Diplomat*, 21 May, http://thediplomat.com/2014/05/chinas-response-to-the-us-cyber-espionage-charges/.

Tiezzi, Shannon. 2014. 'The New, Improved Shanghai Cooperation Organization', *The Diplomat*, 13 September, http://thediplomat.com/2014/09/the-new-improved-shanghai-cooperation-organization/.

Tiezzi, Shannon. 2014. 'China's Push for an Asia-Pacific Free Trade Agreement', *The Diplomat*, 30 October, http://thediplomat.com/2014/10/chinas-push-for-an-asia-pacific-free-trade-agreement/.

Till, Geoffrey. 2014. 'Outgoing Australia?', *Centre of Gravity* Series Paper, No. 14, February. Canberra, ACT: Strategic Defence Studies Centre, Australian National University.

Tisdall, Simon. 2013. 'Shinzo Abe: Is Japan's PM a Dangerous Militarist or Modernizing Reformer?', *The Guardian*, 16 December, www.theguardian.com/world/2013/dec/16/shinzo-abe-japan-pm.

Tow, William T. 2001. *Asia-Pacific Security Relations: Seeking Convergent Security*. Cambridge: Cambridge University Press.

Tow, William T., and Brendan Taylor. 2010. 'What is Asian Security Architecture?', *Review of International Studies*, Vol. 36, No. 1: 95–116.

Tow, William T, Michael Auslin, Rory Medcalf, Akihiko Tanaka, Zhu Feng and Sheldon Simon. 2008. *Assessing the Trilateral Strategic Dialogue*, NBR Special Report, No. 16, December. Seattle, WA: National Bureau of Asian Research.

Tsai, Frederick. 2008. 'The False Binary Choice between Unilateralism and Multilateralism', *SAIS Review of International Affairs*, Vol. 28, No. 2: 45–8.

Turley, William S., and Jeffrey Race. 1980. 'The Third Indochina War', *Foreign Policy*, No. 38: 92–116.

Unidjaja, Fabiola Desy. 2002. 'Indonesia Looks Forward to Reinstatement of IMET Program', *The Jakarta Post*, 30 November.

Uren, David. 2007. 'China Emerges as Our Biggest Trade Partner', *The Australian*, 6 May.

US Department of State. 2005. 'US To Resume Select Military Assistance to Indonesia', *usinfo.state.gov*, 25 November, www.fas.org/asmp/resources/govern/109th/MilAidIndonesia22Nov05.htm.

Usher, John A. 1997. 'Variable Geometry or Concentric Circles: Patterns for the European Union', *International and Comparative Law Quarterly*, Vol. 46, No. 2: 243–73.

Van der Kroef, Justus Maria. 1971. *Indonesia after Sukarno*. Vancouver, BC: University of British Columbia Press.

Van Evera, Stephen. 1994. 'Hypotheses on Nationalism and War', *International Security*, Vol. 18, No. 4: 5–39.

Vance, Cyrus R. 1983. *Hard Choices: Critical Years in America's Foreign Policy*. New York: Simon and Schuster.

Vanstone, Amanda. 2012. 'Does Labor Really Think It Started Our Engagement with Asia?', *The Sydney Morning Herald*, 12 November, www.theage.com.au/federal-politics/political-opinion/does-labor-really-think-it-started-our-engagement-with-asia-20121111-29689.html.

Wanandi, Jusuf. 1978. 'Security in the Asia-Pacific Region: An Indonesian Observation', *Asian Survey*, Vol. 18, No. 2: 1209–20.

Wanandi, Jusuf. 1996. 'ASEAN's China Strategy: Towards Deeper Engagement', *Survival*, Vol. 38, No. 2: 117–28.

Wanandi, Jusuf. 2002. 'China after the Communist Party's 16th Congress', *The Jakarta Post*, 21 November.

Wanandi, Jusuf. 2002. 'East Asia, Terrorism and New Global Rules', in Frank-Jürgen Richter and Pamela C. M. Mar, eds., *Recreating Asia: Visions for a New Century*. Singapore: John Wiley and Sons: 22–33.

Wanandi, Jusuf. 2004. 'The Effects of Leadership Changes in East Asia (Part 1 of 2)', *The Jakarta Post*, 27 January.

Wanandi, Jusuf. 2005. 'ASEAN and China Form Strategic Partnership', *The Indonesian Quarterly*, Vol. 33, No. 4: 328–31.

Wanandi, Jusuf. 2005. 'The Need and the Challenge for an East Asian Multilateral Regional Institution', *Asian Affairs*, No. 6: 91–102.

Wanandi, Jusuf. 2006. 'The Importance of the One-China Policy', *The Jakarta Post*, 2 November.

Wanandi, Jusuf. 2008. 'Indonesia's Foreign Policy and the Meaning of ASEAN', *PacNet*, No. 27, 15 May, http://csis.org/files/media/csis/pubs/pac0827.pdf.

Wanandi, Jusuf, Gerald Segal, Yukio Satoh and Jin-hyun Park. 1998. 'The Security Setting Part 1: Thinking Strategically about Security in Pacific Asia', in Hanns Maull, Gerald Segal and Jusuf Wanandi, eds., *Europe and the Asia-Pacific*. New York: Routledge: 207–34.

Wang, Hongying. 2000. 'Multilateralism in Chinese Foreign Policy: The Limits of Socialization', *Asian Survey*, Vol. 40, No. 3: 475–91.

Wang, Hongying, and Erik French. 2013. 'China's Participation in Global Governance from a Comparative Perspective', *Asia Policy*, No. 15: 89–114.

Wang, Qi. 2012. 'China and US not G2, but C2', *Sina English*, 4 May, http://english.sina.com/china/2012/0503/464519.html.

Wang, Yuzhu. 2013. 'The RCEP Initiative and ASEAN "Centrality"', *China Institute of International Studies (CIIS)*, 6 December, www.ciis.org.cn/english/2013-12/06/content_6518129.htm.

Wang, Zhi, William Powers, and Shang-Jin Wei. 2009. *Value Chains in East Asian Production Networks: An International Input-Output Model Based Analysis*, Office of Economics Working Paper, No. 2009-10-C. Washington, D.C.: US International Trade Commission.

Weatherbee, Donald E. 2009. *International Relations in Southeast Asia: The Struggle for Autonomy*, 2nd edn. Lanham, MD: Rowman and Littlefield, 2009.

Weatherbee, Donald E., Ralf Emmers, Mari Pangestu, Leonard C. Sebastian. 2005. 'The Third Indochina War', in *International Relations in Southeast Asia: The Struggle for Autonomy* (Lanham, MD: Rowman and Littlefield, 2005), pp. 75–82.

Weck, Winfried. 2011. 'ASEAN and G20: Indonesia's Foreign Policy Objectives', *KAS (Konrad-Adenauer-Stiftung) International Reports*, No. 2.

Weisbrot, Mark. 2014. 'US Foreign Policy in Latin America Leaves an Open Door for China', *The Guardian*, 31 January.

Wesley, Michael. 2006. 'The Dog That Didn't Bark: The Bush Administration and East Asian Regionalism', in Mark Beeson, ed., *Bush and Asia: America's Evolving Relations with East Asia*. London: Routledge: 64–79.

Wheatcroft, Geoffrey. 2011. 'Who Needs NATO?', *The New York Times*, 15 June.

White House. 2014. 'U.S.–Japan Joint Statement: The United States and Japan: Shaping the Future of the Asia-Pacific and Beyond', *The White House: Office of the Press Secretary*, 25 April, www.whitehouse.gov/the-press-office/2014/04/25/us-japan-joint-statement-united-states-and-japan-shaping-future-asia-pac.

White, Hugh. 2011. 'Power Shift: Rethinking Australia's Place in the Asian Century', *Australian Journal of International Affairs*, Vol. 65, No. 1: 81–93.

White, Hugh. 2012. 'Indonesia's Rise is the Big Story We're Missing', *The Age*, 29 May, www.theage.com.au/it-pro/indonesias-rise-is-the-big-story-were-missing-20120528-1zf72.html.

White, Hugh. 2012. *The China Choice: Why America Should Share Power*. Collingwood, VIC: Black Inc.

White, Hugh. 2014. 'Japanese Collective Self-Defense: Abe's Changes Won't Help', *Lowy Interpreter*, 4 July, www.lowyinterpreter.org/post/2014/07/04/Japan- collective-self-defence-abe.aspx.

Wihardja, Maria Monica. 2011. 'Second-Generation Reform in Asia', *East Asia Forum*, 18 August, www.eastasiaforum.org/2011/08/18/second-generation-reforms-the-key-to-deeper-regional-cooperation/.

WikiLeaks. 2011. 'Confidential Section 01 of 02 Singapore 000852 SIPDIS Department for EAP/MTS – M. Coppola E.O. 12958: Decl: 09/04/2019 Tags: Prel, SN Subject: Singapore MFA's Tommy Koh Talks China, SE Asia with STAFFDEL (Keith) Luse Singapore 00000852 001.2 of 002 Classified By: E/P Counselor Joel Ehrendreich for reason 1.4(d)', in 'Singapore, Malaysia and the WikiLeaks', *Asia Sentinel*, 20 January, www.asiasentinel.com/politics/singapore-malaysia-and-the-wikileaks/.

Witular, Rendi A. 2014. 'Jokowi Launches Maritime Doctrine to the World', *The Jakarta Post*, 13 November, www.thejakartapost.com/news/2014/11/13/jokowi-launches-maritime-doctrine-world.html.

Wong, John. 2012. *East Asian Economic Cooperation: Lessons for South American Regionalism*, EAI Working Paper, No. 160. Singapore: East Asian Institute, National University of Singapore.

Woodroofe, Thom. 2012. 'Is the East Asia Summit Rudd's Gift to the World?', *Australian Policy Outline*, 12 January, http://apo.org.au/commentary/east-asia-summit-rudd%E2%80%99s-gift-world.

Woolcott, Richard. 2009. 'Towards an Asia Pacific Community', *Asialink Essays*, No. 9. Melbourne, VIC: Asialink: 1–4.

Wright, Thomas. 2009. 'Toward Effective Multilateralism: Why Bigger May Not Be Better', *The Washington Quarterly*, Vol. 32, No. 3: 163–80.

Wright-Neville, David. 2005. 'Fear and Loathing: Australia and Counter-Terrorism', ARI No. 156/2005, 21 December. Madrid: Real Instituto Elcano.

Wu, Friedrich Wu, Poa Tiong Siaw, Yeo Han Sia and Puah Kok Keong. 2002. 'Foreign Direct Investments to China and Southeast Asia: Has ASEAN Been Losing Out?', *Economic Survey of Singapore 2002* (Third Quarter): 96–115.

Wu, Guoguang. 2008. 'Multiple Levels of Multilateralism: The Rising China in the Turbulent World', in Guoguang Wu and Helen Landsdowne, eds., *China Turns to Multilateralism: Foreign Policy and Regional Security*. Abingdon: Routledge: 267–89.

Wu, Shicun. 2014. 'Preface', in Wu Shicun and Nong Hong, eds., *Recent Developments in the South China Sea Dispute: The Prospect of a Joint Development Regime*. Abingdon: Routledge: xv–xvi.

Xia, Liping. 2001. 'China: A Responsible Great Power', *Journal of Contemporary China*, Vol. 10, No. 26: 17–25.

Xinhua. 2014. Xi Eyes More Enabling Int'l Environment for China's Peaceful Development', *Xinhua*, 30 November, http://news.xinhuanet.com/english/china/2014-11/30/c_133822694_2.htm.

Yahuda, Michael. 2005. *The International Politics of Asia-Pacific, 1945–1995*. Abingdon: Routledge.

Yamazawa, Ippei. 2009. *How to Meet the Mid-term Bogor Goal?*, ISEAS Paper, May, www.iseas.edu.sg/apec/D1S1S3_Paper_Yamazawa.pdf.

Yamazawa, Ippei. 2010. 'Has APEC Achieved Its Midterm Bogor Target?', *www.pecc.org*, 13 December, www.pecc.org/blog/2010/12/13/has-apec-achieved-its-mid-term-bogor-target/#more-165.

Yao, Shujie. 2009. 'China Will Learn its Lessons from the Chinalco Fiasco', *The Age*, 18 June.

Yee, Albert. S. 1996. 'The Causal Effects of Ideas on Policy', *International Organization*, Vol. 50, No. 1: 69–108.

You, Ji. 2006. 'East Asian Community: A New Platform for Sino-Japanese Cooperation and Contention', *Japanese Studies*, Vol. 26, No.1: 19–28.

Young, Oran. 1991. 'Political Leadership and Regime Formation: On the Development of Institutions in International Society', *International Organization*, Vol. 45, No. 3: 281–308.

Yuan, Jing-dong. 2000. *Asia-Pacific Security: China's Conditional Multilateralism and Great Power Entente*. Carlisle, PA: Strategic Studies Institute. US Army War College.

Yudhoyono, Susilo Bambang. 2012. 'Keynote Speech by H.E. Dr. Susilo Bambang Yudhoyono, President of the Republic of Indonesia, at the Launching of the *Strategic Review Journal*', New York, 26 September.

Yuzawa, Takeshi. 2006. 'The Evolution of Preventive Diplomacy in the ASEAN Regional Forum: Problems and Prospects', *Asian Survey*, Vol. 46, No. 5: 785–804.

Yuzawa, Takeshi. 2007. *Japan's Security Policy and the ASEAN Regional Forum: The Search for Multilateral Security in the Asia-Pacific* (Abingdon: Routledge).

Zagoria, Donald S. 1982. 'Regional Organization and Order in South-East Asia: Understanding ASEAN', *Foreign Affairs*, Vol. 67, No. 1, www.foreignaffairs.com/articles/36778/donald-s-zagoria/regional-organization-and-order-in-south-east-asia-understanding.

Zakaria, Fareed. 1997. 'The Rise of Illiberal Democracy', *Foreign Affairs*, Vol. 76, No. 6: 22–43.

Zelikow, Philip. 2000. 'American Engagement in Asia', in Robert D. Blackwill and Paul Dibb, eds., *America's Asian Alliances*. Cambridge, MA: MIT Press: 19–30.

Zhang, Xiaoming. 2006. 'The Rise of China and Community Building in East Asia', *Asian Perspective*, Vol. 30, No. 3: 129–48.

Zhao, Dingxin. 2009. 'The Mandate of Heaven and Performance Legitimation in Historical and Contemporary China', *American Behavioral Scientist*, Vol. 53, No. 3: 416–33.

Zhao, Hong. 2014. 'China's Evolving Views on the TPP and the RCEP', *ISEAS Perspective*, No. 28, 8 May, www.iseas.edu.sg/documents/publication/iseas_perspective_2014_28_china_evolving_views_on_the_tpp_and_the_rcep.pdf.

Zhong Sheng. 2011. 'ASEAN Plus Three cooperation is driving force for East Asia', *People's Daily Online*, 16 August, http://english.peopledaily.com.cn/90780/91343/7571027.html.

Zhu, Ying. 2012. 'Australia's Engagement in Asia', paper for the CPA International Forum for Academics, Melbourne, 28 June.

# Index

'n' refers to chapter end notes.

*à la carte* multilateralism 8, 64, 76–9, 122–4
A2/AD strategy *see* anti-access/anti-denial strategy
Abe Doctrine 75
Abe, Shinzo 63–6, 73–6, 77, 80, 84–5n
ADB (Asian Development Bank) 100
ADMM-Plus *see* ASEAN Defence Ministers' Meeting Plus
advisory institutions 10–11
advocacy, China 139
AEC *see* ASEAN Economic Community
Africa 88–9
Afro-Asian Conference *see* Bandung Conference
AFTA (ASEAN Free Trade Area) 133
AIIB (Asian Infrastructure Bank) 100–101
Alatas, Ali 137, 140
alliance system, US 120
America *see* United States
AMF *see* Asian Monetary Fund
anti-access/anti-denial (A2/AD) strategy 99, 114
APC *see* Asia-Pacific Community
APEC *see* Asia-Pacific Economic Cooperation
apex arrangement 155, 160
APT *see* ASEAN Plus Three
'architecture' term 50, 51
ARF *see* ASEAN Regional Forum
ASEAN *see also* Association of Southeast Asian Nations
ASEAN Defence Ministers' Meeting Plus (ADMM-Plus) 42, 54, 72, 76, 79
ASEAN Economic Community (AEC) 29, 133–4
ASEAN Free Trade Area (AFTA) 133

ASEAN Plus Three (APT): China and 95, 106n; formation 22, 157; Indonesia and 140–1; Japan and 70, 72
ASEAN Post-Ministerial Conference (ASEAN–PMC) 21, 157
ASEAN Regional Forum (ARF) 9–11, 156–7; ASEAN management 22; Australia and 48, 49–50, 53; China and 91–2, 97; command multilateralism 160; Europe and 158; founding of 21; functional multilateralism 162; Indonesia and 137, 139; Japan and 69, 71, 76, 79; US and 121
'ASEAN Way' 116, 137
'Asia pivot', Australia's 42–6
Asia-Pacific Community (APC) 6, 49, 53, 95, 157–8
Asia-Pacific Economic Cooperation (APEC) 11; ASEAN and 20–1; Australia and 46–7, 48, 52; Bogor Goals 162; China and 91–2; formation of 156; Japan and 67–8; Track 2 complement 32; US and 114, 116–18, 122
Asian Development Bank (ADB) 100
Asian Infrastructure Bank (AIIB) 100–101
Asian Monetary Fund (AMF) 70, 116
assertive diplomacy 64, 66, 74
Association of Southeast Asian Nations (ASEAN) 18–40; Australia and 42, 51–2, 54–5; centrality of 18–19, 22–33, 115, 158–9; China and 88–91, 93–4, 95, 97, 105–6n, 133, 150n; as convenor 25–7; focus on 155; as hub/node 27–8; Indonesia and 130–7, 138–46, 147, 152–3n; institutional design 5, 9–12; Japan and 66–8, 71, 76, 78; laissez-faire multilateralism 164; marginalization

161, 163; non-stakeholder countries 156, 165; power of 19–20; as progress agent 28–32; as regional leader 24; role 160; US and 110, 112–13, 115–16, 118, 120–1, 123, 127n
attitudinal change constraints 30
Australia 20, 41–62, 156–7; 'Asia pivot' 42–6; China's relationship with 88, 95, 99; communities/concerts and 48–53; Japan's collaboration with 67–8, 70–1, 83n

Baker, James 47
balance of power system 138
balancing: across institutions 8; Japan 64, 74–5, 79; regional states 7
Bandung Conference 115–16, 131
'between-ness', social network approach 28
bifurcation, Australia–China relationship 44
bilateral relationships: Australia–US 44; China–Asia 139; China–US 25; effectiveness 7–8; 'hub and spokes' model 112; Indonesia–China 138; Japan–US 63, 76, 78; US–Asia 111–12, 116, 118, 120
Bogor Goals 11, 162
'bottom up' processes 4, 159
Brazil 136
Brezhnev, Leonid 111
'BRICS' countries 136
Bull, Hedley 150n
Bush, George H. W. 113, 116
Bush, George W. 117–18, 122–3

Cambodia 26, 32, 37n, 90–1, 121, 134, 142
Canada 58n, 157
Carter administration 112
Central Asia, secretariats 17n
centrality: ASEAN 18–19, 22–33, 115, 158–9; as expedience device 32–3
Cha, Victor D. 167n
change constraints 30
Chen, Jian 87
Chiang Mai Initiative (CMI) 117, 157
China 87–109, 156; APT dominance 157; ARF engagement 48; ASEAN relationship 26–7, 150n, 159; Australia's engagement 41–4, 47–9, 52–3, 55; challenges 151–2n; charming to offensive 94–8; command multilateralism 161; dealings with ASEAN 31; free trade agreement 133; Indonesia relationship 134, 137–42; Japan's relationship with 63–6, 68–9, 71–2, 74–6, 77–9; laissez-faire multilateralism 164; 'new normal' 98–101; US relationship 25, 110, 112, 114–15, 117, 119, 121–4, see also 'BRICS' countries
Chinalco-Rio Tinto deal 45
CICA (Conference on Interaction and Confidence-Building Measures) 101
climate change agreements 122
Clinton, Bill 113, 116, 123, 129n
Clinton, Hillary 48–9, 75, 113–14, 119, 121, 128n, 162–3
'closeness', social network approach 28
CMI see Chiang Mai Initiative
coalitions, Japan 65
coercive diplomacy 78
Cold War: ASEAN's role 20, 23, 25–6; Australia and 46; China and 90–1; Indonesia and 137; 'new regionalism' 4; US and 110–13, 115, see also post-Cold War era
collective action, regional states 6–7
command multilateralism 49, 159–61
communism 90
communities, Australia 48–53
community-building approach, China 88
competing visions, Asia's architecture 158–64
concentric circles 9–10, 28, 55, 161
concerts, Australia 48–53
Conference on Interaction and Confidence-Building Measures (CICA) 101
Conference for Security Cooperation in Europe (CSCE) 47
'confidence diplomacy' 144
confrontation policy, Indonesia 131, 139
consensus-based institutions 9–10
'constructive engagement' 141
consultation, Indonesia 132
containment 64, 139
convening power 34n, 132
convenor role, ASEAN 25–7
cooperation basis, China–ASEAN 91
'cooperative regionalism' 136, 139
Council for Security Cooperation in the Asia-Pacific (CSCAP) 72
counterterrorism, US 117
CSCAP (Council for Security Cooperation in the Asia-Pacific) 72

CSCE (Conference for Security Cooperation in Europe) 47

Declaration on the Conduct of Parties in the South China Sea (DOC) 94–5
decolonization 112
defence white papers, Australia 44, 49, 53
'degree', social network approach 28
deliberation, Indonesia 132
Democratic administrations, US 111
democratization process 31, 130, 140, 145–6
Deng Xiaoping 87, 90, 96
Diaoyu/Senkaku islands 75
diplomacy: ASEAN 21, 105n; Australia 42, 48; China 88; Indonesia 134, 144; institutional design 10; Japan 64–5, 69, 74, 78; middle powers 154n; power and 41; US 120–1
directional leadership 65–7, 76, see also quiet diplomacy
dispute settlement, ASEAN 12
DOC (Declaration on the Conduct of Parties in the South China Sea) 94–5
Doha Round 117
Dosch, Jörn 152n
'dynamic equilibrium' 140

EAC see East Asian Community
EAS see East Asia Summit
East Asia: APT and 22; ASEAN relationship 24; China and 95
East Asia Summit (EAS) 22; Australia and 51–3; China and 95, 157, 164; economic integration vehicle 162; expansion of 161; Japan and 64, 66, 70, 72, 76–8; 'steering capacity' 158; US and 114, 118, 120–1, 122
East Asian Community (EAC) 70–1, 83n, 95, 140–1, 160
East China Sea 65, 75, 89–90, 96–7, 121, 142
economic cooperation: Australia 45; China 88
economic growth, Indonesia 149n
economic integration: China 96, 102; EAC as vehicle for 162; Indonesia 133, 136
economic mechanisms: Indonesia 147–8n; Japan 77
economic recovery, Japan 65
economic regionalisms 24, 46
economic reliance, China–Australia 41, 44
economic resources, Asia 41

economic revival, Japan 73
efficiency: apex arrangement 155; functional multilateralism 162; institutional design 5–6
Eisenhower administration 112
Eminent Persons Groups (EPGs) 17n
entrapment, Japan 75, 84n
entrepreneurial leadership 20
EPGs (Eminent Persons Groups) 17n
equity: apex arrangement 155; institutional design 5–6
EU see European Union
Europe–US isolation 111–12
European Union (EU): ARF membership 158; China and 89; EAC based on 160; regional integration 4
Evans, Gareth 43, 46, 47, 52
expedience device, centrality as 32–3

facilitation role see convenor role
feedback mechanisms, institutional design 11–12
financial crisis 68, 70, 72, 92, 116
Ford, Gerald 112
foreign policy: Indonesia 132, 135, 140, 143–6, 149n; Japan 87; US 112–13, 118
Fraser, Malcolm 44–5
free rider problem 10, 102
free trade agreements (FTAs) 27, 54, 95, 100, 127n, 133
Free Trade Area of the Asia-Pacific (FTAAP) 99
FTAs see free trade agreements
Fukuda Doctrine 66–7, 82n
functional cooperation, China 93
functional multilateralism 50, 159, 161–3

'G2' partnership 52, 121
G20 see Group of Twenty
Gillard, Julia 43, 44
global war on terrorism (GWOT) 113, 117–18, 124n
Gorbachev, Mikhail 111
gradualism process, China 93
Group of Twenty (G20) 6, 78, 136, 142–4
Gus Dur (Abdurrahman Wahid) 146
GWOT see global war on terrorism

HADR see humanitarian assistance and disaster relief
hard balancing 7, 79
Hashimoto, Ryutaro 70
Hatoyama, Yukio 71–2

## Index

Hawke, Bob 46–7, 67–8
hedging 7, 44, 64, 79, 140
historical context, Australia–Asia relations 45
hub concept, ASEAN 27–8
'hub and spokes' model 112
humanitarian assistance and disaster relief (HADR) 79, 101
hybrid regionalism 52

ICJ (International Court of Justice) 145
identity, Australia 45
IMET (International Military Education and Training) 137
IMF see International Monetary Fund
immigration 45
India 53, 120, see also 'BRICS' countries
Indo-Pacific region 144
Indochina Wars 90
Indonesia 130–54, 156; ASEAN founder 18; aspiration without ability 131–6; Australia and 53, 54; China and 89–90; command multilateralism 161; Japan and 78; US and 118
industrialization, China 101
infrastructure projects 100
input-oriented legitimacy 6
institutional design 4, 5–6, 8–12
institutional efficacy 162
instrumentalism 163
intellectual leadership 20
inter-stakeholder dynamics 6–7
intergovernmental institutions 9, 30, see also 'top down' processes
International Court of Justice (ICJ) 145
International Military Education and Training (IMET) 137
International Monetary Fund (IMF) 92, 111, 116–17
International Tribunal for the Law of the Sea (ITLOS) 99
internationalism: Japan 66, 73; US 111
Islam 146
isolationism, US 110–12
ITLOS (International Tribunal for the Law of the Sea) 99

Japan 20, 39–40n, 46–7, 63–86; China's economic ties 102; China's FTA 95; existing arrangements 155–6; foreign policy 87; pressures on ASEAN 157; Sino-Japanese condominium 160; US and 112

Jokowi administration, Indonesia 134, 144

Keating, Paul 42, 44–5
*Kemlu* (Indonesian foreign ministry) 143–4
Koh, Tommy 50, 51
Koizumi Doctrine 73
Koizumi, Junichiro 63, 66, 70–2, 83n
*konfrontasi* (confrontation) policy 131, 139
Kuching Consensus, 1990 21

laissez-faire multilateralism 50, 159, 163–4
Latin America 104n, 150n
LDP see Liberal Democratic Party
leadership: ASEAN 20, 24, 130, 132, 156; China 87, 97, 107n; Japan 65–8, 76; US 113, 115–16
legitimacy: ASEAN 31; institutional design 6
Liberal Democratic Party (LDP), Japan 74
liberalism 66, 122–3
liberalization of China 88–9

Majapahit 131
Malaysia 18
Malik, Adam 132–3
Mao Zedong 87
maritime powers, China 99
maritime Silk Road 98–9
Middle East 115, 117
middle powers 147, 154n, 161
Miki, Takeo 67
military alliances 41
military capabilities, Japan 74
military deterrence, US 63
military expenditure, Japan 76–7
military normalization 63–4
military power, Japan 73
military security, US 65
'mini-lateral' arrangements 8
Monroe Doctrine 150n
'multi-multilateral' architecture 4, 5–8
Muslims 146
Myanmar 32, 118

Nakatani, Gen 64, 71–2
Nakayama, Taro 69–70, 72
NAM see Non-Aligned Movement
'national resilience' 145
nationalism 63, 66, 71, 88–9, 152n
NATO (North Atlantic Treaty Organization) 111
'natural economic regions' 8
naval control, Australia 47

neoconservatism 122
neoliberal economic system 48
network nodes, ASEAN 28
neutrality, ASEAN 26–7, 136
'new regionalism' 4
New Zealand 54, 70
nine-dashed lines map, China 96
Nixon, Richard 112
nodes in networks 28
Non-Aligned Movement (NAM) 131, 137
non-traditional security (NTS) 92
'normal nationalists' 63
normalization: China 87, 98–101; Japan 63–4, 73–6
Norris, Stephen 147–8n
North Atlantic Treaty Organization (NATO) 111
North Korea 68
NTS (non-traditional security) 92
Nye, Joseph 122

Obama, Barack 74, 98–9, 111, 113–15, 118–23
open regionalism 46, 48
output-oriented legitimacy 6

'PACINDO' area 144
'patchworks' 167n
PD see preventive diplomacy
'peace state', Japan as 65–6, 73
peaceful coexistence 92, 140
People's Republic of China 90
Philippines 18, 113
Phnom Penh fiasco 134, 142
pivot terminology 42–6, 114, 119
'pluri-lateral' arrangements 8
policy changes, China 97–8
policy differences, Australia–Asia 45
post-Cold War era: Australia 41, 47, 58n; China 90–1, 93; Indonesia 137, 140–1; Japan 67–8; US 111, 113, 116, 119–20, 122
Powell, Colin 125n
power: ASEAN 19–20, 24, 34n, 132; Australia and 41–2, 51; balance of 138; China 87–8, 98–9, 102, 141; diplomacy 154n; Indonesia 147; Japan 65, 73; US 110, 116, 122, 123
pragmatism: China 90; Indonesia 135; Japan 63, 71
preventive diplomacy (PD) 48, 69, see also diplomacy
process-driven regionalism 30

protectionism, Indonesia 134

quiet diplomacy 64–5, see also directional leadership

rapprochement, China–ASEAN 91
RCEP see Regional Comprehensive Economic Partnership
Reagan, Ronald 112
rebalancing terminology 114, 119
reciprocity, China–ASEAN 90
Regional Comprehensive Economic Partnership (RCEP) 25, 29, 33, 54, 100, 157
regional convenor, ASEAN as 25–7
regional hub/node, ASEAN as 27–8
regional leadership, ASEAN 24
regional progress, ASEAN as agent of 28–32
regional states' collective action 6–7
regionalism: ASEAN as driver 18–19, 23, 24, 30, 32–3, 42; Australia and 46, 48, 52; China's engagement 89; Indonesia and 136, 138–9; paradox of 4; US and 117
regulatory institutions 10–11
Reiss, Mitchell 125n
religiosity 146
Republican administrations, US 111, 114
resource constraints, Australia 44
results-based regionalism 30
'revisionists' 63, 71
Rice, Condoleeza 113, 117
ROOs see rules of origin
Rudd, Kevin 6, 44, 46–7, 48–53, 69–70, 95, 161
rules-based regionalism 30
rules of origin (ROOs), RCEP 100
Rumsfeld, Donald 117
Russia 22, 47, 51, 96, 157, see also 'BRICS' countries; Soviet Union

SAARC system 15n, 17n
SAFTA (South Asian Free Trade Agreement) 17n
sanctions, China 97
SCO (Shanghai Cooperation Organization) 95–6
sea agreements 78, see also East China Sea; South China Sea
SEATO (Southeast Asia Treaty Organization) 111–12
secretariats 12, 17n

security concept, non-traditional 92
selectivist approach: Japan 64; US 111
Senkaku/Diaoyu islands 75
Shanghai Cooperation Organization (SCO) 95–6
Shanghai Five 96
Shanghai summit 68
Shangri-La Dialogue (SLD) 22, 64, 71–2
shuttle diplomacy 134
Sing Tel 45
Singapore 12; APEC meeting 21; ASEAN founder 18; China and 94; EAS dispute 51, 53; Sing Tel 45
Sino-Japanese condominium 160
SLD *see* Shangri-La Dialogue
smart power 122
Smith, Stephen 50
social network approach 28
socialization, China/Indonesia 139
soft balancing 7, 79
soft power 122
South Africa *see* 'BRICS' countries
South Asian Free Trade Agreement (SAFTA) 17n
South China Sea 27, 31, 89–90, 93–7, 121, 140–2, 151–2n
South Korea 39n, 75–6, 99
Southeast Asia: Australia and 54–5; founders of ASEAN 18; US and 112, 120, *see also* Association of Southeast Asian Nations
Southeast Asia Treaty Organization (SEATO) 111–12
sovereign states, ASEAN 138
sovereignty 39n, 48, 145
Soviet Union 98, 157, *see also* Russia
Srivijaya 131
strategic partnerships, Australia–China 44
'string of pearls', China 98–9
structural change constraints 30
Suharto presidency, Indonesia 130–1, 134–5, 138–9
Sukarno presidency, Indonesia 131
Sukma, Rizal 143
Sunnylands summit 98
surveillance 45

TAC *see* Treaty of Amity and Cooperation
Taiwan Straits 90
Thailand 18, 32, 142
Tiananmen Incident, 1989 94

TIFAs (trade and investment framework agreements) 127n
'top down' processes 4, 159–60, *see also* intergovernmental institutions
TPP *see* Trans-Pacific Partnership
trade forums 46, 48, 68, *see also* Asia-Pacific Economic Cooperation
trade and investment framework agreements (TIFAs) 127n
trading partnerships, US–China 88
Trans-Pacific Partnership (TPP) 25, 68, 77
Treaty of Amity and Cooperation (TAC) 95, 120, 142
Trilateral Strategic Dialogue 163

UK (United Kingdom) 43
UN (United Nations) 111
unilateralism: Japan 74; US 118, 123
United Kingdom (UK) 43
United Nations (UN) 111
United States (US) 22, 110–29; and/in Asia 111–15; and/in Asian multilateralism 115–22; ASEAN centrality 158–9; Australia's engagement 41–2, 43–4, 47, 53; China's relationship with 25, 88, 92, 97–9, 107n; command multilateralism 161; EAS membership 51, 157; existing arrangements 155–6; Indonesia's relationship with 137, 140; Japan's relationship with 63–4, 66, 69–71, 73–5, 76–9, 80n, 84–5n; Latin America and 150n
utilitarianism 111

variable geometry 9, 71, 163
Vietnam 26, 32, 91, 99, 113
Vietnam War 112, 120
voluntary arrangements, institutions 11

Wanandi, Jusuf 136, 141, 143–4
'Washington consensus' 48
white papers, Australia 55, *see also* defence white papers
Whitlam, Gough 42
World Trade Organization (WTO) 88

Xi Jinping 87, 97–8, 100–1

Yang Jiechi 121
Yoshida Doctrine 65, 67, 73, 81–2n
Yoshida, Shigeru 63, 71
Yudhoyono presidency, Indonesia 144

# eBooks
## from Taylor & Francis
Helping you to choose the right eBooks for your Library

Add to your library's digital collection today with Taylor & Francis eBooks. We have over 50,000 eBooks in the Humanities, Social Sciences, Behavioural Sciences, Built Environment and Law, from leading imprints, including Routledge, Focal Press and Psychology Press.

**Choose from a range of subject packages or create your own!**

**Benefits for you**
- Free MARC records
- COUNTER-compliant usage statistics
- Flexible purchase and pricing options
- All titles DRM-free.

**Benefits for your user**
- Off-site, anytime access via Athens or referring URL
- Print or copy pages or chapters
- Full content search
- Bookmark, highlight and annotate text
- Access to thousands of pages of quality research at the click of a button.

**Free Trials Available**
We offer free trials to qualifying academic, corporate and government customers.

# eCollections
Choose from over 30 subject eCollections, including:

| | |
|---|---|
| Archaeology | Language Learning |
| Architecture | Law |
| Asian Studies | Literature |
| Business & Management | Media & Communication |
| Classical Studies | Middle East Studies |
| Construction | Music |
| Creative & Media Arts | Philosophy |
| Criminology & Criminal Justice | Planning |
| Economics | Politics |
| Education | Psychology & Mental Health |
| Energy | Religion |
| Engineering | Security |
| English Language & Linguistics | Social Work |
| Environment & Sustainability | Sociology |
| Geography | Sport |
| Health Studies | Theatre & Performance |
| History | Tourism, Hospitality & Events |

For more information, pricing enquiries or to order a free trial, please contact your local sales team: www.tandfebooks.com/page/sales

**www.tandfebooks.com**